Karen,

Thank you for your years of excellence and dedication. We will miss you.

Best wishes,

Jane Franklin

May 1999

CENTENARIANS

EDITED BY BERNARD EDELMAN

Dear America: Letters Home from Vietnam

CENTENARIANS

The Story of the 20th Century
by the Americans Who Lived It

Bernard Edelman

FARRAR, STRAUS AND GIROUX / NEW YORK

Farrar, Straus and Giroux
19 Union Square West, New York 10003

Copyright © 1999 by Bernard Edelman

All rights reserved
Distributed in Canada by Douglas & McIntyre Ltd.
Printed in the United States of America
Designed by Abby Kagan
First edition, 1999

Grateful acknowledgment is made for permission to reprint the following: Excerpts from Miss Ethel
Remembers . . . *by Flora Ethel Andrews, with kind permission of Glorious Shenton. Copyright © 1991
by Flora Ethel Andrews. Excerpts from "Thank You, Mr. Block Island," published on July 27, 1986,
with kind permission of* The Providence Journal-Bulletin. *Copyright © 1987 by* The Providence
Journal-Bulletin. *Excerpts from* A Money Mind at Ninety *by Philip Carret, with kind permission of Fraser
Publishing. Copyright © 1991 by Philip Lord Carret. Excerpts from "The Struik Case of 1951," published
in January 1993, with kind permission of the* Monthly Review. *Copyright © 1993 by the* Monthly Review.
Excerpts from I Shock Myself *by Beatrice Wood, with kind permission of Chronicle Books. Copyright ©
1985 by Beatrice Wood.*

Library of Congress Cataloging-in-Publication Data
Centenarians : the story of the twentieth century by the Americans who
    lived it / Bernard Edelman.
        p.   cm.
    ISBN 0-374-17678-7 (alk. paper)
    1. United States—History—20th century—Anecdotes.   2. United
States—Social life and customs—20th century—Anecdotes.
3. Centenarians—United States—Interviews.   I. Edelman, Bernard.
E742.C45   1999
973.91—dc21   98-34198

FOR MY FATHER AND MY MOTHER,

who weren't blessed with the "long genes"

FOR AIDAN,

who sparkles my life

AND FOR ELLEN

Contents

The past? I want to talk about it and remember it,

but I don't dwell on it. Some people keep looking back

all the time: "Oh, oh, oh those days are gone!"

I'm just the opposite. I can always look into

the next day. It keeps you going.

— RENATA BURT

Born December 24, 1895

Brown County, Wisconsin

As the clock winds down on the twentieth century, we seem to be hurtling through a media-fueled din of anticipation and speculation to greet the new millennium, charged by the symbolic significance of it all.

Most of us will reflect, no doubt, upon how far we have come as we contemplate where we are going. Certainly there can be little dispute, particularly in the Western world, that this century — *our* century—has seen extraordinary technological advances and social progress, as well as unspeakable destruction and construction, precipitous economic ruin and rebound, appalling environmental degradation and redemption.

Of some 271 million Americans alive today, only a handful were around at the dawn of the century. They have benefited from its transformations; they have been wounded by its excesses. They have persevered. They are America's centenarians. Some 63,000 Americans are now living who have hit the century marker, members of an exclusive club, admission to which is automatic. The only requirement is longevity.

Some have achieved a modicum of fortune and fame, though not, perhaps, the fanfare of such celebrated centenarians as George Burns and Irving Berlin and Grandma Moses. Most have lived lives of relative anonymity. Some have lived lives of privilege. Others are no strangers to poverty. Many live today on a modest fixed income made possible in part by Social Security. Others are well off, their retirement cushioned by well-recompensed labor and well-placed investments. Minuscule though their numbers may be, they are part of the fastest-growing segment of the population: the over-eighty-five set, the "oldest old." They have *endured*. They have lived twice as long as they might have expected to live when they were born, when the average life expectancy in the United States was forty-nine years. To a person, they did not seek the longevity with which they have been blessed. Their long lives simply happened.

Half of all centenarians live in nursing homes, victimized by failing bodies and/or faltering minds. Senile dementia afflicts half their number. Yet perhaps thirty percent, reports Dr. Thomas T. Perls, principal investigator of the New England Centenarian Study, still have acute recollections; another twenty percent or more have short-term memory deficits. Women outnumber men, by about five to one.

Many have profited by better nutrition and advances in public health. But this does not account for their longevity. "For whatever reason," Dr. Perls states in the January 1995 *Scientific American,* "some people are particularly resistant to acquiring the disorders that disable and kill most people before age ninety. Because of this resistance, they not only outlive others, they do so relatively free of infirmities. . . . They possess traits that enable them to avoid or delay the diseases that commonly accompany aging." They may also have "an unusually low complement of deleterious genes," he notes.

Or, as Lucy Somerville Howorth of Cleveland, Mississippi, put it, "I guess I was blessed with the long genes."

Consider what they have witnessed in their time: Horse-and-buggy days and the space age. Kitty Hawk and the Concorde. Jules Verne and Neil Armstrong—and Sally Ride. Unpaved roads and the interstate highway system. The outhouse and the Jacuzzi. The Springfield rifle and the starlight scope. Hucksters' cure-all potions and MRIs, interferon, and laser surgery. They have lived through two world wars and countless nasty little conflicts; the Spanish influenza pandemic that in little more than a year killed more than 21 million people worldwide, 675,000 people in the United States, and 43,000 servicemen—more soldiers than fell to Axis firepower; the experiment with Prohibition; the devastation of the Great Depression; the rise and demise of Communism. In their youth, women who achieved professional careers were uncommon, and it was only as they came of age that women were finally accorded the right to vote. For much of their lives, "colored" people were, for the most part, second-class citizens.

They have witnessed progress that has transformed society. They have seen America embrace social policies such as Social Security, once considered dangerously radical and now sanctified as practically untouchable. They have been part of the emergence of a prosperous nation, a superpower that has realized middle-class aspirations and dreams for the vast majority of its citizens. They have lived to see the advent of cyberspace, the World Wide Web, virtual reality.

And they have stories to tell. "When you start thinking back," says Ella May Stumpe, now of Frederick, Maryland, "one memory will trigger another and bring up something that you hadn't thought about for years."

To compile a book based on the recollections and reflections of centenarians, I had to find, first, those who were willing, and still able, not only to share their memories but also to tell stories. No computerized central registry of centenarians exists; there is no roster of the oldest of the old. I tailored hundreds of letters, and made scores of phone calls, to labor unions and business associations, ethnic groups and veterans organizations, professional societies and agencies for the aging. Friends across the country sent me clippings from local papers. I started to compile my own modest database. After doing preliminary interviews, over the phone, of many centenarians, members of their families, or caregivers, I scheduled trips when I could group potential interviewees in a geographic cluster.

I conducted the first full-fledged interview in September 1995. Through a friend of my wife, I learned of the oldest resident of a small city in Pennsylvania less than an hour from my home in western New Jersey. I organized and oriented my questions, wondering how I could plumb the depths, as opposed to simply skimming the surface, of one hundred years of living.

The first interview was a disaster. The woman was unresponsive. She was tired. Her memories were indistinct. She could tell no stories. When I left her home on a gloomy Sunday, I hit a wall of doubt: What if all centenarians were like her?

Then, for my second interview, I met Milton Ward Garland. His answers were precise, his recall of events that occurred eighty, ninety years ago astonishing. He still went to work. Five days a week. For seventy-five years then, he had been employed as a refrigeration engineer for the Frick Company in Waynesboro, Pennsylvania. (He has since been cited as the oldest known worker in America.) When I left his modest, well-kept, neatly furnished home, I was elated.

Milton Garland, I came to learn, wasn't the only one who still went to work at age one hundred. Audrey Stubbart, another whom I interviewed early, was a proofreader and columnist for *The Examiner* in Independence, Missouri—a thirty-seven-year career *after* she left her job as a copy reader at a publishing house when she reached the mandatory retirement age of sixty-five. Philip Carret, who in 1928 established one of the first mutual funds on Wall Street, was still going to work every day at Carret and Company, the current incarnation of his investment-counseling business. Dr. Leila Denmark, a pediatrician, was still seeing young patients six days a week in her office in Alpharetta, Georgia. Beatrice Wood and Helen L. Smith, both creative spirits of very different demeanor and notoriety, had worked at their art into their hundredth year. Aaron Birnbaum and Alfred Levitt, artists also, were prolific as they neared the end of their first century.

In the course of compiling this book, I have spoken with some ninety centenarians. They bear testament to a sometimes not so self-evident truth:

All people are interesting. Or, as St. Paul put it: "There are, it may be, so many different kinds of voices in the world and none of them without significance."

Their stories are tilted toward their early memories, when, perhaps, their lives were most intense. I was struck by how many of them had grown up on farms or had emigrated to the United States in search of a better life. Few spoke in terms of grand themes—the war against Communism, the birth of a vibrant American middle class, the emergence of women in the workplace. Most told simple stories with detailed recollections, illustrating many of the key themes and watershed events that have marked the passage of the twentieth century.

In editing these interviews, I have taken liberties. In many instances, when the recounting of an incident was disjointed, or truncated, I've smoothed out the language and added transitional phrasing to aid the flow of the narrative. In a few cases, a son or a daughter translated or recounted the stories their mother or father had told them; in these cases, I in turn transposed a third-person account into a first-person recollection. In one instance, I melded material from another tape-recorded source: Chester Hoff, at 105 the oldest surviving ex-Major League baseball player in 1997, was interviewed shortly after his hundredth birthday by the Baseball Hall of Fame, which lent me a recording of that interview. In other cases, I have integrated written material into the narrative. Eight of those whose stories follow—Flora Ethel Andrews, Philip Carret, John Dodge Clark, Rosie Gries, Erich Leyens, Dirk Struik, Ella May Stumpe, Beatrice Wood—wrote, in their tenth decade, memoirs of their lives. The most compelling, perhaps, is John Clark's single-spaced, typewritten, forty-seven-page account of his experiences as a lieutenant in World War I.

More than a few interviews were frustrating affairs. "Oh, a few days ago I could have told you a lot of things," 104-year-old Elsie Gordon, of Moosehaven, in Orange Park, Florida, said to me. "Today, it seems like things have faded somewhat." For many, however, the recollection of details—even of conversations from their youth—was nothing less than extraordinary. I recognize, of course, that memory plays tricks, that age can confuse. As Sarah Hunter Jackson of Johnson City, Tennessee, said, "Nobody can prove whether I tell the truth or lie. I can just tell anything. People will believe what I say happened, or they won't believe it. The ones who know, they're all gone now."

Most of my conversations with centenarians took place between September 1995 and November 1997, with a last burst of interviewing in March and April 1998. Several of these centenarians have since passed on. Many are still living, and thriving, taking each day as it comes, some with an aura of resignation, others experiencing the joys and satisfactions a new day can bring. Few are enraptured by the prospect of greeting the new millennium. One of the most remarkable centenarians whom I've met, Ella May Stumpe, exudes a reassuring optimism despite the infirmities of age. "You know," she said, "the Bible says I might live to be 120. And that's what I'm trying to shoot for."

Theirs are the true voices of America in the twentieth century. Their recollections, their reflections, their reminiscences tell us where we have been, how far we have come. And, perhaps, how far we can go.

BERNARD EDELMAN
Finesville, New Jersey

First Memories

Listen, I remember very well what

I did ninety, ninety-five years ago.

What I did yesterday, I forget.

—EMIL GLAUBER

Born November 12, 1895

Tachau, Austria-Hungary

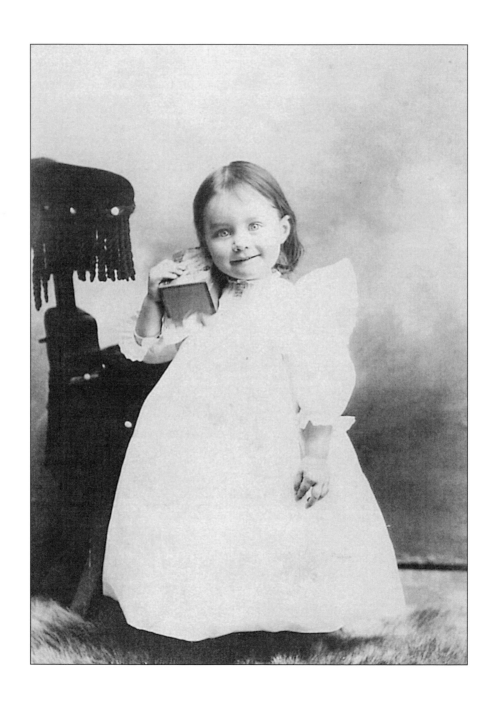

What is my earliest memory? It's impossible to say, because one doesn't know whether it's something one remembers or merely remembers having been told.

When I was four years old I ran away from home. I didn't get very far, only about two blocks, and then they caught up with me. My father was a conveyancer—he examined titles to real estate—and he went to his office in Boston every day. I'd never been to Boston. I was curious. I wanted to see what it was like.

—PHILIP L. CARRET

Mother was feeding Myrtle—she's eleven months older than I am—and Poppa was carrying me in his arms. We went into a store. Poppa opened the door for Mother, who had my sister by the hand.

There was a woman there that was blind, and Poppa went over to her and said something about that I was his baby. And she said, I'll have to see her face. She had to feel my face all the way around. Oh, Mr. Morford, she said, she's just as round—

That's where I got the idea that my face was round.

When I began to be aware of things, I must have been close to three years old. I'd be nursing, and I'd see the pain start coming in Mother's eyes. I didn't want to hurt her; I just wanted her to notice me. Mothers nursed their babies as long as they could then because they didn't think they'd get pregnant during that time. They had no protection.

—AUDREY STUBBART

When I was five years old, I went to a church service in my father's granary with George Clark, who was five, too. It was a time of the year when there was no grain. The neighbors that wanted to start this nucleus for a church, they brought the chairs. It was my mother who said to George and me, You two get outside now and go hunt eggs.

The granary was back by the pastures and the chicken coop—we didn't

◄ *Mary Nell Dosser (Mary Nell Dosser Keller), Jonesborough, Tennessee, September 1896* have a henhouse—with maybe a couple dozen hens. They were supposed to lay their eggs in that coop but they didn't. They'd get out and lay in the tall grass. Every day my two older brothers and I had to chase through that grass and hunt eggs. So from this church service I was sent out to look for eggs with George Clark.

—ELLA MAY STUMPE

We were living in Kenova, West Virginia, and my sister—the next one younger than me—was a tiny little baby. I had a little girlfriend that lived just a couple of doors from us. One day, my mother was busy with my sister, and she missed me. She started to look for me, when my little friend's mother happened to catch me just as I opened her door to walk in to see my friend. She brought me home. Oh, I was just heartbroken, because I thought my friend's mother didn't want me down there.

But the reason she didn't want me was my friend had diphtheria, and she didn't want me to catch it. And my little friend, she was so bad she died. 'Course, they didn't tell me too much about that at the time.

—ADA TABOR

My grandparents' house in Frederick, Maryland, had a back porch, and I'd crawl under there and make mud pies and all kinds of neat things. And I'd sit out there, under the trees, drawing like mad. I could sketch and draw before I could write; I was always at it. Of course, paper was very rare. I had to use slate.

—HELEN L. SMITH

My dad's mother died, and he wanted to go back home. So we left the farm in Eden Valley, Minnesota, and took the train to Kentucky. When we were in Chicago, my folks were doing some shopping and we kids were riding the elevators. We thought that was great, getting to ride the elevators. That was wonderful excitement. I was six years old.

—FRIEDA GREENE HARDIN

When I was about three years old, the family rented a house in Seattle that had a picket fence around about two or three lots. We lived in the big house and the people who owned the property lived in the little house.

They made a small boat—they called it the *Ivy*—and put it on top of their house.

About ten o'clock in the morning, I'd go out to play, and along came a man singing. And I *knew*. They never told me, but I knew. And I ran into the house and told Mama: Here comes the man that sings the naughty songs. He was drunk. They used to laugh about that: Here comes the man that drinks and sings the naughty songs.

—IVY FRISK

When I was still wearing dresses, my father made sorghum molasses for the family and for the neighbors that grew cane. The mill was down behind the barn, about a hundred yards from the house, and I had to go through a wire fence to get there.

He was down there working one morning and as I crawled through the fence I cut my arm on a piece of the cane stalk. It was sharp as a knife. One of the men that was working there with my father come over, and when he saw the cut on my arm, he said, Oh, you're gonna have to go to the doctor. I got scared, and I crawled back through the fence and ran back to my doctor—my mother. She put some Petro-Carbo salve on my arm and bandaged it.

—HARLEY POTTER

Harley Potter at age four, with Miss Kate, his teacher

I was exploring a hole in the middle of the street in Milford, Nebraska, where I was born. They were grading the road. My mother looked out and saw a big steam roller bearing down on me. She rushed out and pulled me out of the hole. Then she took me into the house and changed my diaper.

—VICTOR MILLS

When I was three, I had long curls. My mother would take the curling iron, heat it and curl my hair, and put a ribbon in it. Before I went to school, of course, my dad had to cut those curls off, 'cause I wouldn't dare to go to school that way.

—AL KRAUS

We were living in Chicago, in this house next to the church—my father was a minister—and I saw him chasing a rat in the house. He caught two of them. He put them in a cage. He put the cage in the bathtub. He turned the water on and drowned them.

—JOHN D. CLARK

When I was about six or seven, we was livin' in Bishop, Georgia. One day, me and my little brother was outdoors playin', and my ma was in the field. Then it got so dark we couldn't see one another. And my ma was ahollerin', tellin' us to go in the house.

We couldn't see to get back in the house. We couldn't *see*. We couldn't find the doorstep. So we just got together and hugged up on the ground. Chickens was aflyin' and *oooh!* they was acrowin', dogs was arunnin', people in the field was ahollerin'—they didn't know which way to go or what to do. And we didn't move, 'cause we were scared.

When you talkin' about dark, it was *dark!* I couldn't see my brother, and he couldn't see me. One of the dogs got down next to us. We couldn't get to the house and get in the bed. We thought if we went in the house, we could cover up in the bed, and it would be nice.

And then it passed. The moon, they say, crossed the sun. My ma said if the moon crosses the sun, after you got old you'd come back to life.

—FANNIE LOU DAVIS

I couldn't have been more than four or five when the city of Tacoma was covered with smoke from a forest fire. And ashes were all over the streets. You had to have your lamps lit during the daytime in order to see, it was that dark from the smoke and the fire.

—OSCAR C. WEBER

We could look out of our front window and see what we called the River Jordan, a small creek. This was in Allentown, Pennsylvania. One Sunday, members of a religious sect came there and baptized some members in the water. They walked into the water and the minister sort of dunked them. Then they came out with their clothing all wet. It seemed so irrational to see people all dressed walking into a river.

—JOHN SAILLIARD

John Sailliard with his mother, Marie Leonie, and his sisters, Emilie and Rose, Allentown, Pennsylvania

I was on a farm in Italy, near Naples. We didn't have nothin' to eat. But there were a lot of snakes, snakes all over the place when I was goin' to school. I didn't want to go to school no more. I didn't like it.

—JOSEPH LICCARDO

When I was six years old, my father took me to a school. It was on a farm near where we lived in Kreuzburg, Latvia. It had only about twenty pupils. At lunchtime, they found out that I was Jewish, and they knew that a Jew is not supposed to eat ham. So they started to force ham in my mouth. When I came home, I told my father what happened. So he says, It looks like you cannot go back to that school. And that was the end of my schooling.

—SAMUEL D. SCHNEIER

I was five years old when my mother died. I was next-to-the-youngest one, who was still an infant. The three of us older children had to attend her funeral. That was a must with the old people in that day.

I sat there on that front seat with the rest of the family, right in front of the casket. I couldn't shed a tear. I will never be able to understand how I felt inside. But in later years I learned that that was the grief. Some people could let it out in tears, some of it, anyway. I didn't shed a tear. But I had that terrible feeling.

—JULIA TYLER

Oh, Lord! I was five years old. I had the typhoid fever and I like to die! Dr. Lewis, he was the doctor in Jackson, North Carolina, he give me up. They dressed me to die. My father had the typhoid fever, and my brother had the typhoid fever, we all of us in the same house. My mother was livin' and my mother's youngest son was born in that typhoid fever all of us had. But she didn't get it and neither did the baby. The baby was a boy. They named him Sam Ransom.

—SALLIE JORDAN

Like all boys, smart alecks that we were, the nastiest thing we could do was start to smoke. We didn't have money and couldn't buy a pack of cigarettes. What we did, we'd take a piece of newspaper and roll our own. We would always find newspaper, because people threw their garbage out in the back yard. Everybody did in those days. So we'd scavenge.

Or we'd use leaves from a grape arbor in our back yard in Trenton. We'd get a big leaf off the grape arbor when it turned brown and we made our cigarettes out of it. That beat the newspaper.

—ARTHUR W. HAMER, SR.

I lived in Baltimore on a street that those streetcars ran on. They ran on tracks about the same gauge trolleys used to run on, only they were pulled by horses. The horsecars gave way to cable cars and then to electric cars. In the early days of electric, there were all kinds of wires falling down and killing people. Why didn't they kill birds on the wire, people wanted to know. It was really amusing.

—ALBERT M. COLEMAN

My father took me to a big political gathering at the train depot, where the President's train was coming through. He was able to get a place right at the rear of the train. The President came out to speak. My father lifted me up. And I shook hands with President McKinley.

—KARL LONG

Starting Out

I have asked myself several times:

How can I still remember that?

So many things have happened when

I was young that I remember yet today.

ARTHUR W. HAMER, SR.

Born May 10, 1896

Trenton, New Jersey

My father, Micajah Warren Leonard—"Cage" to all who knew him—filed on a homestead eight miles as the crow flies from Dunseith, North Dakota, in 1885. He built a one-room shanty, dug a well, and began his cultivation of the soil with a one-furrow plow pulled by his oxen. He had no farm machinery, so he planted his small plot by sowing the wheat by hand. This is known as "broadcast": to scatter the seeds wildly. The grain he cut with a scythe and threshed with a flail. During this early period, he did trucking, by wagon train, between Dunseith and Devils Lake, a distance of one hundred miles. He would take a load of furs there for shipping to the eastern market, and he would bring back basic supplies for a developing community. This was his source of income while he was converting virgin soil into farmland.

Cage added two rooms to the sod shanty in 1890 when he married Mary Ann Bigham, my mother. She was seventeen when her mother died in childbirth, leaving a baby boy and seven other children. As the oldest girl, she assumed the responsibility of homemaker and mother to her family. Two years later she married and had a

The home in Dunseith, North Dakota, where Ella May Leonard (Ella May Stumpe) was born

daughter. But this marriage had its problems, and ended in divorce. The problems had to be very grave for a Presbyterian lady to choose that action, when divorce was a sin. Jeanette was five when Cage and Mary Ann married.

Guided and nurtured by the gentle manner of a Quaker father and the strict discipline of a Presbyterian mother, I entered this picture, preceded by two brothers and, of course, Jennie. I'm sure I was delivered by the local

◀ *Leila Daughtry (Leila Denmark) in her mother's arms, in a Daughtry family portrait, Bullock County, Georgia, about 1899*

doctor. And he should have made out the paperwork to record my birth. But I think they were very careless about it in those days. He could have made it out and given it to my folks to send in and it could have been lost there on the homestead. If anybody asked me to prove my age today, I couldn't: there is no official record of my birth.

—ELLA MAY STUMPE

My folks were married in 1891, the first year of four years' drought. They were a young couple just starting out. They put everything they had into stocking a farm. By the time the drought was over, they had nothing.

Poppa went to work down in Lincoln, in a meat factory, but he couldn't take working as a butcher. Then he went down to Texas; that's where my oldest brother was born. But he couldn't stand it, picking cotton with the Negroes. So he went back out to Malvern, Iowa, and then out to Gordon, Nebraska. The census taker one time said to my parents, You folks must have traveled an awful lot because you have four children and each one of them was born in a different state.

I was born five years after the Battle of Wounded Knee in Newman Grove, Nebraska, population I have no idea. It was up north of Lincoln. I don't even know whether or not it's on the map anymore.

It was on a farm—this wasn't the place I was born—where life really started for me. It was just at the end of the Rosebud Reservation, where they drove the Sioux Indians.

One day Poppa came in and said, I'm ready to leave, and I want you to take this money. You may need it while I'm gone.

I said, I won't be going anywhere. You keep the money. You might need it before you get there.

No, Poppa said, you take this money.

Mother was baking bread after he left that day. She turned out a fresh baked loaf on the table by the door. And if there's anything more inviting than fresh bread, I don't know what it is.

Well, the Indians evidently thought so, too, because here came a big Indian up on the porch. He opened the screen door and reached in and picked up the loaf. He put a bill down beside it. Mother said, I don't have any money and I can't make any change.

And I said, Oh, Mother, you remember all that money Daddy left you?

Audrey, Mother said after the Indian left, I wish you would learn to keep your mouth shut. Now the Indians know that your daddy's gone, we're alone, and there's money in the house.

We spent all the rest of that day moving our quarters into one bedroom where she could keep track of us. Every time I'd wake up in the night, there was Mother sitting in one corner of the bed with a shotgun across her knees. And there was her brother sitting at the other corner of the bed with a rifle across his knees. They were keeping track of the Indians out there on the other side of the field. They were dancing around a big fire, cooking something to eat.

That made such an impression on me, seeing those Indians. They didn't have hardly anything to eat. And here we were telling such terrible things about everybody being afraid of them while we were trying to run them off their land.

People's ideas about the Indians had been more cultured and colored by fiction than by reality. Because I lived among the Indians. We didn't have trouble with them. My father died when I was seven years old; it was an Indian woman that came with Mother and took care of us.

—AUDREY STUBBART

The seventeenth of September I was born, in 1892. On Verona Plantation, 'tween Seaboard and Jackson, right here in Northampton County, North Carolina. That's where my daddy was born and raised, born by the rich man, General Matt Ransom. In slavery time, he belonged to General Ransom: my daddy was his slave. And my mother was George Mason's nigger child. She stayed in the house with his children; she never had to get out in the field and work. In slavery time, Nannie Mason belonged to him, and he kept her in his house till she was grown and married to my daddy.

When George Mason found my daddy askin' could he marry, he sent my mother away to a place in Wilson, North Carolina, and wouldn't let my daddy see her over twelve months. She was eighteen years old then. But my daddy didn't give up, and my momma wanted to come home and marry him.

The white man my momma belonged to lived a little bit more decent than General Ransom did. General Ransom had the most money but he was stingy. But he was a man you couldn't outdo. And George Mason told General Ransom that my momma couldn't cook on the fireplace 'cause she had never seen nobody cook on a fireplace. My momma had never made an ash cake before—that was a bread made with water and wrapped up and baked in the ashes in the fireplace—she had never even had that. The home my mother was raised in had a great big old stove.

So General Ransom bought them a cookstove.

The Masons didn't like corn bread: that was slave food. The Ransoms did. So the General had to promise to give my momma a barrel of flour every four weeks of her life so she could have flour bread.

And she and my daddy weren't married until the General had built them this little frame house and furnished it all for them to live in.

So the Mason girl married the Ransom boy and they had four sons and four daughters. And that's who I am.

—SALLIE JORDAN

I grew up in the farmhouse I was born in, six miles from Saluda, South Carolina. Father, who was in the Confederate War—he had walked all the way home after the battle at Gettysburg—grew corn, oats, wheat. Cotton, of course, was the money crop. Mostly Father did well, but there were hard times, when cotton went down to five cents a pound. That doesn't seem like much, but people worked then for fifty cents *a day*. And they didn't work from 9 a.m. to 6 p.m. They worked from sunup to sundown. But we didn't one time dream that we were poor. We had chickens, so we had eggs. Father kept a cow, so we had all the milk we could drink, and butter.

Of course, things cost a lot less then, too. You didn't make much, but you didn't have to pay much, either. A letter cost two cents to mail. You weren't supposed to pay but a penny for a postal card. When one of my brothers got a job in Columbia, I used to write to him real often. And I wrote real small. Now, I don't know if he was teasing, 'cause he was a great tease, but he said he went to the post office one time to get his mail and my postal card was so full of writing the postmaster made him pay another cent.

Father made us work for the money we spent for things we didn't need. Every Saturday, he paid us for the chores we had done. Mother didn't believe in hiring help if the children were able to work. The only colored help she ever hired was a washerwoman. But Mother made us iron, and oh, I hated ironing! We had to sprinkle all the clothes with water, and roll them up overnight. Next day we'd have to make a fire in the fireplace, even on the hottest day of the summer, put five or six irons in front of it to heat and then switch irons to keep them hot. My younger sister could iron just beautifully, but when I'd iron a garment, wrinkles would come in it by the time I'd pick it up to iron the other side.

We girls would also do some babysitting. My brother-in-law had a law partner who would come sometimes to Saluda from over where he lived in

Edgefield. He'd bring his young son with him—the boy was only two or three years old—and he'd spend the day with my sister. She had no children, so she would call Ruth and Edith and me to come down there to entertain the boy. He loved horseback riding, and they had a very gentle horse. So all we had to do was take that boy out on that horse. Well, he was a darling little boy. I never did know him when he was a teenager; he was twenty-five miles from us and those were horse-and-buggy days. But later on, he was always a good friend for the family. Still is. And do you know? I have a clipping from a magazine that was printed in Cairo, Egypt, that one of my cousins found while she was traveling. It was a clipping about how I was a babysitter for Senator Strom Thurmond.

—LOIS CROUCH ADDY

I come from Edgecombe County in eastern North Carolina. The county was, and still is, fifty percent black, fifty percent white. But it wasn't just "black" and "white." We had upper blacks, middle blacks, and lower blacks; all the lower blacks did was cut ditches. The whites had the same thing: upper whites, middle whites, and lower whites, the poor whites.

We had no trouble with most of the white families, and the white families had no trouble with us. The only people we ever had any trouble with were the lower whites. But there weren't any of the strongest, most influential, and most moneyed people in Edgecombe County who didn't recognize and acknowledge what was accomplished by the blacks in Edgecombe County. And my father—he also was York David Garrett—was well thought about by all the best colored people and all the best white people in the county.

My father was conceived before the Emancipation Proclamation in 1863. His parents were slaves on a 700-acre plantation. His mother cooked for the family, and lived with the family, and she had excellent status. His father, the first York Garrett, was a leather man, one of the best harness makers in eastern North Carolina. His father never considered himself a slave even though he belonged to these white people.

Their name was Powell, but he never took that name. My father never knew him, never even met him. And here's why: Mr. Powell had sent my grandfather out on a job, and he was a week later coming back than his owner thought he should be. So Mr. Powell said, York, why you so long gettin' back here?

What you mean? Did you get any complaints on the job I did?

No.

Did the people like what I did?

Yeah.

So what's your complaint?

I had another job that I was gonna put you on last week, he said. And because you was late gettin' back here, I couldn't put you on it. So I'm gonna give you a whippin', so next time you gonna be back here on time.

My grandfather told him: I'm not gonna take any whippin', 'cause I haven't done a thing for you to whip me for. You're not gonna use the lash on me.

And he never did. Because my grandfather left and he never came back.

Now, my father was telling me what his mother had told him his father had said.

My father was in business for himself long before I was born. He owned a grocery store on the main street in Tarboro, across the river from Princeville, where I was born. There were ten of us children—I was the eighth child—but all ten didn't live. My father moved us to Tarboro in 1901. He bought a lot and built a house. He used the best artisans, the best carpenters and bricklayers. They were all colored, and they were the best.

If he hadn't been a good merchant and a good salesman, his store wouldn't have survived for thirty years. He called it the Plain & Fancy Grocery. He sold meat, flour, sugar, butter, lard, canned goods, and liquor. At least half of his customers were white: he had more white people spending money with him than he did colored.

My father was one of those Negroes that white folks felt was "all right people." These were colored people they knew, and they treated them like decent people because they *were* decent people. The only difference between my father and other businessmen was that he was colored and they were white, and his children had to go to colored schools. My father knew a good education could give you the chance. So he sent his children to good schools—good *colored* schools.

My oldest brother, the one that I was so crazy about, went to Shaw University in Raleigh straight from Princeville grade school. He didn't have any high school first, so he finished it there. And then he wanted his college degree. In four years he got his B.S. degree. And then he wanted medicine. But he had bad luck, just like my sister did before him. He had tuberculosis. He got sick in his junior year. He finished Shaw in June and died in August.

Eight years later, when it was time for me to go to college, my mama said, You're going to college but you're not going to Shaw.

But Mama, I said, that's the only school I want to go to, that's the only school I love. My brother went there, my sister went there. And all of my closest friends went there.

She said, Yeah, but you're not going there. It killed two of my children. It's not going to kill you.

—YORK GARRETT

We were taught by our mothers to be very respectful of the Confederate flag and the Confederate holidays. We were also taught that we were Americans, and to be respectful of the United States flag, and to celebrate the Fourth of July. You see, after the Civil War, there was a good deal of squabbling about whether the Fourth of July was a Southern holiday or not.

But my mother always said, We are all Americans now, and we must recognize that and be respectful of the past, but not let it dominate us.

My mother, Nellie Nugent Somerville, was a very wise woman. She had a very fine brain. She went to college, which in that day and age was unusual. And the president of this college by good luck was a bishop in the Southern Methodist Church. He spotted my mother as having a superior intellect. He encouraged her. By the help of this bishop, and other people who spotted her intellectual abilities, she had a better education than most of the girls of her generation.

My mother was quite ambitious when it was quite ambitious for women to go into public life. She ran for the legislature when it was an unheard-of thing for a woman to do. And women up and down the Delta rallied around and elected her. She was the first woman to serve in the Mississippi legislature. She served just one term, though; she didn't think she had enough support to run for reelection.

My mother was always campaigning for something and traveling around, and she didn't want to leave me at home with the servants to look after me. So she took little me with her—she was going to women's meetings and the ladies, either out of kindness or sympathy, would pick me up, give me little candies, take me to some little party. They would all make a to-do about this cute little girl. Maybe that spoiled me; anyhow, it got me accustomed to having attention. And I got the gift of meeting strangers, and keeping my poise; it made me willing and able to take front stage every once in a while.

My mother was a suffragist she didn't like the word *suffragette*; that was a British word—and she was president at one time of the National

American Women's Suffrage Association. She helped organize first in Mississippi, and then all through the South. She was a great friend of Anna Howard Shaw, a Unitarian minister who became a leader of the Women's Suffrage Movement, partially because some of the ministers in the church snubbed her. They thought men should be the only preachers. Well, of course, that didn't suit somebody like Anna Howard Shaw, who had been converted as a child and was convinced that she could preach. She would go out to the woods and stand on a stump and deliver a sermon. Because that was supposed to be—and I think it still is—the best training for a public speaker. You stand there on a stump with no people applauding you, and you talk to the bushes and the trees. You've got to be good if you can keep going.

My mother thought Anna Howard Shaw was a great person. But the suffrage movement got to a stage when some of the people thought they needed fresh, stronger leadership. So they asked Carrie Chapman Catt, who was a wealthy woman, to take over the National American Women's Suffrage Association. She—I could now understand later in life, it sounded selfish then—she said she would do it if Anna Howard Shaw retired. My mother admired Anna Howard Shaw. And, of course, little me trotted along after my mother, so we kind of resented Ms. Catt. But after I was grown, and learned more about leadership, I could understand that if she was going to take over, she had to have a clear deck.

A child, you know, doesn't have a sense of history. At least this one didn't. It was just exciting being with my mother, taking part in suffrage and meeting some of the ladies who came to see my mother, and going to conventions with her. I learned a lot about how to get along with people, just watching her.

We were on a train once. And a group of young college boys began to make some derisive remarks about votes for women. Well, that's bad manners, but that doesn't stop them sometimes. So my mother called the fruit-and-candy vendor and asked him how much his basket would cost. She handed him that money and said, Now take this and distribute it among those boys. Well, those boys changed their tune right away; from making fun of votes for women, they began cheering votes for women. I learned a lesson then that the way you win somebody is not to oppose them, not to downgrade them, but to give them a little lift. It's been very valuable.

And when the Nineteenth Amendment kicked in, oh, I'll never forget the morning we first voted. My father was in for breakfast, and my mother and I came down. He said, What are you all dressed up for? This is just breakfast.

No, she said, it's breakfast, but I'm going to vote with you after breakfast.

Oh, he said, you never voted.

Well, I said, that's all changed. Now we all can vote.

So he changed his tune.

—LUCY SOMERVILLE HOWORTH

Before women went to vote the first time, some men, I heard, would park themselves at the voting places and make not pleasant remarks when the women were trying to vote. They felt women were just stepping outside their bounds. There was a lot of antagonism. And a lot of women wouldn't vote, because it would agitate their husbands.

—HELEN L. SMITH

Ada Tabor, age twenty-three, in Florida, circa 1919

I didn't pay any attention to elections till we went to Logan and I was gettin' big enough to notice them. Before women could vote, the men, they'd get in a big argument and they'd fight. Every now and then, somebody'd be killed over the election. I thought that was awful. Oh, here in West Virginia, they took it very seriously, the Democrats and the Republicans.

Now, women didn't go out on the street, unless it was necessary, come election day. When women were finally allowed to vote, I was old enough to vote. And my dad, he had never wanted us to go out when it would be dangerous before that, but now he said, I would like for you and your mama to go and vote.

And I said, Dad, I want to stay away from the polls.

No, he said, there's one class of women that will go to the polls and vote. And, he said, I think that all decent women should go and vote.

That's the way he reasoned it out. And that was the first time I voted.

—ADA TABOR

I was born at home—that's the only place they were born in then—in Norton, Virginia. It was just one of those little coal towns, mostly depending on the coalfields for income. I guess, oh, seventy-five or eighty percent of the total income in that whole area was due to Westmoreland Coal Company. They owned the whole southwest Virginia area, lock, stock, and barrel—banks, churches, schools, everything. But not Norton, which was an independent town.

Wasn't anything easy then. We didn't have electricity until we moved to the farm over in Powell's Valley in 19 and 4, when I was ten. Before that, we used oil lamps. We went out in the woods to go to the bathroom. Had to walk quite a ways to school, there was no other way to go, and never even missed a day on account of the weather. We'd bathe in a washtub once a week, on Saturday night. My mother heated water on the cookstove. We used soap she made herself. When we used to kill hogs, which was my job, we saved the grease to make soap.

I had to get out of bed at five o'clock in the mornin' to grind coffee beans to make coffee for breakfast to get my father off to work by seven. Coffee beans came green. Mother'd put them in a bread pan and roast them in the oven. I'd put the beans in the mill and grind 'em and make the coffee. My father was a carpenter. He made hardwood floors, he put in mortice locks, he did a whole lot of building all over town. He walked to wherever he worked, carrying his toolbox and his plans.

Back then, the younger'd kind of take care of the older with whatever they got. And they didn't have much, to tell you the truth. It was just son takin' care of daddy or daughter takin' care of daddy when he got too old to do anything else.

—ORLANDO F. MORLEY

The child-labor laws of that day were made by our mother. The dishes had to be washed. The woodbox had to be kept filled. The water pail frequently needed filling from the well. The eggs needed gathering. The young calves needed care.

When calves were taken from their mothers, they were tied with a rope and fed from a pail. They had to be taught to drink. Teaching them was our job. With a pail of milk, you approached, stuck your hand in the milk, and offered it to the calf, which grabbed it, sucking on your fingers. If you did this a couple of times, it would follow your fingers to the pail with its eyes, stick its nose in, and the task was completed.

And since those calves were tied up to keep them away from their mothers, they had to be exercised frequently. That was a lot of fun, running around the yard with them on a rope. It was fun until they had grown to the size and strength where they could pull you off your feet and drag you through the weeds. It was time then to add them to the herd in the pasture.

We would spend a lot of time at the pump handle when the cattle came in to drink. We knew each one by name, and we learned the special traits that set one apart from another. We had a daily special duty: to go to the pasture with Ring, our sheep dog, and bring in the milk cows in late afternoon. This was a real pleasure when snow was on the ground and we could take our sleds. We would run up and tie our sled to the last cow's tail and get a free ride back to the barn. This went on for some time until one day an unruly heifer broke from the herd. Ring was on the job; to get the heifer back in line, he nipped her heels. She broke and ran, spooking the herd. They stampeded for the barn. Each cow turned the corner neatly, but the sled did not. It hit the barn with a force that threw two scared kids into a snowbank.

That was nothing to the scare we got when we dusted ourselves off and saw that the cow's tail was still tied to the sled rope. We finally solved the dilemma of what to do by burying the tail in the snow. We were fortunate, though, that Father was a gentle man. When he opened the barn door and he looked down the row of tails, he saw that one was much shorter than the others. We had pulled off her tassel, and she would never again be able to brush flies off her back in the summertime. Our remorse was the hardest part of the punishment. But we did not get any more free rides, either.

—ELLA MAY STUMPE

On my daddy's farm down in Henry County, Georgia, we grew corn, pepper, peanuts, and peas. And cotton. When I was a little girl, I cried to go to the field. I didn't know what it was all about. And before it was ended, I cried not to go. Pickin' cotton, your back is hurtin', you're all bent over and when you stand up you ache. Mama used to tell me, You're too young, you ain't got no back. And I'd say, Well, back here, I don't know what you call it, but it's hurtin' me plenty from pickin' cotton. I rather chop cotton than to pick it.

We used to start out early in the morning. We picked till eleven-thirty or twelve o'clock. We'd stop for dinner. Then we'd go back to the field at one o'clock and pick till sundown. Sure was hard work. *Hard* work.

We lived in a four-room wooden house. It had a storeroom, a dining room, a living room, and a front room, they called it. We rented it from Cora Wise. She was a rich woman, a fine woman. I loved her.

I wanted to become a schoolteacher, but my schoolin' ended after the seventh grade. Mama and Daddy, they was gonna send me home with Miss Alberta Williams—she was our teacher—and she was gonna put me through school. But when she left to go home, I was down with the measles and I couldn't go. So I worked with the family in the field, sortin', gatherin', pickin' cotton, choppin' cotton, washin' cotton, bunchin' cotton, droppin' corn, pullin' corn, pullin' fodder. You name it on the farm, Jessie done it.

—JESSIE TURNER

My father was a watch inspector for the N&W railroad company in Kenova, West Virginia. It's hard to tell where Ceredo ends—I was born in Ceredo—and Kenova begins; the two towns are jammed together. After his turn was up there, we moved to Matewan, but we were only there for a while, for this reason: When the men got paid off at the mines, they'd all come in to Matewan to celebrate. They'd get drunk, and they'd fight, and I mean bad fights; they'd run up and down the streets on Saturday night, fighting. And my brothers were getting up to the age where they were beginning to catch on to things, and Mom and Dad didn't want them raised seeing all that violence. So they decided to move, even though my daddy had a jewelry store there, and my mother had a store on the order of Lerner's, you know, ladies' ready-to-wear, and they were making good money, both of them.

We moved first to Peebles, Ohio. Dad had a watch-making place there, and he was doing pretty good. Then a house caught on fire and most of the town burned. There was nothing left there for him to make a living at. With six children, you know, you have to work.

So we moved again, to Wheeling. There we went through one flood. It just ruined everything, and it threw Dad out of work again. That was a bad flood. We got word that the water was coming up. We lived on the island, and my uncle called and told us to come to his home. And we all lived upstairs, on the second story; all we had to cook on during the flood was a little bathroom heater out in the hall. But we managed. Then the building next door caught on fire. And there we were: water all in the downstairs. A boat came to take us out through an upstairs window. I was ready to get in that boat, when they got the fire out. And that's why we left Wheeling.

Dad usually worked for himself. When he was about middle age, he got interested in eyes and eyeglasses. He became an optometrist. When he finally put in his own grinding plant, a traveling salesman told him that he had the biggest business in West Virginia. And I believe that, because back in the days when things were cheap, I worked in his office, and it was nothing unusual for us to take in at least $500 a day.

He would give the examinations, and then he would make the glasses. I think he gave away 'bout half as much as he took in. One time there was a man come to him, an old man, and he wanted to know if he could make him up a pair of glasses. He had saved fifteen dollars from the money that his children had given him for tobacco money. And my dad said, Bill, I think maybe I could fix you up something for that.

And do you know what he did? He fixed up a pair of glasses for that old man. He gave him a fine pair of frames, the best kind of lenses. And the man put on those glasses, he looked around, and he said, Oh, I can see things that I didn't even know existed. And he says, Are you sure it's fifteen dollars to pay for these?

Dad said he didn't even want to take the money, but he knew the old man would feel bad if he didn't. And that old man never did know the difference. Dad was always doing something like that. He would help anyone he think needed it.

—ADA TABOR

I don't know anything about my father. My mother, she might have been partly colored, for all I know. I was four years old when she sent me to an orphanage in Boston. From there I was sent to live with people named MacKenzie in Dover, Massachusetts.

I got along all right. I learned easily in school and I always knew the answers to the questions the teacher gave me. We used to have to go down quite a ways to get a bucket of water to drink. One day, I went down with a fellow, he was a grade or two ahead of me, a bigger boy, and along the way we picked up some apples that fell out of a tree. I got a bigger apple than this fellow. He knocked it out of my hand. We had a fight.

Anyway, the MacKenzies had a daughter. She saw us fighting, and she went home and told old man MacKenzie. She indicated that I beat up this guy even though he was bigger than I was. When I got home, he gave me a helluva going-over in the barn. Knocked me down and kicked me around. I went back to the house, crying.

Mrs. MacKenzie said, What's the matter? I told her. When MacKenzie came in the house, she said, You beat the boy up?

Yeah.

Don't you ever touch him again. You do, I'll kick the stuffings out of you.

And it seemed to me that she could do this.

When I was eight years old, in 1903, I was sent to live with the Milliken family on their farm on Block Island. After the steamship arrived, I had to wait for the Millikens to pick me up. I wandered around down by the dock and I met this boy my own age named Avard Steadman. He had a stick of peppermint candy and he gave me some, talked to me. Afterwards, I was downtown one Sunday and a bunch of boys wanted me to fight some-one—this Steadman. He was my best friend! This is something that happens just about anywhere when a new boy comes into town; they test you. I couldn't say it was done because of my color. If I hadn't met Avard, it might have been different.

—FRED BENSON

My mother was into her forties when I came along. I was the youngest of six children, ten years younger than the next oldest child. My oldest sister was married before I was born. I got a big kick out of making my nieces and nephews who were my age—some were even older—call me Uncle Karl.

Before I was a year old, my father had to sell his farm and we moved to Cedar Falls, Iowa. First he ran a butcher shop, but the shop went broke. Then he took a job as Mr. Fixit at what was then Iowa State Normal School, which later became Teachers College. It was a practice school for students who were planning to be teachers.

My father was fifty-four when he met his death. Ice had accumulated on the roof of one of the buildings and was causing flooding. To alleviate the trouble, he climbed up to the roof, ax in hand. He was chopping ice when he slipped. He grabbed a nearby wire and was electrocuted. The electric company had put up exposed wire; it had 2,200 volts in it. Mother got $2,000 in settlement from them.

Mother sold our home and married this guy who had been one of her suitors back in Ohio before she married my father. He was out in California, but they had kept track of each other. He proposed to her by mail, she accepted, and in 1907 we moved to San Jose. I was eleven years old.

But Mother was very unhappy and the marriage did not last. She walked out on him and decided to go to Montana, where my sister Maud and her husband, Clarence, lived.

On the train to Billings, a tall, white-haired man sat alone opposite Mother and me. He signaled for me to join him and Mother said okay. All afternoon, riding through Wyoming, this interesting man told me stories about the West. At Cody Junction he said goodbye and took the branch train to Cody. Mother then told me I had been entertained by Buffalo Bill.

Billings then was a wild town. With over a hundred thousand people there for the annual government land drawing, holdups and murders were commonplace. I delivered the Billings *Gazette* in early morning. My territory was Minnesota Avenue, the street of houses of ill repute. One morning a man asked me to deliver a letter to a certain woman in a certain house. He said she would be up. I did and she was. I gave her the letter. The man gave me a quarter. That was my only contact with the inmates of Whore House Row.

Maud and Clarence, Mother, and my brother Dwight, who came out from Chicago, drew a 160-acre tract in the drawing. Mother financed the homestead, which was in the Valley of the Bighorn. A Bostonian named Beebe became a partner. They homesteaded and bought river-bottom land east of Custer. I helped them build a log house. We lived in a shed until it was built. Among the many chores was cutting ice on the Bighorn and putting it in the icehouse for summer. A chunk of ice slipped and crushed Beebe, who died. From then on, Clarence ran the ranch. It was hard work, trying to make the land productive. Three years in a row, the crops were lost. They never did make much money.

I worked fourteen, fifteen hours a day, six days a week, with only Sundays off. One of the jobs I had was to bury bones. The homestead was near Blackfoot Indian territory, and the Indians used to take care of their dead by wrapping them in some kind of cloth and leaving them up in trees. Well, here we were, down below the trees, and we wanted to build a house and we didn't want to have all these skeletons around in all these trees. There were maybe fifty of them. I climbed up and cut them down. I

*Karl Long with brothers Dwight, left, and Charles,
and his mother, Woodbine, Iowa, 1895*

suppose they'd been up there a hundred years or more. We got a pile of
bones and buried them very respectfully. We never saw any live Indians
around, so we figured the bones were of no value to anyone. I also found
caves where the Indians had buried children with their toys. I would look
at them but I'd never touch them or disturb them because of the sacredness
of the place.

Most of the time, I rode Birdie, a horse of small stature but my best
friend. We had to fetch the five milk cows in from the open prairie
where they were grazing. You would think the cows would come home
to get milked. Not these creatures. I had to ride miles and explore gullies
and creeks and one time, long after dark, I came home without them.
Another time I chased a coyote into a hole. Knowing the bounty on a
coyote was five dollars, I decided to stay and guard the hole. I knew
Clarence would come looking for me and the cows. After dark, Clarence
came and congratulated me on my wisdom of staying and rode back to
the ranch for a shovel and a shotgun. I stayed guard. About ten o'clock
that night we had five coyotes, which netted twenty-five dollars. That
was real money.

In the fall of 1909, after about twenty months on the ranch in Montana, we had a visitor. My brother Charles was a salesman working for the Eli Lilly Drug Company. His territory followed the Northern Pacific from Chicago to Seattle.

On his way back to Chicago, he stopped off in Custer, hired a horse, and rode out to the ranch. He was certainly sore and pretty tired from his trip, and he looked silly all dressed up in a suit of clothes and a hat and necktie, riding a horse. He was greatly disturbed when he learned that I was not in high school—we didn't have one closer than Billings or Miles City, fifty miles away. I'm going to take you back to Chicago with me, he said, and you're going to go to school. So I put on clean overalls, put my few belongings in his suitcase, and went with him.

When we got to Chicago, he rented a room for two dollars a week. He didn't keep a place there; he was on the road all the time and he lived out of a suitcase. As soon as we got settled in, he had to leave town. While waiting for the next semester to begin, I got a job as a flunky in a drugstore for one dollar a day. I worked seven days a week, ten hours a day, sweeping and cleaning and delivering and waiting on customers. And bottling whiskey. The druggist had black-market liquor down in the basement. There was one barrel of whiskey and it went into a whiskey bottle or a Scotch bottle or a bourbon bottle. The same stuff. The price depended on what kind of bottle it was in. Some of the poorer customers, they poured it in a fruit jar and could have it for a quarter.

—KARL LONG

My father was a teamster for a brewery. Back then, there were considerable fights among the union labor and what they called scabs. I guess it was pretty rough. My dad used to go to union meetings wearing a pair of brass knuckles.

Tacoma was really a live town in those days. There were lots of people riding horses, cowboys and the like. See, we had an awful lot of what we called horse barns, and wild horses were brought in there by the carload and the cowboys were there to break them. That used to be a big deal on weekends, to go down there and watch all these guys breaking the horses.

A lot of the people carried their guns around on their hips, and they didn't think anything of standing on the street corner and pointing their gun up to the sky and shooting. Of course, the horses would get all excited. There were saloons all over the place, and on Saturdays or on holidays my dad would take me along to kind of hold the reins and try to hold the team. Of course, the only time I ever went into the saloons with him was when I had to go to the bathroom.

—OSCAR C. WEBER

I was five when my mother died. She was thirty-three years old. She left four of us. Each of us went to live with relatives. I was sent to an aunt who had gone to that now notorious, I call it, Atlantic City, New Jersey, which was a beautiful beach resort then. She and her husband were taking care of an estate for two bachelors who had decided that they'd had enough of their rich life and retired. Her husband had worked for them, so they gave him a few years to live on the place free.

They lived out in the country, in a place named Pleasantville. The nearest house was a mile away. The country store was a couple of miles away. You made a path through the woods to go from place to place. That was where I grew up.

Nobody earned much money. If you needed a nickel or a dime or a quarter and I had it, you could get it until you could pay it back. We had a grocery store where you could go and they'd give you a book to take note of what you bought and the price. At the end of the week, if you could pay it all, you did, and if you couldn't, you paid what you could.

My aunt sent me to the store one day with a note for what she needed. She said, Ask Mr. So-and-So to send me twenty-five cents. I thought to myself—because I couldn't ask questions; you weren't supposed to ask questions—she's getting money from the store? He gave me the twenty-five cents, but it was on the book.

My aunt would take in laundry at home. It took time and strength. She did the laundry with a washboard and tub. The ladies wore petticoats and they had two ruffles on them, and those ruffles had to be starched and ironed with a flatiron that had to be heated on the stove. My aunt also did what they called day's work. When she worked away from home, she earned one dollar.

My uncle was a laborer. He went to Atlantic City every day to work. When he could work, repairing streets or whatever, he earned one dollar and fifty cents a day. When the weather was bad, that was a dollar fifty that he didn't get at the end of that week.

We wore picked-up clothes. Before I was six I had one Sunday dress, for Sunday school and church. Once I went to school, I had one school dress. I'd put that dress on in the morning last thing before I left the house, and I'd take it off first thing when I came home and put it away for

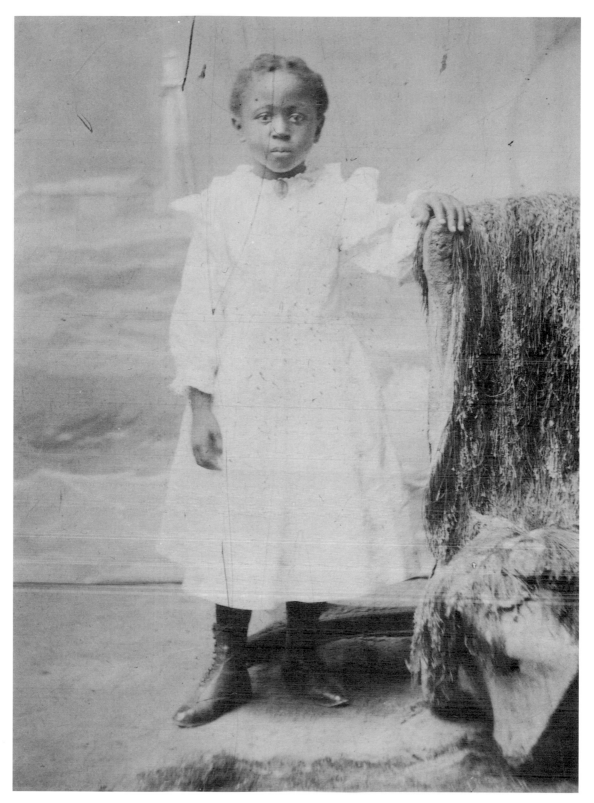

Julia Estelle Pendleton (Julia Tyler) in her Sunday dress

the next day. I had to wear that same dress all week. Shoes cost a dollar and a half, and I had one pair for when I was going somewhere, or in the wintertime. Other times, we went barefoot. And it *was* barefoot; it wasn't sandals.

—JULIA TYLER

We lived on a ninety-acre farm in Clinton County, Missouri, about forty-five miles north of Kansas City. My first job, I was no more than six years old, was to haul the wood from the woodpile into the house for the cookstove and the heating stove. I had a little red wagon that we got for Christmas, and I had to pull a load of wood regardless of whether it was muddy or snowy or freezing. And I had to milk the cows and feed the stock—the cows and hogs and horses.

I began helping in the field at the age of seven. My job was to run the corn planter. This was a one-horse drill that had a hopper on it that seed corn was put in. My brother Madison would furrow out the corn rows on one side while I was going down the other side, planting in the little furrow that he had just made. I worked with an old horse that didn't need any guiding: she knew when we got to the end of the field to turn around on her own and go to the next furrow.

As I grew older, I handled most of the farmwork alone, as my three brothers were then working for other people. And I had to do plenty of work. I would get up about four o'clock in the morning, have breakfast, go down to the barn to feed the horses and milk the cows, then harness up and go to the field, sometimes as early as a quarter of six. I'd come in at noon or so, stay for about an hour while the horses ate a few ears of corn, then go back to the field and work to 6:45 p.m., come back and do some other chores around the barn and the house. It was a very long day.

In those days the farmers had no mechanical help at all; most of the work was done with horses or mules. Corn was planted in four-foot-wide rows, which is not done nowadays. We cultivated the corn two or three times before it matured. The cultivators were drawn by horses between the rows to uproot the weeds and grasses that had grown there. Nowadays, that's all done by chemicals.

We had a big orchard with all kinds of apple trees. One time, Dad had me take a wagonload of apples to the cider mill, which was six or seven miles away. We ran the apples through the mill and had two barrels of cider. One of the barrels had been used before, though, and had some vinegar left in it. When I got back home, I parked the wagon outside of the house. The next mornin' Dad went to open up the barrel that had had some of the vinegar in it. When he pulled the plug, it blew his hat off, it had fermented so much.

—HARLEY POTTER

I was on my own quite early in life. My father always wanted to try farming, and he bought a little farm down in Kansas. It was a colossal bust. So he gave it up and went back to preaching in Nebraska and left my mother with a couple of recalcitrant teenage boys. We stayed in Kansas, and I went to high school there, in Norton.

I just barely got through high school. I was living away from home, no discipline whatsoever. I applied myself, but I also got into a bit of mischief. One April Fools' Day, I set off a bunch of firecrackers. I had to go before the school board and apologize for that one.

When I was in high school was the only time I was ever really sick in my life. I had smallpox. One morning, the man who managed the rooming house I was living in couldn't get in my room. I was flopped on the floor beside the door, too weak to do anything. Well, he got in, and I had to spend twenty days in the pesthouse. It was an old, rundown place out on the edge of town that had been a bawdy house at one time. Anybody that got a contagious disease and didn't have some way to be quarantined in their own homes they'd send there.

I had to walk there, a good half mile, maybe longer, on a chilly, windy, cold March morning. I may even have still been in my pajamas. The doctor could have taken me in his buggy, but he didn't. That doctor, you know, was finally kicked out of the Army. He did the same thing with his troops. One of the stories was, he made all the men in his command stand stark naked out in the March weather for what they called short-arms inspection. He was a real sadist.

Anyway, I was with two other men in the pesthouse. One was one of the town barbers, the other was just a tramp. There was an organization called the IWW, the International Workers of the World, but they were always referred to as Wobblies, and he was one of 'em. He enjoyed living in the pesthouse. Got three meals. Pretty radical.

—VICTOR MILLS

When I was a sophomore in high school, I got a job as a lamplighter in East Reading. I had forty-eight gaslight lamps in the city park that I had to light every evening by the time the sun went down. And I had to put them out every morning when the sun was up. I got fifty cents a light per month, twenty-four dollars a month. That was pretty good for a youngster of fifteen.

I had a dog, and he always went with me, morning and evening. I had a stick about twelve feet high with a hook on the end of it which I put up through the hole to pull the lever on the lamp. This dog carried that stick. He would go to every lamp and wait for me till I got there. And when I got there, he'd jump up, grab the stick, and off he'd go to the next lamp. That dog would carry that stick right down the center of Perkiomen Avenue. In the morning he would not move out of the way for the men going to work; they had to move around him. They did. And they laughed.

— WILLIAM G. HINTZ, JR.

I was fifteen years old in 1910 when I went to work in a bicycle and motorcycle shop. At that time, there were so many bicycles in use and so much horse traffic that the bicycles and horses got mixed. I'd go in the shop after school and the man that ran the place, he'd give me the bicycles to fix. The wood rims usually would be broken, maybe a horse had stepped on them or they'd been smashed up somehow. I removed the wheel and unstrung the spokes, laying the good ones in one pile and bad ones in another. Later on, I learned to string the wheels and insert the spokes. But I didn't true them up. After a while, I graduated to where I could do that.

At first I was only helping repair the bicycles, but I soon got to helping repair motorcycles. This shop had the Indian Motorcycle agency. Indian was made in Springfield, Massachusetts. While I was in my sophomore year, the owner of this shop received notice that the Indian people would accept trainees. I made application to the school principal if I could get off for two weeks. The school agreed. And I went to the Indian Motorcycle factory by train and took their two weeks' course.

Now that I had taken that course, this man was willing to pay me fifty cents an hour because I could handle anything in connection with the repair of a motorcycle. I could time engines, time camshafts, things like that. When I told my father what I was going to be earning—of course, I only worked after school and on Saturdays and then full-time in summer—he really hit the ceiling. That's not right, he said. Here's these men working over at my shop at the railroad and they're only getting twenty-three cents an hour and here's a kid like you getting fifty cents.

Well, when I went to college—my transportation from Harrisburg to

Worcester, Massachusetts, was my motorcycle—I only had enough money for the first semester. I had to work. But I could get good money. While there were lots of good mechanics who knew how to take an engine apart, if they lost a timing gear or something and went to put in a new timing gear, they didn't know how to time the engine. But I knew. So I was even being hired by some of the best automobile shops. Because I had learned that at the Indian plant.

—MILTON W. GARLAND

My Uncle Crystal was partner with von Roentgen at the university in Heidelberg, Germany. Both of them were researching the X-ray. We were living in Baltimore, and my uncle introduced it at Johns Hopkins Hospital there.

They didn't know then the radiation would hurt him at all, but he lost four fingers, then he lost his hand up to his wrist, and the last he lost was up above the elbow. He wore a velvet scarf right around the end. He and I were inseparable.

Uncle Crystal wanted me to follow what he was in and he would pay for everything. But I said, Uncle Crystal, I want to be a businessman. I said it so many times he said finally, Well, Ernie, if you don't want to be a minister or a dentist, why, that's up to you. But whatever you are going to be, be sure of one thing.

I said, What's that?

Maybe it might be a little hard for whatever you select, he said, but persevere. Be committed and don't stop halfway.

After my mother died, and with my father, a traveling salesman, being on the road ten months out of the year, I went to live with my aunt, who was well past seventy years old when she took me in. She had been in Ford's Theatre when Booth shot Lincoln.

The second year after that, I enrolled in the Baltimore City College. I had never been to school before. Until I was ten, you see, I had never gone to school. I was a blue baby, and they didn't expect me to live, so I was always carried around by my father and then my mother. I was always sickly and they didn't want something to happen to make me worse and set me back. Well, I finished high school when I was fourteen years old. It just went along like a breeze.

I interviewed for a job at the U.S. Rubber Company. The president of the company said, Young man, you have a wonderful attitude, but you have to be twenty-one to work here.

Well, I said, I feel like I'm well equipped.

No, you have to finish high school.

Sir, I said, I have something that I'd like to show you. I pulled out my certificate from Baltimore City College. I said, Look over that. And he hired me on the spot.

—ERNEST C. DEETJEN

I lived with my parents on the second-floor apartment of a three-floor walkup in South Brooklyn, where I was born. It was a typical Brooklyn neighborhood. There were stores. There was a park. School was at the corner and the church was on the next block. We had gas for light, a coal stove for cooking, and outdoor plumbing. There were trolley cars and trains and, of course, carriages drawn by horses. When a horse would die, they would come and pick it up, though not very quickly.

In our neighborhood, we had the Sicilians living down near Degraw and Sackett Streets. The Neapolitans were further away. We had several scattered Irish families. No blacks. American families didn't live there. It was a neighborhood of recent Americans. A Jewish man, Mr. Schindler, ran the grocery store; he had all Italian goods for the Italian people.

I went to a Mother Cabrini school. We were three of us in a seat—we had a hundred in the first- and second-grade classes. When some people kept telling my mother that the Catholic schools were no good, that they weren't teaching well, she took me out and sent me to public school. I lasted one week. I detested it. I was used to the order and discipline and prayers, and that didn't exist in the public schools. And I liked the sisters very much. They would take me to the convent, they asked me to go to the chapel where they said Mass and had the Exposition of the Blessed Sacrament. I was happy when I was there. I went back to the sisters' school.

I first saw Mother Cabrini when I was ten. She had piercing blue eyes. She was determined and you knew that she wanted what she said when she spoke. She was always praying and talking about God, and her love for people, and helping people who needed help. She founded the school in Brooklyn. It was a parish school when it was first opened. She would come around and visit each class. When she went on missions, her sisters carried on the work. It was Mother Cabrini who established the solidarities of the parish—the Children of Mary for the older girls, the Holy Angels for the younger people, and St. Aloysius for the boys.

I decided I wanted to be a sister, like her.

Anna Lawrence Infante (Sister Ursula Infante), circa 1915

I wanted to join her when I was fourteen, but my parents wouldn't let me. I was an only child, and they didn't want to lose me. Mother Cabrini said to wait until I was eighteen, and then I could enter without their permission. And that's what I did.

Meanwhile, I went to business school and took up stenography, typewriting, and other business subjects. I knew I had to have money to go into the convent to get my clothes. When I graduated, I got myself a job in Meehan's Detective Agency at 42 Broadway.

This agency, they used to shadow the diplomats who worked for the government of Nicaragua, which was our client, see what they did and who they got in touch with. And private people, husbands and wives, we'd shadow them. All I had to do, though, was take notes and type and receive people. I worked there for almost three years.

Then I was ready to go to the convent. Mother Cabrini set the date for my entrance into the Missionary Sisters of the Sacred Heart: July 21, 1915. When the time came, I wanted to go to the convent modestly, so I put on this suit. My mother said, What are you doing with a suit on? I said, I feel a little cold. She thought I was going to work, but I had given notice two weeks before. I left a note in my room that I had gone to the convent. I guess you could say that I snuck out.

I took a ferry over to Manhattan, and two sisters met me and we went to Mother Cabrini. Her Institute of the Missionary Sisters was all the way up in Washington Heights, near Fort Tryon Park. When we got there, we rang the doorbell at the Sacred Heart Villa, which was a boarding school and a sisters' convent. Mother George answered. Mother is waiting for you, she said. We went into the parlor, and Mother Cabrini came down. She took off my suit. She dressed me in a postulant's habit, and covered my hair. She took me to the chapel and then to the Community of the Novitiate.

The next morning my father came to the convent and wanted to take me home. Daddy, I told him, if I were a boy, I'd have to go to war, and I could die. Here I'm safe and I'm happy. He left. My parents accepted my decision.

That day I spent a little time with Mother Cabrini. During the evening prayers she sat next to me and explained the points for morning meditation. The next day she was called to Seattle. I never saw her again. She died of malaria in Chicago two years later.

—SR. URSULA INFANTE

The guy who's given credit for being the first one to get to the North Pole was named Peary. He was a real son of a bitch. The American Museum of Natural History asked him if he'd bring an Eskimo back from one of his trips to the Arctic. So he brought back a whole family. That first year, they all died except two. One of them was named Mene Wallace. He was given his last name by an employee of the museum who adopted him.

When we lived in Morris Heights, my father used to play golf with this guy Wallace, who lived in University Heights. They were good friends. Mene was maybe a couple of years older than I was, and he used to come down to Morris Heights sometimes with his father, and I used to play with him.

I didn't see him after we went to Brooklyn. Until 1916. I was home from college, and Mene came over on a Sunday to see us. He had gone up to Greenland in 1909, and this was the first time he'd been back. We had dinner, and then he and I walked up Bushwick Avenue.

How come you came back? I asked him.

Actually, he said, the bright lights of Broadway appeal to me more than the Northern Lights of Greenland.

Then he told me: I know the story of who actually got to the North Pole, because I spoke to Eskimos who went with both of them.

See, in addition to Peary, there was Dr. Cook. It was Dr. Cook who said that he had got to the Pole first, and got a big reception in Denmark. Then Peary went and said that that was a lie, that he had got there first. So there was a big hoo-doo about it. When Dr. Cook came home, my father was one of the Committee of 100 to meet him at the dock. After a while my father had him out to the church and he gave us a lecture about his adventures.

And Mene said to me, I know the truth. But I'm not going to tell it. If *Collier's* magazine wants to give me a couple of thousand dollars for my story, I'll tell them.

He didn't get what he wanted, from *Collier's* or any other magazine. In 1918 he had gone to some place up in New England, and he got the flu there and died.

Nobody ever got the story from him.

—JOHN D. CLARK

To America!

In Europe, we heard that America was

the Country of Immense Possibilities.

Immense possibilities!

—DIRK STRUIK

Born September 30, 1894

Rotterdam, the Netherlands

I started working as soon as I started to walk. I used to go around with my father, who was what I call a foot professor. He knew how to examine somebody's feet to prepare the material to build a shoe mold. This was back in Latvia, where I was born.

My father died very young, in his forties. And my mother had a store, even with five children. One day, I must have been maybe twelve years old, this hunter came in to buy some tobacco. He put his gun down in the corner. My mother asked him if the gun was loaded, and he said no. So I picked it up and aimed it at my sister. I was only playing, of course. Lucky I was a bad shot, because the gun went off. There was so much smoke in the store you couldn't see.

I never went to school. To get by, I used to go out to the peasants in the countryside to buy pigs' hair to sell to make brushes. I bought and sold calf skins, and sheep. But I had no chance for a living there, only to be abused by the *Antisemitem*. As Jews, we couldn't go here and we couldn't live there. They used to come and make pogroms all the time and kill the Jews and rob them. So when my cousin sent word to come to America, I was glad; I was happy to leave when I was leaving.

—SAMUEL D. SCHNEIER

I was eight years old when I came to America from the province of Messina in Sicily. My father was already here. He came to America with my oldest sister after my mother died giving birth. She was twenty-nine. The baby—it was her fifth child—also died. A lot of women died giving birth then; their blood got poisoned. So my grandmother took care of us.

In America, my father was a carpenter and then he was a bartender. He would work and make the money, and whatever relative was coming to America, he would have them bring another daughter. A cousin was coming to America, so he took me.

We were in steerage, in the bottom of the ship. The women and children were in one place, and all the men were in another. The women were frightened. I was alone down there in the ship with all these screaming

◄ *Immigrants arriving in America aboard the* S.S. Kaiserin Augusta Victoria, *1921*
(Culver Pictures)

women, and all the children were crying because the mothers were crying. I didn't know why they was crying, but I was terrified. So my cousin came and took me where he was with the other men.

When I got to America, I felt kind of lonely; I didn't know what it was all about. When I came, I was wearing country clothes; my dress went down to the ground. The young children in America weren't dressed like that. So the first thing, my sister, Antoinette, she takes me to a store to buy me a new dress, a short dress. I'm standing there on my toes, trying to make the dress longer, and my sister gives me a little slap in the legs. You can't wear a long dress, she says. We don't dress like that here in America. But I didn't like that short dress; it came above my knees! I didn't want to go out into the street. I felt undressed because I had never worn a dress like that before.

After a while, my father opened up his own business, a little café in Greenwich Village where he served coffee and wine. That's where we lived, on the fourth floor of a walk-up tenement on Sullivan Street. When we were young, we weren't allowed to go by the window, because good girls didn't go by the window. There were boys downstairs, and they'd serenade us from the street.

My father was very strict. One day, he told my sister, Dora, When I call you, drop everything you're doing and come to me. So later she was drying the dishes. She had all the family dishes in her hands when he called her, and she dropped all the plates on the floor and they broke into smithereens and she ran to her father. But he didn't hit her or anything, because he had just told her to drop everything when he called, and that's what she did. He had to keep from laughing.

—VIRGINIA REALE

My full name I have now is Florence Moretti. But to begin with I was Filomena Pezzullo from Bellegra, Italy.

We came to America in 1900. Coming over, it was fourteen days on the water. It wasn't too cramped, but it was bad enough. I was only five, six years old, and I had to take care of my brother that was only a baby. He got measles on the boat, we all got them; he got an infection in his mouth, too. My mother would put me in front of him in the chair and say, When he opens his mouth, you put two fingers in and pull out whatever you can get ahold of. That's how he got better.

We came to America because we had a brother, Luke—he was named after one of the Apostles—and he wanted to come. We first settled with my mother's sister. Only they didn't get along at all. Then we were living near the Holy Ghost Church in Providence. We had to live near a church because my mother had to go to church every morning. We'd get up and she'd say, Come on, we're going. And I had to be dragged along with her all the time because she wouldn't go alone and leave me behind, even though there were others in the family.

When I was little, I learned how to sew. I made all my clothes, or I wouldn't have them. There were stores, but we didn't have the money to buy from them.

I went to school. The only thing was, my sister that was six years older than me, she crept out of the window one night on a stepladder and went off and got married without asking my mother and father and they disowned her. And my mother the next day, she took me out of school because she says, You're gonna do the same thing, so there's no need of keeping you in school. I was twelve. Then they weren't so fussy if the mother insisted upon having a child leave school.

I went to work in the mill, in the same wool mill my father worked in. In those days, there was only mill work. I had to walk there and walk back home, quite a little ways. They used to have machines that would spin the yarn and that's what I did to begin with. I worked in the mill not too many years. Then I learned how to go to the stores for the people around me. I used to run errands for the neighbors, and they'd always hand me ten cents or something. I needed the money, so I did it. I had to go to work, and work and work and work, and that's more or less what there was.

—FLORENCE MORETTI

They had just put up the Statue of Liberty when my father, Antonio Salimeno, came to America. He and my mother were from Terranova, in Calabria, about an hour and a half from Naples by horse and buggy. My father, he used to say, Everybody America, America, America, let's go in America. But my mother didn't come until seven years after.

When he came here, he used to shoot dynamite for the railroad. He'd go all over. I was born where we lived, in a tenement on Mulberry and Elizabeth Streets in New York City. We were nine children in the family. My mother named two of them Rose and two of them Millie. When one would die and the next baby would be a girl, she'd name it the same.

We moved to Westerly when I was a year old. You know why we landed here? In those days this was a summer resort for big shots. A friend of my father said, Why don't you open a little shoe stand and shine shoes? You'll make good money.

So from March till September he used to do that. My mother thought we were like millionaires compared to the others. They used to make, what, four, five dollars a week? My father used to make more than that sometimes in a day. He was so good when he'd do their shoes, he'd brush 'em up and the big shots would tip him fifty cents, a dollar. He used to average eighty dollars a week, a hundred sometimes.

Then my father had to sell everything and we had to go back to Italy 'cause the doctor told him, If you want your wife to live, you've got to take her back to her native country. He said the air here didn't agree with her. My father said, If that's going to save my wife, we'll go back.

The morning after we got to where we had to go, my mother went to a doctor. Doctor, she said, I just came yesterday from America. Now, see what's wrong with me.

What's wrong with you? You haven't got anything wrong with you, he said. Oh, you've got a little inflammation, but you could go back tomorrow.

What? she said. I've moved the whole family here.

Well, you didn't have a doctor, he said, you must have had a shoemaker.

After a year, we came back to America.

In Westerly we had Italian and Jewish and a few colored. We all mingled in together. Jewish was our best friends. I used to write the language for them. And on the Sabbath I'd light the gas lamps. They wanted to pay me, but my mother said, No, no, we Italians don't get paid for little things like that. We're neighbors, we're going to get paid? She was very old-fashioned. I used to say, But Ma, he wants to give me ten cents. To the Jewish neighbors she'd say, Any time you want my daughter, you call her.

For a long time we were the only ones had a telephone. Because my brother was an interpreter for the court, and if they needed somebody, they'd call him. Or even me. Anybody got hurt on the railroad, New York to Westerly, they used to call me. They used to get hurt a lot years ago, you know, working on the railroad.

We had one neighbor, Mrs. Lubinotsky, she had a sister on Narragansett Bay in South Westerly. She got a call once on our phone and I had to get her to come and talk. Oh, gracious! she says, those are the devils that are talking. She was afraid. Those are the devils, she said. How can the thing talk over here and my sister's way over in Narragansett Bay?

My father bought a grocery store. It was on the first floor of a tenement. He couldn't read or write, but he had a memory like I don't know what. He would remember everything. He'd extend credit to all people that he knew.

He knew that sooner instead of later he was going to get his money. He had to pay his bills, too, and people understood that that was one bill they had to pay or they wouldn't eat. He always knew who owed how much. To the penny. Never once did anyone come in and say, Your father made a mistake.

We were always a little better than the next one. 'Cause my father used to make good money. In the summer he used to stay in the store. In the winter he used to stay in the store. At night he used to stay in the store. And my mother would help. How they did it, I don't know.

Back then, we didn't have any gangsters in our neighborhood. But they used to come by. This young fella came in the store once and I knew he was a Mafia. I might have been seventeen, eighteen, and he was twenty-two, twenty-three. I didn't like what he said to me. So when the head one of the gang came in—he knew me; he called me "Little Godmother"—I said, Gee, you know, that fella, he wasn't too nice.

He said, What? Say that again.

I said, No, he didn't say anything bad.

He said, Because if he did—

What he meant was, he would cut his throat. I said, No, he didn't say anything bad.

They never bothered you, you never bothered them. That's the way we looked at it.

—THERESA NIGRELLI

Skole, the small town in the Carpathian Mountains where I was born, was a part of Austria. The biggest battle in the First World War was near there; over a half a million Russians were killed or captured by the General Hindenburg. After the World War, it became part of Poland.

In my time, if the snow fell during winter, nobody cleaned and it formed ice. In the wintertime, the men wore beards, and on the beards there were icicles from the cold weather. By Easter, you'd still walk on ice maybe two or three foot high.

We didn't have no electric, no radio, no nothing. We didn't have no money. The only enjoyment for young kids was ice skating. I used to make sleds myself, and my own ice skates. From wood. So all right, they didn't last long, but that's what the enjoyment was.

The summertime was beautiful! We used to go out in the woods, pick mushrooms, make fires, pick all kinds of berries. You cannot starve if you go in the mountains over there. When you looked at them you was thinking, if you go up on this mountain you'll reach the sky.

My father went to America. Quite a few people went to America to better their life. He was a tailor. My mother was a tailor also. She used to make clothes for the women; they liked her work very much. She used to have like a little factory, with five, six girls working for her. My mother made money. She bought a house; the house had a few tenants.

My mother, she had five children. And taking care of the sewing, taking care of the girls, giving work, and then cooking and shopping, she was always busy. My father was in America. I was raised, you can say, by myself.

I went to learn a trade, to be a men's tailor. I was there not even a year's time, and they were talking about war. Russia, with Austria, with Germany, they were not on good terms. They could make a war any time that they want. So my mother sent me and an older sister to America in 1913, a year before the World War.

We came to Ellis Island. They don't give you a chance to look around. You sit, and you wait for your next. And that's what it is. The doctor examines you. A lot of people were sick and were sent back. But if you were all right and if there was somebody to take care of you, they give you over to the person that waits for you.

This new world, it was beautiful to me. It was a new life to me. The first place I lived was in Ludlow Street in the Lower East Side. A few months later, my mother sold the house and she came with the other three kids. Not long after, they killed the Crown Prince of Austria, Prince Ferdinand, and the World War started. If she would stay there a few months later, maybe they would be killed.

When I came over here, I had an aunt living over here and my father had a room in her apartment. They made for us a place to live also. When my mother came with the children, we took an apartment right away. Because she sold the house in Europe, she came here with a nice few dollars. My parents bought a two-family with a store in East New York. That's in Brooklyn. So my father, instead of going to work, he took that store and he was doing the tailoring there. We took one floor, and one floor they rented.

My father took me in his shop. But men's tailoring didn't pay good over here. So I went to ladies', it paid a little better. Naturally, I got acquainted with the work and I started to make money, and I went to designing school and I learned designing and I worked for a few firms as a designer. Then I made a few dollars and I went in business with a partner. Then I was in business by myself.

I went to night school. Too much education I haven't got because I was always busy working, working, working. It was a struggling life, a very struggling life. And that's what it is. Running factories and making styles. Always work and worry, work and worry. But I felt it was better to be by myself than to work for somebody.

Then there was no unemployment insurance, no Social Security; all this here things was not in existence. People used to work in the shops, but no steam in the cold weather, they used to go home because it was too cold to work. And no work, no pay. Most of them worked piecework.

Now, the thing is this: people used to come here from Europe, they didn't have no trade. So, what is to do? They gotta eat. Say they became a watchman in a shop. A watchman used to get three dollars a week. But he didn't have to pay rent because he was living there. And the people who had an old pair of pants, plenty patches on it already, they used to give it to him and he used to wear it.

So, the three dollars a week was this way. You used to buy, it was five cents a herring. And you used to go in the bakery shop and get the stale bread, rolls and everything, a full bag for ten, fifteen cents. The baker was glad to get rid of that and you got something to eat. So, you had enough bread and the herring you used to divide for three times. Then, during the week, you used to buy another herring, or two herrings. So it didn't cost you even a dollar to live for the whole week. And the rest of the money you sent to Europe. And over there a dollar was two dollars. So they got rich already on two dollars. This is no baloney.

So that's what life was.

AARON BIRNBAUM

My father's name when he came to this country was Anyolik. In fact, some members of the family still use the name Arnold.

But where did he get Goldstein? He came through Hamburg. That's where he got on the boat that took him—steerage, of course—to the United States. And he looked at it and he said, 'Tis a good omen, 'tis a good omen. I'm going to the land that is said to be paved in gold. I will be successful. I will say when they ask me: My name is Goldstein.

My mother told me that story. And if my mother told it to me, you can be sure it's the truth.

Another story my mother told me: She was pregnant and she was beginning to feel pain. Then the pressure subsided for a while and my father started to say special prayers. So the pain subsided and he kept on and kept on and on. Finally she said, I cannot stand it anymore. Do run, please. Please! So he stopped saying his prayers and ran to the hospital for the

Joseph Goldstein on his father's lap, Boston, Massachusetts, 1895

doctor. We had no phone, of course. Before he returned, she was holding me on her lap.

My father was a really thorough Orthodox Jew. I'll tell you how Orthodox: on Saturdays he'd read the Bible in the *shul*; the *shul* was just a little room somewhere. But when he came home, he read it a second time. I said, Pa, why do you read it a second time? You went all throught this in *shul*, I was sitting there with you. And he said, Son, maybe I made an error the first time.

There were eight in the family eventually. I was born in the North End where immigrants, Jewish and Italians and Polish, all got mixed together and all got along—and all were poor. I had my bar mitzvah in the North End. From there we graduated to the West End in Boston. Climbing up the ladder. From the West End we moved to Dorchester. From Dorchester to Brookline. The family was frugal. We got along all right. My father started as a shoemaker, and he was a darn good shoemaker. Do I say it because I saw his handiwork? No. Other shoemakers said that to me as I was growing up. From that, he got into the retail shoe business. Before my bar mitzvah, I became a clerk in the retail shoe store. And I was a good one at it.

In Dorchester High School, I was on the track team. The leader of the Laurette Avenue Gang—Brett was his name, Chester Brett—I heard him say to the other kids in the gang who were on the track team, Leave Goldie alone; he's winning points for us. So they never bothered me. And I earned my sweater and my letter.

—JOSEPH GOLDSTEIN

Three of my brothers had been in America already several years. They insisted that the whole family emigrate, and they had saved enough money to buy the tickets for the whole family to come here. They prepared an apartment for the arrival of their father, mother, sisters, and brothers. Fourteen children we were in all. My father had been married twice. He didn't know of contraceptives. It was a question of a man doing what he has to do, and the result was babies.

The first thing I saw when we got to New York was the Third Avenue El, which came down to Battery Park. My God, look at this! It was amazing. And buildings reaching the moon! What the hell did I know, a little kid, sixteen years old, coming to a great country like this from an isolated little spot in Russia, without any exposure to the world? It was a dream, an awakening. Every little thing around me was an invention I never even conceived of seeing.

I came from a small town called Starodub. I never saw the ocean. I never saw a wave hitting up against rocks. There were a couple of lakes in my little town where I'd go swimming and fishing. But never waves! I'd never even visualized this before.

We got on the Elevated. For five cents. Five cents! We rode all the way to the apartment, on 103rd Street near Park Avenue. There we were squished together, but we were happy because the family was there.

Harlem was mostly a Jewish section in those days, from Ninety-sixth Street up to 125th Street. That was the dividing line between color. If you wanted to see black, you had to cross 125th Street and you were right in a world of black people. This was a great surprise for me: I never before saw a colored man. But I didn't cross that line, 'cause I'd feel strange and I didn't know what to do. And few black men came over the other way to visit white people.

Harlem was a very lovely place, with beautiful shops. There was a streetcar with rails in the street, no electric wires, that ran right through 110th Street across the East River and into the Bronx. There were a lot of horses, especially in the wintertime. When the streetcars couldn't run in the winter—too much snow—horses would pull the cars. And Central Park: there was a lake in the park where we used to go ice skating in the winter, and swimming and boating during the summer. Coming from a small town in Russia, with all of the privileges taken away from us, I had the freedom to go in and swim with everybody, to rent a boat for five cents. Hey, it's beautiful!

Alfred Levitt, standing in the middle, Starodub, Russia, August 1911

The question was, What were the boys going to do? How were they going to find a job to help the family? I was the oldest of the three boys in the apartment; it fell upon me to do something to bring in some money.

I came from a family that made carriages and painted carriages. Despite my father's craftsmanship and mechanical abilities, the selling of a carriage in a small town in Russia was an almost impossible job. We were always very poor. Over here, they said, Why can't you be a painter? Paint houses, paint flats? That I won't do. I'm essentially a poet. I'm going to look for something in consonance with my feelings. But they didn't understand that. They thought that I was a lazy boy who didn't want to work. I paid no attention to my father or my mother.

My conscious drive when I got here was to escape the rigors of poverty, to become somebody of importance. This I don't mean economically, but someone who can justify his presence on the planet. I wonder: Who am I? What am I here for? At seventeen years, the first question for me, though, was: What was I going to do? What will I become?

It was very difficult. I didn't know enough. My schooling was very limited. I did go to school in Russia; I learned some Yiddish and some Russian. But when I came here I felt totally incapable of communication. It was my drive to forget my Russian antecedents and become an American and communicate with people that we lived with. And that's what I did.

I made up my mind, as young as I was, that I'm going to amount to something in the world, and I'm not going to continue being one of those who starve. After all, the natural need is to fill the stomach, and mine was empty on many occasions.

So I got a job painting buttons on women's coats. At that time, women wore coats with cloth buttons, and the buttons were rimmed with a metal strip, and the metal strip had to be painted to conform to the cloth. I was an aspiring artist and I knew what to do with color, so they gave me the job. Columbia Button Works. I was earning eight dollars a week. And eight dollars in those days was a lot of money. My mother was very happy.

—ALFRED LEVITT

I came from Dundee after the First World War. Over in Scotland, everybody thought the United States was wonderful. I had an aunt in Brooklyn. She came and brought me from Ellis Island and I stayed with her.

I says to her, I got to go to work. I have to work. And I got a job at the Plaza Hotel in New York as a domestic servant, a helper, making the beds, and all the bath work. I worked every day, even Sunday. I used to go to church in the morning, at St. Patrick's Cathedral, then come back and go to work.

The Plaza was quite a place. All the big shots was there—the Vanderbilts and the Astors, the Guggenheims. All wealthy people. I got fifteen dollars a month, and my food. We'd eat in the kitchen. I slept there, on the sixteenth floor, with all the help that worked in the Plaza.

I met a nice girl there; she worked with me. And she says to me, Would you like to go to Coney Island?

And I says, Where is that?

That's where there are a lot of amusements. You and I will go Sunday; we've got a day off.

We went to Coney Island. We were walking along the Boardwalk when she says to me, Don't look around, but we've got two guys followin' us. The two guys came up to us and said, Hello, girls, would you like to go someplace to eat? Oh, of course, yeah, we went with them to get something to eat.

So, they asked us, where did we live. And the girl says to me, Don't tell them we live in the Plaza. Just say that we live in an apartment.

And they said to us, Oh, well, we'll come to your apartment when we come back to New York. And the girl says, Don't say nothing.

Coming back on the train, I says to her, I'm not going with you. She says, You and I, we'll duck them; we'll go to that big store, Macy's, and we'll tell them to wait outside for us. Well, we went into Macy's and out the back door and we went back to the Plaza, and the two guys was still standin' outside of Macy's, waiting for us.

That was when I learned a lesson: I had to watch myself. After all, I was only a young girl. I had to be very careful, very careful, because I was alone, you know.

One day, a guest at the Plaza came out to me and says, You want to come in and help me pack because I have to go to Europe? And I says, I'm sorry, but I don't do that kind of work. I knew what he wanted. But I was wise enough to know to watch out for stuff.

I lived in the Plaza until I got a job in Newport. A nice woman who worked for the Astors said, Would you like to be my kitchen maid? I said I would like that.

So I went with her to Newport. The Astors came back from Europe, after the *Titanic* went down—Mrs. Astor lost her husband—but I never saw them. We was always in the big, big kitchen, with all the pots and pans hanging on the wall.

Oh, they had an awful lot of help. They had four butlers, and a housekeeper, a gardener, the caretaker. I couldn't keep the job because the work was too heavy for me. The housekeeper—she was the head over us—says to me, You're a nice girl. But you have to be strong to work in the Astor home. See, they wanted a big, heavy woman, one that can whip up the work. In a home like that, you gotta be on the go, on the go. Because they entertain an awful lot. They have big parties.

—CATHERINE AVERY

I arrived in New York from the Netherlands in early December 1926. There were no airplanes at that time for civilians between Europe and America. I traveled on the steamship *Minnekahda*. It took about a week and it was very pleasant. We danced; we had good meals. I knew English from high school, but here I learned some more spoken English.

Professor Dirk Struik

I came to the Massachusetts Institute of Technology in Cambridge. I was there for a year as a lecturer on differential geometry. I wanted to find out if I liked America—I knew there were very sharp confrontations between capital and labor, and that there were the very rich and the very poor—and if M.I.T. would like me. It turned out satisfactorily on both sides. So I stayed there as a professor, and began to study very seriously finding out what kind of a country I was living in.

We settled first in Cambridge, and after 1935 in Belmont. My wife and I came here childless; we eventually had three daughters. Acclimatization was not very difficult because there is no deep cultural gap between the Netherlands and the U.S.A., the kind of gap that confronts a person from, let's say, Nigeria or Cambodia who comes here. In Dutch high school I had learned French, German, and English as well as Dutch. I also had learned some American history—about Washington and the American Revolution, Abraham Lincoln and the Civil War, Woodrow Wilson and World War I.

In our early days in America, there were some things that struck us about this overwhelming country. The amazing fact that the police were armed gave us an idea of the state of violence in this country. In peaceful Holland, the worst thing police had was a nightstick. In the second place, the universities, like M.I.T., had for undergraduate students much more of a high-school aspect than a university one. At Leyden, where I got my Ph.D., we had two exams in four years (with some *tentamina* with individual professors), and we were otherwise entirely on our own. Here you had a test every two weeks.

You have, of course, here an enormous country compared to such a small country as that from which I came, with far different kinds of political and economic problems. We began, by and by, to understand some of these, to participate, and get more of an idea of the history of this country.

What is being an American? I don't know. But I remember finding out what a Yankee is. I had heard the term, but in the European sense: Yankee refers to the whole of the United States. Here, Yankee means a person from New England. That led me, in a book that I published, to study New England from the point of view of its scientific and technical developments in the first century of the Republic. I called it *Yankee Science in the Making*; it was published in 1948, twenty years after my arrival.

— D I R K   S T R U I K

I had to leave Italy after Mussolini, Il Duce, changed course, acting on the best Macchiavellian principle of expediency. Soon after the "pact of iron" was made between Italy and Germany, a law was proclaimed which was incomprehensible to the Italian way of thinking: all Jews who had immigrated after 1921 had to leave the country within six months.

Before leaving, I went to the Italian part of Switzerland, the Ticino, and called on the highest political official. I introduced myself with two letters, which eliminated the ubiquitous suspicion of the time that I could be an impostor, a *cavaliere d'industria*. In one letter, on the stationery of the Senate, I was praised, in not little exaggeration, for my more than four-year-long successful work on a process for keeping raw milk fresh. The Italian senator, Silvio Crespi, eventually offered to give witness in no uncertain terms to whatever authority about my ability and character. In the second letter, on the impressive stationery of the Vatican, its Governor, Count Ratti, wrote how much he regrets my decision to leave Italy and with his wishes for my future, etc.

With the two letters and documents for my rights about two patents—the milk process and a new kind of zipper—the national counselor went to President Motta himself to explain the value of the patents for Switzerland. I got immediately the right of residence in Lugano. Negotiations soon followed for the exploitation of the zipper patent that would give work to many hundred mechanics of a closed watch factory nearby. After almost a year of preparations, I was called in to see the chief executive of the large corporation—half owned by the government, I was told—of which the new factory was a part. There my faith in Switzerland was shattered. I was told that the solemnly notarized contracts with their promise of security for my future were cancelled. A new contract would have to be signed. This was an ultimatum. If I'd refuse, I'd be brought to the German border. That would mean deportation and certain death.

Well, I survived again. I had found a real friend in the national counselor, who declared he would start legal action against the powerful firm with which he had previously been associated. However, this good, politically powerful man died within three months. Shortly thereafter, President Motta passed away. But what timing! A visa arrived for me. My alarming letter to friends in the United States helped. But it was an emergency visa for Cuba, not the U.S.A., where I had applied in vain for more than six years.

My happiest time in Lugano occurred early one morning rowing back in a boat from Morcote. There I heard the unmistakable voice of the Nazi minister Goebbels informing the world of the "victorious" invasion of Russia. There was no doubt in my mind: this was the turning point of the war. On the shore, I saw a group of wounded prisoners of war, probably Polish, who looked at me with incredulity as I shouted at them what I had just heard. Their expressions changed to real happiness. Their reaction was the same as mine. The Russian giant would not be conquered like France.

The decisive change in my life soon followed: my departure from Europe.

The *S/S Magellanes*, a luxury liner, had as passengers a *Schicksalsgemeinschaft*—companions in fate. It was easy to recognize the pale, emaciated faces of those who had come from jails or had escaped from concentration camps. Most of the other passengers were emigrants, too. All of them had to leave their homeland to save their lives. After a few days on a calm sea under sunny skies, the miracle of human resiliency became visible. People started enjoying themselves; normal social contacts were made; the play of the dolphins and the flying fishes were admired; there was even singing and dancing. Romances started. My intention to be deaf-mute, to concentrate on learning Spanish, was quickly foiled by a young lady from Budapest.

A hurricane altered this happy atmosphere. For three days, the ship was tossed around. Nuns wailed on their knees. Pious Jews chanted death prayers. My young lady and I were behind the lifeboats, in desperate happiness, but also prepared to jump into them if the ship had to be abandoned.

Erich Leyens in his passport photo

We did arrive safely, eventually. We were detained in Tiscornia, the Cuban Ellis Island. Many of the immigrants had to remain for months there awaiting a visa for the United States. But I made a discovery that set the course of my nine months in Cuba: adjacent to the barracks area where we were detained was the *campamento infantil*, an orphanage of more than a thousand children. I was amazed to observe that they were doing nothing. I managed to get acquainted with the director of the camp, to whom I suggested an "occupation therapy"—training the listless children for light work.

My initiative had fortunate consequences. I was introduced to ministers to whom I explained the milk process, which could transform the surplus of milk in Cuba for export. After nine months of strenuous, often frustrating, and sometimes amusing negotiations, I was given to understand that Cuba didn't have the industrial capacity to produce the containers needed to keep the milk from spoiling. Then my visa for the United States arrived, almost seven years after my initial application. I felt deeply grateful that at last I was to be admitted to a country which had become for millions around the world the "promised land," a country of which one of its Presidents once said: We are all immigrants; we are all refugees.

It was not the Statue of Liberty that welcomed me on my arrival in Miami. Nor was my arrival without unexpected complications. I was whisked from the plane to a large room where I faced three officers of the Armed Forces. The confidence I had in my linguistic abilities was quickly shattered. These stern and suspicious-looking men commenced a tough cross-examination. I am sure Ponce de León could better understand the language of the Seminoles in Florida when he was searching for the Fountain of Youth than I could grasp their questions. They read from a fat dossier, but to me it seemed obvious that most of their questions had nothing particularly to do with me. I was anxious and confused. There were two questions I never have forgotten:

What did you do with your yacht?

I never had one, I said.

They admonished me to stick to the truth, indicating the big dossier about my life. Well, it dawned on me that I may have been asked about an old boat I once had that had sunk under me in the river Rhein. Was I now a liar in their eyes?

Would you also deny that in Germany you were a hero?

Again I was flustered. I had not heard the word "hero" before and asked for a spelling. Then I grasped the meaning. After all, I had lived in Switzerland. In good conscience, I declared that I never had anything to do with Hero marmalade.

What followed was warm, hearty laughter. They obviously came to the conclusion that I was a harmless idiot and not a spy smuggled in at the beginning of the war. This was my first lesson that ignorance can be a blessing! The previously stern officers came down from their intimidating podium to shake hands with me and, with genuine smiles, wish me luck in my new country.

When I reached New York, I made my way to the recruiting office. I was politely given to understand that my forty-four years would disqualify me from military service. I did, however, find a modest outlet later on in the U.S. Army Ambulance Corps. I was mighty proud to wear Uncle Sam's uniform—if only at night in emergencies.

Some years ago my friend Odette from Lausanne returned to me a letter I wrote to her after my "discovery" of New York in 1942 and '43. The great miracle, I had written, was that you were permitted to work and you could find jobs when you tried hard enough. I had already six different ones, I had written, and in each I had learned more than the work: I had learned the language, more than in the free evening school. People are friendly here and like to communicate, I wrote. You even can strike up a conversation with a girl you aren't introduced to, without getting into trouble. A pity that they all look alike, have the same way of dressing, same makeup, even use the same words in talking.

I found it noteworthy that there were effective fans against the heat and that the showers sprayed diagonally instead of vertically. The President,

Franklin Delano Roosevelt, appears in this letter a God-like figure, and the "Little Flower," our Mayor La Guardia, is described with affection as the best example of how wrong the Cubans were to say that they were only poor pupils of the corruption in the States. For the first time since childhood, I wrote, I felt tears when I read carved in the frieze of the New York State Supreme Court building: *Equal Justice Under Law Without Regard to Color, Creed, Sex or Race.* Today I realize how profoundly shaken I must have been. Equality before the law was abolished in Hitler's Germany, and the judiciary was a tool of the Nazi Party. At that point in time began my abiding love for the country and the almost religious meaning the "Pledge of Allegiance" had for me.

One of the most important and proud days of my life was the day I became an American citizen. How carefully I prepared, learning thoroughly about American history. Waiting to be admitted to appear before the judge, I heard stories like these: One frail old lady was asked, Tell me, please, who was the first President? Her prompt answer: Franklin Roosevelt. Well, said the judge, when you came by ship to New York, you must have seen the large statue of a lady who greeted you. Can you tell me who that is? Came the reply: Eleanor Roosevelt. Congratulations, the understanding judge said to the trembling old lady, now you are an American citizen!

The next applicant was a self-assured former history professor from Germany. To the question, When did the War Between the States occur? he responded for one half hour with a learned lecture about that war. Another lecture ensued when he was asked about the American Revolution. Then the judge asked, Who is the most popular sportsman in the country? He got an indignant answer; the professor was not interested in sports. To which the judge said, I suggest that you inform yourself about that important part of American life and come back after half a year.

It is irrelevant whether this story is true; what fun it was for me, a Dodger fan—when the Bums were still in Brooklyn—to hear it. In our happy celebration of the wonderful day, "liberty and justice for all" was the prevailing refrain.

—ERICH LEYENS

Hearth and Home

Oh, my land, you children

don't know about living

back yonder. But we lived,

and we lived well.

—F. ETHEL ANDREWS

Born November 13, 1888

Shady Side, Maryland

There was no telephone on the farm for years. How did we reach help if help was needed? Go to the pasture, catch a horse, and we always had a choice: harness it for the buggy, or put on a saddle. Distance would determine the decision.

There was no electricity—no radio, no TV, no VCR. What did we do for entertainment? We had no time during the week for frivolity. We met with our family and friends after church on Sunday and on holidays.

There were no electric lights at that time. We used candles, and kerosene lamps. Those lamps had to be cleaned every Saturday—filled with kerosene, wicks trimmed, and globes washed and polished.

There was no plumbing. Water was carried in from the well in a bucket for the family needs. Dishwater, bathwater, and other water not consumed would be carried out in a different bucket.

There was no washing machine. The wash boiler, washtub, washboard and homemade soap were every Monday morning necessities. Washday was all day—with intermittent breaks to rest by doing other things.

There was no electric dryer. Clothes were hung on a line in the yard to dry, if you had enough clothesline. If not, hang them on the fence, and watch out that the barbs didn't snag something.

There was no refrigeration, no ice maker, no ice. For cool storage there was the cellar. For keeping things really cold, you put it in the old oaken bucket and with a rope let it down into the well.

There was no vacuum cleaner. No cleaning lady. The kitchen-dining room floor was scrubbed every Saturday on hands and knees. And during the week it was swept after every meal, with a broom.

The kitchen stove was wood-burning: no thermometer, no timer, no microwave, no electric coffeepot, no toaster, no electric waffle iron. There was no Mixmaster, but there was no need! A better angel-food cake was never made than the one that came out of that old stove oven: thirteen large egg whites whipped on a meat platter with a wire whip. And that never failed!

—ELLA MAY STUMPE

◄ *A wood-burning kitchen stove, before electricity (Culver Pictures)*

My daddy was a farmer in Bishop, Georgia. He rented the land he worked; he had to pay the man half of what he made.

Our house was made out of wood plank that Daddy would whitewash. My ma had to seal it up with newspaper. One time, my little brother was playin' and he set fire to some of that there newspaper. Me and my older sister, we hollered for my daddy to come, and he just grabbed up some white dirt and put out that fire.

We didn't have no well water. We used to get our water from a hole my daddy had dug out the side of a spring. Me and my little brother had to go way down to the spring to get water for my ma. That water was good, but every time we went down there, water snakes done crawled over there. We sort of got scared of the little snakes, but we'd get the water. Then me and him would go get more water and Ma would come in from the field to cook.

—FANNIE LOU DAVIS

Momma would go in the woods and dig the root of the dogwood tree for to make quinine for the plantation Negroes to take when they had chills. She'd dig that root out of that dogwood tree, she'd bring it home and wash it and dry it. Then she'd put it on the big kitchen stove and boil it three or four days. Then she stopped and let the water set at the bottom: that was the quinine. When we got sick, if we had a chill or an upset stomach, we had to take a drink of that quinine. And I hated it so bad. Ooh, Lord, it was bitter! It was the worst medicine I ever take in my life, but I had to take it. 'Cause as long as you were a child you had to mind your parents—and you better be sure you didn't give 'em a back word.

We had to drink water off the ground. See, we didn't have pumps and they didn't have runnin' water. So we'd drink any kind of water out of a ditch, or they'd dig a well in the yard and we'd drink out of that little well. We also had springs on Verona Plantation, six springs at one place. They wouldn't let children go there 'cause they afraid the children'd fall in the springs. But bein' a child, I wanted to go there.

One day, I was picking cotton. I couldn't pick much cotton, but they carried me into the cotton field with 'em 'cause I was too little to be stayin' home by myself. I slipped out the cotton patch and went to the springs and got me some water out of the barrel where they watered the teams and the cows. And I commenced havin' chills. I got mighty sick with typhoid fever.

There was a doctor in Jackson, Dr. Lewis, and they called him 'cause I couldn't stop havin' them chills to save my life. And they found out that I had drank water out of the wrong spring. Dr. Lewis tended me and he told 'em that I would be dead before daylight the next mornin'. So they fixed my clothes to bury me in. But I was tough. I didn't die. The next mornin', I woke up. And so, when the doctor came back, he looked at me and he said, You ain't dead yet? Sallie, you ain't gon' never die. If you didn't die last night, you gon' live a hundred years.

And I been wakin' ever since.

—SALLIE JORDAN

People were born and waked at home in those days. Funeral parlors were not in existence. It was not unusual to walk down the street and see a drape hanging outside on a front door, which meant that someone there just died, or there's a funeral being conducted.

—ARTHUR W. HAMER, SR.

When I was a child, a few of the things they didn't build in houses were bathrooms and closets. They all had nice chifforobes and things like that.

Our houses had high ceilings and big windows. The house I was born in had seven fireplaces in it. But I never saw a fire built in any except my mother's room, unless the preacher was there to preach in the parlor. In south Georgia we had something called lightwood, and you could build a fire there that'd warm up the country.

—DR. LEILA DENMARK

I grew up in an old weatherboard farmhouse out near Frederick, Maryland. It had a big kitchen and, of course, we were in the kitchen an awful lot. We didn't have running water. We had a bench and a big bucket that you carried the grandest water that ever existed. We had a great big old iron stove that had a tank at the side next to the heating chamber. So we had lots of really hot water for washing and cleaning. We had baths in a washtub in the kitchen, the same one we'd do laundry in. And we had an icehouse. The men used to go down to the creek and cut ice in the deep end and bring it up and stack it in the icehouse.

In the evening, we'd all sit around the dining-room table, especially during the winter. Father would read the newspaper, mostly out loud. Or the *Farm Journal*, that was gospel, you know. Mother would be at the other end of the table embroidering or sewing or mending. And the kids would be scattered.

Mother's parents looked after me. A lot of evenings I'd sit around with them at their house. There was a stove—they had no furnace, of course—that would feel good to sit by when it was cold out. And we'd make lamp-lighters. They were long rolls of paper that we'd turn over at the end to keep from unrolling. We'd put 'em in this old spoon holder that stood on the mantel or in these glass vases. When we wanted to light a lamp, we took one of 'em and stuck it in the stove and lit it and used it to light the lamp. No switches. Who ever heard of light switches? Who had electricity?

In our house, we were four girls, and the room over the dining room was our bedroom. It had two beds and a bureau and washstand with a bowl. We had to carry a bucket of water up for everything. My two brothers each had one of the smaller rooms.

There was no plumbing, of course. We had a chamber pot under the bed for quickies. But we also—I know this doesn't sound civilized—used to get wooden buckets some kind of fish came in. We put that out in the hall in the wintertime and you just went out and sat on that if you had more drastic things to do. Which you didn't very often, you know. Of course, we had an outhouse, and that was very busy with a family of eight.

—HELEN L. SMITH

I stood in the yard and watched Gordon, Nebraska's banker, put the first indoor toilet in his house. I was not yet eight years old. What are they going to do, have the toilet in the house? I thought, That's just awful.

—AUDREY STUBBART

My first cousin across the street here in Saluda, my father's nephew, was a lawyer, and he always made good money. One day, Mildred, my little daughter, and Mother and I were digging out a magnolia tree, and Cousin Ben came over and said, Aunt Ida, I've come to tell you not to vote for the waterworks. In two months' time, he said, you'll lose your house, the taxes will be so high.

Well, now, Mother said, Bennie, I am going to put in waterworks, and I'm gonna have two bathrooms. His mouth was hanging wide open.

Ben, he'd had one bathroom upstairs; he was one of the few people in Saluda that had waterworks. He said, Just think, Aunt Ida, now every Tom, Dick, and Harry will have waterworks, and I won't enjoy mine.

Now, wasn't that selfish?

See, until then, we'd had an outhouse out back of the garden. And we had to clean it out every now and then. Ugh! Those were awful days when you had to do that.

—LOIS CROUCH ADDY

We made a fire around a great big black washpot. We washed the clothes in the first tub, and put them in the pot, and boiled them, took them out and rinsed them through three waters, then hung them on the line.

We made our soap, too. You'd put a little water in the washpot, then you'd put your grease in there, let it get hot, and then open your potash and pour it in there to make potash soap. You could make three to four pots full, accordin' to how large the pot was. Mama always made two pots of soap. She cut it in a block and lay it on a plank in the smokehouse. It'd get hard, then you could use it like you do bar soap. Those two pots would take care of us for three or four months.

—JESSIE TURNER

Around the time that I was born, there was no mail service; there was no rural free delivery in North Dakota when I was growing up.

A bag of mail might come in maybe once a month by courier from the nearest railroad, which was a hundred miles away. It would be dropped off at the general store, which had some pigeonholes on a wall. The mail was shoved into those. When you came in—there was no self-service—you went to the counter and you gave your order to the clerk, who would write it down and go assemble it. And he would tell you if there was a letter for you.

My father had family in Minnesota, and they kept in touch about once every six months. A letter would come and he would send one back. He would leave it at the general store. And it would stay there until they had enough letters for a courier to take them to the railroad station.

We got no printed material by mail at all then. It was around the time when I was in the eighth grade, around 1909, when my father started getting the socialist paper, *Appeal to Reason*, in the mail. My mother got a magazine, the *Woman's Home Companion*. We kids were not allowed to touch those papers.

So that was the mail system: There was none. Any news, anything happening in the community, you jumped on a horse and you rode a circuit around and let everybody know. You went to the first neighbor and said,

So-and-So's in trouble. You go and alert the rest of 'em. That's the way they took care of one another, and that's the way they spread the news.

—ELLA MAY STUMPE

Father was one of the first to have a telephone. With a family our size, he felt he had to be able to get to the doctor in case something happened. And he had to be among the first to have a telephone. We needed one or two extra posts to lead the line into the house and he had to furnish that himself. There were seven or eight families who shared one line. The telephone hung on the wall, and when it started to ring, you had to listen to see if the call was for you. Ours was one long and three short.

There were three old maids—they were Father's and Mother's age—that lived up the road. Oh, they were snooty people! They'd have liked to have shown off more, but they didn't have much money. And always when we heard their ring, we'd run and listen because it was always rich. We would nearly die! The oldest one, Jane, had kind of a squared-off face. Father called her "The Bulldog." They had a farm, but it wasn't too big, and they'd always try to save their money. Later on, they had columns put up so they'd look very colonial.

The phone was for Father and Mother and they didn't linger much talking on it. They were busy. It was an event when I got to talk on it. And we'd never make a call without permission. Oh no, oh no, oh boy, would they have slam-banged us! You weren't that familiar with anybody anyway.

—HELEN L. SMITH

The first telephone we ever had, we had half a dozen people on the same line. Of course, it was not considered proper to eavesdrop.

—VICTOR MILLS

We raised more than we needed and we always had plenty of milk; everybody had a milk cow. We didn't have a variety of food but we didn't go hungry, either. We made our hominy in a big iron kettle that would lie out in the yard. Everybody butchered their own meat. It got so that it didn't bother me, but that first chicken, that was a bloody operation. Because I didn't know the first thing about it. I'd seen Mother, she'd swing a chicken by its head until its neck snapped, and then it went sailing off in the yard. She'd go get it and dress it, and we'd have chicken.

I never knew the intimacy until you get down to where you've got to have something to eat. Out on the ranch, we did what we had to to survive. If we had to have porcupine hamburgers for Christmas dinner, it was a lot better than the alternative. And if you never ate one, don't knock it.

—AUDREY STUBBART

My mother always had a large garden, but she needed it, because you didn't freeze anything then. You preserved it, pickled it, or canned it. The canning process then was to put what you were canning into a big boiler of water and boil it for about two hours. That was supposed to kill everything that would spoil it. Mother also made hominy from seed corn, and preserved ham, bacon, and sausage. She made real mincemeat for pies, pickled pigs' feet, and made headcheese. She made her own horseradish. The only fruits native to North Dakota were the chokecherry, highbush cranberry, and the Juneberry, a wild blueberry. She picked and preserved them when she could find them.

Mother would share her garden with anybody that was in need. She always planted a large patch of rhubarb, much more than our family could possibly use. I think she might have planted it just for people to come and help themselves. And they did.

One day at the noon hour, when the hired men were on their way to the house, a hobo appeared at the kitchen door asking for something to eat. Feeding hoboes at that time was pretty frequent after the railroad was built through our farm a quarter of a mile from the house. Hoboes riding the rails would drop off and come up for food. Our compassionate mother never refused food to anyone, but she always struck a bargain with those she thought were able to work. That day, she told the hobo, I always need wood for my woodbox, so if you will go to the woodpile and split a few chunks of wood, you may eat dinner with the men who are coming in.

The hobo said, I want something to eat, and I want it now. And he reached for the handle on the screen door, which was locked.

My mother said, Just wait a minute while I get something. And she turned quickly, grabbed the boiling tea kettle from the stove. She almost caught up to him before he reached the front gate.

—ELLA MAY STUMPE

Once, just after we moved out to Foster from Seattle, my mother was going to teach our neighbor how to row a boat. As Mama was showing him, out there in the middle of the river, a great big salmon jumped right in the boat. Just jumped right in! Mama unhitched the oar and hit it on the head. That was the end of the rowing lesson that day because they were so busy cleaning and cooking up the fish.

I know this happened because my little brother and I were sitting on a log watching Mama and this neighbor. Were we ever surprised!

Now, my brother and I, we went out in the rowboat, fishing. It wasn't easy to catch fish. But Father had a net, and he'd put it out at night and, boy, we'd get some big ones. We'd have a feast and my mother would can some of it. Just about the only food we bought was coffee and sugar and crackers and hams—great big hams and slabs of bacon that Father hung in the meat cool room.

—IVY FRISK

My father was a farmer and blacksmith. Rainy days and winter days, he had to do blacksmith work, sharpenin' tools and makin' 'em. He had to make 'em: not much was store-bought then. He'd make his own fish gigs, too. And when these here creeks would freeze up and we'd be skatin', my father'd cut a hole out in the ice and sit there with his homemade gig and he'd get a bunch of fish runnin' up the stream. They were just fish back then; you didn't have no thoroughbred fish.

—W. F. JARNAGIN

I was in the fifth grade when I went to live with my grandmother. She was still cooking with a coal range. Finally, Grandfather bought her a gas range. He ran the line in from the cellar, where the meter was, and installed the range where she could cook on top and bake in the oven. But Grandmother never used it. She was afraid it would blow up.

—ALBERT M. COLEMAN

In our house, there was a meter for gas. You put a quarter in a slot to get the gas. Gas was piped overhead in certain rooms; the light fixture was a Welsbach burner, a woven burner in the shape of my fingers. To set it off, you had to touch it with a match and it made a little flame. Then you could turn the gas on with a match, and it gave off a beautiful light.

Electricity came on when the electric company expanded. You know what they did? They advertised. At first, they gave away electrical appliances for free to encourage people to go into electricity. It was feared, I think, by a great many immigrants: electricity will shock you, they thought. Bulbs were exchanged for free. But there were still meters, and you still had to put a quarter in. If the light was on and it began to dim, that meant—oh, quick, quick, put a quarter in.

—JOSEPH GOLDSTEIN

I must have been sixteen when we got electricity. Of course, it made a big difference. I could read late at night and do a lot of things that I couldn't do before because Mother wouldn't let the kerosene lamps be burning all the time. We could only be up a certain length of time and then we had to turn them out because she didn't want to fall asleep and not have all the lights out in the house.

You'd never imagine the joy we had when we got our first electric iron. My dad came home with this present for Mother. It was an electric iron. And I ironed everything: the wrinkles of my pants, my dresses, everything. I never seemed to get tired. Because before then, you had to have a good fire going and the irons on the stove. It was hard work, ironing without electricity.

—IVY FRISK

We were the first ones in the neighborhood to have electricity, and, oh, my gracious sakes' alive, people from all around the neighborhood came in to see what it was like to live under those lights. I can't say exactly that it made our life better, but it sure made life easier, especially in the evenings when we had to do our homework. We didn't all have to sit around the same table under a lamp to see what we were doing. Now we could sit mostly anyplace in the room.

That was in 1907. But we didn't get a refrigerator until years later. Until then, we still had nothing but iceboxes.

But where refrigeration really made a difference was in my grocery store. Around 1927 I had a Frigidaire unit put in. Before then, all my refrigeration was ice, and I decided to remodel the store and put in a refrigeration system. I had this Frigidaire put in down in my basement, and it was large enough and powerful enough to run all of the refrigerant I needed in the store.

Before then, you never had things really cold; they were just kept reasonably cool, where with the Frigidaire I could keep the meat case down to thirty-three degrees and the ice cream cabinet down to ten below zero and the milk cabinet down to thirty-four. So that was a marvelous thing.

As far as I know, that old Frigidaire is still in operation in a store out in Northampton. It's what was called a water-cooled system in those days. Boy, that really was a wonderful thing.

—OSCAR C. WEBER

We didn't have a refrigerator in the apartment we were renting, and the landlady said that she would get one eventually. When I came home from school one day, I found that she had had one put in, and she was so pleased because I think she kind of liked us and wanted us to stay as her tenants.

She was happy and so was I because I liked ice cubes. Before this, we had a card that we would put up on the window telling the man who came along with the wagon with the ice whether to bring in fifty pounds or whatever, and put it in the icebox. The refrigerator was so much better.

—ANNETTA GIBSON

All I knowed about growin' up was Verona Plantation and Occoneechee Neck. I had never lived no better, so how'd I know there *was* any better? We couldn't go to Weldon and buy food. There was no bridges across the Roanoke River. We had to go on a flatboat. Had a man that run the flat; he would pull a rope and a chain would carry the flat across.

In them days, we didn't get food or clothes by train. We got it from a boat. People in Norfolk owned a big store and two times a year they had a boat bring groceries and clothes to Occoneechee Neck for the people that lived on this side of the river. My daddy was the overseer of that farm there—it was hundreds and hundreds of acres and it took a lot of help to run it—and he would get a notice when the boat was gon' come in. And when he'd hear it blow he knew it was in Weldon. If he had gone to bed and he heard that boat blow, he would get up and dress and go down to the river with carts and wagons to bring in the load of groceries and clothes.

—SALLIE JORDAN

Most everything we ate, or had, was homemade. For a mattress, we'd fill some heavy material with straw. Us kids had the straw mattress on the floors only. We'd make quilts mostly out of clothes we couldn't wear anymore. We'd cut the pieces out and sew them together. That's what my mother always did: made quilts. And not only that, she spun the wool and made yarn to knit socks and mittens.

'Course, we also shopped by catalogue, from Sears, Roebuck; Montgomery Ward; and the M. W. Savage Company. You'd always go through the catalogue, even if you didn't always get what you wished. You could get almost anything in them catalogues: dry goods, farm equipment, clothing, shoes. Whether the shoes fit or not, you'd still wear them.

—LENA STANLEY

Mama was too busy to sew, so she hired a lady to come for a week or ten days in the spring and then in the fall. They never thought of buying clothes already made. They bought material—Mama had stacks and stacks of material—and the lady would come and sew for Mama and me.

I had pants made of "Centennial Best"—hundred-pound sacks that our flour came in. For Sunday school, I had other dresses with lace on, but around home, I had these Centennial Best flour pants. Oh, and I had black satin bloomers, too. My mother thought they were better for me than pants because I was always climbing fences and so forth, so she fitted me out in those black satin bloomers.

My father, though, looked after my shoes. My mother and my sister had corns and trouble with their feet, and he never allowed them to have anything to do with my shoes. And I thank Father many times, because I haven't any trouble with my feet. But Mama, it was a pity. Whenever they went to go out, always they had to soak their feet in hot water and soap. And that was before spiked heels.

—IVY FRISK

One piece of clothing some of the girls wore then was called the hobble skirt. There was a little poem:

> *Come on, fellows, if you want to flirt,*
> *Here comes a girl with a hobble skirt.*
> *You can hug and squeeze her all you please,*
> *But you can't get her skirt up above her knees.*

That skirt, you know, it used to be so tight, when you had to walk up a step, you couldn't. You had to be so careful or you'd break your neck.

—THERESA NIGRELLI

Theresa Salimeno (Theresa Nigrelli), age seventeen, Westerly, Rhode Island, 1911

Our store was a general grocery store that gave us a chance to serve the local public year 'round. It carried items suitable for every need. People had to buy here in Shady Side or sail to Annapolis, or go by horse-and-buggy over roads that were a loblolly of mud.

The store building was much longer than it was wide. At different times we had built three buildings for use as the grocery store in different places within one hundred feet of the Rural Home, the resort business my parents operated. Counters ran down each side with a wide-open space between them. There was a stove in the center of the room. In the early days, these buildings were lighted with large oil lamps which hung from the ceiling and which could be pulled down to be cleaned and filled. We heated with stoves that burned either wood or coal. At the height of the winter, the fires were made with coal because it lasted longer. In spring and fall, fires were laid with wood and allowed to go out once the place was warm.

In the northeast corner of the store were sou'westers, long yellow oilskins and boots both high and knee-high for men. There were rubbers for both men and women. Some of these were on the shelves, some on the floor beside kegs of nails of all sizes, dipped by hand and sold by the pound.

Bolts of fabrics called dry goods—calico, gingham, percale, bleached and unbleached muslins, linen, taffeta, satin, nainsook, and corduroy—lay in order on the shelves. Blue material that looked like sailcloth, similar to the denim of today, was sold for overalls. White laces and ribbons of all colors were in glass cases on the counter. A tall case was filled with spools of thread, mostly white and black but with a few of every color. ONT furnished this case for the thread. To this day I don't know what ONT stands for.

Every once in a while I would look at a beautiful piece of white lace about wide enough to make a skirt for my doll. My china-headed doll needed a new dress. I thought that lace would make her a beautiful skirt and looked at that lace again and again. It was just right. I quietly removed it from the case, went upstairs to my attic room and reached for my doll. Busily, I made that skirt by hand, sewing up the seam and put a band in and gathered the top. No hem was needed. I had a white blouse that matched. She looked so pretty! But my mother missed that lace from the case and often said, Where in the world did that lace go? I never answered. The result was that I could never dress my doll in that skirt any place except in the attic, where Mama couldn't see it.

Yardsticks used for measuring lay on the counter. Also, black-ribbed cotton stockings of all sizes were sold. The kind I wore cost ten cents a pair. There were no ready-made garments among the merchandise. All women had treadle sewing machines bought through salesmen and shipped in on the steamship *Emma Giles*. They bought the fabrics and made all the clothes for their family: underwear, children's clothes, dresses for women, pants for men, coats for both, bed linens, tablecloths, and napkins. The store sold no furniture, so people in Shady Side either made their own or went to the city to shop. Another item not sold in the early days was toilet paper. Everyone saved their newspapers for use in the privies.

On the west side of the store, the counter began behind the cracker barrel. The meats were served from there. We sold slabs of bacon, pork, hams both fresh and smoked, fatback, sausage, and highly seasoned western meat. A quarter of a beef was kept in the meat-keeping case. There was no refrigerator. All of this meat had to be cut and wrapped by the pound. The paper was kept on a roll and was white and shiny. My sister Annetta and I often had to slice this meat using the cleaver and the butcher's knife.

Further down on the shelves were canned vegetables and fruits and seasonings like nutmeg, cinnamon, and pepper. Chewing tobacco, wrappers for cigarettes, tobacco to be used in the cigarettes, cigars and snuff were next to the canned goods. On the west side even further down were medical supplies: paregoric for diarrhea, quinine pills for malaria, and laudanum for pain. Vaseline and olive oil were always kept with the medicine. Often in the middle of the night we would be awakened by someone whose family member was ill, and Papa would have to get up and go into the store and get the medicine. There were also the fifty-pound cans of lard that had to be divided into pound packages and put into little trays made of wood, similar to the wood used in cheese boxes.

Under the counters, or behind them, were huge barrels of sugar, yellow cornmeal, white flour, and ginger snaps. Crackers, square and large and saltless, all had to be weighed by scales and put into pound bags. That was a tiresome and tedious job. Every product was sold by the pound, put in a paper bag and tied by twine from a ball on the counter.

A great big roll of cheese was kept on the counter in a wooden box, from which we lifted the wooden top. We cut either great hunks of cheese or nice slices. From October to May at the close of an oystering day, the oystermen in their workaday clothes, often very muddy from the culling of the oysters, filed in to buy cheese, crackers or ginger snaps and sometimes large pickles. They stood around the big stove in the center of the store with the sandwiches they had made. Uncle Billy Moreland was a big black man, jolly, always laughing. Uncle Billy would take two very large ginger snaps, put slices of cheese between them and stand at the stove, laughing and enjoying eating them—no matter the kind of the day, no matter the small catch, no matter the difficulties of mud and dirt, there was always laughter everywhere in the store with dear Uncle Billy leading it.

Men gathered around the stove every day around 7 a.m. and remained until the store closed at 10 p.m., telling stories. Nearby was a table on which a checkerboard lay. There was often a scrap as to who was going to get to play checkers. I think there were dominoes there, too. There were no cards because my father wouldn't allow a pack of cards to be in the store.

—F. ETHEL ANDREWS

Verona Plantation had locust trees. And they'd take the juice from the locusts and make beer. They had a machine to put it in and press it and let it set three or four days and then they'd strain it out and that'd be beer. They'd put brown sugar in. Oh, it was good!

—SALLIE JORDAN

I used to make the best beer there was. We never sold it, though. But I was going to try to one time. I went over to the Hand Brewery Company, it was called. They were very nice people, they took me in and they showed me all the barrels. I said, My Lord, anybody falls in there, they're going to get drowned. The barrels must have been built right in there in the building, you know, 'cause you couldn't get 'em through a door.

But I used to make it just as good as theirs. Oh, it was nice. No sediment down in the bottom, just bright and nice. I used to make it for my husband. I used to have someone come and take the baby out 'cause the smell of the hops might make him sick. It took a lot of work, let me tell you. It had to go through one barrel, then through another barrel, and then finally to the bottom, where I'd bottle it. And I'd put a little bit of sugar in it. I used to make it once a week. I'd get it all ready, then at night when my husband came home he would bottle it up. I couldn't do that; that was a man's job.

Of course, all the families used to make their own wine. I thought it was terrible. Did they wash their feet? They used to stomp on the grapes with their feet down in the cellar.

—THERESA NIGRELLI

When I was a small child, my mother would give me a glass of water with a spoonful of wine in it, which to me that was a glass of wine. As I grew older, the amount of water versus the amount of wine in the glass changed, until finally it got so that I was drinking pure wine.

My father made some very good wine. Of course: he was a Frenchman. One day, a commission merchant came around. He told my father that he had received a shipment of high-quality grapes that were overripe. They weren't wine grapes, they were table grapes, good grapes, and he offered to sell them for a rather low price just not to lose money. My father said that he would have to consult another Frenchman, because it was a tremendous amount of grapes. The other Frenchman said, Sure, buy them, we'll pay for them together.

So they bought a roomful of grapes. They were all over the cellar, crates of them. My father put them in this grinder, which he put on top of an empty barrel that had no top so this ground-up mix would fall in there. And every day my mother would go down with a lighted candle and lower it into the barrels. If the light went out, there was fermentation going on. But the day the light stayed lighted, that was the time to get busy. The first thing you did was to drain all the liquid through a spigot at the bottom of the barrel and put it in bottles. Then you had left this mess that you put in the press and you'd squeeze out every last drop of moisture. That, too, was put in bottles. Our French neighbor took his half, and we had our half. It was very good wine, too.

Then the question came: What should they do with this dry residue? Well, the thing to do is to bury a cheese in it. The theory is that it imparts to the cheese a taste which is out of this world. So they bought a wheel of raw cheese and buried it in this stuff. Well, one day, my father came home from work and my mother said to him, You know that residue down there in the cellar? It was beginning to attract flies, so I told the garbageman to take it away. My father was shocked. His pipe dropped out of his mouth. But he didn't scold my mother, because it was his fault. He should have told her that there was a cheese buried in that residue.

—JOHN SAILLIARD

Sundays and Celebrations

Since I was a kid, I walk five, six miles

to go to church every Sunday. Always

I tried to be the most close to God

I can be over my life.

—TRINIDAD HUERTAS

Born June 3, 1896

San Lorenzo, Puerto Rico

My father was dedicated to Sunday as a day of rest. When a little church was started in his granary, my mother would get us all ready; we always had to be clean and have clean clothes on.

Even though he didn't go with us, he had his routine. He would get up, go out and feed the horses, come in and have breakfast, go back out and turn them into the pasture for the day, pump up water and fill the water trough so that the animals had water. Then he would come in, clean himself up, and put on a white shirt. I never saw my father on Sunday without a white shirt. And that was for all day. He didn't change into casual clothes for comfort. He never played ball or anything like that. Not on Sunday.

Sunday was a day of meditation. Sunday was a day in which you showed honor to the Lord by the way you dressed and the way you observed the day. My father would never put his work crew into the fields on Sunday—not even if the grain was ripe and a storm was threatening the crop. Friends or neighbors or other members of the family might come by and he'd sit on the front porch with them, just sitting and visiting. That was Sunday.

When I was quite small, there were a few very important holidays, like the Fourth of July, days when the farmers "laid by" their work and went to town to celebrate. They took picnic lunches, baskets filled with fried chicken. Right at the edge of town was sort of a park at a place we called Willow Creek. We were down there one time—I must have been about thirteen then—and my father went into town and when he came back he had a bunch of bananas. We had never even seen bananas before! Then again, we didn't get any produce. We had to grow everything we ate, except for maybe a can or two of something.

—ELLA MAY STUMPE

I was raised a Methodist and we always went to church on Sunday. But Ma made two of us stay home with the baby 'cause Ma didn't carry her little babies to the church. And seems like there always was a baby around 'cause there was fourteen of us. And then the next Sunday two others of us would stay with the baby. That's the way she'd do it.

◄ *Christmas morning around the turn of the century (Culver Pictures)*

For the special days, the church would get a hog, and a deacon would keep that hog and fatten it. And when that day would come to take our dinner to the church, the deacons would kill the hog. And then some of the men would get it in a barbecue. The women would bring cakes and bread.

The preacher would stay at our house for a week, and the next week he'd stay with someone else. 'Course, we all had to pay the preacher. My daddy, he give fifty cents, and my ma would give him a quarter, and they'd give us a penny or something to put on the table. That's the way they'd do it.

—FANNIE LOU DAVIS

We walked ten miles to church and Sunday school every Sunday. We'd walk from Verona Plantation to Salem Church on the other side of Garysburg. We'd get up Sunday mornins' and my mother would dress us and put us in the road and we'd walk to Salem Church barefooted. When we'd get there, she'd tell us to go back there where two people lived back of the church and wash our feet and put on our shoes. They were high-topped, lace-up shoes, no linin' in 'em at all. I didn't know what a shoe was called a slipper till I was about grown. But mostly we didn't have no way to ride to Salem Church 'cept on the Sundays that my daddy could get off. Then he would carry us on a double wagon with two mules pullin'. Oh, I loved to go to church.

We didn't know nothin' 'bout holidays. My daddy didn't allow us to celebrate holidays. Except for Christmas. We'd get fruit. The General's brother was in Texas and he always sent a load of fruit to Verona Plantation to give to the men and the women that worked on the plantation.

My mother was going to Santa Claus to bring me dolls. And he'd always bring me dolls with a china head. But I didn't like 'em. So I broke the head.

—SALLIE JORDAN

Poppa would stand behind the counter just before Christmas, wrapping goodies, candies, and nuts and pickles—everybody loved pickles—in little paper bags to distribute among the Negroes. There was a section in Shady Side then that was a whole field of Negroes. And Poppa, he got those packages as a gift to every Negro that bought from our store because he saw that they couldn't afford to buy for Christmas.

On Christmas morning, everyone in Shady Side was up about 4 a.m. In our house, we were awakened by Murray Leatherbury, my sister Jennie's husband, shouting at the top of his voice, *"Christmas gift!"* and carrying in his arms a large country ham of his own curing. All of us rushed to the top of the steps and answered the call. Murray had entered the front door which, of course, was unlocked. My father and two brothers busied themselves with getting black gunpowder and matches. They walked out to a Revolutionary War cannon in our yard, rammed it with powder, touched the bunghole with a roll of lighted paper. It exploded and the sound reverberated through the village, announcing to everybody that Christmas had come. Just as this reverberation passed throughout the village, sounds of firecrackers were heard coming from outside the homes, for firecrackers were fired at Christmas, never on July 4th.

Now that we were fully awake, we opened our black cotton-ribbed stockings. We found candy sticks of peppermint, lemon, sassafras, and horehound flavors. We also had tiny assorted candy drops. No chocolates. We always had an orange in the toe of the stocking, and we looked forward to it for oranges were only available at Christmas, and to have an orange we didn't have to share was a treat.

What do you suppose we had for dinner? The same plump turkey we have today, but raised in the back yard and stuffed with homemade bread. No one went to a store to buy a turkey. Several people raised them to sell. Some people substituted other meats, chicken of their own raising or wild ducks or geese caught and killed from a hunting trip, or their own prepared ham. We had vegetables kept from the fall garden and stored in kilns: potatoes, a steamed cabbage, and boiled turnips seasoned with bacon or butter. We used homemade jams and jellies, grape and damson, instead of cranberries, which were not available to us. Lots of people made their own mincemeat for pies. Sweet-potato pie was a favorite and served widely since sweet potatoes kept well in the late garden.

Christmas holidays lasted a week. All kinds of parties were held for groups—sometimes families, sometimes adults, and sometimes children only. At each home, we had the same entertainment. We sampled the cakes on the table which were made before Christmas. They were spread out on Christmas day and remained until New Year's. The batter was usually the same, the icings were all different. Chocolate and coconut were the favorites. Accompanying these cakes, homemade lemonade was served from cut glass pitchers. There seemed to be no scarcity of lemons. Occasionally there would be a bowl of eggnog in one or two houses.

When I was a teenager, if we had a heavy snowfall at Christmas, Fernando Weems would hitch two horses known as a double team to what we called a "drag." It was a long, narrow wooden body with runners. As many as twenty-six of us, each with his own blanket, would sit on the floor and sing all the Christmas songs we knew. Fernando, reins in hand, would shout *Giddyup!* and those spirited horses would start off to the tune of *Jingle Bells*. We would ride about three miles up the road, singing all the way. Beautiful moonlight, sleigh bells ringing, we would come back to my home, go into the kitchen, get out utensils and implements for making taffy out of black molasses obtained from a huge barrel in our store. We boiled it on the wood range to a right consistency, tested it often by dropping a drop in water until it formed a ball, let it cool and then taking a part in our hands, we pulled it until it became a golden yellow. We then ate our fill. Each person would go out singing into the moonlight.

—F. ETHEL ANDREWS

At Christmas, Santa Claus'd bring me one apple, one orange, two what I call "niggertoes"—Brazil nuts—and one little stick of candy that he'd put in our stocking. That's all I got. We didn't have no Christmas tree; we didn't know what a Christmas tree was. Santa Claus didn't come see us like I see Santa Claus come today and bring the children a heap of things.

We didn't celebrate no other holidays. I didn't even know when Easter came. Birthdays just was.

—FANNIE LOU DAVIS

Juanita Friedly (Juanita Dudley) with her brother, Enoch, and her mother, in their home, near Helix, Oregon

On the farm we grew up on in a canyon in eastern Oregon—we called it North Cold Spring—there was no trees for us to have a Christmas tree. So, on Christmas Eve, Mother used to take a straight chair and we'd hang a stocking on it fastened with a clothespin. I had one, and Enoch, my older brother, had one. That was our tree.

On Christmas morning, we'd wake up early and run down to see what Santa Claus had brought. And every Christmas I usually found a doll sitting in the chair. Our stockings would be full of fruit. That was the only time of the year that we'd get fruit, like oranges, and nuts.

I believed in Santa Claus until I was seven or eight. Dad used to kid me about that. I wanted to believe.

—JUANITA DUDLEY

At Christmastime, when we were kids, we believed in Santa Claus for a while. But the year that I found a toothbrush hanging on the tree, I figured it wasn't Santa Claus that time.

—JOHN D. CLARK

We always had fried oysters for Christmas-morning breakfast. And Mother's sweet rolls. She baked bread three times a week. One time she said that in heaven there were three things that she wouldn't have to do and one of them was to bake bread.

In the parlor we would have a Christmas tree, because it was cold in there. There'd be things under the tree, mostly clothes that Mother had made. One Christmas I got a beautiful doll. Mother made a suit for it, and it had a kind of Gainsborough hat on.

Birthdays were never a big thing, but Mother would always let us have the dessert we wanted. I always wanted Tyler Puddin' Pie. I often wonder if that goes back to President Tyler. It was a popular thing, kind of a custard pie, only it's much better than custard.

We always had a big family picnic every summer, and the family would all be together. And there were a couple of picnics that we would go to in the summer. Mother would fix a clothes basket full of food and we would take it to the picnic and spread it out on a tablecloth. On the Fourth of July, our neighbors to the north of us had a sister who was married in Baltimore and she and her husband would come up and visit with her children and they'd bring sparklers and firecrackers. We didn't hardly celebrate most other holidays. Thanksgiving wasn't especially big. New Year's Eve? Probably didn't even know it came and went. Halloween? We never went trick-or treating; never even heard of it then.

—HELEN L. SMITH

One Halloween, we were living up in Turney, Missouri, after Dad had traded the farm for a hardware store and sixteen acres and a nice house out on the edge of town. My brother Matt and I were workin' in the store on Halloween night. Well, there was one fellow, he was kind of rough on the kids around town. In front of his house was a sidewalk that was made out of wood with wire down the edges; each piece of wood was nailed on to this wire. We thought we'd pull a joke on him. We took some wire cutters and went over and cut a section of his sidewalk off and started to pull it away.

Just then Mr. Shelton come out on the back porch and he was gonna take a shot at us. We dropped his sidewalk and ran around back of a building nearby. As we rounded the corner and started down the alleyway, we saw this outhouse, and we thought we'd bounce around it and make our escape. Only somebody had turned it over and we didn't know it. We fell in. Fortunately, I had a key to the hardware store, and Matt and I, thanks to Grandmother Potter, who believed we should stay dressed in our Sunday best on the Lord's day, we had extra clothes in there for playing baseball on Sundays.

Turned out the prank was on us.

—HARLEY POTTER

Fun and Games

We didn't have to buy our fun.

We made our fun. Kids don't

make their fun nowadays.

—SARAH HUNTER JACKSON

Born July 13, 1895

Johnson City, Tennessee

I'll tell you what we did for entertainment. It all depended on the time of year. One of the things that we loved to do, we'd get our mother to take homemade molasses, boil it down into a real thick syrup. Then we'd put butter on our hands to keep them from blistering, and we'd take that hot taffy, we'd pull it till it just got so white and creamy, and then we'd cut it off so that it looked like a little pillow. The longer you pulled it, the better it was.

In the fall, the boys would go to the hill and gather maybe a bushel at a time of walnuts and hickory nuts and chestnuts. My mother would put those away for winter. In the evening, we'd build up a big fire in the fireplace, we'd sit around it and crack nuts. We'd put the chestnuts in the fireplace and rake the hot coals over them. You'd take those chestnuts out, and oh! were they delicious.

In the summertime, we'd get out in the yard and play until it got dark. We'd play hide-and-seek and drop the handkerchief. We had one silly game we used to play. We'd cross questions and silly answers. We'd take boys and girls and put them in two lines. One person gives one line secret questions and the other line secret answers. So when one side asked a question that they had been told to ask, the other side had to give the answer they were told to give: Would you like to kiss me? *You look like a pig.* Or: Are you coming to the party tomorrow? *Well, I don't like chocolate.* That was silly, but so were we.

—ADA TABOR

On Verona Plantation, we played ball and shot turkeys. We played seesaw. Now, the boys did that more than the girls. But girls would slip in and do it with the boys unbeknownst to the parents. The boys would go in the woods and cut down a dogwood tree and leave the stump. They would take the tree limb and limb it up and put it on the stump. That was a seesaw. You got on one end and the other children got on the other. I can't tell you, but that was fun!

So was lookin' for money. Now, after the war ended, when the Northern

◄ *Children at play around the turn of the century (Culver Pictures)*

states took the Negroes from the white Southerners, they didn't have banks to put the money in. So they buried the money. When they lost the Civil War, the money was no good to the United States, don't you see? And on Verona Plantation was where General Ransom planted all his money. He had my daddy and his white brothers haul that money out and put it in ditches. After the war, it was their job every day to get that money out of those ditches. The paper money they burned, big barrels full of it.

But the coin money was brass. A penny was bigger than the middle of my hand. When we was growin' up, my daddy told us what ditch they had buried that money in. And when we got old enough, we would go there and sometimes we'd find a penny big around as a silver dollar. We would try to find as many as we could. But the water had washed most of the money all through the canal.

—SALLIE JORDAN

We used to play with little wagons. After we had worn out four of them, a friend of mine had outgrown her wagon and she offered it for sale. I asked Father for the money to buy it. No, he said, that's something you don't need. I'll buy you what you need, but anything like that, you've got to make your own or make the money.

So I went to a neighbor and offered to pick cotton for him. I told him, I want to make some money, buy me a wagon. He was thrilled enough to get his cotton picked, and I was able to buy that wagon. There were three of us, three little sisters, and I sat in the front and we'd go scootin' down the hill. Sometimes we would land in the ditch, and that's how we wore that wagon out, too.

Father let us climb trees and put up swings. When I was ten years old, Father gave me all his carpenters' tools that he used to keep up all the buildings. When people would ask me what I was gonna do when I got grown, I said, I'm gonna be a carpenter.

Oh, they said, whoever heard of a woman carpenter?

I'll tell you what I said: If you kiss your elbow you'll turn into a boy, then you can be a carpenter. And you know, my arm was sore three days I tried so hard to kiss my elbow so I could be a carpenter.

—LOIS CROUCH ADDY

On the farm, we did what we could to amuse ourselves. We had these round iron rings about twelve inches in diameter. I'd take a stick, a two-by-two or two-by-one, and nail a crosspiece on the bottom of it, and then I'd roll this stick up and down the road. The thing to do was to keep it going. It was good exercise. I also had a sharp piece of metal, a prong from an old hay fork that I had sharpened down to a very fine point. I'd sneak around and wait for the rats to come up into the corncrib through the spaces between the boards, and I'd spear 'em. In wintertime, with the snow on the ground, we played what we called the fox hunt, a big circle in the snow and one of us would be the fox and he'd have to get into the circle chased by the "hounds."

My cousin Earl and I would do a lot of things together. I was over at his house one time and there was about a five-gallon crock of cider out on the back porch. It was what they called a hard cider, it had really fermented. We started drinkin' a little of it and we kept on drinkin' and finally we left, even if we didn't know just where we were goin'. Earl got on a horse and started to town and I followed him. We finally ended up at the church. The horse ran up to the hitch rack and stopped and Earl fell off. We had a hard time gettin' him back on and gettin' him back home.

Another time, the stationmaster of the train had gotten us a case of beer out of Kansas City. We took it home and found a place with clear cold running water and set this case of beer down in a hole there. Then we'd be workin' in the woods cuttin' logs and we'd go and get us a bottle of beer. The next day, Earl's father was checkin' on the logs that we were cuttin'. What's the matter with you kids, anyway? he said. Don't you know the length of a log? We hadn't been able to figure out just how long we should have cut 'em. I don't think he ever found out about the beer, though.

—HARLEY POTTER

There wasn't much to do on the farm for entertainment. When night came, after we'd got our chores done, we'd take our shoes off, sit by the stove and read, and about nine o'clock we'd go to bed. People would gather at neighbors' homes, play cards, even move the furniture out of the way and have a dance.

We would play sandlot baseball games. We'd mark off a place in somebody's cow pasture and one little community would put together a team and play a team from another community. It had to be passed around by word of mouth that we were going to be playing.

Well, we'd all gather and outline the diamond. Of course, we had to do a little scraping to get rid of some of the cow droppings, and pretty soon we'd have a game. Usually we'd take a gunnysack, fold it over, and fill it with straw for the bases. For a ball, we were lucky in getting some that had been used for practice games that somebody would get from a friend who had an association with a league. I don't think we ever had any new balls. We had our leather gloves, but we had no masks or chest protectors. A few of the neighbors would sit there and watch us.

—AL KRAUS

Karl Long, mascot, Iowa State Normal School, Cedar Falls, Iowa, 1902

I loved all sports. The director of physical education at the Normal School was a fellow named Affleck, who had been a classmate of Naismith at Springfield College in Massachusetts. Naismith, of course, invented basketball. Mr. Affleck had brought basketball to Cedar Falls: the Normal School had the first basketball team west of Springfield.

He took a liking to me and made me the mascot of the football and the baseball teams, just about all of the school teams. When the teams would travel on the train to play teams from neighboring schools, the players would hide me under the seat when the conductor would come through, so I wouldn't need a ticket. A man named Joe Wright, whose father was one of the professors, was one of the star athletes at the school. I guess you could say that he was my hero.

So I saw basketball just about from its beginning. And I loved playing. In the wintertime, though, we couldn't play ball outdoors. We had a big hay mow in the barn on our property. We didn't have any animals, and the barn was empty. So we put up baskets—we used peach baskets—at each end against the wall and we played basketball up there. Our baskets were ten feet up, which made them official. Our court wasn't full-length—the hay mow wasn't ninety feet long, only about seventy-five—but it had to do. And we had an "official" basketball. I think we made it out of a bladder. Our barn was a regular playground. All the kids in the neighborhood came over to play.

—KARL LONG

York Garrett, front row, left, on the Howard Academy football team, 1915

I was always very sports-minded. I loved baseball, that was my game. I started playing when I was twelve years old, in Princeville grade school. When I went to school in Elizabeth City, I was on the baseball team there, too. When I got to Howard University, I played on the Howard Academy team. I was lucky enough to have a good bat, and hit .400 when I was captain of the team. I also played on the Howard Academy football team, but I couldn't make the varsity. I wasn't big enough and I wasn't strong enough.

When I got back to Tarboro, I was too far up the line to bother about doing anything for fun because I was in business then, trying to make a living. But Tarboro was a good baseball town, and some of the best black baseball players around were from Tarboro and Rocky Mount.

We had a black league there, and I umpired some. That's how I came to know Buck Leonard when he was coming up. In one game I was umpiring, I called him out. You didn't have more than one umpire for a game then, and he stayed behind the pitcher. And any time a player didn't like a call, he could complain. So Buck Leonard said to me, Doc, that weren't no strike.

And I said, Don't tell me it wasn't a strike.

He argued some more and I said, You want me to throw you out of the game?

No, he said. But next time, if I don't go for 'em, you don't call 'em.

—YORK GARRETT

There were a lot of fairly new houses in Reading. There were a lot of children and we all played together—bat the wicket, hopscotch, jump rope, jacks. We went roller-skating. We ice-skated in the city park above the reservoir. There was an area there that they would flood so that we could go skating. There was always somebody who could play the piano and we'd get together and sing:

> *Spain, Spain, Spain, you ought to be ashamed*
> *for killing all the sailors and blowing up the Maine*

and

> *There'll be a hot time in the old town tonight.*

And we hopped ice wagons. In those days, your ice was delivered in wagons. You'd buy, say, fifteen cents' worth of ice, they'd chop off a chunk and bring it in and put it in your icebox. There were all these little pieces of ice that chipped off. We'd jump in and get them and suck 'em. That was our candy.

—LAURA HOCH

On our block in Westerly we used to play hopscotch and marbles. I used to play marbles so much that I had a little hole in my thumbnail. From flipping. Oh, I was a good player, too.

On Saturday afternoon, I used to go to the movies. This friend of mine—we called him *Gumbada*, that was better than your brother—he would deliver different things around. I'd say, *Gumbada*, would you do me a favor today? I'd love to go to the show, but who's going to stay in the store? Don't worry, he'd say, I'll get up early and I'll do my route and I'll be here for you to go to the show. Once a week he used to do that for me.

It was a big treat to go to the movies. Of course, I wasn't allowed a lot of the things that the other girls did. My mother was strict. She wouldn't let me go if they were having dances. No, she was old-fashioned. Oh, let me go, Ma, I'll go with Rose or Mary. No, she'd say, forget it, you're not going, and that's all there is to it. So I couldn't go to no dances. But when somebody's child would be baptized, or somebody'd get married, you went with your mother and father. There I could dance. Oh, I was a wonderful dancer, too. There would be a list that would be filled out before you even entered the hall. Different boys would write their names, they wanted to dance with you. They used to respect you, too. But my folks, if they were there, all right, but if they weren't there, they didn't want you to go alone. Or even with the other girls. There weren't too many mothers and fathers like that. Mine were like what you call really strict.

—THERESA NIGRELLI

I was fourteen when I started to dance. I was working in a toy factory then. I got acquainted with a young girl named Suzie, I met her at the Odd Fellows Hall down in the city of Bedford. Suzie, I said when the band started playing, I don't know anything about dancing.

I'll teach you.

So Suzie, she put up with me. You know, when you don't know anything about dancing, you're a little bit clumsy on the floor. But before the evening was over I was doing quite well and from then on I used to go dancing quite often. And I've been dancing ever since. From Nova Scotia to Florida I've been in dance halls. I love it. You accomplish two things. First, you meet a woman and then you enjoy what you do in dancing, and then it's a chance maybe to date or get together. Besides, I was a good-lookin' guy in them days.

Oh, I love the dance floor! You know what I love about dancing, the best thing? I love to hear the orchestra, the music itself. Yeah, I fell in love with that. Although I was quite good with my feet, when they'd start to play waltz-time music, that soft, quiet music, I'd just love to sit down and listen.

When I was a kid, I used to like Wild West pictures. That was a favorite of mine. That was in the silent days. Over in New Bedford was the New Bedford Theater. It was a big, big, big, big place. It had downstairs, first balcony, second balcony, and the third. We called that "nigger heaven." That was the cheapest; you could get a seat for ten cents. Down on the first, it would be twenty, twenty-five cents. Some of the silent movies had music from a piano playing along. One picture I enjoyed one time and it's lived with me since is *The Face on the Barroom Floor*, I think it's called. *'Twas a balmy summer's evening and a goodly crowd was there, 'twas nigh on Joe's barroom on the corner of the square*, and it goes on and on. This man, he was an artist, he falls in love with a woman and at the end he leaps across the picture, dead. Somebody stole his wife from him. It's quite a story. Oh, I just loved that picture.

—EDDY KINCAIDE

We'd go to the movies, the silent pictures, but we didn't know there were stories, with a beginning and an end. And we didn't know that these stories weren't true. So we would cry and cry, if somebody died. We thought they had *really* died.

—VIRGINIA REALE

Canal Fulton, where I grew up, was a small town in Ohio with about a thousand people. We had about six churches, three saloons, a couple of grocery stores, a meat market, and the usual blacksmith shop.

We kids would play tag and hide-and-go-seek. We played Indians and white men and all. But not cowboys: the cowboys came later, in the movies.

One fellow brought a movie screen there. He would show a movie in a room with chairs and an old piano playing. There were no long stories, no serials. In one film, a woman was in the kitchen ironing or laundering some clothes and a fire broke out. In another, somebody was tied to the railroad tracks by the bad guy and made a narrow escape. It was all crazy stuff; it was just silly when you think of it.

But it was something new, so it was kind of exciting.

—MARION W. HARMAN

When the silent movies came along, one of the boys in my class rented an old saloon that had closed up and showed silent movies. While the movie was going on, he and his partner would be standing behind the screen. They'd be yellin' at one another so that it would appear they were talking on screen.

That was the beginning of talking pictures for us. That school chum and his friend ended up eventually operating three theaters for the *real* sound movies.

—ALBERT M. COLEMAN

I was never, you might say, crazy about the movies. But I did like vaudeville. They had a vaudeville theater down in Harrisburg, and when I was old enough I liked to go to it. Vaudeville shows were singing and music and dancing. They would have a magician and sometimes a minstrel act. Usually there was about five or six acts in a show. Sometimes you might see a chorus who sang popular songs as well as some of a more formal nature. I liked the different variety.

—MILTON W. GARLAND

Bob Lyle was a friend of my sister, Fanny Rhea. One night they had a date to go to the Ringling Circus in Kingsport. Well, Mary, the biggest elephant in the circus, got loose and killed its trainer. People were running everywhere, and my sister lost a shoe trying to get away from the wild elephant. The next day they took that elephant to Erwin and hung it from a derrick.

—MARY NELL DOSSER KELLER

I had the upstairs bedroom, and when I got old enough to go to parties I came home kind of late. My dad wanted me at the breakfast table at nine o'clock, but I overruled that and stayed in bed.

So he went up to the barnyard every Sunday morning and caught the bantam rooster and his hen and carried them down and then let them go right outside my window. Oh, they cackled and

Ivy Frisk, about twenty-three years old, Seattle, Washington, around 1920

scratched something terrible! And Dad would laugh when he saw a shoe flying through my window. Bantams, you know, can make an awful lot of noise for such a little bird. And they don't scare very easily, either.

—IVY FRISK

Flora Ethel Nowell (F. Ethel Andrews) in a dress she made herself, California, 1912

I was born in 1888, the same year my parents opened a boarding house. People from outside Shady Side came from the nearby cities of Baltimore, Washington, and Annapolis to spend their vacations at the Rural Home, so named by my sister Jennie.

Beginning about the middle of June, at the close of school, whole families began to arrive, bringing their belongings packed in very big trunks, having come on the steamship *Emma Giles*. Those trunks had to be brought by either sail or rowboat up the creek and onto our pier. What a tough time my father with his helpers had lifting them and getting them up into the bedrooms on the second and third floors of the Rural Home. Many of these people stayed until school began in September. The husbands went back and forth on the *Giles*, often spending a few days from work with their families. We never used the term "weekend" until many years later. The *Giles* made three trips a week: Monday, Wednesday, and Friday. Later it began to make a trip on Saturday. That's when the term "weekend" began to be used, probably around 1918.

Our guests enjoyed bathing all summer. The women wore black suits, long-sleeved and knee-length, with long black stockings and beach shoes. The suits were big and baggy and did not cling to the body to reveal body shape. Most of the women wore rubber bathing caps. The men wore black suits with short shirtsleeves and knee-length pants. No one worked to get sun-tanned. It was stylish to keep our winter complexions.

The large living room invited guests for card playing in later years: euchre, bridge, five hundred, and pinochle were popular; while the upright piano in the open dining room allowed the people to sing and dance at all times. Among the guests there was always a talented piano player who played the current tunes. My sister Annetta and I danced all the time, and Saturday-night dances were the zenith of entertainment in the area. There were seven boarding houses from which the people came by land and by sea to trip the light fantastic, the dining-room floor made slippery by the use of cornmeal. Our lawn was a veritable fairyland! The whole lawn was illuminated by fifty Japanese lanterns strung on ropes on the lawn and among the trees. Music was furnished, first by an accordion player, later by a guitarist, and finally by two Naval Academy band people, by violin and piano.

These are the tunes played on that old piano that come to mind: "Hot Time in the Old Town Tonight," "After the Ball Is Over," "Shine On, Harvest Moon," "In the Good Old Summertime," "Yankee Doodle Dandy," "Sidewalks of New York," "When the Moon Comes Over the Mountain," and "Wait Till the Sun Shines, Nellie." In the early days we danced the two-step and the waltz. We danced the Virginia reel and at times attempted the minuet. For special entertainment my sister and I danced the cakewalk. We never square-danced. When ragtime came, we changed the rhythm of our dancing, and later we jazzed.

—F. ETHEL ANDREWS

The first radio I ever had we made. We took a Quaker Oats can, wound it with wire—magnet wire they called it—over an area about half an inch wide. We scraped all the insulation off. Then we had what was called a cat's whisker that used to go to a pair of receivers and we could run that thing and pick up a radio voice coming in. The first words I ever heard over one of those things was: *This is WBZ broadcasting.*

We used that for a long while until they came out with the vacuum-tube sets. With those sets, of course, we could pick up more distant stations.

—ALBERT M. COLEMAN

I got my first radio around 1927. It was just a little bit of a thing. You had to sit with one ear right up to it to hear anything. Then there was no local programming here in Tacoma or Seattle, but we could pick up programs from San Francisco. They were mostly talk shows.

A few years later came the good shows. Like *Amos 'n' Andy.* When *Amos 'n' Andy* was on, why, people would be standing on every corner listening to it. Companies would have a radio hooked up to a loudspeaker.

Then, during the Depression, President Roosevelt broadcast his Fireside Chats. I'll tell you, people sure listened to him, you bet they did. He was listened to so well, he made four terms.

—OSCAR C. WEBER

I was in high school when Mother got a radio. We were living in Pendleton, Oregon, then. One day, Mother was sitting out on the swing on the front porch and the radio was playing. Well, there was one lady who lived on down the next block, and she came along. She looked at that radio, and she said, I don't believe it. I still don't believe it.

—JUANITA DUDLEY

Another thing that was considered amazing was an ordinary camera that an ordinary person could use. You didn't have to be a trained photographer. You could take snapshots; you just pressed the little button and bingo! Of course, you took the film to the store to have it developed.

My first camera was what they called a box camera. It didn't fold. I was very good at taking pictures, and then I would develop them myself. We used to go out sometimes on picnics, a lot of young people. I would take this camera along and take pictures, and then I would take orders and develop the pictures for the rest of the group. And you know how they paid me? They knew that I wore suspenders, so they bought me a pair of what were called President Suspenders. They had little strings on each side. They were supposed to be flexible and move with the body.

—JOHN SAILLIARD

My first television I put together myself. As a side thing, I'd assemble radios, you could buy these kits. And my first TV was a kit. Of course, like all of those kits, they worked, but then later on when something went sour, you couldn't buy parts.

—MILTON W. GARLAND

My husband took me to the 1939 World's Fair in New York. And he says to me, Ma, you want to go in the tent to see something?

Well, what will I see?

He says, You're gonna see something that you never saw before.

I says, What is it?

He says, It's a television.

And I went in the tent and he says, This is a television, Ma. You're gonna see this in your house someday.

And I says, That thing? You mean to tell me that we're gonna see that thing in my house someday?

And he says, Yes, Ma, you're gonna have television in your house.

That's the first time I'd seen a television. I couldn't believe you could see a television in the house.

—CATHERINE AVERY

Reading and Writing

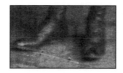

My mother saw to it that

we studied in school. She insisted

that to get a good education

was absolutely necessary.

— O S C A R   C .   W E B E R

Born October 8, 1897

Tacoma, Washington

My sister was born the fourth of December, six years before I was. I was born on the twenty-third of December. We were "planned" that way. That was the quiet time of the year, see, and by the time it was spring's work time—gardening time, housecleaning time—we were about three months along.

In those days, the teacher stayed near the country school where she taught, and she usually stayed with us. The schoolhouse had one room, with two outhouses, the woodshed, a stove. The teacher, of course, had to start the fire, and we had to help keep it going. We had to carry a pail down to the neighbors to get water to drink, 'cause we didn't have a well.

We walked to school, it was only a half mile. In real bad weather, my father would take the team of horses and a bobsled and take the teacher to school and the kids along with it. I would tag along, and, at four, I was sitting in the front seat listening to the recitations of the kids that were in fifth, sixth, seventh, even eighth grade. They sat at a long bench in front; most of the work was on a blackboard with a chunk of chalk.

The school year ran about eight months. During the early fall and the late spring, the older boys didn't come to school; they were too busy on the farm.

—AL KRAUS

We lived for a while in Morris Heights in the Bronx, which was not well built up then. I began school there, although I wasn't a very good boy in the beginning. They sent deficiency blanks home on me. I was a little bastard, really, in the schoolroom. I did all sorts of things: I wrote pictures in the books. I took things off of desks. When we'd walk back to school from lunch, if I saw my teacher coming, I'd get up and walk along the fence, which was next to a steep embankment, just to scare her.

But for some reason my first-grade teacher saw something good in me, apparently. She gave me a medal for effort. I still have it. And that made all the difference in the world. From then on, I wanted to prove, I guess, that I was good.

—JOHN D. CLARK

◄ *Schoolroom in New York City around the turn of the century*
(Jacob Riis, from Corbis-Bettmann)

I was just five years old when I first went to school. See, the teacher allowed any of the students to bring a little brother or a sister to visit, so they could kind of get an idea of what school was going to be like, and one day my older brother, Bill, took me to school with him.

I had taken two apples—one for the teacher and one to eat at recess. I put my apple on the desk. It was by the window, and it was spring, and the window was up.

Well, somebody's cow had got loose that day. And I was so proud to be in school, I was busy lookin' all around the room, when my brother punched me and pointed. That cow had stuck her head in the window and was tryin' to get my apple. She couldn't reach it with her nose, so she had stuck her tongue out, and I'm telling you, her tongue looked like it was a yard long!

But she didn't get that apple. I beat her to it and snatched that apple off of the desk. I laughed so hard! Imagine seein' a cow's great big long pink tongue out after my apple. That was something I wasn't gonna put up with, that's for sure.

—ADA TABOR

I started attending school when I was five. My first school was about a four-minute walk from home. My first day, I went to the school and sat on the edge of the porch. I do not know why I didn't go inside, because I have never been shy. George Hallock, an older pupil, called for me to come into the classroom, where the teacher sat at a desk on a platform. The first-graders had to sit around the edge of the teacher's platform because the school was so crowded. The teacher was Miss Mary Heller of Annapolis. She wasn't pretty at all, with red hair and a freckled face, but she was kind and considerate. After one day's schooling, I went home and told my mother that I was going to be a teacher.

Throughout my elementary schooling, my teachers were patient and taught us the necessary fundamentals, each grade going higher in the study of these fundamentals. Nearly all our teachers were eighth-grade graduates from nearby schools. Each teacher had to teach all subjects from grades one to eight. We were taught reading, spelling, arithmetic, penmanship, grammar, geography, history, and physiology. We had no physical education, art, or music teachers. We had no science as such. School was opened every day with a reading from the Bible, saying the Lord's Prayer, and singing a patriotic song.

All my teachers maintained strict discipline through setting up rules for our behavior that were usually followed. I never saw a teacher use a hickory stick. Instead, they used a ruler, with which they cracked knuckles. The only other punishment I saw was when a teacher washed out a boy's mouth with soap and water when he used cuss words in class.

I missed many days of school because I caught every disease that my classmates had: chicken pox, measles, scarlet fever, yellow jaundice, and whooping cough. One aggravation that annoyed our parents more than anything else was dealing with black lice that got in our hair. My mother treated our heads with mercurial salve, which was considered poisonous. She would wrap our heads for the night, and we would wash our hair before go-

Flora Ethel Nowell (F. Ethel Andrews) at age twelve, Shady Side, Maryland, 1900

ing to school. Nothing stands out as being a more horrible thing to endure in my life than having the treatment necessary to get rid of the lice. In the fall, many of us had malaria, caught from mosquito bites. We had no screens in our windows. We had to take quinine pills frequently at school. We lined up at the water-bucket shelf to take our pills, passing the water dipper from one to the other. Malarial attacks came on about 3 p.m. I'd come home with a shaking chill followed by a high fever. Sometimes I would have such a high fever that I would become delirious, seeing angels instead of children swinging on the front porch.

—F. ETHEL ANDREWS

I didn't go to school until I was six years old. I didn't have a desk, although there were desks behind me for the older kids. I sat on what would be a picnic bench today in the front row of a crowded room, just under the stern eyes of the teacher. He had an easel that he brought out and set in front of me. It was a black oilcloth or whatever it was they used. On it he wrote, "A, B, C." He gave me a piece of white chalk and told me to copy what I saw. That was my first lesson. As I progressed, another letter or two was added, and numbers followed. I did not have my own book until my second year. It had been used the year before by a second-grader with unwashed hands. Pioneers had large families and could not afford to buy books.

—ELLA MAY STUMPE

I went to school in Lithonia, Georgia. I only went through the fourth grade but I got up to where I could read pretty good.

When I first went to school, I had a man teacher, Mr. Stroud. We would have to stand up and he would call out a word to us. If you couldn't spell it, he'd whup you in your hand with the blunt end of a stick.

For lunch, Ma would put at least two biscuits in a tin bucket along with a cup of cane syrup my daddy had made. Well, one year we had this other teacher, Miss Hall, and every time she'd turn us out for recess, she would go in every one of our lunches and eat something. When we got ready to eat, we thought Ma had not put the food in there. That teacher, though, she didn't have no home. I told my ma, She don't bring nothin' to school to eat.

Well, my ma wrote a note askin' her why the children was goin' around with no lunch. And that teacher, she never did write back to my ma.

—FANNIE LOU DAVIS

I went to a one-room school, and it was a good walk, too. But that was all right. I could hike like mad. The road we'd take went on past the school, and there was a creek along the other side of the school.

In the spring, the snakes would come out, little garters, and sun themselves on the rocks. The boys loved to go down there and get them and wind them on a stick and chase the girls. And the girls would scream like mad and run into the schoolhouse. One day, my cousin Earl, he stood there with a snake on a stick, looking at me, and he gave it a pitch. Didn't land on me, though, and I didn't scream or run. That gave him quite a shock. It wasn't any fun for him.

There were only four or five children in a grade in that little country school. We all sat at our desk and we had to have one hand on the top of the desk and the other one under the desk, so we couldn't get into mischief. Or we would have to stand in a row at the teacher's desk, and she would ask questions about whatever we were learning. Or we'd do arithmetic on the blackboard. Friday afternoons we had to sing or recite.

We had these double slates. They were two slates that touched each other and were wrapped with wool around the edge, which kept them from breaking if they fell. And on those four spaces, I drew. I'd been drawing I don't know why, from the time I could hold something to draw. Nobody ever showed or told me anything, I just did it.

Now, the *Ladies' Home Journal*, that was Mother's pride and joy. There wasn't much to circulate and give you ideas and all, but she swore by that magazine every month. It had a design on its front cover and I thought, I want a design on *my* slate, too. So I made a design that I kept, then I did my work inside. Some of my friends wanted pictures on the fronts of their slates, and they'd bring them to me. I had to decide what to draw because they didn't have any ideas. And if it got smeared I just did a new one.

I had never had any instruction whatever. Father subscribed to the *Farm Journal*. And I guess I read everything there was to read, 'cause in it they offered a prize one time for the best drawing of a tree. There was a group of locust trees down in the field that I thought were so pretty. I always liked looking at 'em, but I'd never drawn 'em. I didn't go around drawing things around me very much; I draw more from my mind.

Well, I drew them and sent it in. And I got the prize! That was a competition all over the country. I don't think they wrote and told me I'd won, but I went out to the mailbox one day and here was this package. It was a box of watercolors. I doubt if I'd ever even seen a box of watercolors, much less had one, or a brush, even. I was so ecstatic. I don't think my feet touched the ground!

—HELEN L. SMITH

My father was a Tuskegee Institute professor. But he did not insist upon his children getting an education. *His* dad, who was a slave, insisted upon him goin' to school. But he did not insist upon his children goin' to school. His wife died when I was seven, and he had four children, and we had to take care of him. We were sharecroppin', and all of the children worked. He didn't have time for us to go to school.

—CHARLIE LUE MOSLEY

I was never much for going to school. We lived on Grand Street in Trenton, just across the fields from the Roebling School. My father and my mother woke up my brother Jim and me early one morning—it might have been late in the evening—and they took us over to where my grandfather lived, on Beatty Street. And we sat in the parlor of my grandfather's home and watched the school burn. No more school! But we didn't lose any more than a day or two of school. Class was held in the basement of a church.

I never made it through high school. I quit. In those days you could leave school at fourteen. I walked to school in the morning, then I'd walk over to the Centennial Inn, I took a lunch with me, I had to sit at some place. It comes time I think that school's starting again in the afternoon, I'd walk back. All I did was walk and walk and walk. I hooked a ride one time on the step of the back of an ice wagon; when I jumped off, a dog bit me.

My father got after me. You really gotta get to school and you gotta study, he said, or you gotta go to work. I said, Dad, I'll go to work, I don't want to do any more of this walking. So I went to work, doing carpentry like everyone else in the family. I was thirteen. That was not unusual. Very few children in my day went to high school. Very few.

—ARTHUR W. HAMER, SR.

Once I got a job after we first came to America, my next drive was to learn English as Americans speak it. And to lose my accent. So I went to Public School 83 in East Harlem. There were about fifty foreign-born boys in the classroom. I wasn't too satisfied; I wanted to hear English spoken, not other foreign languages.

So I went to the principal of the Harlem Evening High School. I came there and he received me.

What do you want? he says.

I'd like to become a student at your school.

He says, I'll give you two questions. If you answer them, I'll admit you.

Okay.

The first question: Spell "accident."

Two c's. What's the second question?

He says, Give me two-thirds of fifteen.

Ten.

You're admitted, he says.

And that's where I began to learn my English.

As I was leaving the school one day with a friend of mine, he says, Alfred, do you know that there's an art class on 107th Street and Madison Avenue? It was at a school called the Ferrer School, which, I learned, was organized to memorialize Francisco Ferrer, who was executed by the Spanish government for being too radical. I'd like to see it, I says. So we walk into the building. We ring the bell. A woman comes out. What do you want?

I'd like to know whether I can join the art class?

We're not open today.

Why not?

We have no money to pay for a model.

I says, Don't worry about it. I stripped my pants and I got on the stage.

That's when my art got started. Of course, I knew what paint was because my father painted his carriages. I wanted to be an artist. Well, she says, we'll start the class today, and you model. As a result of that, as a compensation, she allowed me to join the art class free of charge. So I became a member of the class, to which one of the great American painters used to come, Robert Henri. He taught me color. He taught me art.

That's where my life got started.

—ALFRED LEVITT

East Orange, New Jersey, was a progressive town. Our neighborhood was mixed, black and white, a lot of immigrants. But people got on. We knew everybody and everybody knew us. Everybody looked out for everybody else's children.

East Orange had a first-class school system. But if you were black, you weren't encouraged to go on to high school. It was tacit. Nobody in the upper administration would ever come out and say anything like that, but it was pretty well understood by those who came in direct contact with "undesirable" people. They did the dirty work. The underlings told me, You don't need to go to high school. They told me I couldn't have my diploma from elementary school unless I promised not to go to high school. So I promised. Of course, everybody in the upper administration would deny categorically that they promoted such a thing.

But when September arrived—this was in 1913—I went up to high school and they were asking me, Why are you here? We know nothing about you; you're not supposed to be here. I told them, I'm going to take a commercial course. And I had a sponsor. I walked dogs for a woman who was a professor at one of the local colleges, an activist for women's rights, who had a son who went to East Orange High School. I told Mrs. Flynn what was happening. Mrs. Flynn went up there—they thought she was coming to see about her son—and she said, No, I'm not here about Roger, he's a very average student, he'll do whatever he needs to do and make out. I'm here about Delia Harrison. She convinced them that I was very bright and had every right to go to high school.

So I took that commercial course. I learned typing and shorthand, and I graduated in 1917.

—DELIA HARRISON-MARTIN

When I was in high school on Block Island, I had a man teacher named Parks. He said to me one day, If you're not gonna do better than you're doing, you don't belong here. He told me I didn't know nothing. But the thing of it was, I was the only kid in school that became a teacher. Parks, he lived alone in a shanty out there in the woods. It caught fire. He was burned to death.

—FRED BENSON

I walked to high school and back a mile and a quarter each way. I did my studying after I finished work. Got an "A" in gym, a "C" in everything else. I went to that school from February to June, and then I worked all summer. One afternoon, while I was delivering prescriptions, I ran into my mentor from Cedar Falls. I was walking down the street and a great big man stopped me.

Aren't you Karl Long?

Yes. Who are you?

Joe Wright. I know you because you walk like your father.

He said no other person except Karl Long could walk like I walked.

That meeting changed my life. I managed on my supper hour to visit the Wrights. They had an apartment nearby; I knew Mabel, his wife, from Cedar Falls. He was head of boys' physical ed and she was head of girls' physical ed at Francis Parker High School, a wonderful private school, very progressive; it was financed largely by the McCormick family. He helped me get a full scholarship to Parker for my junior and senior years.

The summer of 1911, my brother Charles quit the traveling and got a job running a drugstore in Chicago, and Mother came from the ranch. Charles rented an apartment near Parker and I got a job in the school as assistant in the woodworking shop. I made twenty-five cents an hour. This was more money in fewer hours than I made in the drugstore. I was way behind my classmates in academic work, way ahead of them in making a living for myself. I was so proud when I won a letter from Parker as an athlete. It was on a wool sweater. Mother washed it and it shrunk, so that I couldn't wear it. That just broke my heart.

After I graduated in 1913, I went to Springfield College, which was my dream since Cedar Falls. I worked my way through college at twenty-five-cents-an-hour jobs, in the dining room, in town. Each summer I worked in playgrounds and saved enough to pay my $150 tuition.

In my senior year there, I made the varsity football team. I once played against Paul Robeson when we played Rutgers. He was a big player and I was fairly small, only five feet seven inches. I'd go underneath the bigger players. I'd get underneath Robeson and carry him for a couple of yards on my back. Well, I had a bad boil on the back of my neck, and Robeson hit me there while he was tackling me and it hurt so bad. I guess I didn't feel very kindly toward him for a while.

—KARL LONG

After we moved to Cambridge, I spent two years at Cambridge High and Latin, a public preparatory school. I'm physically clumsy and I've never been athletic. The one sport in which I participated was debating; I was captain of a three-student team. The only physical activity that ever intrigued me at all was hiking and mountain climbing. Otherwise, my attitude toward exercise is I think that of Mark Twain, who said that when he felt like taking exercise he went and lay down until the feeling went away.

In 1913 I took the entrance exams for Harvard. While I was dimly aware that there were other colleges, it never occurred to me to think of going anywhere else. I received my degree at the end of three years. I had started out on a possible career in science, and I spent many hours in classrooms and laboratories gaining some proficiency in chemistry. Unfortunately, the laboratory was a stinking place, redolent of sulfur, and I couldn't see spending my working life in such a miserable place. But the idea of making money had great appeal, and I abandoned chemistry in my senior year and went to the Harvard Business School. Since I was socially immature and had practically no social life as an undergraduate, it was no great achievement to attain an academic rank somewhat above average, and to graduate cum laude, lowest of the three levels of distinction.

At best, my social life at Harvard would have been difficult because of my age. A sixteen-year-old freshman might be able to cope with his instructors but was less able to make friends with classmates a year or two older. Though I did acquire a few very good friends, none was a member of the social and financial elite who comprised the roster of Harvard's social clubs. At most colleges then, undergraduate social life revolved around fraternities. At Harvard, only two national fraternities had chapters—Delta Upsilon and Sigma Alpha Epsilon. In my junior year I received an invitation to join Sigma Alpha Epsilon. The invitation carried one stipulation: that I ditch my Jewish roommate. To reach a decision took no time at all. I told them to go to hell. Until we graduated, David Hoffman and I roomed together in harmony and friendship.

—PHILIP L. CARRET

Getting to the Maryland Institute of Art, that was a miracle. Father was tight to begin with, and no way did you get any money or anything. But Uncle Travers, Mother's oldest brother, he found that there was an art scholarship to that college for Frederick County. Every county had a scholarship to the Maryland Institute. He found out about that. If nobody else applies, he said, you won't even have to take an exam. Well, nobody did. I had that scholarship all four years.

'Course, just getting down to Baltimore was a miracle. I went on the train. Mother had a younger brother who lived there. And so Uncle Travers—there was no stopping him when he got a notion—made Uncle Detro promise they would take me in for a very minimum amount that Mother paid. Mother did it with her egg money. She didn't have much money, but she had her eggs, and she did a lot of things with those eggs. Every so often, she'd send me a five-dollar bill for the trolley.

But, oh my, you have no idea what a country person endured. I went there and Uncle Detro took me to the Maryland Institute the Sunday before I was to start classes. We took the trolley. I wasn't used to trolleys. We walked two blocks up for the trolley and took it past all these big houses and everything. I was scared out of my senses that I wouldn't know where to get on and off. I was almost frantic. Then we got off and walked two blocks to the Institute. I tried to look at buildings so hard but everything was so strange.

The next day, I went to the school myself. I went early. A lot of students were coming, and so many of them knew each other, and they were having so much fun and all. I stood there like a lost soul. I climbed up this very beautiful stairway—I thought, well, I'll go up there, it's better to be by myself than with all these people I didn't know—and I kind of peeked in the schoolrooms. It was all so overpowering, sculptures of all these great big Greek gods standing around.

For me, it wasn't easy. Not the classes, though. Everybody did the same thing. You didn't get to choose. Every morning it was charcoal drawing of plaster casts, little specks of ears and noses and lips and all that you have to learn to draw. Then we had a little bit of design; we designed and made wallpaper.

My money was going fast on nothing but the trolleys and materials. I had this blue dress I wore the better part of that winter and it had a little white collar on it that you could wash. At that time it was the style to wear a little crepe tie on the collar. They were a quarter. I couldn't have one. I thought, oh, I would love a yellow one of those. Just a quarter, but I had to buy tickets to go on the trolley. You have no idea of the misery.

I thought, I'll try it one more day. Then, in our charcoal class, we were drawing a plaster hand that was over the top of a book with the fingers clasped. And our teacher, I'll never forget her, she was Scotch: thin and straggly and red hair scooped up in a knot on top and you'd better not do any fooling around around her. She said, of all these drawings around the room, there's only one that shows the pressure of the finger on the book: mine. What do you know about that? I just drew what I saw. But from then on, the world was mine. I'd needed some kind of a boost and that sure did it.

I never forgot it.

—HELEN L. SMITH

Love and Marriage

When I called to take her out once,

my future brother-in-law said, "Don't

do anything I wouldn't do." Jesus,

I wanted to punch him in the nose!

Because I wouldn't touch a girl,

I wouldn't hug a girl, if I didn't really mean it.

—JOSEPH GOLDSTEIN

Born March 1, 1895

Boston, Massachusetts

Girls were girls until the age of sixteen, when we became "young ladies." We wore longer skirts and blouses with higher necks. Braids circled our head and "buns" decorated the lower back. We used hairpins and fancy combs of colored shell. At sixteen, young ladies were eligible for marriage. By eighteen, you had better be looking. And at twenty-five, well, you were an "old maid" and on the shelf.

Little boys wore knickers until the age of sixteen. Then they were put into long pants and referred to as "young men." They were expected to remain at home until age twenty-one. That was known as "coming of age," when they could vote, acquire property in their own name, and get married. Should a young man wish to get married before he came of age, he had to get parental permission. That was often accomplished by the "shot-gun march" preceding the celebration of the wedding ceremony. Young men were considered rich if they could leave home with a horse and buggy. Most, though, would leave with a horse and saddle and think they were well off. A lot of them would go riding around the country until they found some farmer that needed work.

—ELLA MAY STUMPE

The story I like to tell happened at one of the beach places a little bit north of Boston. It was in winter. The girls would come out and stand around, and the boys would come out and stand around. And one night, unknown to me, the girl who would become my wife took out a block of cement and camouflaged it. I came whistling along, tripped, and fell into the pit. She lassoed me.

I was going to Harvard. I took a course at M.I.T. because Harvard wasn't running it: oil geology. I was offered a job by the Standard Oil Company in South America, in Venezuela. But I didn't take it. Because I had interest in this girl. I was already roped and branded.

When I knew we were going overseas to the war, I went to my little girl and I said, You want to get married? And she said, No, I'll wait till you come back.

◄ *Young love in the pumpkin patch around the turn of the century (Culver Pictures)*

When I came back from the war, it didn't take too long before we got married.

—JOSEPH GOLDSTEIN

Joseph Goldstein, left, at Revere Beach, Massachusetts, with the young woman, to his left, who was to become his wife, just before America entered the First World War

Before I sailed for Europe in July 1917, a college roommate told me that a girl from his town, Emma Zangler, was a nurse in the Roosevelt Hospital unit and urged me to look her up. There was no chance to do this on shipboard because the nurses, along with the doctors, were rated as officers and lived on the first-class deck, whereas the rest of us were buck privates confined to a lower deck. But at Vittel, a popular watering place in the Vosges Mountains where we luxuriated until we were assigned to a French military hospital, Bill Taber, another Amherst student, and I managed to lure Emma and another nurse to an ice-cream sidewalk café, the first of many subsequent dates.

At Christmastime, I managed to obtain a three-day pass to Paris, where Emma and several other nurses were on temporary assignment at a privately sponsored hospital for American officers. On that visit I persuaded her to wear my fraternity pin in lieu of a ring. Since then we had kept up a steady correspondence, which for me was a mixed pleasure. The officers at General Headquarters understandably craved feminine companionship and organized dances and other social functions, to which they invited some of the nurses. And it would not be an exaggeration to state that Emma, who was a beautiful girl with an attractive personality, was the belle of the ball. She enjoyed the various functions as a relief from arduous nursing duties, but I did not particularly enjoy reading about them in her letters. Too often, from my standpoint, her particular partner was Colonel Xenophon Price, at twenty-six the youngest colonel in the A.E.F.—the American Expeditionary Force—and a favored member of General Pershing's staff.

On July 16, 1919, I sewed on my fourth service stripe. We sailed from Brest on the twenty-fifth and arrived back in the U.S.A. on August 4. I had sent radiograms to my parents and to Emma, who had already returned to the States, letting them know that I would be disembarking at 11 a.m. on that date at the Bush Terminal in Brooklyn. When I landed, there were my father and mother and Emma, escorted by her brother-in-law. When I introduced Emma to my parents, I said, This is the girl I am going to marry.

As Emma told me later, she was a bit taken aback by my announcement, since she had not given her assent up to that time, but she did not want to embarrass me. By the most unlikely coincidence, the ship on which Colonel Price was returning was arriving on the same day. He had sent a radiogram to Emma, asking her to meet him on his arrival at Hoboken at 11 a.m. When she did not appear, he tried to reach her on the phone at her home in Croton-on-Hudson, but Emma had instructed her mother to state that she was not available. After trying for a couple of days, he finally gave up. I have sometimes wondered whether, if Colonel Price's ship had docked a day earlier, our roles might have been reversed.

Emma figured that it would be wise to wait a year before getting married in order to insure that ours was not just a wartime romance. We were married in September 1920.

—JOHN D. CLARK

I was born rebellious and romantic. I was willful and had an intensely independent, almost wild, nature. When I was in my teens, the world glowed in a dream of romance. But the dream had nothing to do with reality.

Reality was my rebellion against my mother, a dominating, aristocratic woman who devoted herself to protecting me from life—both its miseries and ecstasies. Determined I should remain a virgin, perhaps forever, she dressed me in lace, taught me to curtsy and to remain silent unless spoken to. As my dear but rather passive father stood by, my mother and her two sisters, my aunts, attempted to turn me into a porcelain doll. But I was no doll beneath my childhood lace. At fourteen, my secret accomplices had been Dostoevsky, Tolstoy, de Maupassant, Colette, Shakespeare, Freud and Oscar Wilde. I have no idea how I found out books by such writers existed, but I lost my virtue reading *Madame Bovary* by a spirit lamp.

Deep down I longed for the carefree life an artist, and imagined living in a simple garret, free of pompous antique furniture. Artists were not interested in material things, as my mother's friends were. In the dark, secret dreams of my youth, I envisioned resting my head on a man's shoulder and leading an immoral existence, whatever that might be.

Every time I mentioned painting and living in a garret, my mother threatened suicide. Finally, to appease me, I was sent to a small village in France, chaperoned by Miss Osborne, a spinster of thirty whom I detested. Artists and peasants lived in the village of Giverny, with one tired horse and buggy as the town's only means of transportation. The great painter Monet, by then an old man, had his home and enchanting garden there. Once I peeked through the leaves and saw his glorious head with its white hair as he painted in his flower beds. I trembled as I spied on this master.

Miss Osborne agreed to start painting with me each morning at nine. She was not, however, able to organize herself. After three days of waiting, I set out for the fields alone. A few days later we quarreled over a spider, so I picked up my gear and moved out to the inn where a few students and models lived. The owner did not want to accept me as a tenant, but my eager face, diminutive figure, and heavy paint box won him over. He confessed there was an attic left, reachable only by a ladder. It was a large space with a ceiling at uneven angles and small windows that allowed just enough light to create shadows, like in a Rembrandt painting. It was "full of promise."

At last! Alone with art, living in a garret like a real artist. This was paradise. I lifted my arms to the sky, picked up a paintbrush and attacked the canvas. An outdoor scene in the morning, a still life in the afternoon, a fantasy at night. The walls quickly became lined with paintings, and more were stacked on the floor. All disasters. But it did not matter. I lived in an attic and was blissfully happy.

Everything would have been wonderful except that Miss Osborne wrote my mother and soon, without notice, she arrived. A beautiful woman with great style, she came from a world of servants and Pierce Arrow cars; she didn't approve of smocks and turpentine. Slowly she climbed up the ladder, her high heels clicking as she ascended, her black dress with tulle at the throat rustling, and the ostrich plumes on her French hat bobbing up and down. She had never been in an attic before.

As she surveyed the room full of the ghosts of Botticelli, Whistler, and Sargent, and dreams of gold medals from the Academy, I awaited her exclamation of approval at the evidence of my talent.

How can you live in such filth? she exclaimed. Look at those cobwebs!

Mother took me back to Paris . . .

Two years later I tried to run away again. This time my mother consented to let me study with Gordon Craig in Italy. I was eighteen and mad to be an actress.

Gordon Craig was one of the great figures in theater, the first to abolish stiff canvas scenery and replace it with curtains and footlights. I had read about him, and knew my talent would blossom in the presence of such a great man. I went so far as to tell my mother that Gordon Craig was the son of Ellen Terry, one of the esteemed actresses of the nineteenth century—although I did not tell her that he was illegitimate, nor that he had fathered one of Isadora Duncan's children.

Mother exchanged proper correspondence with Mrs. Craig, the tuition fee was paid, and my railroad ticket was in my hands. Two days before my planned departure, some woman at the American Club in Paris filled my mother's ears with gossip.

Mother strode ominously into my room. Did you know that Gordon Craig was an immoral man? You are not going. I have cancelled your reservation.

But he has a wife there! I meekly protested.

I never heard of such a thing, she said. And with a glance of fury she walked out of the room, shuddering as if I were a lunatic.

Throwing myself on the bed, I wept for twenty-four hours. Gone were my hopes for a creative and worldly mentor. So what if Craig was immoral? I had read that most men were immoral. Besides, since everyone had to be seduced once, I would rather be seduced by a wit than a dullard . . .

My mother hoped I would give up the idea of acting, but after two years of study abroad, I was determined to prove myself onstage. My ambition had shifted from being the great woman painter of the age to becoming the great actress of the day.

Having studied in Europe with teachers from the Comedie-Française, and still wearing my beautiful clothes, I had no trouble getting into the French Repertory Company which was then being organized in New York. It appeased my mother to have me act in French.

I wish I could say I was good, but except for my youth and beautiful clothes, I was ineffectual. From 1914 to 1916 I played over sixty parts, but in only one of them did I move the audience. It was a love scene—of course—with the company's leading man, Reuben. He was the only actor who ever paid any attention to me, although he was the real-life lover of the leading lady. Each time we played our love scene, the audience responded loudly to the passionate vibrations, while the leading lady stared with beady eyes from the wings.

Our onstage embrace inspired someone to write my mother—anonymously—that I was having an affair. In public life we cannot avoid gossip, I told her with regal dignity. Nevertheless, when the repertory season was over, she insisted that I make a social debut and begin my life in earnest.

Mother simply could not make me the popular debutante she wanted. I was the flop of the season. People invited me to parties and I would not talk. I was too timid for small talk and the only subjects that interested me were art and literature. All businessmen were pitiful sloths sunk in materialism and I refused to hold conversations with them. I was so naïve about social customs that when a Wall Street tycoon, whom my mother hoped I would marry, took me to the Plaza Hotel for dinner, I volunteered to pay part of the check. I was accustomed to artists who had no money . . .

I met a Frenchman by the name of Henri-Pierre Roché. He was tall, with keen eyes and a large nose dominating his narrow face. He was cultivated, well traveled, and worked in the French diplomatic service. He was a writer as well as an art collector. One of the first to collect modern art, he bought the works of Pablo Picasso, Georges Braque, and Constantin Brancusi before anyone else did. Roché had also traveled extensively in India and been art advisor to a maharajah.

I invited Roché to Sunday dinner. He conversed easily with my mother and other guests and fit in so well I actually relaxed and had a good time. Besides, he was much more interesting than the stockbroker my mother was conniving to have me marry.

After Roché's visit, Mother came into my room and said, You are falling in love with that man.

Too shy to dare acknowledge such a thought, I was shaken that a secret part of me should be so violently invaded by my accusing mother. The next time Roché phoned, asking to call, I casually replied, This time I'll come see you.

Taken aback, he protested, But I live in a very simple room.

I don't mind.

I took the subway and walked two blocks to his address. He let me in without a fuss and watched as I stood taking in the fine books on the table, the single rose on his bureau, and the meticulous order of the small objects about the room. The late-afternoon sun came in through cheap window curtains and transformed them into gossamer webs. The room was luminous and calm. I stood motionless for a time, not knowing what to do or say.

Come, take off your hat.

No . . . I think I will keep it on, I replied, clinging to it as protection against myself.

Beatrice Wood, age fifteen, circa 1908

He took a step closer. Then I will take it off. I wanted the sensation of happiness that came over me to last forever. Without another word, we were in each other's arms. I offered no resistance. He carried me to the bed. And I was loved by a man of tenderness and passion, unequaled in understanding and consideration.

Older than myself, at times he acted like a *vieux-papa*, talking to me for hours about art. Often we had dinner in his room. We made a wonderful vegetable soup together, served with dark peasant bread and cheese. From the beginning we behaved like an old married couple. Every remark was surrounded by the unspoken language of love. If he said, The knife is there, it meant, I adore having you near. If I answered, Where is the butter? it meant, I waited more than twenty years for this to happen and it is more wonderful than I dreamed.

He took me everywhere with him. We had gay dinners at bistros or big hotels. We talked and talked—as if we could never find time to tell each other all the things that mattered. He was excited by the quality of my mind. When you are an old lady, he said, you will talk just like you do now. You will never age, and I will never tire of listening to you. You have something untouchable. Events of all kinds will happen around you, but they will roll off like water on a duck's back.

He insisted that I become an artist. I did not care about being an artist; I was only interested in love. Roché had released me from prudish views about sex, and made it a loving and creative experience. He impressed upon me: It is important for a woman to have a fine relationship with a man the first time, for it marks her for the rest of her life.

—BEATRICE WOOD

In Edgecombe County, if you came from a certain section, or if you were a certain complexion, you had your own group. That was strong in North Carolina. There were places in Edgecombe County where nine-tenths of the people were octoroons. My wife, Julia, had only one-eighth black blood in her family. Her father was an octoroon, her mother was an octoroon. However, a bunch of people my complexion or a little darker felt like they were the chiefs, that they could get anything they wanted because a lot of the white people dealt with them.

My wife's father had a barbershop. Nine-tenths of his customers were the rich white people—not just white people but the *rich* white people—of Edgecombe County. My wife's father and mother were high up in the black-white community: blacks that were white. They were black and they knew it. They didn't go around and try to pass for white. In their community, a man would choose a woman that he wanted to be his wife, and he had all his children by that one woman. The more they mixed, the lighter they got.

One of the men that I knew in Tarboro was a white doctor. He liked colored people. And he had four or five children by the same colored woman. They were all colored, but they looked like they were white. He took care of them, sent them to school, did everything for them. In fact, there were three big families in Tarboro that had three sets of children: an all-white set, an all-mixed set, and another set that was dark. One of these was a prominent doctor from a group that all down the line had had colored women as their wives. And they brought those children up and they put them through school and took care of them. Now, I'm not blaming them, I'm not unblaming them. That's just the way it was.

On the other hand, some black folks did not like it too much if you mingled with the white colored group. And if you were going to do that, you might not get a break that you would have gotten otherwise.

When I came back to town after I graduated, I had a whole lot of good-looking colored girls. I had three nice-looking girlfriends who were brown-skinned and two more girlfriends who were white-skinned. And I was having fun with all of them. They all wanted to know which way I was going. So when *I* thought I was going to marry Julia, nobody in *her* family thought I was going to marry her. But she decided that we were going to get married. She was in New York, working, and she came home on a vacation, and looking like she was looking, I said, This is it. I had not planned to marry then, but when she went back to New York, we were engaged.

She gave up a whole lot to marry me. She had boyfriends by the dozen, from Atlanta to New York. Nice people, from good families. But I had as much trouble getting out of my group as she did getting out of hers. My mother and father and two sisters asked me a whole lot of sixty-four-dollar questions: Do you know if you and Julia will make it? You've got five other girls you're going with and four of them have good jobs teaching. What has she done that the other ones haven't done? I said, She loves me. And she was going to give up everything she was used to having and doing to be with me.

And so we were married.

We decided that the thing to do would be not to try to live together until we could have our own home. I had said, I'll never spend a night in your father's home. And she said, I'll never spend a night in *your* father's home. When we get together, it will be in our own place. So my father built a house next door to where we had grown up and turned it over to us. But until that house was fixed up, I went back and forth to New York to see her.

Now, I was going to let her teach that year. But it just so happened that this other thing happened: a brand-new baby boy. My first child. She was in New York with her brother, who was a barber, when that pretty baby was born. They got in touch with him when she was having trouble and they rushed her to the hospital, where she had the baby. When the hospital people saw her, and they saw him, and they saw the baby, they didn't ask any questions, they just assumed her brother was the father and the baby was white. It said so right there on his birth certificate.

Most everybody in her family except two had left North Carolina and had gone to New York. They didn't go to visit New York. They went to pass for white. Julia didn't "go white," but she did have to make up her mind: Was she going to marry into the white group, or was she going to marry into the middle group or was she going to marry into the black group? And she decided that we had fallen in love, and I was the one she married. From then on, that was going to be her life. You know, the color we are is the color we are together.

—YORK GARRETT

Before I married, I went to New York to hunt for a job. Hilda Evans, my dearest friend, had a job with Wanamaker's there, and was living in Greenwich Village with three other girls. She invited me to join them in the apartment, so I lived with them and found a job at Macy's.

One time, this young man invited me to go to his apartment for breakfast. This was one of the things I wouldn't even consider doing at home in Johnson City; my family was a strict family, and they probably wouldn't have approved. But you get in Greenwich Village and you think it's all right.

—MARY NELL DOSSER KELLER

I never was a girl for boyfriends. I was afraid of men, I'm gonna tell you the truth. But anyhow, there was two of them that I walked and talked with after I came home to Fredericksburg to live. One thought I was gonna be his wife, he told me after I was married. But I liked the one I married better, although I didn't have any idea in my mind of marrying him.

One day when we were talking, he said, Julia, we like each other. We gon' get married.

I said, We are?

He said, Yes, don't you think it would be a good thing?

I said, I don't know. I'll have to think about that.

He kept repeating these words at intervals. I said, This boy—I still thought of him as a boy, although we were both in our twenties—this boy is getting serious. This is something I have to pray about. I have to ask God about this.

And God gave me the right answer.

We had a lot of enjoyment in our married life. My bringing up told me that people didn't have to fuss and quarrel and have hard words with each other just because they were married. My aunt, I never heard her argue with her husband. If they had a disagreement, I never heard anything about it.

Well, one day we had something important to settle, and he didn't agree with me and I didn't agree with him. He was getting uptight, and I saw he was getting angry, he was raising his voice. I said, Cut it off right there. I said, We're not gonna have that. I didn't grow up with it and I'm not gonna live with it. I said, If we have to live with confusion, somebody's moving out. (I said "somebody" because we were living in the house that his grandfather built and I knew *he* wasn't gonna move out.) So I said, We'll just lay it on the table. And when you're in a good mood, we'll talk about this. Later on, we settled it agreeably. And from then on we never had a cross word.

But, oh Lord, that name! He had an aunt that had been a schoolteacher in a rural community, and she was a great reader of history. This is the name she gave him: Gosnold—G-O-S-N-O-L-D, if you've never seen it— Wymath Bartholomew Tyler. Some people used to say then, you don't have anything else to give children, give them plenty of name, and she believed it.

—JULIA TYLER

I was fifteen going on sixteen when I got married. I was married in February and I was sixteen in June.

We both went to school at Lamoni, Iowa. We had started school in the fall. Mother had sent us girls there from Malvern because we had no school near our ranch. She was teaching us at home, and she thought it was time for us to get in school, so she sent us back to stay with Grandpa and Grandma. Then during the year while we were gone she sold the ranch there in Nebraska and bought a place at Lamoni and moved there.

We had a neighbor up on Ruby Hill, she wanted us to go swimming. We didn't swim; we didn't have enough water in Nebraska to hardly have a drink, let alone take a swim in. But we went up to the pond, and here was that nice young man. He was teaching the kids how to swim. I didn't want to go into the water, but he said, Come on, I'll show you how. He held me and had me paddling my feet and hands for a while. Then he let me go and I just went to the bottom. So he gave me up as a bad job. That's the first time I saw him.

Then when I saw him when he was all dressed up, he was the handsomest thing I had ever seen! He was in the eighth grade and I was in the sixth, but he was five years older than I was. We went through that year and didn't see much of each other, only when we went on a hayride. Everybody went for a hayride, and he brought me a little can of Nabisco's. I've still got the can.

He just always kind of picked me out. And I let him; I acted like a fool, but that's the way I felt. He finished eighth grade and went away to the ninth. And I finished the eighth grade there, too. Then the doctor told Mother she wasn't very well. Hadn't been for a while. He said if she'd just go down to the mountains, she'd feel a lot better. Well, she just took all the money she had and moved us all down to Seymour, Missouri.

After we left Lamoni, John got so lonesome for me he packed up and came down. Stayed with us all winter. February came around and the pastor came over and talked to Mother, and they decided that it would look a lot better if we got married. So John went and got a marriage certificate, and the pastor performed the ceremony. His wife was there. Mother had a lovely linen tablecloth, and she folded the corners together and pinned them in place. She brought some Christmas cactus she had in bloom. Those were my wedding flowers: Christmas cactus.

We lived with Mother until John got the call that his mother was ill. He caught a ride on the train at Cedar Gap and was there when she died. He stayed there with his father then. He got a job hauling lumber and he wrote to me to come on up. We'd live in his father's house and take care of his grandmother.

His father was a missionary in the Western states, and he went off. And he wrote and said that they'd opened up the resurvey there for homesteading, and if we'd come out and take 320 acres, he'd take 320 acres joining it. We'd build a little cabin, and he'd live there right across the fence from us. He would missionary, then come back and stay with us, and hold his claim down.

I told John when we went to Wyoming—I lived in a tent and took care of my two children while he worked at the sawmill to get roofing and flooring—I said, I don't want to be a transient. I'll come with you, I'll stay with you for the seven years it takes to prove our promise, and then we're going to get settled. But I'm not going to be a transient. My mother and father traveled and changed ten times in the years they were married, and I'm not going to live that kind of life.

We stayed there twenty-eight years.

—AUDREY STUBBART

I can sling hash with anybody. I began right after my father died, in 1908. I worked every place I could. I started first in a hotel, then on to different restaurants. In Williston I worked for Charley Lam Lee, a Chinaman. We only worked thirteen hours in a shift, on our feet—in high heels, no less—all day. We got corns, bunions, ingrown toenails. For four bucks a week, plus room, board, and horse feed, we used to say. I waited tables better than seven years, from the time I was fourteen till I was twenty. Then I got married.

I met my husband when he came in to eat and I waited on him. He came in three or four days before I met him, before I really met him. Anyway, a couple of friends of mine, they were going to this little shindig, a home dance. I didn't want to go, but they talked me into it 'cause I liked to dance. And a little while later Jack came along and he asked me to dance. So then I danced with him. He was a good dancer, too.

Who did you come with? he said.

I followed a couple.

How's a chance to follow you back?

I said, Okay. Just like that. That's the only one I ever went with after that, my Jack.

He worked out around Scobie, that had opened up for homesteading. People went out there and filed their claim and, naturally, they had to have water. So well-digging was a good business and that's what he done. It was about two years before we got married, in 1915. Two years later he went into the Army. I think from the time he went over there until the war was over, I had about six letters. And I made up my mind, if he ever come back, there would never be another one.

—LENA STANLEY

The first time Mr. A and I met was at the dinner table of the Rural Home the day I got home from teaching in California, planning to stay in Shady Side for good.

To tell the truth, when I met Alexander Andrews, I knew I was going to marry him. Before this time, I had had two proposals. One of my suitors got down on his knees to me. How different my life would have been if I had accepted him. He was deep in Democratic politics. The other proposal was more casual. As we were walking across the lawn, he said, Miss Ethel, will you marry me? I said a vigorous, No! I knew I would have been bored with him.

Mr. Andrews was an exciting person. The first night we met, he proposed to me. His proposal was a simple: Will you be my little girl? He didn't have to ask me twice. I never regretted my choice. It wasn't all perfect; we had our high points and our low points, but our relationship survived and improved as we shared our lives.

The very night I came home, at supper where we always had strangers at the supper table, I sat opposite a tall thin gentleman with blond hair and blue eyes who talked of a new philosophy of life, spiritual in nature and emphasizing positive thinking. His talk pleased me. I felt related to it and to him. After supper Mr. Andrews and I went across the hall into the parlor and became acquainted. He was a typical Yankee from Massachusetts. Speaking with a broad "aah," that brogue foreign to a Marylander back from California, made me like him as well as liking his thinking so akin to my own. He and I loved each other that very night. We knew it when we kissed, although we didn't talk of love for many months.

Mr. A was a salesman for Le Page's glue products. He traveled as far southwest as Texas, and when he was traveling south I wouldn't see him for four months, but when he was living in Gloucester he visited me twice a month. He came by steamboat on the side-wheeler *Emma Giles* from Baltimore, would land at Shady Side on West River and walk the mile to my home. There was a window in my classroom by which I stood while teaching a ten o'clock English class. Through it I could see the steamboat road. On the Fridays when Mr. Andrews had told me he would be coming to visit me, I kept a sharp lookout to see if I could catch a glimpse of the Yankee coming up the road. When I spied him in his dark blue suit, three-inch-high starched collar and stylish cap, my whole being was filled with happiness.

We had a long engagement—four years. I told him I would not leave my teaching nor the village of Shady Side. I convinced him that he could be a successful real estate agent and that we could have a happy life here. I received a letter from him every day. About 4:30 p.m., after school closed, I would go to the post office and see if my letter was lying on the desk. And there it was—the joy of my life.

On a cold March 9, 1918, Mr. Andrews at my side and my niece accompanying us, we went to Baltimore by boat, train, and trolley car over to the old Caroline Methodist Church. We entered the church door and were met by the pastor who married us. We picked this church because it was the one popular at the time for walk-in weddings. Nobody at home knew we were to be married. I thought I was too old for a formal wedding; I was twenty-nine and Mr. A was thirty-three years old. I did invite all my friends to a reception in June when school was out.

The fact that my husband was a Republican didn't change my politics. I was the daughter of a staunch Democrat who thought that there were no good Republicans. My father asked me, Are you going to marry a Republican, the scum of the earth? However, he grew very fond of Mr. Andrews and forgave him his politics.

—F. ETHEL ANDREWS

I didn't really care for my husband at first, I got to tell the truth. It was another fella that I liked. But my father didn't like him because he was dark: Sicilian. And my father couldn't see it. He's too black for you, he used to say. You go out with him, they think you married a colored boy. That's the truth. But my husband loved me. And he wouldn't give up. So I finally had to consent.

I met him in the grocery. I used to be in the store a lot, you know. I used to do all the bookkeeping at night. Santo would come in there and buy his cigars and cigarettes. I use to tell him, Don't bother buying 'em here, go to some other store. He'd come the next night just the same.

We got married in 1917. We drove to the church in a horse and buggy. Cars were around, but I said, Nothing doing, I want a horse and buggy. There was about four feet of snow on my wedding day. Dr. Scanlon, he said, Theresa, what made you come in that? I said, Doc, that's what I wanted. I didn't want the limousine, I wanted my old-fashioned horse and buggy.

After we got married, we had to live with my mother. She got crying, You're going to leave me; you're going to leave me.

Well, I'm getting married, I said. I don't want to stay here.

No. You've got a lovely bedroom here and the nice dining room. And a living room, she said, you can entertain in.

No, I said. But we finally had to consent to stay. After my first son, Clarence, was born there, I said, Ma, I'm going whether you like it or not. I got mad one day, I told my husband, Listen, either you pack up, or I'm going to leave you. So he packed up and we went. We moved in my mother-in-law's house. She had an empty apartment in her tenement. But we paid rent. And then we built this house up here on Granite Street.

—THERESA NIGRELLI

I met Mary when she was twelve. I was twenty. I was workin' in a mine in Clymer, Pennsylvania, and I was boarding with her sister. She was living with her mother. When we decided to get married after a year, her father spoke for her: he said she was sixteen, so she could marry me.

After the ceremony, we had no money to go on a honeymoon; we didn't know about no honeymoon. I took three days off. We had a party downstairs, and we went upstairs. That was the honeymoon. And then I went back to work.

—PAUL ONESI

Paul and Mary Onesi, Clymer, Pennsylvania, 1917

One day, I delivered a case of eggs to a customer, he had a party in the house. He took me and brought out this good-lookin' girl and he introduced her to me. Ida is her name, he says. She was visiting, from Brooklyn. And I married her.

Lucky for me, I didn't get married before. I had one customer, a wealthy man, he says to me one day, if I marry his daughter they'll give me a house, with furniture and everything. So, you know, I kind of accepted; it looked pretty good. But they were trying to buy me with a lot of money. Right away they wanted to show that she's engaged, so they demanded I should give her an engagement ring. I went and I bought her a thousand-dollar diamond ring. Then, being that they fixed me up the home and everything else, they wanted to make an engagement party. So at the engagement party she started giving me orders, what I can do, what I can't do. I says, Now wait a minute, this is not what I bargained for. So I broke the engagement. And I went broke because of her: she kept the ring.

—SAMUEL D. SCHNEIER

Samuel and Ida Schneier

I got a job in Red Bank, New Jersey, at the Governor's house. I was a maid there, a kitchen maid. It was a better job; the work was not so heavy as at the Astors' in Newport. They were wealthy, but it was a smaller house, a smaller kitchen, and I didn't have to work so hard.

They had two chauffeurs, one for the help—who would take you shoppin' and take you to church, or to the shore—and one for the boss. I was working in the kitchen when a boy came in to see me and he liked me very much. He was the chauffeur's brother. He came in from Paterson, and he says to his brother, She's a nice girl. I'd like to see that little girl. So then he says to me, Would you like to go for a walk?

And I says, I don't know who you are.

Oh, I'm the chauffeur's brother.

So he talked to me. And the next thing, I was getting married to him.

—CATHERINE AVERY

I knew my husband from Italy when we were children. We were distant cousins and we lived in the same community. He came to America with his two older sisters when he was about twenty.

I didn't want to go out with Salvatore at first, because I was older than him by three years. I used to tell him, I'm too old for you. Get somebody young. And he'd tell me, Don't you worry about it. I don't want the younger ones, I love you.

He was a shoemaker. When they started making shoes with machinery, he opened his own shoe-repair shop in Greenwich Village, but he still would make shoes for me and the family. And during the war he was always very busy because no one knew how to fix shoes. But he could take them apart, he could put platforms in and take them out; he could fix crippled people's shoes.

After we got married and we had our reception, we went home for our honeymoon. The whole family came with us to the apartment, playing music in the streets. The next morning, bright and early, they all came back and woke us up with their serenade.

When we were married five days, my husband's sister moved in with us. She could have stayed with her sister, and she didn't even give us a week. Since my husband was the brother, it was his responsibility to take care of his sister, even though she was older than he was. She lived with us for two years, until she got married.

— VIRGINIA REALF

After I pursued a girl all the way to Cleveland that didn't work out, it wasn't very long until I met an American girl who married me. This was in 1920. Jerry—her name was Gertrude, I called her Jerry—was a good woman. I met her in Central Park at a musical concert. One day, a friend of mine said, Alfred, let's go and hear the music. So we did. When we came there, there was a group of girls sitting all around in one spot, and we sat down near them. And naturally, you speak to the girl alongside of you. After the concert, the gentleman that I believe I was had to take her home.

I never stopped seeing her.

One day, we eloped. To Washington, D.C. There we stayed in a hotel for a couple of nights. That was the fountain of youth. We experienced it and we went home. The question arose: What are we going to do? We weren't married legally, we didn't get a license. Because we just decided to sleep together, that was all. So then we decided to live together. Without marriage. We rented an apartment on Fourteenth Street between Seventh and Eighth Avenues. We shacked up, without her telling her parents.

After a little while, her father came to me, threatening to have me locked up. What did you do to my daughter? I said, I didn't do anything that she didn't want done. And her mother asked Jerry, Where is your marriage license? So Jerry says to me, Alfred, we've got a problem. I says, A problem? We have no problem. I'll marry you. We went to a rabbi and he married us. So she brought the license to her mother and put it on the table. Here you are; we're married now.

I liked her because she was very hungrily acquisitive of knowledge. I introduced her to the library, museums. They gave her an understanding of what art is. I made her an appreciator of what I was doing. And she sharpened her sensibilities.

I don't know if we ever had any hard times. I never wanted to have money. Consequently, not having it was not hard. I never knew what it meant in the first place, so why worry about it? I had a nice little place, a lovely place, well organized, with all the books I wanted. And I had a good-looking wife who pleased a man as a man should be pleased. I never worried about anything as a man. That's how we got along so beautifully.

—ALFRED LEVITT

I was working in Seattle for a firm dealing in municipal bonds. It was there that the most important event of my life occurred. A letter from an old and cherished friend informed me that her friend, Florence Elisabeth Osgood, had just moved to Seattle, and gave me her address.

On November 20, 1920, I called at the boarding house where she was staying. I asked for Miss Osgood and gave my name. Word came back that the young lady was undressed, about to take a bath, requested additional identification. I mentioned my friend, Marion Sawyer. After an interminable wait, a beautiful black-haired girl appeared and we greeted one another. An exploratory conversation suggested to me that here was a girl with whom I might happily spend my life. However, I had already struck out twice. I did not want to strike out again. Prudence suggested that I should see Miss Osgood as much as possible over the next six months. Then, if my first impression was confirmed, I should ask her to marry me.

On weekends we frequently took picnic lunches and sat under a tree in a park, exploring one another's personality. At the end of five months I was absolutely sure that this was the girl for me, and so informed her. Betty felt it necessary to communicate with her family and the official engagement was postponed for a month.

It seemed sensible to Betty and me to return to New England. Upon our arrival in Boston, Betty went home to her parents in Clinton, Vermont, to spend a year acquiring housewifely skills. It never occurred to either of us that she might hold down a paying job after we were married. The two-income family was unknown to the so-called middle class in 1921.

On September 4, 1922, I was married to my lovely Betty and began what can properly be called an idyll. The wedding took place at a girls' camp in Vermont owned by my parents-in-law. In the afternoon my bride and I left for a honeymoon in Canada in a decrepit Chevy which I had bought for $125. This unsuitable vehicle broke down twice and was eventually abandoned on the return trip from Quebec.

One incident during the honeymoon stands out in my memory. One day we sat on a park bench on the Plains of Abraham, where Wolfe's little army defeated the French General Montcalm, securing Canada for generations as a jewel in the British Crown. Still somewhat curious about the strange individual she had married, Betty started fishing in my pockets. She came upon my key ring. Why do you carry so many keys? she asked.

Phil and Betty Carret

They're to lock and unlock things, I said.

One by one she requested an explanation. Soon she came upon a key whose identity I could not recall. If you don't know what it's for, why do you carry it?

Good question! Dramatically, I said, I'll discard it! and immediately threw it over the cliff. Betty disclaimed all responsibility when we got back to Cambridge and discovered that the discarded key was necessary to open my Army locker trunk. We forced the lock, and the trunk was then also discarded.

—PHILIP L. CARRET

I was married twice, so "Matheny" comes in between "Crouch" and "Addy." I lost my first husband, Marvin, during the flu epidemic. I had met him, my Prince Charming, at a Sunday-school convention. All the people were Christians and the schoolteachers never had a minute's trouble, because back then if a child was punished at school they got another switchin' when they got home. That was the way of the times.

Anyway, I was fifteen years old and he was eighteen. I was staying with a cousin, and Marvin was a pal of her brothers. Well, he just parked there after he met me. His father was in politics and Marvin would take me with him off to campaign meetings. Two years later, when I was ready for college, we became engaged, with the understanding that we would not get

*Lois and Marvin Matheny
had been married four years
when he died in the
influenza pandemic,
January 1919*

*Lois and Sam Addy
were married
thirty-nine and a half years*

married until I got a college education. He waited for me. I was twenty-two when we were married, in 1915.

When the war came, we had two children. If you had at least two children, you weren't drafted. Then I lost the baby. She was seven months old, she had whooping cough and pneumonia and she died. And it wasn't two weeks before the board wrote us that Marvin would have to go in the next draft 'cause we just had one child. I think that was really about the most frightful time in our whole life. But then the peace came and he didn't have to go.

It wasn't soon after that he died of influenza.

Just as soon as he began to feel bad, we sent for the doctor. It was two o'clock at night. And when the doctor came—we were living on the farm—he pronounced it flu. The doctor did not know what to do for it. Mildred, our little girl, was not quite three years old, and she took ill the same hour that her daddy did. She began to get better after three days. But Marvin died, on the ninth of January 1919, after taking ill on New Year's Day. The only thing that I had consoling me was that he died at home.

I was a widow five and a half years. Then Sam Addy wrote me a letter asking me to correspond with him. His wife had died and he was left with two little children. But I didn't want to 'cause I had loved my first husband so. I didn't think there was another person living that could come up to him. Sam told me not to tell anybody if I chose not to answer him after two weeks. I gave Sam some serious thought, but I didn't really want to answer him. At the end of the two weeks, I finally told Mother.

You answer that letter, she said. I don't know a finer young man anywhere than Sam Addy.

I said, Well, Mother, I'll answer him on one condition: You let me invite some friends over for Christmas—neither of them ever married and both of them were just as sweet as they could be—and I'll invite him for Christmas supper and I'll turn him over to one of them. Lo and behold, by the time Christmas came, I didn't want him to meet either one of them, I was so in love with him.

Sam was a banker. I had security and all the love I could ever want. I'd always heard that you could not love like you did after the first time. Well, that's all a fib. You certainly can love just as hard the second time as you did the first. Don't ever say you can't. We not only loved each other, we appreciated each other, because we had both lost our mates. He used to tell me that the Lord made me especially for him, but what he couldn't understand was why we didn't find each other the first time.

He already had kids and I had one and he said, These are not *your* chil-

dren and *my* children. They're all three *our* children. We never used the
word "step" in our house; they were *our* children.

—LOIS CROUCH ADDY

One night, I had an unintentional sexual encounter. The next day I went to
see Dr. Mary Halton, a gynecologist who took care of many literary and
theatrical women. Edna St. Vincent Millay, one of her patients, told me
about her. Bluntly I announced, Yesterday I was immoral. Will you please
see if I have a venereal disease. I want to protect others if I have.

It had never occurred to me to worry before. Roché was a gentleman.
Besides, it was a love affair.

She laughed. It takes longer than a day for venereal disease to develop.
Since you have come to see me, I will give you protection.

Beatrice Wood, Paris, circa 1915

A marvelous woman, thin as a pencil, with black hair, probably dyed,
and a sharp nose, Dr. Halton was one of the first to supply birth control to
women. Every night she dressed formally and dined at the famous Brevoort
Hotel, where the artists and literati gathered. She told me she saw so much

misery during the day that the ritual helped to change the rhythm of her work. She felt women had a right to lead their own lives and told patients if they knew of someone in trouble to bring her to the office, any time of the day or night. She protected unmarried mothers. Edna, myself, and others put on a yearly ball to maintain a private room in one of the hospitals. Here Dr. Halton's patients could have privacy, for in those days an unmarried mother was put into a public ward, made to scrub floors to earn her keep, and was watched over by police, who, after the baby was born, returned her to her hometown, whether she wanted to go or not.

—BEATRICE WOOD

Getting Around

My father began with a team of oxen

—the mode of transportation

common in the time of Jesus. For

two thousand years we were dependent

upon beasts of burden for our mobility

and to keep in touch with our fellow man.

—ELLA MAY STUMPE

Born July 12, 1895

Rolette County, North Dakota

The first time I ever seen an automobile I said, Daddy, a buggy's comin' down the road that ain't got no mules! He laughed and laughed. But I was scared. I didn't know no better. I was too scared even to sit down in it.

—JESSIE TURNER

Before cars, we'd get around in stick wagons and a buggy, and a carriage for Father and Mother. As a youngster, Father said he used to take the heavy stones from the old stone fences and bang them into the dirt roads to keep their wagon from sinking to its hubs in the mud. See, in those days, if you had a heavy snowstorm, the county didn't take care of it; no one came out and plowed you out. 'Course, we lived on a fair-sized farm and Father'd get his great big wagon out and hook up two or more horses to it and the boys and men would get in the wagon with their shovels and go down the road, and when they'd come to a great big drift, they would get out and shovel it.

Father had an older brother who was something of a daredevil. Uncle Will used to show off to Father and Father would almost have a fit. One time he came out in a Stanley Steamer. I was a little thing and I just stood around and listened and watched what they did. I didn't get in the way. And then when they were ready to take off, they put me in the back. The step that you took to get in wasn't at the side, it was across the back.

We would drive to a hill out here near Feagaville. It was very steep and if you could get up it in your car without busting a button, the car's engine was good. That day they went to test this Stanley Steamer on that hill. When we were all ready to go, they had to let it run awhile and steam flew out, to build up power. I don't know how it worked, but I was there. I sure was there.

Then, around 1900, Father got his first car. It had a lot of brass—trim and lamps and rods—and of course it had no glass. No, no, no, no. It had curtains that you could button onto the frame. Father was so proud of it. We had a garage around the barn and he'd come around and the sun would shine on that brass like mad. And you know what he'd do? He would drain

◄ *Travel by horseless carriage was often interrupted by flat tires that needed fixing (Culver Pictures)*

the water out of the engine and every time he was going out he'd have to take water for the engine. If it was in cold weather, he would take hot water out.

Father learned to drive himself. He took the car out on the road and experimented with it until he could work it. He didn't know he had to have a license to drive. He went running around in it for I don't know how long before he found out he needed a license.

Hardly ever did you go anywhere that you didn't have a flat. But that was all right because you had a kit. The roads were not paved—they were very, very rough—and the tires were like bicycle tires. You had a kit, and you just put a patch on the tube and blew it up. 'Course, you also had to pull off the road if you met a horse, the kind that reared and scared. You had to stop and maybe help lead it past the car.

—HELEN L. SMITH

I was riding bareback up the Twenty-fifth Street hill toward Tacoma Avenue—this must've been around 1905—when I thought I could hear something that sounded like *put, put, put, put, put*. And I started thinking, Now, what in the dickens is that? I found out a few seconds later: me and the horse and an automobile met right at that corner. And that horse just stopped right there in its tracks and I went over its head and I landed in the middle of the street.

That little automobile, it looked just like a regular buggy, only without the horse. The engine was under the seat and it was set so that the chain from the motor went to the right rear wheel; I guess you would say today that it was a one-wheel drive car. And it didn't have a steering wheel; it had a steering bar.

—OSCAR C. WEBER

When we were in northern Iowa, Mother's brother Walter had made a good bit of money on his farm and he had bought a new Maxwell car. Took all of us for a ride in it. Of course, we thought it was pretty wonderful to be able to get out to the road that fast. But he spit out the window and it came right back in the back seat where I was.

—AUDREY STUBBART

The first cars that came out on the road, the horses were terribly afraid of them because they had a very poor muffler and they made an awful noise.

And I guess the poor horses, not seeing horses in front of this strange craft, thought it was a big bug or whatever. And, oh, they'd get up in their hind legs and rear. The people that owned them would start cursing. But, of course, little by little automobiles increased. Delivery wagons became automobiles. And the horses disappeared. Nobody was sorry to see the horses go; they left a lot of dirt on the streets.

But you had to make sure when you drove that you had a supply of gasoline. The grocery stores didn't have it, and there were no stations. I think the drugstores kept the gasoline at first. Because most stores weren't going to sell anything for which there was no demand.

—JOHN SAILLIARD

When I was about six years old, my dad got a French car, what they called a de Tamble. When I was eight or nine, I was drivin' it. Then, of course, I just kept goin' from there. Whenever he got a car, I could drive it. Back then, you never needed no license or nothin'.

The early cars, you had to hand-crank 'em. But you had to know *how* to crank 'em, else they'd back up on you. Break your arm if you wasn't careful. The roads then weren't paved for years. When it rained, they were all mud.

One of the difficulties drivin' was, there were no gas stations around, and very seldom you could find a grocery store where they would have some. That was where you would get gas: grocery stores would have a little tank out near the garage there. Gasoline then was only eight or ten cents a gallon.

—JAMES M. DAVIS

We bought an old Model T Ford, our first car, in 1913. I was the only one in the family who could drive it.

The salesman sold you the car, and of course the Model T was very simple. He showed you how to push the pedals, shift gears, go into reverse. That was it. No problem. It was a very primitive car. You sat on the gas tank with a cushion between. If you wanted to know how much gas you had, you pulled the cushion up and unscrewed the cap and put a dipstick in to measure. When I was in college, a friend of mine and I were taking the same physics course, and we wasted a lot of time trying to figure out how you would create a gauge on the dashboard or the instrument panel that would tell you how much gas you had. We never could figure it out. I still don't know how you can get that measurement from a gas tank in the rear of the car to the instrument panel. But someone figured it out.

—PHILIP L. CARRET

The first time I ever drove a car, we were living in Huntington and my daddy had traded for a little old one-seater Ford. I didn't know anything about driving. So naturally, when I went out to look at the car, I said, Dad, how do you start this thing? He showed me how. He cranked it up and I got behind the steering wheel and I started creeping up the alley and out to Jefferson Avenue. I went I don't know how many blocks, only I didn't know how to stop it. Daddy showed me how to start it, but he didn't get around to showing me how to stop it.

Well, I found if I moved the wheel I could make it go however I wanted. But it was Sunday morning and people was beginning to come to Sunday school and I was afraid of hitting somebody. So I turned to the right, I went out a block, down a block, back in on Jefferson. How I ever crossed that avenue without running into somebody, I don't know.

So I came creeping back down Jefferson Avenue and I thought, How do I stop this thing? When I got to where I got in on Jefferson, I turned back into that alley, and I thought, Well, all I can do is keep goin'. I knew if I ran out of gas I'd have to stop. Well, there was a log laying out in that alley. I saw it, but I couldn't avoid it. But when the car went over it, it give it such a jolt that it stopped that car, right on our back gate. I got out. I'd been gone so long Mom and my two sisters were out lookin' for me. Anyway, I had a good ride.

—ADA TABOR

My first car was a Velie. It was a company that bought parts and put 'em to-gether and sold you a car. It was second-hand when it was bought after the war. Cost about $150.

Back then, roads weren't paved. All of 'em wasn't. You could get up to twenty, twenty-five miles an hour. That was speedin.'

—ORLANDO F. MORLEY

A lot of people used to go up on Bellevue Avenue opposite the Newport Casino to see Reggie Vanderbilt drive his Red Devil, which then went at the tremendous speed of forty miles an hour. That was a big public spectacle.

—EDWARD J. CORCORAN

I taught up in Umatilla County for six years before I got married. The second year I taught, I had to go up on the train—there was no road in—to a town called Duncan. Duncan was a post office. There was no town; there was just a station for the train to stop, and a post office. It was isolated, but I just loved it there; I taught there three years.

It cost only a dollar to go from Pendleton to Duncan. One time, when I brought my younger sister up, I told her, Now, if you're five years old, you have to pay a fare. So you tell the conductor you're four. And when the conductor asked her how old she was, she said, I'm really five, but my sister told me to tell you I'm four.

—JUANITA DUDLEY

After my first husband died, I went on a Western trip with some friends. We were going through Colorado and I was thoroughly enjoying myself. We decided we were going to sit in the observation car. Now, this car didn't have a top to it, didn't have windows or anything; it was just a flatcar with little seats on it. Well, I don't know how long we were on it before we discovered we were getting as black as tar. When we'd be going through all the tunnels, the cinders and all that black smoke would just settle on us. You talk about embarrassed!

—LOIS CROUCH ADDY

My first airplane ride was out at Brush Lake, just west of Grenora. There was an aviator taking riders up; barnstorming, they called it. Well, my brother-in-law had a free ride coming. He said, I'm not going up in that. I said, I'm going to.

I went to the pilot. I said, My brother-in-law doesn't want his ride, but he said I can have his turn. And the pilot says, Just as soon as I get another passenger, I'll take you.

So we climbed in, just went in and sat down, nothing over us, nothing to hold us down. I didn't know enough to be scared. And that pilot, he flew all around. Oh, it was beautiful, to see down on earth like we seen at that time.

That was in 1925. I had this chance and I wouldn't turn down a chance like that for anything. Jack, my husband, would never do it. Over in France, during the war, he told me, they could have gone up for a package of cigarettes. But he wouldn't go up, he said. He was scared.

—LENA STANLEY

When I was a youngster, I built little airplanes. I'd put them on a kite, fly 'em, cut 'em loose, and watch 'em maneuver as they'd glide. If I could find 'em, fine; if not, I'd get another one. And back in '14 or '15 I saw the early flights of the plane the Wright Brothers made in Dayton, Ohio. It got maybe a thousand feet high.

But the first time I was up in an airplane was back in '18 or '19. It had an open cockpit and it could hold twelve people. We were in Los Angeles, and a gang of us got up there, it didn't cost hardly anything. We had to climb up a stepladder to get into it, and they flew us down along the ocean a little ways, turned around, and brought us back. That's all there was to it.

In '20, I flew a little biplane. This fellow by the name of Burns, we raced motorcycles, and I says to him, Want to go up to the lakes?

He says, What you want to go up there for?

I says, Somebody said there was a guy runnin' 125 miles an hour up there. We oughta go up to see him.

Do you wanna drive up?

No, I says, let's fly up.

Fly?

Yeah, I says, we'll go over and buy one of these airplanes: $125 for an airplane and they'd run. And a guy had a pile of 'em.

So we go in and I says, Hey, have you got a good one here?

He says, Sure. You guys fly?

Yeah, we fly.

So we bought this little biplane and we pulled it across the street into this little airport, which I think is the site of the big airport out in Los Angeles now. We got her across the street, and the guy put gas in it for us, and I says to Burns, All right, you wanna fly it or you want me to fly it?

You paid for it, maybe you'd better fly it.

'Course, neither one of us had ever flown before. Oh, we'd watched the fellows how they operated 'em, but we'd never actually been behind the controls in one. So we get out on the runway and the fellow says, Are you *sure* you guys can fly?

I says, Oh, sure. Well, we went down that runway and lifted off just like a professional. We didn't have enough horsepower to get over the mountains, so we had to find a pass. Then we wormed our way up through the pass. We followed the road 125 miles up to the lake. That's where they were runnin', in the middle of a dry lake.

So now the problem was to set down. No, I says, that won't be no problem, we just come in and coast right down. Well, we got over one of them concession tents and we almost went into it. We dropped about a hundred feet like that—bam! Blew one tire out and broke the struts off. When we left the lake late that night, we left that plane set right where it fell. Never saw it after that.

In the motorcycle industry, nobody cares anything about airplanes. My wife and I took one of the first commercial flights ever on TWA, coming back to Ohio from Los Angeles. Cost $150 then, a two-day ride. We flew outta Los Angeles to Clovis, New Mexico, rode the train out of Santa Fe to a little place right outta Wichita, Kansas, and picked up the other flight.

Now, these were Tri-Motors we were flyin' in. They only held twenty-six people. They had a toilet in the back. I went back in the toilet and raised the lid up and, hell! you look right straight down at the ground! Whatever goes in there goes out. I'm tellin' my uncle about this, he's a doctor in Riverside, California. Oh, he says, that'd be awful if somebody was constipated and then let loose.

—JAMES M. DAVIS

I was the first person at Procter and Gamble to travel on commercial flights. They frowned on that. It cost more than a train trip, and they made me pay the difference. And I was too stupid to point out to them that I'd saved a lot of time—and a lot of meals, too. I look back and wonder why in the world did I let that get by?

—VICTOR MILLS

Pride and Prejudice

Did I experience discrimination?

Nothing else but. Oh, yes,

nothing else but.

—JULIA TYLER

Born June 26, 1888

Fredericksburg, Virginia

My husband's daddy, Richard Jordan, was a half-white man. That's what they called them, you know, when the mother was a white woman and had a child by a colored man. His mother was a rich white woman, but she didn't want white people to be knowin' that she had a child by a Negro man. So she gave my little daddy, I called him, to a black man to raise, a man by the name of Jordan. And when that child got grown, he went with the colored folks, but he looked like a white man. And I married that man's son.

He was a man that everybody thought a lot of. He was a man treated everybody right and white people loved him even though he couldn't go white. He was a churchman, belonged to a church in Margarettsville. And he was a big man in the Odd Fellows. So he goes to this meetin' down in the church one Saturday night. This was when my oldest child was a baby, goin' on eighty years ago. Well, while he was at that meetin', a colored man come in town and told him that his son and another colored boy was in a white man's henhouse stealin' chickens.

Next mornin', these white boys in Seaboard —they was grown men; one of 'em was married and had a child—they made up their mind to go on down to Richard Jordan's farm and get the boy. So these white men come to his house to tell him they was goin' to search his henhouse and see if the stolen chickens weren't there. And Richard said to them boys, Well, I just got home from my meetin' and I don't know where's any chickens in my henhouse or not that might belong to you. But if you go in my henhouse and don't bring no chickens out, then I tell you to get out of my yard. 'Cause don't you come here sayin' my son has stole your chickens.

So one of those men, Nate Harris was his name, told him, I'll shoot you 'fore I get out your yard.

Richard said, No, I ain't gon' have no trouble with you. Then he turned 'round to come back in the house. And that white man shot him and killed him.

His son was in the bed upstairs. He said to his momma, He's killed my daddy and I'm gon' kill him. He grabbed a gun and he shot and killed that man half in the gate goin' out the yard.

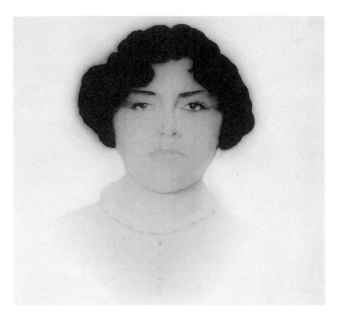

Sallie Ransom (Sallie Jordan) at age nineteen, around 1912

Well, then they was gon' kill that boy. A doctor's son—he was with the bunch of boys that went to get the black boy—he come home and told his father that somebody had killed Nate Harris. So the doctor went on down there, and sure 'nuff, Henry's daddy was layin' half in the yard and half on the porch and the white man was layin' half in the yard gate and half out. And he told the boy he better get away. That boy, he went away and nobody ain't never seen him no more.

Here's the thing: Then, you did anything the white man didn't like, they'd lynch you. They'd of put that boy in jail and gone to the jail at night and got him out and hung him over a tree.

—SALLIE JORDAN

In Georgia, Ku Kluckers would go around and whip some niggers. But they never did bother my father.

My daddy, when he wasn't workin' the field, he'd go around and work for white folks. For a quarter he'd do what they'd need done. But they wouldn't let him come in the house. When they would give him something to eat, they would hand him a plate out the back door, and he would have to sit outside and eat. When he got through eatin', he had to get him some water to rinse that plate out before they'd take that plate back into the house to wash it.

—FANNIE LOU DAVIS

As soon as I was old enough to read, I had a Bible. And I read my Bible and tried to understand what the Bible said. I read about Creation: God created man in His own image and likeness. Everybody that He created was one of His children. I grew up with that embedded in me, and although I was pushed aside and called names and all that sort of thing, something within me told me that there was nobody any better than I. And I felt that way all through my life.

My aunt taught me—she sat me down and talked with me when I was ready to go to school—she said every child, except maybe two or three, beside you would be a white child. She said, You're gonna be called names; you're gonna be tossed around in a way. Nobody won't have anything to do with you. But, she said, mind your manners, and when you answer somebody, choose your words before you speak. Don't bring any bad language you hear into this house, and if you hear it I don't want you to repeat any of it. God gave you that piece of red flannel, she called it, in your mouth to use, she said, but you don't hear any fussing and quarreling in this house. You don't hear anybody called "fool" or "nigger" or a liar.

And I have lived by what she taught me.

—JULIA TYLER

When I was comin' up, we didn't have any trouble with black and white. Tennessee is a border state. Most of our black people are pretty high-class. 'Course they do have some trouble with the youngers comin' on, but back then we played ball with them, and ate with them. Black people lived on the same streets with white people. We'd go by old Sola Harris's house, go in and eat with her. That's the way we came up. It's different now.

—SARAH HUNTER JACKSON

Shady Side was unique because all the men, black and white, did the same kind of work. They went out oystering and fishing and crabbing. And when you work on the water, if one person gets in trouble, everybody goes and helps out. There was no color there.

—F. ETHEL ANDREWS

A long time ago, white people recognized that the colored was human just like they was. We're all human, just different colors. We're all born the same way, and we all die when the time comes. Ain't no difference, it's just different in the color.

We had a white neighbor lived right next to us. We come up with Miss Anne's children. I'd get up every morning, eat my breakfast, go to her house, and play with her children, and later in the day, or the next day, her children would come over and play with us. When we'd go to Miss Anne's to play and we'd get into a fight, she'd whup us just as she would her own children. And when we got home, Mama whupped us again. That's right.

One time a storm blew the top of our house off, and I was always nervous for thunder and lightning. When it would get thunderin' and lightning, I'd go to Miss Anne's house. And when the cloud passed over, I'd go back to my house. I'd go to Miss Anne's house just 'cause that was Miss Anne. She was white; it made no difference. People looked out for people then.

—JESSIE TURNER

Homestead, Pennsylvania, was a mixed neighborhood. There were a lot of Slovaks, blacks, Mexicans. Everybody worked for U.S. Steel and lived in houses U.S. Steel owned. The houses had a common yard out in the back. We all got along. One lady—her name was Mary Darko, she was Hungarian, and she had at least twelve children—if Mrs. Darko told one of my kids, Now you cut that out or I'm gonna slap you, well, she would just take her slappin' and that was it. 'Cause if she told me, she was gonna get some more.

Someone was askin' my daughter a few years ago, what did she know about prejudice. Well, she knew nothin' about prejudice because we were all poor, and everybody helped everybody. If one neighbor made pigs in a blanket—that was a dish made of cabbage and ground meat—they would send us over some. And when I'd make hot rolls, I'd send them over some. I'd make the bread, and everybody could smell it all around, and I had to make it because we didn't have enough money to buy it.

—CHARLIE LUE MOSLEY

We had to pay a poll tax in order to vote. And we had to pass an examination before we could vote. I was one of those that was crossed off, which I didn't care. But some of the people that were crossed off were schoolteachers and such, and they knew they had answered those questions correctly.

After they came with the poll tax and allowed us to vote if we paid the tax, my husband said to me one day, I want you to go with me to sign to vote.

No, I said, I'm not gonna sign up and I'm not gonna vote.

He said, Peg, that's your privilege, to vote. But we do have to pay the tax.

I said, I'm not going to vote.

I knew what went on. I had worked for politicians, for people that were up in politics, and they had charge of these polling places. I knew the dirty rotten game it was.

He said, You have a privilege and a right to vote as you choose, whether what you choose succeeds or not. He said, Now, come on, don't be stubborn, come on and vote.

I said, All right, it's your dollar, not mine. I wouldn't pay the dollar.

—JULIA TYLER

For a long time, there was a law in North Carolina that said that no store could serve both races. A colored store could only serve colored people. A white store couldn't serve blacks *in* their store. The way it worked, no colored folks could go in a white drugstore with a prescription and sit down and wait for it to be filled like the white folks did. If a colored person came in, he had to go outside and wait thirty, forty minutes and then come back and the prescription would be ready. Because the law didn't allow them to serve any blacks in the store.

Where colored folks could go to the store wasn't the only thing the white people controlled. Hospitals were white, and no colored doctor could work in a white hospital. A white doctor could admit his colored patient to the hospital. But she couldn't go to the hospital unless her doctor said she could go to the hospital, and then she had to be in the basement.

They also controlled who could vote. They put in new laws that prevented most black people from voting. They put in a new requirement that you had to read from the Constitution to the satisfaction of a registrar. I knew a lot of educated colored folks who could read better than the registrar could, but couldn't read to the registrar's satisfaction. Now, if a white person couldn't read or write, he was protected by the "grandfather clause": any person could vote if his grandfather had voted. Of course, none of our black grandfathers voted, because they had all been slaves.

But they didn't intimidate my father, and they never bothered me. When the voting time would come up, he would go there to vote. He'd tell them, I'm York Garrett. I come to vote and I'm gonna vote or I'm gonna raise hell. And he never missed a chance to vote in his life. But they intimidated a lot of colored people.

My father was a staunch, staunch Republican. The first time he almost dropped dead was when I voted the Democratic ticket. He said, You can't do that. Do you know who Lincoln was? He freed the slaves. And you mean to tell me you're not going to vote for him?

But, you know, my father taught me a lot. And one of the things he taught me is that some things I have to make my own decision on. And I decided I'd rather be voting for the other side than the side that has done all the discriminating and putting us out of business.

—YORK GARRETT

I don't remember much about movies, but I'll tell you about a show that I had seen in New York City. The name of that show was *Peg o' My Heart*, and the star in the show was a young girl. It was a musical comedy in a way, and she was full of pranks and things; she was very alert and active.

So that movie came to Fredericksburg. And I told my husband I wanted him to see it because I had enjoyed it so much when I saw it in New York. But he wouldn't go without me. I could see it again, I said, but it's no use buying that extra ticket; I was always thinking about the financial part of things.

He said, Well, I won't go unless you go. All right, I said. And he told me afterwards, he said, That girl was so full of mischief I'm going to give you her name. So he nicknamed me Peg.

Oh yes, the movie theaters were segregated. Where we saw this *Peg o' My Heart*, they had this opera house, and it had an upper part—they called it the gallery—and that's where colored people could sit and look at a show.

That was accepted. We had to accept it or else not see anything.

So, it was *Gone with the Wind*, the movie that was made from that book, that came to Fredericksburg. My husband bought the tickets downstairs at the window, and we went upstairs. Well, there was a white fellow up there showing us where to sit. I looked at him and I looked at my husband. Gossie knew what was coming so he looked the other way.

I said, Why do we have to sit on this back seat?

The front part is reserved tonight for white.

I said—listen to what I said; it didn't sound very nice—I said, I am *not* going to be Jim Crowed in this dirty little pit. I was gettin' angry. My husband said to me, Come on, Peg, let's go. He took hold of me and, Come on, Peg, let's go! And I said, Yes, we're going, 'cause I am not going to sit here.

So we went downstairs and he went to the ticket window and asked for his money. Everybody that was up there ahead of us followed on. They saw what he was doing and they went to the ticket window and asked for their money.

The man who had charge of the place—his name was Benjamin Pitts—whoever was selling the tickets called him. Benny, come here, he said, all these people comin' downstairs askin' for their money. Benny, he said, Well, you'll just have to give it to them if they're asking for it. Just give it to them. Benny, he was a lovely man.

There were two colored stayed up there that night. One worked for the newspaper and the other was a doctor, our colored doctor, and they both had complimentary tickets. The girl's name was Fannie. Fannie told me afterwards, she said, When we went up there we heard them talkin' about the colored people walkin' out.

I said, Fannie, I'm sorry, I started it.

She said, I heard about you.

I said, Maybe some other people would have stayed up there today if it hadn't of been for my big mouth.

Well, we got to see that movie afterwards. See, this man that built the theater, he had a decent place. We were on the second floor, of course, but we could sit anywhere we wanted to sit up there.

—JULIA TYLER

One of my daughters got grown, finished high school, went to college. She had a friend lived in Norfolk, Virginia. Well, she said, Momma, you never been to Norfolk; I'm gon' take you to Norfolk. So we got on the boat. Well, that boat had a place for black folks to sit, and a place for white folks. The black folks had to sit down close to the water and the white folks sat above. When I got on the boat, I said, I ain't gon' sit down near that water, I'm gon' up on top.

She said, Momma, they ain't gon' let you.

I said, They ain't gon' hit me.

So I went on with the white folks. And they didn't put me off.

Then I went to Richmond to see my sister, she was in the hospital. This was during the wartime. We come back that night on the train to Weldon. Well, Negroes had to go up three flights of steps to wait for the train. When I got to the train station, and I walked up the stairs, there was a whole big thing of black soldiers layin' all over the floor, waitin' for the train to carry them to German places to fight. There weren't no place to sit. And I didn't know what they might do. So I said, Well, I ain't sittin' up here. And this other woman up there, she said, They ain't gon' let you sit downstairs where the white folks sit.

I says, They gon' let me sit down there.

So I went back downstairs and got me a seat and sat down. The white people was eatin' and havin' a good time. When the train come, I got on a car with the white folks. Didn't nobody say nothin' to me, and I didn't say nothin' to nobody.

Before I was grown, black folks didn't have nothin'. The white man let 'em farm his land, gave 'em food to eat all the year. And when the crop was in, he'd take your half to pay back what he let you have to live. But, you know, we black folks now ain't gonna take what we used to take. 'Cause the white man don't own black folks no more. I don't mind tellin' you 'cause it's the truth.

But I didn't have no trouble with the white folks. I don't mean to treat a white man no better than I treat a black man, if you treat me with respect. But you got to treat me with respect. If you don't treat me with respect, I don't have nothin' to do with you.

—SALLIE JORDAN

There was this little black boy lived across the street from where I had my grocery store in Tacoma. His father and mother were a really nice young couple. But nobody played with this little boy. He was a serial loner, you might say.

Well, I decided one day that, well, gee whiz, maybe he'd have a little fun flying a kite. So I made a kite for him. And myself and one of the delivery-men coming to the store early in the morning, we got out in the street and were flying the darn thing before I presented it to him. Oh, his mother and father never got over the fact that here was a white man who would actually make a kite for a little black boy.

—OSCAR C. WEBER

My wife and I couldn't have been a better couple from this standpoint: most of the things she liked and the things I liked were the same. For every year of our marriage, two or three times a year, we'd go up to New York City to see the shows on Broadway: *South Pacific; Oklahoma; Damn Yankees; Kiss Me, Kate.* From around 1919 up until my wife died, there would never be a show in New York that was worth seeing that we didn't see.

We liked to book into the Taft Hotel. The Taft wasn't taking colored, except celebrities, when we first went up there, and then later on they would take you, but you could only go as far as the second floor. But I got to know all the bellmen there and they got to know me, and they knew my wife just like she was part of their family. So whenever we'd get up there, if any good room could be had, the man at the desk would give us a room and the bellmen would take us to a room they wanted us to have. Because we had the money to pay for it.

New York was New York. It didn't break down easily. There were times I might go to the ticket window to get a seat and they'd say, We're sold out. So then my wife would go to the ticket window herself and she'd say, I want a couple of seats. And she'd get them. They didn't know she was my wife. See, she could get a lot of things in New York that I would have trouble getting.

—YORK GARRETT

My husband served in the First World War. He played the trombone in an Army band. He never had to handle a gun. And he always told his sons: No heroics. Just bring yourselves home intact.

In World War II, Bob was in the Navy and Charlie was in the Army. They came home intact. But when Bob tried to rent an apartment in one of the new garden-apartment projects in East Orange, he was told he could rent only in the black section of the city.

Well, they didn't have the right to segregate any of the projects. They didn't have the right to deny black boys the same recognition as whites vis à vis housing. Any government project, you could not take government money and deny people the right to live where they wanted. I'd long been a member of the local chapter of the NAACP for New Jersey. We fought that through the NAACP. We took it to the courts and we won.

We need to aim for a single standard for all Americans, which still doesn't exist today. There shouldn't be any second-rate Americans.

—DELIA HARRISON-MARTIN

I never did get involved politically. I never allied myself with any group. And there was a reason for that. When I came down to Durham, my best shot was to get the best position I could to help my business grow. With a lot of blacks, you had to go from one side to another. Some folks wanted to bring down segregation. Some talked about making their own separate nation. But for me to go with them, I'd be going against myself, because my store was doing as well as it was. My business was strong *because* I was segregated. Ninety-five percent of all my customers were black. The minute there's no more segregation, I was afraid my store was going to have to close up. So I maintained a neutral position. And I could talk to all sides.

When all the civil-rights agitating came about, I never took part in it. I didn't have to. I could get anything I needed for the other blacks around. For a long time we didn't have black police. But the city was going to give us some black police if that's what we wanted. And the first nine black police we had, they would gather in my store. See, they were going to let us have some black policemen, provided they didn't patrol where white people were.

Now, in my store I had a public telephone. Folks could use it as much as they wanted. One time, a kid I knew, he was eighteen or nineteen years old, came to me and said, Doc, hell's gonna break loose in Hayti tonight. That was the section of Durham where we were: Hayti.

I said, What's going to happen?

We just got a message that at six o'clock tonight the KKK is gonna burn St. Joe's Church down. St. Joseph's was a colored church that was sponsored by the Duke family and all those people that have money.

I said, What're you going to do?

He said, The minute they set the fire on St. Joe's, nine buildings on Main Street gonna be blown up.

Now, this uproar was caused by the killing of a black soldier from Fort Bragg by a white Durham bus driver. The soldier had argued with the driver, saying he was a soldier for his country and he should not be told to sit only on a black seat. When the soldier got off the bus, the driver got off and shot him.

I said, Now, do you know what you're talking about?

He said, You wait and see.

This is a colored boy telling me this in my drugstore. And I knew he was in a group that could do it. I thought, This is going to be hell. So I had to make my pick. He hadn't told anybody but me. He knew me. He knew where I stood and what I was supposed to do. So I got on the telephone and called the president of the North Carolina Mutual Life Insurance Company, a good friend of mine. I told him about the bombings. And he got right on the phone with the Mayor of Durham and told him: We have information that there's going to be a riot here tonight. Do me a favor, he says, put a curfew on. So they put a curfew on right then and it stayed on for two weeks. Nobody was bombed. I did my duty as I saw it. And I changed my mind down the line about desegregation.

—YORK GARRETT

Men's Lives

Sure, twenty-five dollars don't

seem like much now, but when

we were getting twenty-five dollars

a week, bacon and eggs and coffee

cost fifteen cents.

—JAMES M. DAVIS

Born March 23, 1896

Columbus, Ohio

I left grammar school after the seventh grade. Something about school just didn't fascinate me.

I got a job in the shoe factory in New Bedford. I had the lowest-pay job there: nail puller. It paid around six dollars a week. Then I went on to assemble. That was a better job. I got a raise to seven dollars. The assembler job then paid me twenty-three, twenty-five cents piecework.

Every Friday I used to see this Coast Guard ship coming in and the sailors coming off. And the shoe factory wasn't doing too well. Certain times of the year they'd be very busy, other times not. So I see these sailors coming every Friday. I liked the uniforms. I inquired about them. I went down to the pier and asked if there was a job on the ship. There was and I took it.

I walked down to the ship, the *Acushnet*, with a suitcase in my hand. My grandmother was leaning out of the window yelling, Take off your shoes, take off your shoes! Meaning that if the ship was sinking, maybe I could have a better chance to swim without my shoes. I got a bang out of that.

I was a steerage boy. That meant taking care of the warrant officers' quarters. There were four officers on board and I would bring them their meals, clean for them, change their beds. I took good care of them. And I got acquainted with the chief radioman. He come to me

Eddy Kincaide, center, with Coast Guard pals, South Norwalk, Connecticut, 1918

one day. Eddy, he said, how would you like to work on radios?

I said, Well, I don't know much about it.

◄ *Ralph Montecalvo, right, at work making Army boots at Converse Rubber Company, Malden, Massachusetts, during the Second World War*

We can teach you.

He had a second-class man on there named John Ash, a guy from Texas. So I started learning how to receive and send in Morse Code. I was doing well with the code receiving, and Mr. Ritter, the guy that was teaching me, his wife owned a variety store. One day I said, Mr. Ritter, if you want to go home tonight, go home, I'll take your watch. And I stayed up to twelve midnight. He thought that was pretty good. One night, after I served the officers their coffee and sandwiches, Mr. Ritter says, Eddy, tonight you're going to take the midnight watch, midnight to six in the morning. And from now on you are Acting Second Class Radioman. That was wonderful for me. To leave a common ordinary service-boy job to go up to a second-class petty officer, that was pretty good. I was seventeen years old.

—EDDY KINCAIDE

When I was a young man in Puerto Rico, it was very difficult for me to get a job. I never went to school. I had to work whatever was available—in the farm, selling eggs, picking up cans and bottles to sell, making charcoal. But, thanks to God, we were not as bad off as some others. We had our own farm where we raised our own cow and chickens. But it was difficult.

When I got married, I have to do more to provide for my family. I have a couple of dollars saved, so I make my own business buying pants and clothes and selling all around the neighborhood. Then I was eight years a prison guard, in charge of prisoners to go and work in the roads.

After that, I made my living killing pigs and cows. That was a business I established myself. It was dirty work. You have to take the pig, tie the legs and mouth not to make noise, then kill it with a knife. You stab the pig right in the heart. Then we collect the blood. We take the hair off with hot water and a knife. Then we open the pig and take out the entrails, the lungs and the liver and so forth. From that we make sausages. And then the rest of the animal we cut in pieces and sell by the pound.

That was hard work, but not as hard as working in the sugarcane plantation, where I was a foreman. Sometimes I have to get up at two or three o'clock in the morning, walk three or four miles. If it was raining I have to come back home without an hour's work. We start at seven o'clock in the morning and work to seven o'clock at night. Those people that owned the plantation tried to take advantage of the workers, trying to get the most for the least. Sometimes I make thirty-five to fifty cents a day for eight, nine, ten hours. There was no by hour, it was by day. Gradually they start to raise the price by day. Sometimes it came up to seventy-five cents.

Then there was no union, no nothing, only the big corporations "taking care" of the workers. The workers don't have the conscious about working that workers have today. In that era was difficult. A day in the sugarcane plantation was sweaty. It was muddy. It was all that you can say about hard work.

—TRINIDAD HUERTAS

When I was still in my teens, I went to Detroit to learn to be an automobile mechanic. Picked it right up. After I got back to Block Island, I opened my own garage. Called it the Square Deal. But I did a lot of different work—dug ditches, mixed cement, laid cement walks, dug clams, built dories, worked on construction of the Narragansett Hotel. I salvaged wrecks. I made a name for myself catching fish—I got some great swordfish. I kind of caught on to where the fish were, how to find them, how to catch them. If I wanted a job, I didn't have to ask more than once. I just had the ability to do several different things. Some people, they don't see anything; they can't do anything. I didn't have to see something done too many times before I could see exactly how it's done. Then I can do it.

There were always a lot of wrecks off Block Island. There'd be a vessel run aground out there, breaking up, some people on her, some overboard, all trying to get ashore. We'd take a boat out and pick up the survivors.

Anyway, I had my garage for twenty-five years. Then I decided I didn't want to spend the rest of my life crawling around under automobiles. So I took a job teaching—carpentry, boatbuilding. I found it to be easy. I could associate with the students. They weren't rowdy with me. I wanted to teach them, and they wanted to learn.

—FRED BENSON

When I got back to Chicago after my stint in the service, jobs were scarce. I drove a taxi, worked for a bank, then an oil company. I met the woman who would be my first wife on a blind double date. Then I got a job teaching phys ed at Morton High in Cicero. Most of the students there were first-generation Americans. Their parents put a very high value on education. We had a fine industrial-arts program that prepared our students for jobs with local industries.

I taught and coached there about ten years. Al Capone had seats to the football games right on the fifty-yard line. There was a railing that separated the team from the spectators. Capone sat right behind me; I could feel him right over my head. But he never said a word to me, never showed any pleasure or displeasure over how the game was going.

The year we won the basketball championship, 1927, was a big deal. Here's how they wrote us up in the school paper:

Mortonian

Vol. IX   J. Sterling Morton High School, Cicero, Illinois, April 19, 1927   No. 28

Morton Wins U. S. Championship

VERPOWERS ARK. IN FINALS

WINS BY A BASKET

Trails at Beginning of Fray

With the prep basketball ampionship of the United tes at stake, Morton and esville, Arkansas, battled ely in a nip and tuck fight g was anybody's game from t to finish. Batesville d a great team, but it lacked final spurt to overcome a two nt advantage in the final min- , and Morton gained the well- ned title by an 18-16 score.

Each player was introduced by erbert O. Crisler before the ne began.

Mike scored the first point of game, and Pickren retaliated h a short basket. Then Ed ed in two from the foul line, king the score 3-2. Al Car- ter looped a pair of ringers ore the initial quarter closed- atesville was leading at the

1st row—Elmer Hauer, Donald Barton, Coach Long, Arthur Herion manager, Warren Johnstone, Robert Hanzelin.
2nd row—Louis Rezabek, George Fencl, Edward Kawalski, Mike Rondinella, Ossian Nystrom.

DEFEAT FIVE STATE CHAMPS

WINS GREAT FAME

Longmen Swamp City Champs

Morton annexed the most cov- eted prep title in America, that of basketball championship of the United States, after cutting down five state champs and Englewood, Chicago champs at the Ninth Annual National Inter- scholastic Basketball Tourna- ment at the Bartlett Gym. The glory of it all belongs to Morton, and the honor goes to the state of Illinois. This is the first time in ten years that an Illinois team has won the national title or even advanced as far as the quarterfinals. It is the greatest and most glorious athletic achievement in the history of J. Sterling Morton.

Monday morning, March 28, the long hoped invitation arrived from Stagg, and on Tuesday afternoon Durant, Oklahoma,

We helped change the rules of the game. One of my players, Mike Rondinella, was a very skilled dribbler. It took at least two players to corner him. There was no time limit then on ball possession, no center line, no ten-second rule, and a center jump after each basket. Well, my 1927 team had all the ingredients to control the ball—and the game. My center, Ed Kawalski, outjumped every center we faced. He signaled which way he would tap the ball. We always had the ball after each basket. First move: pass the ball to Rondinella. He would dribble around until he was cornered by two players, which left one of my other players free. He'd pass the ball to the free player, who would dribble to the basket and score. Then back to the center. That was our story.

The rules people changed all this. They added a center line; once the team with the ball passed it, they couldn't go back. After a basket, the ball went out of bounds to the other team: no more center jump. And unlimited ball possession was replaced by the ten-second rule. All of which made the game faster and more exciting.

Karl Long, upper left, in one of his first stints in his career as a high-school coach, Bordentown, New Jersey, 1916

I really expected a lot from my kids. Mostly I expected them to be good sportsmen. If there was ever any booing done by anybody, I would call the game. Our cheerleaders wouldn't make noise to upset an opposing player trying for a free throw.

When I moved on to Parker, my alma mater, I still stressed sportsmanship. We had a black player on the team one year and the team we were going to play didn't want to play against a black. Somebody called him a "nigger." Well, my boys got all up in arms and got determined to beat this other team because of the insult.

And we did.

—KARL LONG

When I was a kid, we used to play baseball with anything we could get ahold of. We didn't have no rich parents; we couldn't afford to buy gloves and equipment. After I got out of school, I earned the money to buy my own uniform and gloves and shoes. My parents didn't have nothin' to do with it. What I got, I got myself.

We used to have a local sandlot team. We'd be invited into Sing Sing to play against the convicts. They had some good ballplayers there, too.

Sometimes the Giants would come up, or the Yankees, and the convicts would play them a good game. They used to call Sing Sing "the college": You couldn't get in unless you were three years up.

In 1911, I was twenty years old. I didn't have any intention of playin' baseball. I was out of school, gettin' bigger, fillin' out. And I was filled out pretty good then, about 170 pounds.

One evening, my brother Herbert was over to my house. We were havin' dinner, talkin' about this and that. And he says to me, Let's go out and have a catch. I didn't know he knew somethin' about baseball at the time. I says, Yeah, we'll go out and have a little catch.

So he looked me over pretty sharp. He wanted to see what I could do. After about fifteen minutes he says, I'll be back in a few days and I'll have dinner with you again. He was a salesman, my brother Herbert. When he came over again, we're sittin' at the dinner table and he says, How would you like to go out and have a catch? All right, I says, I'll go for that. So we went out and had a catch.

He went away and he came back on a Saturday. He says, We have a big game up in Croton. Would you like to go along? Yeah. So I went up with him and I pitched the game and won it. The same thing happened the next week. I won again. The next week, the same thing. Then we had another game down in Tarrytown. I pitched and won that one, too.

Well, Herb talked with someone he knew, a Wall Street broker lived in the same town and who also knew me. He went to see the Yankees play twice a week, only they were the Highlanders then. He knew the manager pretty well, Hal Chase. So he says, I have a nice ballplayer up in Ossining and I'd like to bring him down for a tryout. Chase says, What is he, a left-hander? Sure, bring him down.

In three days, he was lookin' me over. The first day, he called over one of the regular catchers. He says, Take this young fella and warm him up, see what he's got. After a while, the catcher went back to Chase and he must have reported I was pretty good. Chase comes over to me and says, You come back tomorrow morning. Same time.

The next morning, I come back. Again Chase says to the catcher, Warm him up. Later, Chase says to me, How do you feel? I says, I'm okay. He says, You feel good enough to come back tomorrow morning? Yeah, I says. I was all excited.

So I did the same thing the next morning. And Chase says, You see that locker over there? Your uniform's in there. You put that on and come out with the regular ballplayers. I looked at him, and he kinda laughed to him-self.

I felt pretty good. I helped the pitcher out there on the mound during hitting practice. I relieved the regular pitcher and I finished up. We got the practice game over, then Detroit came out. They had their practice. Then the game started, and I'm sittin' on the bench with the regular players.

Our best pitcher was pitchin', and he was pitchin' a good game for a while. By the sixth inning, he was gettin' tired. Then Chase says to me, I hate to take him out but I have to. He's lost his stuff. You get ready to go out there for him.

I warmed up. When I went out there, I wasn't a bit nervous. I was just as calm and cool as a cucumber. We got our signals together, the catcher and me. I tossed some warmup pitches and then the umpire said, *Play ball!*

I didn't know who I was pitchin' to. He was a left-hander. I'm a left-hander. I pitched him a couple of fast ones inside. Two foul tips. Then Ed Sweeney, the catcher, called for a pitchout. So I pitched outside; we thought he'd go for it. He didn't. Then Sweeney called for a curve. So I drilled him an overhand fast curveball. A perfect strike! Cut right through the plate. The batter never even got the bat off his shoulder. He stood there in the batter's box as the umpire called, *Strike three, yer out!* Then he walked back to the dugout. He never said a word. When I struck him out, fifty thousand people were cheering in the stands, and boy, could you hear them. Lord, that was somethin'!

The next morning I picked up the New York *Journal* newspaper, there was a big headline, in red ink: HOFF STRIKES OUT COBB. I almost passed out! Ty Cobb, he was the greatest ballplayer that ever was. That's including, by my estimation, Babe Ruth. The Babe, he was good, but he was no Ty Cobb. Ty Cobb could do everything.

Cobb never got mad at me 'cause I struck him out. Just the opposite. He had a barnstorming team he called the All-Stars. When they'd play around New York and Jersey City, he would call me up to pitch them games.

So that's how my career started off. I think I got to the major leagues faster than anybody I ever knew: three days. Without any minor league experience. I just wanted to take a trip to New York, to see the city.

After I was with the Yankees and they looked me over, they thought I needed more experience. So they sent me up to Rochester. I made good up there, too. I was a good-hitting pitcher. I hit .410 for the season. They'd take their regular ballplayers out for me. Imagine that for a pitcher? Out of three hundred and some odd players, I led the league.

Ray Keating played there, too. We had to play two games on Labor Day, the last day of the season, to win the pennant. And we did it. I pitched the morning game, Ray pitched the second game and I played first base. You

know what we got for winning? So long, boys, so long. We didn't even get a cigar. But I was satisfied. I had some money in my pocket, and I didn't have that before. When I started, I was makin' about $250 a month. The best I got was $450 a month. Big pay in them days. It was way ahead of workin' for a livin'.

—CHESTER ("RED") HOFF

*Baseball card of
Chester ("Red") Hoff, 1912,
the year before
the New York Highlanders
became the Yankees*

My dad rode in two or three amateur bicycle races. I don't know whether this set my course or not, but when I was in the fifth grade he bought me a motorcycle: a Yale. He paid $225 for it, and $225 back then was a lot of money.

Racing was what I enjoyed. I was good at it and it hooked me. I got professional in '16. The dealer for Indian motorcycles in Columbus, Ohio, took me to Detroit, to the Michigan State Fair. They had a mile dirt track there. When I lined up with all them professionals, I got off my bike and walked across the track and I was lookin' at every one of them, just to see what they looked like. They looked like me, only some of them were a lot older than I was. So I just figured: I'm gonna go out and beat 'em. And I did. I got off fast at the start and I never stopped. Nobody even got close to me.

Then the Indian Motorcycle Company wired my dealer and asked him if he could bring me to Saratoga, New York. I told the dealer, New York's a long way away.

It won't take you long on the train, he says.

Well, you'll have to call my dad.

Which he did. And Dad says, if he wants to go, let him go.

Which I did.

I was fortunate, I guess. I won that one, too. And I got to thinkin' that maybe I'm pretty good. Well, I won five straight hundred-mile races. We used to run pretty quick back then, around eighty, eighty-five miles an hour. Two or three years later, we're runnin' up around 120. Fastest I ever did go was around 157 miles an hour, but that wasn't till '47 or '49. 'Course, now they got bikes that run two hundred miles an hour easy.

After I got out of the service, I worked at my father's cut-stone company. I raced on weekends. Sure, I could've stayed with the other guys out where we were racin', Toledo, Buffalo, wherever, waitin' for the race on Sunday, 'cause I had a swindle sheet. That's what the company'd give you to keep your expense account on. I called it a swindle sheet from the time I was with Harley-Davidson. They used to have a ticket that said, "Don't be a tightwad. Spend our money as if it were your own." When we were racing for them, they'd give us $300 when we'd leave the plant, but they wanted to know where we spent it.

Between races I went home. Worked in my plant. I never wanted for anything. A lot of the kids that rode, all they had was what the factory paid 'em: twenty-five bucks a week back in '20. And expenses, of course.

One time I was up in Syracuse and the referee was E. C. Smith. We were good friends, we played golf together. Anyway, I had already won three national championships and now we got another comin' up, a fifty-mile event. The way it was supposed to work, the fastest eight fellows ride all afternoon; the rest of them they put in another race, give 'em a chance to get some money. But this Smith, he was also the flagman for this race, he says, I'm gonna start all these fellows in this race.

Well, I says, that's illegal. You helped build this rule that only eight can go.

He pointed his finger at me. You go on the last row on the pole, he says, for insubordination.

Now, I was on the pole in the front row. I tell him, You gotta be kidding!

I am not! You wanna ride, that's where you go.

So I go back there on the last row and get on the pole, and they're gettin' ready to start. This little kid was standin' there over the fence with an old gray sweater on, had a big tear in the front. I says, You wanna trade sweaters?

He says, You mean it?

Yeah, just hurry up.

I jerked my sweater off, a Harley-Davidson sweater, it had green sleeves

Jim Davis on the circuit, around 1925

and a white front and my name on it. He got his off and I got it on. By that time they're startin' to move, Smith didn't even know who I was when I come by. After we got by the startin' line, I backed off and got way out on the outside. When I hit that line, I figured, I'm gonna be full-bore. I figured these other guys wouldn't be 'cause they're gonna turn it on at the line. So I hit that line as he dropped the flag. When I went into the turn, I'm out in front. And when I come around the next time, I raised up in my saddle and hit my button to shut the power off, and I guess I showed Smith up. I thought he black-flagged me the next lap. I thought I heard him cry, *Yer outta here!* But the stands roared. Hell, they saw what he done, and they knew I was the favorite. It ended up I won the race.

Another time I was down in Phoenix. The factory shipped two racin' machines out, and I'm all set to go. But the referee says to me, You can't ride here. They made a new rule over the weekend.

What kind of a rule is that? I says.

We only let two Excelsiors, two Indians, and two Harley-Davidsons ride.

Now, I wasn't riding for Harley-Davidson or Indian then. So I says, Who made this rule?

I don't know, but that's what they told me.

Oh, I says, that has to be wrong. I'm supposed to ride here, too.

Well, you can't ride.

So, I says, what if I get a telegram from the president of the motorcycle association and he permits me to ride. Then can I ride?

Absolutely.

So I go downtown to Western Union and some little girl in there, I give her a box of chocolate candy. There's a phony telegram I want to make for fun, I says. It's all fun. Just put down, "Permit Jim Davis to ride." And sign it "A. B. Coffman." That was the guy's name in charge. Then I give this little kid with a bicycle a quarter. Now you ride up and hand this to me when they're linin' up to begin the race, I says. So he brought it over to me and I pointed over to the referee in the striped shirt and told the boy to take it over to him. He opened it, and he looked at it, and he came right over to me. Well, here it is, he says.

What does it say?

"Permit Jim Davis to ride."

Well, I says, that's what I wanted him to say.

They had four races there and I won all four of 'em, got their money, and went to Los Angeles for the next race the following week. Well, there they told me, Jim, you can't ride here.

I says, That's what they told me in Phoenix. What's the trouble?

I don't know. But I just got a wire that says you're suspended for a year.

Oh, I says, there must be something wrong.

So I wasn't gonna try any more. I thought, Well, I'll go back home. And this Harley-Davidson guy who was running the show says, Why don't you ride the Harley, Jim?

I'm suspended for a year.

Ah, don't let that bother you. The Harley factory'll take care of that.

Until I retired from competitive racing back in '40 I must've run in around 15,000 races all over the United States and out as far as Australia. I won ninety-five championships, ninety-five gold medals. One year, I think it was '35 or '36, they had seventeen championship races all over the country—San Francisco, Portland, Los Angeles, Toledo, just scattered all over—and I won all seventeen. 'Course, I won for the factory, and the factory don't care anything about you: it's Harley-Davidson they publicized, not Jim Davis.

'Course, you never won too much, only like a thousand dollars for a race. You'd get to keep the prize money, though, plus your salary and expenses, so it worked out pretty good. We had everything we wanted.

—JAMES M. DAVIS

W. F. Jarnagin, Rutledge, Tennessee

I come to Rutledge in 19 and 16 and worked in a garage up here about a week for Mr. Nance. Then I was out of work for a while, until my cousin—we was distant cousins, but we was Jarnagins—was huntin' a mechanic to take on a dealership. When he found out I'd mechanic'd some, he got me goin' with him. He contracted with Ford on August the 12th, 19 and 16, and he patched up a place to set up the dealership. But we didn't get no cars till about the first of 19 and 17. Then we got a load of six T models. Come by boxcar. From then on, we'd get a carload of about six cars every two, three months. And we'd sell 'em right out.

Those T models then sold for $625 for the roadster. That was supposed to be a five-passenger, but they's little passengers;

you couldn't get five big 'uns in there. The two-passenger touring cars were a lot cheaper: $425.

'Course, we had to assemble them cars back then. It'd take you a day to set one up. You had about half a gallon of bolts and nuts to put in, and you had to learn where to put 'em. And I got so that I learned to set up six a day. We had to assemble 'em at the railhead, carry the chassis out, and the body, and set 'em on the cross-ties to start with on the railroad up here. Sometimes I'd get me some drivers and we'd drive over to Cincinnati to pick up the cars there and save on the freight. And I devised this thing to lift out the parts of the cars when we was unloading them. I used it 'bout a year before I applied for a patent. Then I had it manufactured in Knoxville, and shipped 'em out across the country.

Those first T models, you had to crank 'em. We got starters come out middle of 19 and 19. Ford shipped us three starters then, complete: starter and generator and relays and battery. The battery by itself cost over fifty dollars, but Ford wanted to get 'em introduced. And we had to install 'em. Forty dollars it cost us for a starter assembly, and we sold it complete for fifty dollars to make ten.

Anyway, we had an old man come in and he's gettin' his first car and he looks one over and he's wantin' a starter. But no, he said, he'd crank it for fifty dollars. I said, All right, you go on out there and I'll fix everything up here and you crank. So he went out and started to crank and he got cranked out. Then he had to pop and blow to get his breath, standin' beside the car there. Now, I cut the switch off, only he didn't know it. I said, You get in there now and turn the switch on and, *k'zipp*, she kicked right off. See, I'd got it all primed and everything. I seen him grin there after he set there for a while. But he still weren't gonna buy the starter, he weren't gonna pay no fifty dollars. I said, Now, you get your arm broke crankin', you lose three months' work and lose your crop. I said, You better get a starter while you can get it, we only just got 'em in. Till then, I hadn't sold a one.

The roads was about as reliable as the power in them days. Even though you could get up to about seventy-five miles an hour in the cars, we had windin' roads all filled with chuckholes. We didn't have no paved roads when I come to Rutledge, just wagon roads: hard-packed dirt. They put the first macadam right there in front of the People's Bank. They used prisoners from the old jail to haul rock up in there, big rock, and they had to beat them rock up with sledgehammers. Then they had to haul dirt and fill the cracks up. That's the only macadam we had in the county, probably no more'n a hundred feet long.

We also started generatin' our own electricity here, 110 volts. It was just a little-bitty plant; we didn't even know what a kilowatt was. We supplied the bank, drugstore, courthouse, and a hotel, too. Later on, we took more people on and got overloaded. Then I had to run the plant all the time. People wanted lights on at night. We had to get real inventive there for a while. They thought we was gettin' rich, and we was goin' broke. So we finally give it up. Besides, bein' in the car business, we had no business bein' in the light business. Gonna finally break us if we hadn't of got over it.

By that time we got Bettis Electric Company in Morristown to build a line over here. But in three years they went completely broke. The Tennessee Valley Authority built this dam over here on the Holston River. On Cherokee Lake, between here and Johnson City. They started stringin' lines then.

In the 1930s, it was a hard, hard sell. We just didn't do no business. And we had to cut our overhead, lay men off. Had to. Couldn't cut prices much; there wasn't much to cut on them T models. No, people that had saved up money could buy 'em and then we'd get 'em financed through the bank. We had to sell tires and refrigeration and electric ranges, just about anything to make a few dollars.

I'd work sometimes all day and all night, catchin' up, you know. Somebody broke down, why, I'd have to go out and get 'em and sleep when I could. We just stayed right on the job. I'd keep mechanics and work with 'em. They don't do that no more, what with overtime and everything they get now. Back then, we used to work a lot of blacks. We'd work 'em in the shop, trainin' 'em, washin' cars, cleanin' 'em up, polishin' 'em. They all gone to the cities now. The old-timers would do anything for you to get somethin' to eat.

—W. F. JARNAGIN

When I came to America in 1913, I came to a relative that had a farm in New Jersey, in Piscataway, and I became a milkman. I would get up in the morning before the sun. The first thing I had to do was hook up a horse to a wagon or to a sleigh if it was in the wintertime. Then I used to go out to deliver the milk. First I had to learn where the customers are. My memory at that time was very good, but I told my cousin that I'm going to deliver the milk myself, I don't need anybody to show me where the customers are. I depended on the horse, see: the horse knew every customer. And when I went out and the horse stopped at a certain house, I remembered just exactly how much milk they were getting. If a customer moved, the horse would still stop at that house, and I'd have to wait until the horse

Samuel D. Schneier with his sister, Rebecca, in New Jersey

was ready to move on to the next stop. That horse was very smart. He depended on me, too, to give him to eat when we came home. So he kind of liked me. I guess he felt: I'm taking care of him, too, you know.

Of course, the milk was in bottles, and the bottles had to be washed and filled and put in an icehouse to keep the milk cold. I did everything. It was the same old rounds every day: hooking up the horse, filling up the wagon or the sleigh with milk, going out to deliver, coming back and washing and filling the bottles. Three years I worked on the farm, until it burned down. My cousin went out of business and I had to look for a job.

I opened a hot-dog place, and a movie theater, and a grocery store. I learned how to read and write and speak English, all on my own, without going to any school, not one day. My common sense dictated to me exactly what to do, how to make a living. Then, after I scraped up enough money to bring my mother, sister, and two brothers over from Europe, I went into wholesale butter and eggs. I had a little business and a lot of customers. I did very good until the Great Depression. Then things was very bad and customers couldn't pay their bills, so I couldn't pay my bills. I had to go out of business.

At that time, there was no jobs available. One day a dairy twelve miles from where I was living had an ad in the paper that they are looking for a driver. So I called them up and I said, I'd like to take that job. They said, Okay. The driver that used to deliver the milk, he showed me where all the customers were.

But I only worked for them one day. They called me in and said if I want to buy the route, they'll sell me the truck and the customers. I said right away, No, I won't take it. I didn't want to be a sub-dealer. So they called up another dairy and asked them to give me a job. They agreed. The job paid $42.50 a week. At that time, it was a good salary.

I worked there twelve years. I felt compelled to work there because I couldn't find another job because of my age. I made a lot of money for them. I did the bookkeeping and everything; I'd add up all the numbers without a calculator. They couldn't believe how fast I was—and I didn't make mistakes. But I always had plans: I'm gonna be a big businessman someday. That's what I wanted to be.

I went into business for myself in 1943. I saw the ad in the paper that there's a little milk business for sale in New Brunswick. The whole business amounted to two routes, one retail and one wholesale, and a small bottling plant in back of a house. I went over right away and I made a deal with them. I was trusted by an awful lot of people. They knew that I didn't have the money, but I had a house that I had $5,000 equity in. I traded the house for the business and borrowed $1,000 from a friend to open a checking account.

I named it Cream-O-Land Dairy.

I always was saying that if I go in business for myself it would have to be the "cream of the land." So right away I called a lawyer and I told him to register that name. My son, Arthur, worked with me right in the beginning. Then he had to go into the service, and he was stationed at first at Fort Dix. He used to come home as often as possible, driving to New Brunswick to help out when he could.

My days never ended. Seven days a week I used to get up early in the morning. The first thing I had to go to the farms to pick up milk in those forty-quart cans that weighed over a hundred pounds. I'd lift them up, put them in a panel truck, go back to the bottling plant behind the house. I'd wash the bottles, bottle the milk, go out and deliver the milk, come back and try to get new customers—because it really wasn't a full wholesale route. It was half a wholesale route, and I had only one driver to help on the retail route. Getting customers was difficult at that time because everybody and his brother was in the milk business.

I did all the bookkeeping myself, the payments to the farmers and the other suppliers, all the reports to the state. I bottled my own buttermilk with a dipper and made my own sour cream. I just kept at it and kept at it. And it kept growing. I bought a lot and put a big sign up: *Future Home of Cream-O-Land Dairy*. See, I didn't have any money, but already I knew I needed a bigger place. Besides, I had to wait until the war was over to start the building anyway.

After we built the building, we kept growing, and we kept enlarging on that building. And my whole family came to work with me: my daughter and my son and his wife and their two boys. The milk is in their veins.

*Samuel D. Schneier with two of his inventions,
New Brunswick, New Jersey*

When I started Cream-O-Land, I was always looking: How can I make it better? I designed a rectangular-shaped milk bottle that I called the Space-master. I had a straight one for homogenized milk and one for the cream top. I wanted it to fit on the inside of a refrigerator door. How I did this, I carved out a piece of Ivory soap the shape of the bottle I figured would be a good thing for the milk business.

I invented a milk bottle that would make a storm over the whole country because it was such a wonderful bottle. It was saving space also in the cases: the cases now that are holding sixteen bottles replaced cases that could hold twelve. I had it patented and we built a lot of retail routes with that bottle before the paper containers started replacing glass bottles. A lot of people were coming out to New Jersey to these new developments, and my son would sit there day and night, seven days a week, looking for people, talking to them, getting to know them. He got a lot of new business because of that new bottle.

Cream-O-Land today is the largest milk distributor in the state of New Jersey, and one of the largest distributors on the whole East Coast.

I guess you could say that persistence paid off.

—SAMUEL D. SCHNEIER

When I came back from the war, I went to work for my dad, manufacturing slippers. I was married and I had to earn money as rapidly as possible. So I didn't have to go looking for a job; there was a door open for me.

We didn't have a huge factory. We had twenty-five, fifty workers, depending on the season, but we made a good profit. One of my brothers ran it. I was the leather buyer.

But I didn't forget what I learned at Harvard: I invented slippers that glow in the dark, and distinguish between the left and the right. That's what I did with my chemistry. I had five inventions. I could make your tie, your shirt, your trousers—stripes on it, let's say—glow. They use that now for toys—phosphorescence, not fluorescence. You've seen toys that light up in the dark? That's my invention.

—JOSEPH GOLDSTEIN

Ten months after I came home from Europe, our daughter was born. My wife's father and mother wanted us so bad to live near them—this was in Waynesboro, Pennsylvania—so I said all right, we'll go up there for a year anyway and maybe longer according to what opens up. They had an A&P in Waynesboro, and my brother-in-law introduced me to the manager. After talking with me about half an hour, he said, Ernest, you're just the man I'm looking for. How would you like to be manager of an A&P store?

I don't want it, I said.

You don't want it? Why?

Well, I said, it's not the pay, but I don't know anything about groceries.

You eat, don't you?

That's how I got with the A&P. I was with them nineteen years. And every year we topped what we did the previous year.

The first A&P I ran was a little place and only had two clerks. They got fifteen dollars a week. The manager got thirty dollars a week and one percent gross over whatever we sold. When the year would be up, I would have netted maybe around five hundred dollars a week. Then they opened a store in Hagerstown, Maryland, and asked me to manage it. I accepted.

This was a larger store. My salary still was thirty dollars a week, but now I got two percent of the gross. When we moved to the old Bickel's Shoe Store is when I made it big. We had sixteen clerks, and I had all highly intelligent boys that worked after school and on Saturdays. We put a doughnut machine in the window and I had one of the salesladies become manager of the doughnut department. People would watch the doughnuts being made, and the aroma made them come out with something they never had before. It wasn't long before my salary went up and they raised my take of the gross to four percent.

Then they wanted to open a supermarket. That was something new. And I said to the president of A&P, Who you going to get to take care of it for you? And he said, You. You will be the manager. You inherited this, and you well deserve it. And you're going to be surprised beyond your fondest imagination when you see what you're going to make in cash money; it'll be more than you ever dreamed of.

When the supermarket opened and I got paid, I went home and I said, Sweetheart, look here. I showed her my pocketbook. She said, Ernest, have you been gambling?

When A&P decided to close the store I managed, I decided to buy out the equipment and open my own market: Deetjen's Independent Market. I thought all my customers would follow me, and they did, for a while. Then they gradually began patronizing a new store downtown. After running my market for three years and losing a few thousand dollars, I made a career change. For the next twenty-five years, I worked for People's Security Insurance. Now, back at that time, they didn't have automobile insurance and all these other insurances. You can get a whole family package of insurance today that one company will cover everything you need. But they didn't have it that way then. The insurance companies would only insure you and your wife.

Now, if they was to call me and ask me to come out to insure Mrs. Brown, I'd say, All right, when will your husband be home?

Oh, he doesn't need to come home. He told me that when I'm taking it out to leave it to you completely.

But we had a strict policy. So I'd say, Well, I appreciate that more than I can ever tell you. And I wish everybody had that feeling. But I will not insure you unless your husband is home there, too.

I'd draw up three different plans. One was a twenty-paid life. The next was a twenty-year endowment which would become cash. The one I liked the best was, you pay it for twenty years and there's two different sets of prices, so if you were younger, you would get it for a whole lot less, because the more elderly you become, the higher the premium is.

So they said, All right, we'll both be home on such-and-such a night. And I'd ring the bell, go in, sit down. I'd take out one sheet of paper, another one and another one, and I'd draw up three plans. I would take the third plan, I would look at them, and I'd say, Now, how old are you? Twenty-eight? Twenty-nine? Well, that's fine. Then I'd show them the policy: You pay twenty years and leave it with the company to invest. Leave it until you're sixty and you'll get a third more than you ever paid in. And that's a nice little nest egg. I wouldn't say, you put a huge amount, that way you'll get back a huge amount. No. I'd say, you put in what you and your wife feel you can afford and no more. Why? Because I don't have anybody cancelling my policies and neither do I want you to cancel. So they were very careful and consequently I had a lowest rate of cancellation of anybody in the company in Washington, Hagerstown, or Baltimore.

The most important thing in my life, I really believe, is that I was helping people. When I was selling insurance, many of them said, We don't have an insurance man, we have a brother. Now, some brothers are not like they should be, but we had the kind that one sticks to another.

—ERNEST C. DEETJEN

I had started working in the Farmers & Merchants Union Bank in Columbus in 1924. I started at seventy dollars a month. I'd've starved if I wasn't boarding out on the farm where I could help my dad weekends and evenings. After I got into the bank, well, naturally, I was interested in watching investments. I had accumulated a little stock and I kind of watched the markets.

Bank robbers, though, were watching the banks. One afternoon, while we were balancing up the day's transactions, we had a call from the protective agency in Milwaukee. What can you tell us about the bank robbery? What bank robbery? we wanted to know.

Turns out the bank across the street was robbed. Four fellows drove up and one of them put his foot in the door just as the janitor was locking up. Evidently they had cased the bank. Two of them went in. They made everybody lay on the floor. They gathered up the money and the securities. Then they ran out and got into their car and started up the street. The fellows in the back seat had several sacks of these big-headed roofing nails that they scattered on the highway, so that the sheriff and those that followed them, all of them soon were settin' on the side the road with flat tires. And here we were, balancing our books, never knew anything about it.

A good many years later, some of that bunch was caught. They found some of the securities way back in New York. They were from one of the organized gangs, Barker-Karpis or Dillinger or one of the break-off gangs.

—AL KRAUS

Paul Onesi, Clymer,
Pennsylvania, around 1917

I came over to the United States from Arquata del Tronto, a village near Catanzaro. My older brother was over here already. He came to make money. I came to make money. I was fifteen.

My first job, I was a water boy when they were building a reservoir in New York. After about a year, when they finish over there, we go to a big town—Indiana, Pennsylvania—to work in the mines. To make money, that was the best place then to go. I had no education; you didn't have to go to school then if you didn't want to. Most of the miners were Italian and Polish, immigrants, young and strong.

It was hard work, oh yeah. Sometime you get up two, three o'clock in the morning to go to work before dawn. You bring your lunch in a pail. It had one place for water in the bottom, bread in the middle, and lunch meat on top. We didn't make sandwiches then.

You work nine, ten hour all the time. The more you work, the more coal you get out, the more money you make: forty cents a ton. Maybe you dig out four, five ton on a good day, diggin' with a pick, kneeling down in little tunnels three and a half, four feet high. Then you'd shovel the coal into cars that would be on tracks that would go out of the mine. Sometimes you work six days in a week, sometimes two; it depended on when the company needed you. And Sunday, Sunday was for drinkin'. All the men used to get together, stay up all Saturday night and on Sunday, we'd go from one house to another, drinkin'.

Always there were accidents, explosions, people gettin' hurt and dyin'. One time, a piece of rock fell down, broke my [pelvic] bone. I go to the hospital. The company no pay nothing. I had to pay. But I no work, I no get no pay. If you didn't work, you got nothing. When the union came, the United Mine Workers, I paid a dollar and a half to belong. The mine owners didn't want the union. One time, the union strike went on three, four months before we had to go back to work. But the union got us a raise, one, two cents more a ton, and more work, steady work.

We lived in a company town. We bought groceries and clothes in the company store. When there was a strike, the grocery store, they trusted you. When you work, you pay them back—they'd take the money out of your pay. They always had you.

Black lung I got from workin' in the mines. A lot of miners died from that. Fourteen years I worked in the mines—Clymer, Ellwood, Starford—till 1927, when I went to work for Union Carbide in Niagara Falls. What did I do when I started there? Worked with the furnaces, shoveling coal.

—PAUL ONESI

The Westmoreland Coal Company had these towns they'd built, they called them collieries, and each colliery had its own superintendent and paymaster, which was my job.

The miners made fifteen cents an hour, nine dollars a week. It was really slavery then. You needed something done for labor. The company's owners didn't welcome the unions, but they came in anyway. There were strikes, and picketing, and fighting all the time. We couldn't join the union, though. We were in supervisory jobs.

But the trouble is the unions won't stop when they get something good and keep things movin'. They go on makin' all these demands. Some of 'em is idiotic, absolutely idiotic. For instance, they had one long-drawn-out strike over the magazine where they keep the high explosives. If you understand mining, they cut the coal with a cutting machine and drill it and order it—they call it orderin'—and they'd use high explosives. The magazine was kept down with the coal party; they had to walk down there to get the explosives. But the union wanted to put it right in the room with them, where if the stuff went off it'd blow 'em into eternity. The company never did accede to this; but they did accede to a lot of things that should have been, just to get along.

—ORLANDO F. MORLEY

My husband and his people formerly lived over near Bluefield before they moved to Logan. He was a mine foreman—a bank boss, they called them.

He was in charge of runnin' the mines. My husband, he never asked a man to go anywhere in the mines that he wouldn't go, or to do any kind of work that he wouldn't do.

The strikes, of course, put him out of work. When they'd come out on strike, he would come home and stay home until he was called back. He never stayed up there during the strikes. Of course, he didn't get paid while the strike was going on. But we bought a house in Huntington and the vacant lot beside it. That give us a great big yard and a great big lot in the back. He put in a big garden in the back of them two lots, and we bought five hundred little chickens and I had a regular poultry business. So we got along pretty good all the time he was off during a strike. We ate good, but the ones that depended on the money from the mines, the ones that lived in the mining camps, they didn't.

—ADA TABOR

At certain times, like during the mineworkers' strike in Ludlow, Colorado, in 1914, many people were killed when the owners of the mines hired goons with guns to shoot the strikers down. Here I come from an aggressive nation, Russia, into a nation that shoots people down. It was a terrific disappointment.

So when we could, some of us acted. I helped the strikers during the Paterson silk strike in New Jersey. There was a woman, much older than I was, and as the strike continued, she wanted to go to Paterson to partake in it. She says, Alfred, come on along with me, I'll pay your way. We went to Paterson. She was greeted by the strikers—she was well known; she was an anarchist. I was enthusiastic, but I was too young to really understand the whole thing.

I followed the strike. When I organized the soldiers and sailors in New York, the Paterson strike was still on, and they had a committee come over to the headquarters of the soldiers' organization to ask us to be pickets. Half a dozen members and I went to Paterson and we were picketing until we were arrested. I knew enough to keep my hands in my pocket. Because there they were known to stick a gun into your pocket. When they'd get you to police headquarters, they'd have you licked. Anyway, my hands were in my pockets, so they couldn't stick anything in there. And they had to let me go because they had nothing on me.

—ALFRED LEVITT

My father was in the construction business. He owned the Davis Cut Stone Company in Columbus, Ohio, and a quarry in Bloomington, Indiana. We'd quarry blocks of stone up to fifty tons for everything from big monuments to whole buildings.

Used to be, we'd blast the rock out. Later we'd drill a hole, run a line down with a weight on it to keep the saw from goin' all over, and just saw right into the stone. Then we'd pick the blocks up with cranes, chip the rough out of 'em, and bring 'em back to our plant. If a customer was gonna make some kind of a monument, we'd use big hammers and chisels to chip a block down to about the size that he needed; then we'd rig it up on a lathe and start turnin' it. For building jobs, we'd machine the stone. We'd roll twenty-foot blocks on a cart along a track and we'd start the saw goin'. In the early days the saws had Carborundum teeth, but they'd always work loose and fly out. Never hit anybody, fortunately. Then we switched to diamond saws.

We only had eight people in our shop, but every one of them worked. They were true and honest, and you don't find that much. We had to deal all the time with unions—bricklayers, masons, concrete men, steelworkers—on building jobs we'd be working on, and we had basically good relations with them. But we weren't a union shop. One union out of Chicago tried to get us to join. I done the talkin' and I says, What can you give us?

Well, if you get in trouble we can come in and fight for you.

I says, If we don't have any trouble, what happens?

We don't have to help you.

I says, Well, what I think is, we don't need your help.

And that was the end of it. We didn't have anybody that really wanted to get in the union anyway. Because in a company that has no trouble, they're not much help.

Cuttin' stone, of course, was hard work. Dangerous work. I talked to the insurance man once. I says, How come my insurance varies so?

He says, Don't you know? You got the worst dangerous business.

Well, I says, we never got anybody hurt, nobody goes blind. The guys are careful. They're told to wear not only safety glasses but other protection all the time, and if I catch 'em without that, boy, I really lay the law to 'em. I know one guy went up told my dad, he says, Your son's crazy down there.

Why? What happened?

He said if I didn't put the glasses on I'd get the gate.

Well, says my dad, he means it, too.

He didn't get no sympathy from my dad.

—JAMES M. DAVIS

My education at Howard University was interrupted when the First World War came on. I didn't get into the Army until the thirty-first of July 1918. The chairman of my draft board—he was the son of one of the strongest families in Edgecombe County—had told my father, When York gets in the war, I'll fix it so he gets the best assignment as anybody. And I did: I was made a company clerk at Camp Green in Charlotte.

After I was discharged, I went back to Howard, which was the best black school then in the United States, and graduated with honors. I went home to Tarboro. My father was having some medical trouble, and I decided he didn't have time for me to be messing around, so I got into business for myself. I opened my own pharmacy, which was something natural for me. Having been brought up in a colored business store, it was just a piece of cake.

A lot of my friends from school went North because they had a better chance to make it. You had a better chance of accomplishing something in a biracial place than you would in an all-racial place unless you had a whole lot of money. Maybe one-third of all blacks that were in the South at a certain time took their chance to go North to get a better break. They went to Washington, to New York, Boston, Philadelphia, to Chicago and Detroit. They wanted to better their status.

I was lucky. I was York Garrett's son and Judson Garrett's brother. Wherever I went—in Wilson, in Charlotte—people would see me and say, You're York's boy? Or, You're Judson's brother? Well, what can we do for you? And I'd say, Anything you want to! They thought Judson was one of the princes of North Carolina. I didn't go anywhere that I asked for something and the answer wasn't: You're York Garrett's boy, of course we'll help you out.

Now, my father was not lucky, he was smart: he did what he had to do to get where he was going. He got very, very much in the societies—the Odd Fellows, the Masons. That was his life. For twenty-five years before he died he was the treasurer of the Grand United Order of Odd Fellows in North Carolina. A lot of black people joined these societies. They had to. Because there were no insurance companies that would take them. So if you could join the Elks or the Pythians or the Masons, you had yourself made: you had people who would help you. Of course, these societies were segregated. But most of them started out as black organizations. They were brought here by blacks from Europe and Africa and Asia. There were a lot of white people who liked what they were doing, and they started their own *independent* orders; the Independent Benevolent Order of the Elks was white.

So I made my way. All the money I got has my name on it. We came to

Durham from Tarboro and did all right. I didn't want to come to Durham, but with the Depression on we were going broke in Edgecombe County. My wife had been in Tarboro all her life, and she wanted to be in a bigger city. I went to Wilmington, Charlotte, Winston-Salem, Greensboro, and Durham to interview people there, doctors and dentists, to see if I'd get their support. I was also looking for a town that had a good school for my kids, because I was thinking about their future.

In Winston-Salem, I ran into a guy who was in medicine at Howard the same time I was in pharmacy. His wife was in Howard Academy when I was there. They had married and had gone to Winston-Salem and were doing real well. And when he found out I was looking for a place to go, he said, If you come here, I'll go with you. You'll get my nephew's support, and So-and-So and So-and-So. But I also went to see Dr. Donell, who was medical director for the North Carolina Mutual Life Insurance Company in Durham. That was the black insurance company. I told him I was thinking of going to Winston-Salem.

He said, I was hoping you would consider Durham.

No, I said, you already have the best colored drugstore in North Carolina in Durham.

He said, You can't reconsider? I'll talk to the president of the Mutual for you.

So he got the other guy to talk to me. He said, If you can consider coming to Durham, we'll give you a good deal. It isn't generally known, he told me, but the drugstore in the Biltmore Hotel is in trouble. Now, there wasn't another decent hotel fit for a black man to stay in between Durham and Washington, D.C.

That's how I found out the Biltmore drugstore was in debt. And I'm leaving Tarboro with no debt. Now, Julia, my wife, said, York, if you can work out something to your advantage, I'll go with you wherever you want to go. But, she said, I know somewhere back down the line something went on between you and one of those girls in Winston-Salem. And she was right. When I was at Howard, I'd gone with this girl. She had a boyfriend, a doctor who was looking for a wife, but she still had some attachments for me. We never did get out of love, see, we just didn't get into love deep enough to get married. And Julia knew that. In a small town, everybody knows everybody. You know the good, you know the bad, you know the indifferent. So Julia said, I'd rather come to Durham and take a chance, but I'll go wherever you decide for us to go.

Well, I got a commitment from Mutual and I took the chance. They told me I would have it made. So I bought that drugstore and we've been in Durham ever since.

But I didn't have it made. I wasn't getting the same breaks from the drug companies that I found out other pharmacists were getting. And I was carrying all these accounts that paid me after six months. Plus the drug company I was ordering from made it harder for me by denying me credit and making me pay cash.

Then I got a call from a representative I knew from the Owen Minor Drug Company in Richmond, Virginia. Doc, he said, we're going to move into Durham. Give me your next order. I'll have it on the express tomorrow morning for you at your door. And you don't have to pay for it for sixty days. He said, I feel you're honest, and I know you'll pay me.

And I did. They have never lost a nickel on my account. I stayed with them for sixty-seven years. In fact, I'm the only person who opened an account with them that long ago who is still living.

—YORK GARRETT

My father and his brother started a stationery store in 1883 when he was fourteen years old. It started as a little store, about ten feet wide, on Penn Street in Reading. They moved three or four times, each move to a bigger store. They developed that store into a school-supply business; that became their big business. There were fifty-eight school districts in Berks County, and Hintz supplied fifty-six of them with slates and chalk and erasers and pencils, everything they needed. It was not my ambition to take over the store, but it did become my livelihood, too.

I wanted to be an architect. I graduated from the School of Architecture at State College in '21. But you're not an architect until you get in business, and I never got into a business that paid the bills. If it wouldn't have been for my parents, I'd've starved.

Well, my father said to me, You better come to work for me. So I did. He put me in charge of gifts and the greeting cards department. From there on, I climbed the ladder as the business expanded.

Selling school supplies became our bread-and-butter. Across the county, there were farmers and businessmen that were on the school board. Well, every time my father went out to one of their school board meetings, it was a gala night. He'd hand out a box of pencils, a cigar, to the men. And to the women, if they wanted one, he'd give them a Hershey bar, something like that, and a box of pencils. Sometimes he'd hand out notebooks. It was like Christmas Eve. And, oh yes, a big bag of peanuts or a big bag of pretzels, and if they were right near a barroom, why, my father would order beer for

William G. Hintz, Jr., in drafting room
at Reading (Pennsylvania) High School, circa 1914

the boys. That was the night we sold the supplies to them. Oh, we had competition. There were smaller outfits, but we were the largest in Reading for many years. We had sixteen, seventeen employees at one time. You needed supplies, you always went to Hintz's.

After my father had passed away, in 1945, I took over the business. Sometime around the early fifties, a man came to me. We're going to start up a mall out here in Muhlenberg Township, he said. How about renting a store or two and moving out?

No, I said, I don't think so.

He said, You'll be sorry. Fifteen or twenty years from now, there won't be anything on Penn Street.

And he was right.

—WILLIAM G. HINTZ, JR.

My father had charge of the wrecking crews on the Pennsylvania Railroad. When he'd come home, he'd tell stories about the people who had gotten killed in a wreck. There were so many horrible stories that my mother vowed she'd never let any of her children work for the railroad. That's one thing she kept preaching all along. Besides, I liked mechanical things like bicycles and motorcycles and automobiles as I got acquainted with them. So I just made up my mind that I wanted to be an engineer.

After I graduated from the Harrisburg Technical High School in 1915, I went to Worcester Tech in Worcester, Massachusetts, to take a mechanical-engineering course. That was considered one of the best engineering colleges in the country. Engineering colleges at that time, you see, were rated by the Navy, which accredited five colleges, because the Navy would give their officers postgraduate work at these schools in their specialty. Worcester Tech was highest-rated in both mechanical and electrical engineering. Their electrical laboratory at that time contained a complete trolley car.

The world then was already changing so rapidly. We had the automobile coming on, we were building bigger and better ships, we were electrifying things. We were getting automatic controls for heating homes. The development of technology was already under way. I was just wanting to be a part of it.

Following graduation in 1920, I found a job here in Waynesboro, Pennsylvania, with the Frick Company. I started with them the first of July. Been working for them ever since.

The Frick Company manufactures industrial refrigeration machinery. While I started with the idea of being an application engineer, their training required that I spend at least a year in the field, installing, which I did. That lasted more than the year before I got back into the office. Then, just three years later, rather to my surprise, I was put in charge of all field installation work. When I first started out, they paid me seventy-five dollars a month, plus living expenses while I was in the field.

When I took over, there was immediately placed under me about thirty-six

Milton W. Garland at his graduation from Worcester Tech, Worcester, Massachusetts, 1920

men. We installed jobs anywhere in the United States, Canada, and Mexico. The installations were in ice-making plants and breweries, cold storage, food-freezing plants, chemical manufacturing plants—just most anyplace where refrigeration was being applied.

I liked my work because there was always a challenge. The challenge here was, what is the heat load? Once the man that designed the reactor told us, I could do a backward computation to figure why the system was failing: Did it fail immediately, when the reaction started, or was it a gradual loss of temperature? Anyways, on the basis of what they told me, I could make my estimate from a scientific viewpoint. They had so much surface, with so much heat they were trying to remove. It was just a matter of estimating the rate at which they were removing heat, and designing the equipment to accommodate that.

Now, I'll tell you, using a computer wouldn't have done us any more good then than it would do us now with that particular type of problem. Yes, I can put it into the computer, but I've still got to tell the computer what this heat rate is going to be. The computer is handy, a good way to go, and maybe faster, but, nevertheless, you only get out of the computer what you put into it.

—MILTON W. GARLAND

I started working when I was fourteen. I was always interested in machinery, so I got a job in the silk mill in Allentown, running looms powered by steam. I moved on to a machine shop in a foundry.

The machine shop ran on rather long hours. We started at 7 a.m. and quit at 5 p.m., except on Saturdays, when we quit at 4 p.m. But we had to come in an hour earlier one time a week to make that hour up. We only had twenty minutes for lunch. We had to bring our lunch, because there was no restaurant there even if we had more time.

While I was working there, I took a course in mechanical drawing and mathematics. That enabled me to get a job in a drafting room of the Ingersoll-Rand Company of Phillipsburg, New Jersey. It was remarkable to work in that quiet, clean drafting room after having worked in that noisy silk mill and that grimy machine shop. After a year and a half, I applied to Bethlehem Steel Company and they took me right away. Their Freemansburg plant, where they sent me to work, made only one thing: shells for the French and British Armies, who were trying to drive the Germans back into Germany. This was in 1915, the beginning of World War I. The plant was running day and night for a while.

John Sailliard at the beginning of his career

After a stint with a company in New York that made aeronautical equipment, I answered an ad in the paper that the Western Electric Engineering Department—eventually Bell Laboratories—wanted draftsmen. I went over there—they were based on West Street, a street that runs alongside the Hudson River in lower Manhattan—and I was accepted.

I enrolled in night courses to take advantage of the opportunities at Bell Labs. Soon I was promoted to chief draftsman. I had twelve men under me, working on improving the printing telegraph, which was replacing the Morse telegraph. In Morse telegraph, the operator sent only one letter at a time. It was terribly slow, and you had to have a trained operator to understand the Morse Code. Our printing telegraph machine was like a typewriter connected to a telegraph wire. It worked beautifully. Finally, Bell Labs—that is, AT&T—decided that it was developed far enough, it was being used, and they stopped all development work.

About that time, talking movies were being developed. The first talking movie had a huge success. So AT&T decided they would spend a great deal of money and develop this talking-movie machinery as far as they could. I was transferred to that job. It was a very urgent job, because every moving-picture theater operator had to replace silent pictures with talking movies if he wanted to stay in business. So the Bell Laboratories and RCA both worked on developing the recording machinery to make talking movies. One of the great problems, of course, is that in the moving-picture machine the film moves with jerks. While it's moving, there's a shutter that cuts off the light; while it stops, the light is allowed to shine. That worked beautifully for silent pictures, but with sound pictures you also want the film to move with perfect steady forward motion. The problem was solved by recording the sound at a spot on the film twenty inches away from where the pictures are recorded. That worked fine and business couldn't have been better.

But then Mr. William Fox, the movie man, bought the American rights to a German patent which he said our invention violated. A tremendous lawsuit was in the offing. We knew that if he won he would take over the rights from the RCA people and he would be a millionaire several times over. Mr. Fox was very clever. He allowed us to develop this machine and install it in theaters all over the country and make a pile of money. *Then* he sued.

The trial was to be held in Scranton. Bell Labs rented a whole floor in the Hotel German. A group of us took all this equipment and installed it up in the hotel, so that the judge could come over and see the actual machinery, if he wanted. Well, he did come over and he looked at it. And he decided that he could not make a decision because he didn't understand the machinery. Send it all over to Lewisburg where I live, he said. Install it in the basement of the post office and I'll be able to study it. We did that. Mr. Judge found against us.

We took the case to the Court of Appeals in Philadelphia. They agreed with the judge. So the only thing that remained was the U.S. Supreme Court. Everything depended on that verdict, because if they found against us, we were going to lose a lot of money.

Well, our lawyer said, They probably won't ask to see any of the machinery, but if they do ask and we don't have it there, it'll look bad for us. So, he says, I want you to send all of this equipment in a huge truck and have it parked in front of the building. And if the court says that it wants to see something, I will give the signal to John Sailliard, he will run out, select it from the truck, and bring it in to show to the court. Well, the court didn't need to see anything, and all I had to do was sit there and enjoy what was going on.

At one point, the lawyer for the other side was pleading with these eight judges—there's ordinarily nine, but one disqualified himself because his son was handling some legal work for Mr. Fox—he said, Now, the patent consists of a number of claims, and if you're taking each one of these claims individually, well, it's nothing unusual, but put all these claims together and you have a formidable patent. And, with that, one of the judges, who I thought had been asleep, spoke up. He said, Isn't that very much like saying that a lame duck could walk well if it had three legs? Well, boy, that upset that lawyer, and it made us feel very good.

When the arguments ended, we had to take all these models and equipment, which had been packed in the truck outside, back to the warehouse. These things were considered so valuable that the president of the trucking company that did the hauling for Bell Laboratories insisted on being the driver of the truck. Well, a few weeks later the court rendered its decision in our favor. Oh, were we happy!

—JOHN SAILLIARD

I had a professor at the University of Washington and he had this good friend in Cincinnati who was with Procter and Gamble. He suggested that I go there. I said, What in the world would a chemical engineer do at an old soap factory? And he gave me a very good answer: They haven't done anything. It's wide open there. That's why it's a good place to go.

For me, it was.

When I first got there, in 1926, somebody took me down a long, long building where they had this huge line of soap kettles, ninety-eight of them, twenty feet in diameter and sixty feet high. It took about seven days, then, to make a bar of Ivory soap. It was a terribly complicated and slow process. I was appalled. I decided right then and there that that had to go. I thought there must be a better way and I got to work and came up with a process of taking the fat and splitting it to liberate the glycerine. The glycerine was a very valuable by-product, so I took it out first, and then they could convert the fatty acids directly into soap, using very small machinery. I got the process down to two hours.

Ivory soap was sort of a sacred cow. They were very proud of it and didn't want to change. So I had to sit down with the chairman of the board. I told him that we who had developed the process thought we had made a mistake, that a bar of Ivory soap would wear away faster. Well, this chairman had come up through sales, and he thought that was great.

In my job at Procter and Gamble, when I could see a weakness in the production of a product, I'd think up ways to correct it. My philosophy was: Can we make a better product more economically? I think that was most of my motivation. I worked on Duncan Hines cake mixes, Zest soap, Jif peanut butter. We made the first really affordable peanut butter. And we had great surpluses of it. Fifty pounds here, fifty pounds there. I put some out for the birds, and the funny part was to watch the way they had to clean their bills after they ate.

I also worked on Pringles potato chips. There was a big market for potato chips. But they were expensive; they were sliced-off bits of potato cooked in deep fat and packaged in big, bulky bags. So I sat down with one of the men in my department and we just sat and talked it over and came up with the idea for Pringles. The way we did it, we packed it under nitrogen. That way, the fat wouldn't spoil. That's why it's packed in little cylinders. Those cylinders are filled under a blanket of nitrogen instead of oxygen, because it's the oxygen in the air that makes anything spoil.

The Pampers story is quite a story, though. Somebody with the company had been over in Sweden and he came back with a "disposable diaper." All it was was a square sheet of paper that would absorb a bit of moisture and had to be pinned together. I said, Well, let's make one that'll fit the baby. This was in 1960. So we worked on it. And I was driving in a station wagon on a highway with my granddaughter. When she needed to be changed, I would simply pull the tailgate down and change her.

My group in Research and Development wanted to try this out on a larger scale. But the trials had to be authorized by the sales people. They got it all balled up. They tested disposable diapers in the middle of a sticky summer in Dallas, Texas. This was stupid. It was a complete failure. Well, I raised a hell of a racket. It was the only time I ever remember going to bat against the people in what we called the city office downtown. I'd advanced far enough in the company that I could make my voice felt quite a bit. You made a mistake in the timing, I told them. Let's try it again. I got them to try it again somewhere else, and it came out all right.

—VICTOR MILLS

At the beginning of 1922, I finally located an opening for which I was reasonably well qualified. I became a financial reporter.

I worked for two remarkable men, Clarence W. Barron and Hugh Bancroft. How C.W. began his career, I do not know—only that he was the founder of the *Boston News Bureau*. At first, the financial news gathered by himself and a very small staff was printed on small sheets of paper, perhaps six inches by nine inches. These were distributed throughout the day by runners who periodically and frequently made the rounds of Boston's concentrated financial district. The subscribers were stockbrokers and banks. In each subscriber's office was a clipboard to which the increasing stack of bulletins was affixed. Shortly after 3 p.m., when the New York Stock Exchange closed, the news thus accumulated was reprinted in an evening newspaper still known to the staff, in 1922, as "the summary." At some point in his career, Mr. Barron bought Dow Jones & Company, publishers of *The Wall Street Journal*, but the *News Bureau* remained first in his affections.

And then Hugh Bancroft, Mr. Barron's son-in-law, for whom I had great admiration, had a brilliant idea: sell the news a third time, at the end of the week, in a magazine which might achieve national circulation. That became *Barron's*. The old man had very little interest, in spite of the fact that he had his name on it. Occasionally he'd write something for it. One dealt with America's railroad network. I saw it in galley proof before and read with astonishment that more railroads served the city of New Orleans than Chicago. And I said, Gee, that doesn't sound right to me. So I got out the Moody's railroad manual. There were twice as many railroads entering Chicago as New Orleans. So I said to Mr. Bancroft, Will you look at this, the old gentleman is wrong. What'll we do about it? Well, if that's what he said, I guess we've got to leave it alone, was his reply. I thought we'd probably get fifty letters pointing out the error. We never got one.

At the newsroom of the *Boston News Bureau* in downtown Boston, I kept busy in my dual capacity as a reporter for the daily paper and feature writer for the weekly magazine. The job was interesting and the news, at times, exciting. For many years American Telephone was a New England institution whose stock was the archetypal widows' and orphans' investment. Its two-dollar quarterly dividend was a fixture, as sacrosanct as the interest on government bonds. Out of a clear sky, with not a rumor circulating in advance, the directors of Ma Bell raised the annual rate to nine dollars. When the news reached our semi-basement quarters, one reporter hastened to write the story. Each of the others grabbed a telephone and placed a buy order with his broker. This was in flagrant violation of the prescribed rules of conduct, but the rules were more cosmetic than binding.

One time I was down in Washington for something else and the head of the Washington Bureau took me to a press conference in the White House. I didn't ask any questions; I just stood there with the rest of them. It was a very different affair from the way they treat the President now. We treated Coolidge very respectfully. It was really very funny. The reporters wrote out questions on little slips of paper. And he had a bunch of them that must have been an inch thick. But if he didn't want to answer the question on top he'd put it on the bottom and go on to the next one. Coolidge, you know, was fundamentally a very smart guy. He knew enough to nap in the afternoon and let the country take care of itself.

One visitor to the newsroom had a great influence on my life. A gentleman named Sherman Adams—not the Sherman Adams who became President Eisenhower's confidant many years later—was exploring the concept of organizing an investment company. He was one of the founders of the first mutual fund. The editor sat on a raised platform, like a teacher in a schoolroom, and my desk happened to be right under his nose, practically. And he used to come over and they'd just think out loud about how you set this up. And I sat there and listened to these conversations as I worked. And I thought, What an interesting idea. So I set up a little investment trust for the Carret family and a few friends, starting with the modest total of some $25,000.

I was soon persuaded to move to New York, the mecca for all ambitious young men in any branch of finance, in 1927. I've been here ever since, working first for Blyth, Witter & Company and then, beginning during the early years of the Great Depression, as a principal for a succession of firms in which I was an officer or partner. I cherished independence highly. Better to be master of one's own destiny at half the income than to be too dependent on the decisions of others.

I am always looking for ideas. I read a great deal. I talk to people. I listen to people in the business. There are very few really original ideas. For instance, a war is very stimulating to some businesses, certainly. Bethlehem Steel in the First World War made armor plate which went into naval vessels. And they were the only company that made it. So they did a land-office business and became a big company as a result.

In 1939, as Hitler expanded the boundaries of the Third Reich and threatened all his neighbors, we had watched with dismay the timid response of Anglo-French leadership. War, we thought, was a certainty. In place of the chronic surpluses of basic commodities and manufactured goods which characterize a free economy in peacetime, war brings shortages. No commodity is more sensitive to such changes than sugar. In tropical countries with abundant rainfall and cheap labor, sugar is usually the principal crop. When World War II finally began, it got off to a deceptively slow start. Raw sugar was selling at about a cent a pound, condemning the laborers on Cuban plantations to lives of misery.

My partners and I felt certain that sugar, the most concentrated form of

Philip L. Carret in Paris, 1951

food energy, would skyrocket. Cuban sugar plantations, for the most part, were owned and operated by public companies. One such was controlled by the Royal Bank of Canada. The company had incurred a burden of debt during the 1920s, had been reorganized with income debentures—interest payable only when and if earned—and a tiny 20,000 shares or so of common stock. Royal Bank owned a majority of the stock. When we stumbled upon the situation, the stock was quoted around six dollars a share. We started buying. As we continued buying the shares, we made a purchase at nine dollars. From a short-term viewpoint, nine dollars proved to be a winner. During the protracted "phony war" period, before Rommel's Panzer battalions outflanked the Maginot Line and raced for the Channel, we bought a few shares at one and three-quarters. As the war in Europe exploded into a struggle so far unmatched in history for the scale of combat, the price of sugar also exploded. Most of the shares we had accumulated for our customers in the one-and-three-quarters to nine-dollar price range were sold at about sixty dollars a share. So our average cost was about six dollars, and our average realization was about sixty dollars. The highest price we got was $200. In seventy years of investing, this is the only stock I have ever sold for one hundred times its cost.

—PHILIP L. CARRET

My father was a builder of horse-drawn carriages. He used to grind his own color and boil his own oil and build the entire carriage from the wheels up by hand. I was young enough to be impressed by that. So I did carry away from Russia a vestige of understanding of paint. Being an artist is another medium of being a poet, only the medium is in color instead of words.

At the Ferrer School, there were artists, promising artists, who were already competent to paint. When I came in there, I didn't know what to do; I didn't know how to make a stroke. So I listened to the lectures. And then I exposed myself to exhibitions in Cooper Union, where I began to understand how you could use a piece of charcoal. I began to fiddle around with charcoal and things began to appear to me.

Then I decided to go to the Art Students' League. Every time I went there, there was a nude model, and you had to study anatomy, because in those days the Renaissance period was still very much the period of art to be studied. You had to know your anatomy. There's a naked woman before you, what are you going to do? How are you going to draw her? So, after so many months, and a couple of years, you began to feel which lines express the various pronounced features of a woman's body.

It was a struggle. I couldn't sell a thing for fifty cents. I just couldn't. I sold apples on Fifth Avenue for five cents an apple. In 1929, I had a basket of apples. In the Depression, I had no money, there was nowhere to turn.

I never wanted to mix up commercialism with the impulse of creativity, no more than I want to mix up hard science with art. Art is the song of a bird. And you can't tell a bird what to sing. That's what art is—good art. The world is full of *schmere, schmere*: paint, paint. Meaningless. It'll never last; it'll never make any contribution. To make a lasting contribution for the next generation to profit by, or to follow, you have to be touching the depth of your feelings and turbulences of life. If there is no depth to your well, there is no water.

Marcel Duchamp and many others realized the importance of breaking away from the Renaissance orthodoxies. And with the debut of the *Nude Descending a Staircase* at the Armory show in 1913, we elevated him to great importance. All of the artists in New York looked at it. Some of them said it was an explosion in a shingle factory. I thought it was great, a great denial of the influence of the Renaissance period.

Marcel lived in a big building on Seventh Avenue near Fourteenth Street. But he paid too much rent, and when there was an empty apartment in my little building, he moved in there. And that's where he lived for sixteen years. His flat was on top, and I was right under him. We became friends. Marcel was always to himself. He was absolutely queer. When he'd meet me in the morning on the staircase coming down, he'd say, Hello, Alfred, good evening to you. Conversely, if he met me going up in the evening, he'd say, Good morning, Alfred.

Sometimes Jerry, my wife, would make a meal and we'd invite him to eat with us. And after that, he'd invite me to play chess with him. We'd go up to his studio. He had a chessboard already in action, never disturbed, because he never finished it. So when we'd come upstairs, he'd look at it and maybe move one piece and leave it there for the next day, until his mind tells him which way to go. He was an exceptionally queer person, but very nice.

Gloucester, Massachusetts, was one of the places to which artists went and spent their summers. It's a colorful fishing town. It attracted me. I rented a room there and found a studio. I stayed fifteen years in that studio in the summers. In the wintertime, we had to come back to work in New York to earn a few dollars.

At that time, I became a student of Hans Hofmann. Hans Hofmann recently came to the United States from Germany and he introduced methods of approach to painting that were entirely radical and tremendously inter-

Alfred Levitt with one of his paintings

esting. Being in the class, I met a woman who came to Columbia University to become an art teacher, to study art teaching. She studied with Hofmann as well. She was young and hungry and very good-looking. We got together. She had no money. She came from a poor family in Bluefield, Virginia, and she didn't know what to do. I said, Don't worry. Let me introduce you to my wife. So I introduced her to Jerry, and they got together. They were friends until the last moment of their lives.

She came in and I said, Don't worry about food. Jerry cooked for three people instead of two. I got her a job. I knew somebody who was a manufacturer of designs for men's ties. I talked to him. And he put her to work. But he never paid her until he sold what she designed. And she starved. So we'd have her over to eat. She had no coat. I took her to a furrier I knew from my connection with Dun & Bradstreet and I got her a coat free of charge. I did everything because she had a great deal of talent. I was jealous of her talent, absolutely jealous. She just filled me up. She moved into our apartment, and she never moved out.

—ALFRED LEVITT

From my nice, clean five-dollar-a-week room on 112th Street in Manhattan I set out in my struggle to "make it." Failure in the big endeavor I had hoped for, yet success in small ways proved to me that this, indeed, is the land of opportunities. If your courage, perseverance, and health are intact, you can regain whatever may have been lost before.

As so often before, courage exceeded intelligence when I made the exhilarating discovery that, unlike in Europe, the chief executives of large corporations would take the time to listen. This was so at Borden and Sheffield, the two giants in the milk industry, with whom I discussed a process for keeping raw milk fresh. Some days after my initial contact, a young engineer who was present when I explained the construction of the containers invited me to dinner. This was marvelous for me at a time when I lived on fifty cents a day. We were sitting in a nice restaurant overlooking Times Square. He told me about the hundreds of millions of dollars his corporation had invested in the present setup in plants and distribution. He noted that wartime conditions would not permit allocation of the material needed to produce the containers. My friendly reception was meant only to gather information from me. Then he pointed quite casually at the traffic and said that traffic deaths are frequent here and not suspected. I think I got the message. Whether my fear was justified or not, I was realistic enough to understand that my milk process was not to be a revolution on the American market.

Without resources, without specific qualifications, without friendly connections, not even able to speak the language satisfactorily, how can I start "making it"? Always I was thinking: I have to take care of my mother after the war. Even then, nobody could have imagined that Germany, fighting a war on two fronts, would set up a giant organization dedicated to the extermination of all Jews. Today, though, we read that our government, as well as the English at that time, already had reliable information about the gas installations in Auschwitz and elsewhere.

For some months I worked in menial jobs, which for me had the great advantage that I could listen to the real, idiomatic language—not the one I learned in the evening school—and talk without inhibition. Reading carefully the newspaper every night, I followed up on an advertisement that guaranteed seventeen dollars a week, the only requirement being the ability to talk! The results of this endeavor were frustrating. Once, though, when I climbed endless stairs to a factory loft in downtown Manhattan, I met again a contemptuous refusal. But I did ask the boss of "Fashions in Leather"—the name was misleading; leather wasn't available for commercial purposes for the duration of the war—if I could have some samples of his wares to sell on my own account. When I returned the next Saturday with my results, he called in all of his salesmen and told them that this greenhorn—me—who couldn't even talk English well, had sold more than all of them. And to me he said, I'll work with you in a way that you'll be competitive. Set up your own firm.

So I did, on Broadway and Thirty-second Street. Of course, I was my own porter, bookkeeper, sole salesman, and receptionist, and in a field I knew almost nothing about.

"Only in America," I think now, is it possible to start an enterprise without means and to grow, in just a short time, from a wholesaler to a contractor and importer of handbags. I engaged representatives in almost all states. I mailed out photographs of new creations twice a month.

The expansion of my firm demanded, of course, employees. Two of them, Hazel Boswell and Lore Wolff, have remained friends now for more than fifty years. We still manage to see each other once a year. They remind me that my working days then never lasted less than twelve but usually ran sixteen hours. Many an evening they stayed, too, and often they joined me Saturdays. Their only reward was that we had lunch together.

The handbag business proved to be so profitable that I felt encouraged to bring my zipper partner and his family over from Switzerland. Their fate is, perhaps, a typical example of a time out of joint: First I was fortunate enough to get them out of Nazi Germany, then out of Italy, and finally, with sufficient capital for their affidavit, to the United States. I had such confidence in the zipper modification unit that I invested all available money in its development, not listening to my horror-stricken, more realistic accountant. In due time, Zips, our trade name, was ready. It made its debut at a national notion show in the Hotel New Yorker. It was a sensation. One trade magazine wrote: There *is* something new under the sun. Two large zipper manufacturers contacted me. They wanted to buy us out, offering the tempting promise of high-salaried positions. What hubris! I had the illusion that I could succeed on a shoestring, without help.

Buyers from across the country were at that show and were eager to place their orders. I refused to accept them. I didn't dare rely on printed materials, which is all I had. I was convinced that a permanent success depended on salespersons who had to be trained. They would learn how easy and quick the cutting of the zipper and the attachment of the end-pieces could be done. With this in mind, I would crisscross the country for years to come.

Informed that the state with the largest sewing population was Louisiana, my Studebaker brought me first to New Orleans. There Honoré Jaubert, head of the most prestigious wholesale firm in the state, followed my request to have one of his salesmen bring me to the most difficult customers.

Later that evening, the incredulous salesman reported that everyone, from the biggest department store to the smallest specialty shop, had purchased the unit. The enthusiasm of the buyers was logical: it saved them the substantial investment of keeping all lengths of zippers in stock and assured additional sales. And a pattern for the future began to take shape. Every day, another salesman went with me to the stores in his territory, in Louisiana, Mississippi, Alabama, south Texas. After three weeks, Mr. Jaubert, a patrician Southerner who hadn't lost the mannerisms of his French antecedents, asked me to write out an order for him according to my judgment. In addition, he said, I didn't need to look for the best wholesaler in other states. The best ones belonged to one association, and on the basis of his report, they would keep their salesmen available for my arrival.

In this way I had the pleasure of meeting all kinds of people in countless towns and cities and villages across the country. How different the Catholic Creoles of the Louisiana bayou were from their neighboring Protestant Texans. One not so young salesman was obsessed with square dancing, a funny spectacle with me in tow. A full-blooded Indian salesman in Oakland, California, was the most gentle person, so long as he wasn't drunk. In Oregon, I was brought by superior salesmen to isolated villages where I met with truly sophisticated, cultured owners of general stores. In Washington, I drove through endless groves of apples with a Seventh-Day Adventist from Spokane. In Salt Lake City, where I learned to admire the community spirit of the Mormons, I was the house guest of John Paul Jones, a bishop in the Church of the Latter-Day Saints. And there I had a living example of how young this country really is: his wife had been kidnapped by Indians when she was five years old.

I spent about two years on the road, sleeping almost every night in another place. At that time, the price of a night's lodging at a good motel was one dollar; a nice guest house included breakfast in the price.

When I returned to New York, I analyzed the overall situation of the firm. In spite of my success, the future did not look promising. Reorders were not coming in. Why?

I went to important clients in key states, not to generate new sales but to discover what was causing this lack of turnover. The results were unexpected. With the development of self-service, there was a lack of trained sales personnel who knew the products. And many salesgirls wished only to hand out packaged goods. From one saleslady in Poughkeepsie, New York, I even got the stern response that her religion did not allow her to cut the chain of a zipper!

How was it possible that I had not anticipated these developments, these psychological factors? In my defense, even the well-established manufacturers had not recognized this or they wouldn't have tried to buy me out at the beginning of my venture. What about the clever merchants, the prestigious wholesalers, the experienced buyers from big department stores who had placed their orders with enthusiasm? But all that was of little consolation. It was I who had lost more than three years and all my hard-earned money. I decided to make a clean cut. The business didn't have debts. I left it all to my partner, who still harbored the illusion he could make it work.

Two engineers in Lugano informed me about a new machine for the ballpoint pen industry. After initial disappointments and disasters, we were able to construct a semi-automatic machine which the expanding American market needed. I was successful beyond all expectations. And another opportunity was on the horizon. As I had to be in Lugano rather often, I visited at the same time a family nearby in Italy. Lino Cattaneo was the owner of a carpet factory created right after the First World War by my late wife's father, who also had to leave Italy after the Mussolini–Hitler pact. I eventually set up exclusive distribution of the factory's production in the East Coast, West Coast, and Canada. Our friendship endures to this day.

—ERICH LEYENS

Women's Work

My hands were never still.

—FLORENCE MORETTI

Born October 11, 1894

Bellegra, Italy

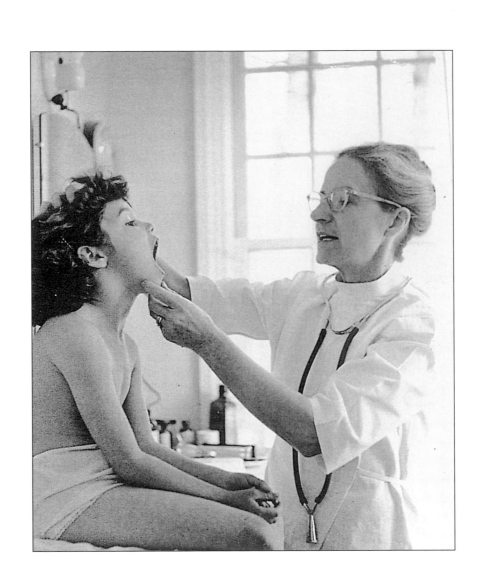

You didn't have much time to do anything but the work that you had to do in order to keep going—laundry and cooking and hand work, all the things you had to do yourself. I didn't go out to work, because I had to be home for the family. At night, when the children were in bed asleep, that's the time I started a new day. I did another day's work from nine o'clock on. I made all my clothes, and all my daughter's. I made all my husband's shirts and I was without a lesson. Then you went to bed and fell asleep if you could. Life came to you and you lived it that day, and the next day.

—FLORENCE MORETTI

My first washing machine, of course, was a Bendix. Now, I had nothing much to say about the purchasing of big items for the home. The Bendix just appeared one day; it must have been about 1930. I said to my husband, Well, what is that?

He said, A washing machine.

I'd heard about them, but I hadn't seen one or experienced one. I said, Well, why are we getting a washing machine?

And he said, So I don't come home to a worn-out old washlady every Monday night.

—ELLA MAY STUMPE

I only went to the fifth grade. Then I went to work finishing furs in a coat factory. I made five dollars a week at first. Every week I would bring my pay envelope home to my father, and he would give me a dollar or two to get by on.

The boss—his name was Izzy Katz—he wanted to marry me. But I was afraid, because he was a different religion. He wanted to come home and meet my father. No, I told him, my father won't hear of it. But I did learn to speak Yiddish, because I worked with a lot of Jewish girls.

I was working there when they had that fire in the Triangle building and all those girls threw themselves out of the windows. So many girls

◄ *Dr. Leila Denmark examining a patient, Atlanta, Georgia, circa 1950*

Virginia Reale, New York City

died in that fire. It was frightening to me because I was working nearby.

—VIRGINIA REALE

Across the street from where we was living was the Triangle Shirtwaist Company. I went there and I offered my services. They were looking for girls. It was after a strike. The workers lost. Then they didn't have a labor union. So they came back to work, take it or leave it. But some of them didn't come back.

I had no idea about sewing; I didn't learn that growing up. They had a machine for me. Just all I had to do was to put a button in and it goes through the waist. This I can do, I don't need good English. I don't know about the conditions. I was there two years, till the fire broke out. I was eighteen.

The company was on three floors of the building. On the eighth floor were the cutters, men, I never even seen them. On the ninth floor were the finishers—mostly women, Jewish women—and the sewing machines. And on the tenth floor were the executives.

Then it was like a clique. There were old-timers and there were healthy girls, European immigrants, and I suppose, with a house full of children, everybody was working to meet a goal. Some girls, they had preference; they were working piecework. For me, for working forty-eight hours a week, I got seven dollars. After two years, I got nine dollars. Nothing extra. We were like slaves. And if you don't like it, you're gone. But I didn't bother with anybody. All I had to do was put the buttons in.

The day of the fire, that was some day. It was about the time to go home, five o'clock. Even before the news of the fire came up, we felt the smell already. It started on the eighth floor. People started to scream and

Rose Freedman, New York City, February 25, 1909

cry and run around. But the doors were closed. The executives didn't want the people to get away with merchandise, or stop working, so they kept the doors locked. Not one person from the tenth floor came down to tell the people what to do. Nobody bothered.

So all that's left is the fire escape. Everybody moved to the fire escape. It was overloaded. It broke. People jumped and fell to the street.

But I'm thinking, What am I going to do? And I'm thinking about my mother—not a damn thing about my father—what will my poor mother do? She wasn't even there; she was in Vienna at that time.

So I'm thinking also, What are the executives doing on the tenth floor? I have to do something. I bent down, covered my face, put my clothes over my head. My eyeballs are gone, I can't see. The walls shook already. I ran up the stairs. Nobody was there. I turned around, I saw three little stairs and an open door, but the flames were coming in. I can't go back down. So I walked up yet two more flights to the roof.

When I came out on the roof, there were firemen. Instead of going down to save the people, they were saving the building. One fireman, he hoisted me up to the roof of the adjacent building. There I walked down ten flights of stairs. Do you think anyone walked me down the ten flights? No. I was sittin' on every single floor, I was so weak. At least I got fresh air.

So I came down to the street. I was looking around. I seen my father. He seen me, and he fainted. The ambulance took him away. I seen another lady I knew and she said to me, Rose, is this you or your shadow? I thought you were dead.

A nice how-do-you-do. She reminds me maybe I would have been dead.

I didn't even turn around when I seen what was happening. One after another would fall. It was awful. Then the owner, he met me and he said he will do anything for me—he meant give me money—to testify in court that I'd saved myself through the door. I said, You're not kidding me, you dirty slob. Nothing doing.

I wouldn't talk about it. I was shaking. It was so scary, how everybody was screaming and crying. One hundred and forty-six women, mostly young, died. So far as I know, I was one of the only women from the ninth floor that didn't.

It was the biggest tragedy of the century.

—ROSE FREEDMAN

We were living in Union Springs, Alabama, when my husband died with the influenza. I had three children. I had a brother in Pittsburgh—it was really in Homestead, Pennsylvania—and he sent for us. Now, my second husband's wife also died of the influenza—the same day as my husband did. And we both had moved to Pittsburgh at around the same time. What had happened was, my brother was married to my second husband's sister, and I guess they kind of decided, Well, these two may as well get married. So we met and married. I had a set of children and he had a set of children and then we had children together: thirteen of them.

My second husband worked in the steel mill. We lived about a block from the mill, and we got so used to the flames coming out of the smokestacks at the mill. Every Saturday we washed windows and we scrubbed the stoops of the soot from those smokestacks. All the children would get up and scrub to get the dust and everything off of the windows and stoops.

But when the mill wasn't doin' too good, when they was layin' people off, I had to work to support everybody—my children, his children, and the ones we were bringing into the world. I worked for a Jewish family up on Squirrel Hill. That was maybe two miles away, the ritzy area. I'd be there every day. Sometimes I would stay on, and my oldest two children would take care of the rest of my babies while I would take care of the Sieffs' children. In fact, my daughter Mary was almost born in that house. Mrs. Sieff finally said to me, Charlie, you're gonna have to go home and have that baby.

—CHARLIE LUE MOSLEY

I had two children when we went out to homestead in Wyoming. I waited eight years and I had another one; he's my bomber pilot. He says he's the odd one in the family. And he is, he's more like me. Then I waited seven years and had two more. We were too busy. My heavens! I was teaching school. I was running the rake, stacking the hay. I didn't have time to stop and have babies!

My husband and his father were carpenters. They built all the new schoolhouses after they opened up that territory. There were several families that moved in there, and they built five new schools. They asked me if I would teach. So I went to Gillette, took the teacher's examination, and got my certificate. I drew the highest wage that they paid then: ninety dollars a month. This was in 1918.

Out there, you had to learn to be self-sufficient. We separated milk with a strainer, a big strainer with a little sieve in the bottom of it. One time I let my littlest one hammer on it with a spoon until he made a hole in it. I threw it away. When John came down, he said, You better save this, it might come in handy someday. You never threw anything away; you'd make it over, and make it do.

You also learned to be self-reliant. Back when we lived at Tabor, Iowa, Mother was sick once and the doctor came—they made house calls then—and he put quinine in capsules for her. He took a knife and he scraped, like, just so much on the blade to go in a capsule. He put it in and put the cap on it. He did this until he had about a dozen, what he wanted for the prescription for Mother. I was so fascinated I decided I was going to be a nurse. That was what I wanted to be.

We had a lot of sickness around in southern Missouri when we lived there, and they always called for Mother. But Mother wasn't able to go one night, and she sent me over in her place. A baby was in convulsions. They had sent for the doctor and he came out. He put her in a tub of warm water and had me hold her head out of the water while he poured hot water out of a kettle around her to warm the water to bring her temperature up where he wanted it, and she went out of her convulsions. She got all right that night, but she died the next day.

Something happened like that years later when we lived on our homestead. One time our neighbor came over the hill: Come quick! My wife's having the baby! I put on my boots, climbed up over the hill, and got there just as soon as I could. And she had her baby. I took the baby and washed it and dressed it and cleaned her up and took care of the bed and went back home. I guess they got the idea that I could do about most anything.

Then one of the fellows that lived up on the top of the hill, their little girl pulled a teakettle of boiling water over on her legs and blistered them clear down. Just blistered them. She went into convulsions. I put her in a tub of warm water and had her father hold her head up top of it, and I heated the water up and brought her out of the convulsions. I did that two or three times. I just picked up what little I knew.

—AUDREY STUBBART

In the fall of 1918 I started teaching in a school west of Goodrich, North Dakota. It was during the time of the war, and teachers were short. I had to walk seven miles a day to school, three and a half miles each way. That was no fun. In winter I dressed warm but I still got cold. I carried my books, water, and my lunch, shoveled the snow, carried my wood, coal, and ashes, cleaned my blackboard, washed desks, cleaned the windows, and kept the floor clean. I never missed a day. No matter how bad the weather was, I was there on time. I was paid $64.35 a month.

I had twenty-three children, from the first grade up to the eighth. When I started out, I told my students, If you behave, I won't be rough. But if you do not behave, I will be. I said, I want you children to know more next spring than you do now. So I had no trouble. I had to quit one year before my term was over; I was sick. And the boys cried just like the girls because I couldn't finish my term.

To be closer to the school, I took a room. I paid twenty-five dollars a month for room and board. I had to sleep in the kitchen at the house where I boarded. I had a single bed with no mattress, just a spring with two gunnysacks filled with straw

Rosie Gries, Goodrich, North Dakota

that didn't cover the whole spring. There was an apple box under the spring, so it wouldn't sag down to the floor.

I was so cold!! There was no heat in that room. There were no covers, either. I took my dress and overcoat and pulled them up over me to keep warm. One night I saw a mouse come up out of the cellar, so at least I had him for company. The family slept in the living room, where there was a stove and some warmth.

I only stayed there a month. It wasn't a fit place. I went back home and walked to school again every day. Many times during the winter, I could hardly see the path because of the blowing snow.

The next fall, 1919, I went to Ashley, North Dakota, to teach. I stayed with such wonderful, kindhearted people. They treated me like a queen. My room and my eats were very good. In 1921 I taught in Eureka. I thought the eighth-grade boys would give me trouble, but they didn't. They were just as nice as they could be.

On Mondays I had to get up at four in the morning and get my dinner and my sausage ready to take to school. I had to go nine miles and it was 11 a.m. when I got there. It seemed the faster I went, the slower I moved. I was just like a grizzly bear, all covered with frost and cold in the below-zero weather.

One time, years later, I was in McClusky. A lady sat down beside me. I looked at her and I said, Seems to me I saw you someplace.

She said, You were my teacher. And you were the best teacher I ever had.

I said, Oh, come on, you had high-school teachers better.

Oh, no, no, no, she said. You helped me and the rest never cared for me.

—ROSIE GRIES

"Art" was next to a dirty word. It had nothing to do with making a living. But I was determined. After I graduated—this was in 1916, when I was twenty-two—I went out to Hood College here in Frederick and got an appointment with the president. Did they have anything I could do in the art department? Well, they were poor as church mice then, but Dr. Atwell took me. I wouldn't ever tell anybody what they gave me, but it was something. And I got a room at the college, my meals, and there was a bathroom at the end of the hall that everybody had to use. I loved it there.

I went in as an assistant to Miss Floie, who was at the head of the art department for twenty-five years. I taught art there, painting and all kinds of crafts. I loved the girls so, and we would have such fun.

I was at Hood eight years. But I was getting so tired of the students. Some of them didn't have much ability. We'd have exhibits and I'd try to boost them and we'd please the parents and they'd think their daughters were very talented. Anyway, I just thought I would like to do work that I could finish instead of this piecemeal work I was doing on my own. And I thought maybe if I could get a cheap storeroom I could have a shop.

So I looked around and I found an old place in Frederick that I thought might work. I found out who owned it and made an appointment to call on them. When I went to their house, they asked me, What are you going to sell? I said, Oh, my paintings. If I said scarlet fever or hydrophobia, it couldn't have been worse. Oh my, such stares! I didn't know how biased people were then.

But people liked to come in. I don't know that I made much money. I sure didn't charge any more than I had to, 'cause, for one thing, people didn't have very much money to spend, and not for things that they didn't have to have, either. But I was there ten years. I lived in a little apartment two blocks down. When I had an urge, I'd go racing down the two blocks to work on something or other. I painted on china, 'cause I had my kiln. But what really took over—and, boy, would some of those department stores have loved to get in on that—was painted brooches.

That first year I was in business, I was so scared I wouldn't make it that I took in pupils at night. Now, that was something, 'cause it was hard work through the day, then I had to, quick, straighten up and put out tables for my pupils and then clean up afterwards. Boy, I sure worked hard! And relax? Who ever heard of relaxing? No, you didn't do any relaxing, you just went ahead and you fell into bed and went to sleep. It was hand-to-mouth a lot of times.

But it made me work so hard. I was always so busy I'd almost go to sleep standing up. I moved to another storeroom, a bit more upscale. I

Helen L. Smith, Frederick, Maryland

lived over the shop. I did all kinds of painting as well as lots of gift-shop things. I had three girls helping me. Barrels of stuff would come in that had to be unpacked and I had to do that. The express people would bring them, and the barrels would stay in the corner until night. Then I'd have to go down and open up the store and mess up the place and get all that material out and checked and priced and shelved and about half of it stored for future use.

I was there five years and I was so worn out I thought I'd just get out of the shop business and maybe, my thought was, I could find a simple little home where people could come and browse. 'Cause I'd built up some trade with my painting, and at that time people were beginning to pull trays and things out of the cellar and the attic that they wanted decorated. And old picture frames. I invested in prints that would fit into their frames. So I bought this place in 1940 and I've been busy ever since.

—HELEN L. SMITH

In Holland, I had been spellbound by the antique stores that lined the squares, and had spent hours picking out copper and silver and tiles. In Haarlem, I bought six plates with a beautiful lustre glaze. Back in Los Angeles, where I was then living, I decided I wanted a teapot to go with them. Frustrated at being unable to find one anywhere, a young actor friend of mine suggested I take a ceramics class at Hollywood High School and make one myself.

The next day I enrolled, expecting to make a teapot in twenty-four hours. I made two plates, both horrors, then modeled two figures which, for some inexplicable reason, someone bought. Thereupon, with my arrested financial brain, I reasoned that if I continued selling my pieces I might supplement my miserable seventy-three dollars per month income. Of more importance, when my hands touched the clay, it was as if a door had opened. I became infatuated with clay and glazes and spent the next three weeks in the library reading back issues of the *Ceramic Society Bulletin*, hoping some of the information would sink into my unconscious. It certainly did, but my primary concern at that time was economic, not artistic. The Depression was on.

In those days no one was making pottery and decent ceramic materials were simply not available. In spite of the crudeness of my pieces and bad glazes, my figures sold. One, representing the Duke and Duchess of Windsor, attracted many to my shop window. I was absorbed in pottery, and at my little shop on Sunset Boulevard in Hollywood I was experimenting with decent glazes and also beginning to make a profit.

We built a house on a small lot on Sarah Street in what is now North Hollywood. The lot had seventy-five feet of frontage, tall eucalyptus trees and a small ditch at one side that we were assured was safe from flooding. Later we added a workshop in back.

It was February 1938. Towards the end of the month rain began falling like a gray curtain. It stormed for two weeks and the ground was saturated.

I walked out under the eucalyptus trees and stood on the wash watching the water slowly running down. To my horror, I saw the earth falling into the water and phoned the Highway Department for sandbags. In the late afternoon it started to pour again. By dawn the wash had become a torrent. I began putting furniture on top of tables, in case the water reached the floor of the house.

The waters grew fiercer, the wash larger. By five o'clock, neighbors conceded that it might be wise to move the furniture and cars to a higher street. In the darkness came a shrieking sound. One of the eucalyptus trees went down like a match, borne away by the torrent. Soon another popping noise and a second tree went down, and a third and fourth. The raging, snarling waters were now at the doorstep of the workshop. A shattering noise of wind arose and in one gulp the workroom disappeared. I watched without feeling—in a disaster, feelings disappear.

Neighbors on high ground invited us to their home for the night. Eleven of us were marooned; bridges were down and no rescue teams could reach us. The night was dark without electricity and the storm shook the house as we stretched out on the floor trying to sleep. At one o'clock in the morning I heard an angry clattering noise and saw a flash of lightning. In that very moment the river took our house in a single gulp.

The next day the rain stopped and the sun came out shining. It was the third of March, my birthday. The trees, workshop, house and even the land had been swept away and destroyed by the deluge. Only a row of flowers was left, defying disaster.

The Arensbergs, who had moved to Los Angeles from New York, volunteered to put us up for the first few days. I arrived mud-splattered, unwashed, uncombed, the sound of roaring water still beating in my ears. At dinner Walter Arensberg remarked, We have been all day with decorators, for we are doing over one of the rooms. You know the color of the wallpaper is very important.

How could wallpaper matter when my home, my workshop, my hopes, my future were gone? Suddenly I saw how relative everything is. Wallpaper is important to one who already has security. I had none. I had fifty dollars in the bank. Yet, never had I felt so free, my only estate being my spirit and the air I breathed. I had faced death; now I faced life and with every breath I felt fulfilled. Gone, I thought, were my ideas of ever making pottery again.

Hearing there was a disaster fund for flood victims, I encouraged Steve, the man with whom I shared a house yet with whom I had a purely platonic relationship, to investigate. He registered for assistance, but when the Red Cross invited him to come to their office, he hesitated. I decided to go myself. The Red Cross officer, Miss Selby, listened attentively as I answered her routine questions. Walking with me to the door she remarked, I will see what can be done. But do not raise your hopes. Maybe we can get fifteen dollars to replace your glazes. I doubt that I can manage much.

Three weeks later Miss Selby phoned. Miss Wood, I am glad to tell you that the disaster fund of the Red Cross is giving Steven Hoag $900 to buy a new lot, $500 for you to start a new workshop, $125 for a new kiln, plus $100 for materials.

Thus, the Red Cross enabled me to pick up the broken pieces of my life. It was a gift that had no measure . . .

Ojai was the pot of gold at the end of a long, obstacle-strewn rainbow. From the moment I arrived in Ojai on March 3, 1948, time ceased. The fact that the house was grim, with unpainted brick walls, did not matter, nor that the rocky acre did not have one blade of grass. The only living thing was an "old man" cactus which I brought in a pot. Before unpacking I planted it, and in the next twenty years it grew six feet. I rushed to a nursery and bought two eucalyptus trees, painted the gray exterior of the house pink and blue, and then did what Frank Lloyd Wright asserted was a crime—I planted rose bushes and vines all over the place to hide its barren and bad architecture.

I arrived in Ojai with only enough money to live on for three weeks. For six months I ate in the workroom, for there was no kitchen, and slept in the exhibition room because there was no bedroom. I did not care. At last I was in Ojai, surrounded by luscious hills.

The very first day someone came and bought pottery and several other sales followed during the month. But I did not enjoy selling my work. One man complained, Tell me something about the bowl. Sell it to me.

Feebly I replied, I don't know what to tell you, and let the man walk out. I could not pressure people to buy; it just was not in my nature to market myself. Sometimes I succeeded despite my nature.

My first big sale was to a short, thin, overdressed man who came with his genial wife. While she chose pottery, he stood by, his face pinched and formal. I tried to talk to him, but he kept backing further into the wall. His wife bought several pieces, amounting to the unheard sum of $450. I acted as if it were peanuts.

After they left, I rushed into Steve's room and, in excitement, cried, What do you think of this check, can it be good? It has a funny name that I cannot pronounce.

Steve put on his glasses and grumbled. What's the matter with you? Christ! It is from Zellerbach. You bet it's good!

Beatrice Wood, Ojai, California, 1961

Zellerbach. Who is Zellerbach?

He is president of the biggest paper company in the country.

And here I had feared they might be con artists!

On another occasion a couple walked in and the wife pointed to a bowl. How much is that?

Seventy-five dollars. Just as I was about to tell her there were less expensive things in the next room, her husband asked about a pair of kissing fish.

I did not want to sell them, so I priced them at an exorbitant $350.

Without batting an eye he announced he would take them. His wife, also without hesitation, took the bowl.

It was such unexpected windfalls that made it possible for me to keep going. I did quite well after an exhibition where a couple had seen some cups they liked. They came to the studio and bought six of them, but as I was packing them up they remarked that they seemed paler than the ones in the show.

That was another set, I replied, made especially for the exhibition. It is very expensive so I put it aside.

They asked to see it.

The gallery had priced the tea set at $1,500 for it had a rare iridescent glaze. I brought it out of the storage area. I did not have the nerve to ask so much money, so I mumbled $1,200 and made a move to take it away.

Twelve hundred? We'll buy it. In addition they walked off with a figure and several gold lustre bowls.

One of the nicest sales I ever made was to a dignified man who announced upon arriving, I have one shelf full of pottery that is five thousand years old and another of pottery one thousand years old. The third shelf is to be modern pottery and I want all of it to be yours.

—BEATRICE WOOD

I started selling Avon products in 1938. One day a lady came to my house and started me in my Avon career. I had no money, but she talked me into it. I had to borrow five dollars from my mother for the samples.

The first year, a tube of hand cream was ten cents. That's what people bought, things like creams for the hands, nothing luxury, no powder, no lipstick. I had $1,200 in sales that first year. I got forty percent of what I sold. And so many called me a dumb fool at first. Days I walked from house to house I was the only one on the street. Carrying two bags. Thirty below. Face wrapped up. Nothing on the street but ice. I had to go to ten places to get one dollar. But I stuck with it. I had to. I had no other income. I had a family.

Six days a week I sold Avon. My housework was done at night. Many nights I never got to bed. When I went out selling I always got up at four o'clock. I fed the chickens and hoed two hours in the garden. By morning my clothes were on the line and my bread was baked. I always made my own dough. There was no bread to be bought in the stores and no frozen dough.

Then I packed my stuff and at eight o'clock I was on the road. I worked from eight o'clock in the morning until six o'clock at night, summer and winter, every day except Sunday. Many nights after supper I went out again. I walked house to house many times when it was ten to thirty below.

The first twenty-five years, I sold Avon walking from house to house. I caught rides to get to the next towns—Hurdsfield, Denhoff, and McClusky. Later they gave McClusky to someone else. That hurt. I lost all my good friends and customers there after I worked so hard to get them.

Later I got a car and I put on a lot of miles. I made eighty miles a day and in the summer it was 100 to 110 miles a day, rain or shine. I paid $150 for that car, which had 96,000 miles. One tire was on the car seven years. It was just smooth, but it never blew up. I could make a lot more money with the car. Some years I drove 12,000 miles, selling Avon.

One time I had a close call with thieves. I had cashed my checks at the bank in McClusky because the bank in Goodrich charged me extra for cashing them there. I had a hundred dollars that I intended to send to Avon the next day.

As I was leaving town, I noticed a car behind me with a man and woman inside. It had California license plates. Every place that I stopped to sell or collect, they were right behind me. I never did catch on. Finally, I started for home.

I always drove slowly, but the car did not pass me until I was two miles out of McClusky. It went around me and stopped. The man got out of the car and stood in the road, trying to get me to stop.

Another car came and I got behind it and drove around the man. When the news came on an hour after I arrived home, it said that a car with California plates had stopped a trucker between Steele and Jamestown. They made him lie on the ground, the woman held a revolver to his neck, and they robbed him of forty dollars. I would have been a dead duck if that car hadn't come by.

—ROSIE GRIES

The first chief justice of the state of Mississippi, Abram Fullerson Smith, was my great-great-grandfather. He was a lawyer, became a judge, went to the legislature, splashed around a great deal over the years of 1800, 1812, 1820. And that had apparently stayed in my brain as I was growing up. I would brag on it every once in a while, you see; my mother was proud of that heritage. My father was a civil engineer and didn't know anything about law, except what it takes to get through life. He graduated from the University of Virginia in civil engineering, and more or less by accident came to Mississippi.

After I graduated from college, I would've studied in New York, but Columbia University wouldn't let me go to its law school. You see, I had a conception in my mind of what I considered the best. The public rated Columbia University very high, and I was anxious to graduate from what I considered the best law school: Columbia. But they got snubby and wouldn't admit me, because they never had any women in the law school. They were keeping it exclusively for men. So I just packed up and said, Goodbye, New York, I'm going back to Mississippi, where they'll let me do what I please and be glad to have me. I knew a lot of people, and my family were known. I knew how to live comfortably. I enrolled at the University of Mississippi Law School.

By good luck, my husband-to-be wasn't in that class, so I didn't have to bash him down. But it was kind of funny: One day, I went into this little club room where students would get together before class. I didn't do this regularly, because there wasn't any other women, and I didn't want the young men to think I was disrupting their recreation.

But I went in that morning, and this young man had a five-dollar bill. I said, What are you doing with that?

Oh, he said, It's going to be mine. I bet it on you, that you will lead the law class.

Well, I said, you're mighty reckless with your money, but we'll see.

I think that was just the little slight stimulation I needed to give me the ambition. And, of course, it ended up that I led the law school that year, and received all sorts of honors and commendations: first woman to graduate, and graduates at the head of her class. That was in 1922.

Like my mother, I served in the Mississippi legislature. I was there in about '32. The legislature's a tricky place, you know. They laugh very much in the legislature. I had the floor once, to get a bill through. And this young man, who was in his first term and whom I had helped to learn some of the intricacies of parliamentary maneuvering, somebody put him up to do some dirty work—whoever was behind it didn't have the nerve to do himself—and try to frighten me.

Here I was up in front of the Speaker, ushering this bill through. And he started asking me these rather impudent questions. Everything he knew, I'd taught him, and he was being so obviously ungrateful. So finally I got fed up and I told him: Sit down, you dirty scoundrel! I don't know, and I don't care, who put you up to what you're trying to do, but you take your seat

Lucy Somerville Howorth, to the right of Eleanor Roosevelt, who is speaking at a dinner held in connection with the Herald-Tribune Forum, Washington, D.C., circa 1944

and keep it. And don't act like you think you can take over the Mississippi legislature! They heard me down at the other end of the capitol, and the other senators came piling in, wanting to see what the racket was. It didn't disconcert me, though; I only got a little ruffled.

President Franklin Roosevelt named me to the Board of Appeals of the Veterans Administration. Later I became General Counsel of the War Claims Commission. I knew that Washington was the center of activity. If you had Washington support, you could go from that to spreading out your accomplishments.

I was a great admirer of Eleanor Roosevelt, and she liked me. Of course, she couldn't spend much time with anybody, she was hopping around so. She landed several good appointments for me. There was a woman in New York that wiggled her way close to Eleanor Roosevelt, and she did give Mrs. Roosevelt some good advice about people to pick up and help. She included me on her list of beneficiaries. Mrs. Roosevelt was an ambitious, fine person. She wasn't going to let her husband be made an invalid in the public eye. She helped train Elliott how to assist his father, and nobody thought about a cripple when the sergeant-at-arms made the announcement: *The President of the United States*. A lot of people didn't like Elliott, and I didn't really very much; he was kind of sticky. But when it came to helping his father, he was a master.

Mrs. Roosevelt had a group of twelve women. A woman in New York told Mrs. Roosevelt she thought some of the younger women in Washington should be encouraged to get into public affairs. She said, I'll pay the costs of their renting a room and arranging to have this group and to pay a leader if necessary to come down from New York to help. So Mrs. Roosevelt selected a dozen women around Washington. She put me in that group. And that was really the first selective process that I was put in that gave me an advanced opportunity, and we began making ourselves felt in Washington.

Washington is, or was then, really not much more than a large country town, and it responded to individual efforts. But if you want to study spite, Washington is a good place to do it. And it hasn't changed that much.

—LUCY SOMERVILLE HOWORTH

On the farm I was born on in Bullock County, Georgia, we had all kinds of animals—dogs, cows, hogs, chickens, geese. I was always doctoring some of these animals; it was just in me. My mother wanted me to learn to play the piano, but I'd be taking lessons and all the while I was thinking about something I was going to do with the animals. I don't know how you'd ever say when I decided to study medicine.

After I graduated high school over in Statesboro in 1918—there was no high school in our town—I went to a Baptist women's college for four years. My father, he could have done most anything he wanted to, but I always wanted to run my own fair, so I paid my way through there by waiting tables and doing things I wanted to do. My last year there, I taught science at the college. One of the professors knew I was interested in science, so he fixed me up with a dissection laboratory, and I learned lots about dissecting different animals.

Then Mr. Denmark and myself—we had been children together—we kind of got engaged, and I decided to give up that idea of studying medicine and get married. I taught science for two years. And then Mr. Denmark got an appointment as a banker in Java. He couldn't miss that opportunity, but he could not take a wife with him—it took three months on a boat just to get there. So I decided to give up the teaching business and go to medical school. I went to Mercer University to get the rest of the credits I needed to get to enter medical college.

I talked to people about going to Emory University. They said if a woman ever went to Emory they'd have to have two schools. So I sent in my application to the Medical College of Georgia. When I didn't hear from them, I decided to go down there and see about it myself. They told me that they wouldn't be able to take me that year—1924—and I said, Well, I'm getting older and I want to go this year. They said, Well, wait till tomorrow and we'll see if we can take you. The next day, they said I could stay. There were fifty-two other students in my class. I was the only girl.

Back then, women weren't doing that; Southern girls didn't do that type thing. They felt maybe a boy might tell a dirty joke or do something untoward. But I lived there four years with those young men, and there was never one thing that went wrong. The professors were awfully kind to me and all of the boys were unusually nice. We had a glorious time.

Seventy-two hours after I finished college, I got married. My idea about medicine, if I had never gotten married, was to probably go to India and doctor the women there; at that time a woman in India could not have a

Leila Denmark was the only woman in the graduating class of 1928 at the Medical College of Georgia—and only the third woman to graduate from the Medical College

man doctor. But we got married and we headed for Atlanta, and my idea of going anywhere else ended. And then, when I got to Atlanta, somebody at the university told me that they might be opening up a babies' hospital, and I should go to see a Dr. Roberts, who would be head of the hospital. So I went to see Dr. Roberts and told him I'd like to be the intern. And he said sure. He didn't question me at all, took me right in, and I stayed there two years. Then I left them, went to Children's Hospital in Philadelphia, stayed there for a while, then came back to Atlanta and went in with another doctor. Then I opened my own office.

When I got to Atlanta, I worked in the colored hospital for a while, until we got Egleston Hospital built. When they opened up Egleston, I went there for two years. And then I started going to Central Presbyterian Clinic, one of the greatest missions I've ever gone on. It was in the Central Presbyterian Church, right in front of the state capitol. I went there every Thursday for fifty-six years to give my time and services as a physician.

While I was there, in 1932, we had one of the worst whooping-cough epidemics we'd ever had. I got interested in that disease, seeing that children were dying with it, and I felt that there was something we could do. I started in the research on that, and worked out the whooping-cough vaccine.

When I opened my office, people were so wonderful to me. And those I treated, they always stayed. Right today, I'm seein' the third generation. I never let a patient's race make any difference. They were never too poor, never too rich, never too clean, and never too dirty. It didn't matter whether they paid or not, because Mr. Denmark made the living—he was one of the officers in the Federal Reserve Bank. I didn't have to practice medicine to make a living. And I never had to charge people much.

—DR. LEILA DENMARK

I just wanted to be a worker. And I *was* a worker. I done every kind of work that was honest since I been born. I worked in the field with the hoe. I worked the garden. I planted cotton, chopped cotton, picked cotton—I could pick as much cotton as anybody. I shucked peanuts. I pulled corn off the stalk and tied it up in bundles. I kept house. I raised a family.

And I was a midwife. I helped black folk and white have their babies. I didn't want to be a midwife, to tell you the truth. But white women that was bringing children into the world thought so much of me they wanted me to help them. I wouldn't do it unless the doctor was with me. And when the doctor went and delivered the baby, he give it to me. I would not cut the labor cord; that's the only thing I would not do.

I was with a white woman one Easter Sunday mornin', and the doctor wanted to go fishin'. So that doctor, he said, Sallie, this damn woman won't have this baby. He said, I'm gon' send her husband away. Well, the man ain't got two yards from the house when that doctor shot the woman harder than he ever shot the mule. I said, Doctor, what for you shoot that woman like that? He said, You shut your mouth. I got to go in here.

Well, when the baby come, he cut the cord and handed the baby to me. And I said, Now, you know you cut the cord too short.

Hell, he said, I don't care, I'm leaving here.

That was the doctor. A white doctor. And he said, I'm gon' leave her to you.

So I dressed the baby and dressed the woman and got everything straight and went to church. When I got back from church, her husband was at me, saying, Sallie, you got to come out and do somethin' with that baby, it's bleedin' to death.

I called the doctor. And he said, I'm damned if I'm comin'. If you don't tend him, he won't get no tendin' by me today. Now, he done delivered the baby, and cut the cord. I didn't cut the cord; I didn't know what to do.

I knowed another doctor. I called that doctor and told him the shape the baby was in. I said, Dr. Parker, this is Sallie. I been with you on many cases. I said, Now, don't you let me down here this mornin'.

And he come and saved that baby. But for that I won't say what he called the other doctor.

That baby growed to be a man and got married and he moved here in town. I was goin' to work one day—I had forgot all about him—and he come out of his house and he said to me, You saved me, and I got to hug you. And this was a white man, married then and had children.

So, I said, Well, I don't know you.

He said, Do you remember the baby that was bleedin' to death and you saved him?

I said, You that baby?

He said, Sallie! And he grabbed me in a hug.

—SALLIE JORDAN

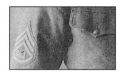

As a teenager, I was a voracious reader

of war books. I thought that

if there ever was another war, I would

rather ride a horse than be a foot soldier.

But, of course, I regretfully figured

there would be no more wars.

—JOHN DODGE CLARK

Born July 19, 1895

New York City

I enlisted in 1916 during the Mexican border dispute. Never got to Mexico, darn it. They told me there's nothing down there but sun, sand, and snakes, anyway. There was this real Mexican hero by the name of Pancho Villa, he crossed the border and killed several American citizens. General "Black Jack" Pershing was put in charge of many troops to get the guy, but they never got him. That's what I missed. A few months later, we went to war with Germany. I'm in uniform. Everybody that was in then wanted out. And most everybody that was out wanted to stay out. They wanted to throw me out, but I stayed all the way through.

Arthur W. Hamer, Sr., 1917

We left out of Norfolk, Virginia, on the *Princess Matoyka*. We encountered a submarine the very first night, just outside of Norfolk. And me, I could get seasick in a rocking chair. Twelve days I'm seasick, until we landed at Brest on a beautiful June day.

Don't ask me about the war, though. I read somewhere that nature provides that your mind does not dwell on the bad things. If you dwell on the bad things you end up in the state hospital somewhere. The worse is the memory of it.

I saw combat. I saw buddies die. Joe McCoy was a friend of ours. I could touch Joey right now. We caught machine-gun fire. Joey has his gas mask across his chest. One fellow right beside him catches a bullet and dies. I go down to the side of his face. Joey goes down about the same time. Joey grabs his helmet and throws it away. *Put, put, put, put, put.* Next *put* gets Joey. They miss me. I'm trying to get that gas mask from under—*put, put, put, put.* I get down even farther. Bullets hit all around. *Put, put, put, put.* Missed me by one-tenth of a split second. Because if it hit me it'd run through the top of my helmet right into my brain. Lucky.

But don't ask me about the war.

—ARTHUR W. HAMER, SR.

I was born in the town of Wesel in the kingdom of Prussia that only in 1870, after a victorious war against France, was incorporated into a united Germany. And the Prussian king was made the German Kaiser (emperor).

What I recall as my very first impression as a child were the ubiquitous glamorous uniforms, the military music, and the high-stepping, breathtaking military parades. Four regiments were stationed within our small city. Through elementary school, through the Gymnasium, or high school, our adulation for our "God-like Kaiser" grew and was systematically indoctrinated. For the average teenager, the heroes—and heroes seem to be needed by people in every country—were not the remarkable industrialists and merchants in a mightily growing nation, nor the poets nor composers of worldwide fame. On top of the social ladder was for us the strutting lieutenant of the Armed Forces.

The three boys in our family were brought up with the "Prussian ideal" of Duty, Obedience, Responsibility. My brother Walter and I joined a new Youth Movement, where we happily toughened up during the long summer vacations. With heavy knapsacks, we often hiked thirty, forty miles in a day, sleeping in our tents or in the barns of peasants. It would be considered "bourgeois"—soft—to go into an eating place; we always cooked our meals in the open. In those weeks we learned that there were still more people living in the country in their traditional way, as self-sufficient as they had been for thousands of years; to us, it appeared that the peasants had more in common with peasants in faraway countries than with their compatriots in nearby cities.

We could see how little the industrial civilization had penetrated their lives. Once we set up our tents close to the forest in the Harz Mountains. Boys and girls from a neighboring village joined us as we were singing around a fire. It was almost dawn when they invited us to come with them to see a miraculous thing. They guided us for well over an hour through the woods to where, lo and behold, a railway train passed!

Sometime later, we ourselves had an equally surprising experience. Near the city of Erfurt we saw for the first time—it was 1911—airplanes: seven of the famous biplanes which just a few years later would play such an important role in World War I. Little did we realize how their development would change warfare and civilian transportation.

When in August 1914 war broke out, when our "peace-loving" Germany was attacked from all sides—so we firmly believed in our love and faith for the country and the "Monarch by the Grace of God"—every able-bodied man rushed with almost ecstatic enthusiasm to the colors. So did we three brothers: Heinrich, then twenty-one, Walter, eighteen, and I, sixteen years old. We survived. But two cousins aged nineteen and eighteen were missing in action and their parents announced their deaths *in stolzer Trauer*—in proud mourning.

This will be a short, cleansing thunderstorm, said our Prime Minister. And our beloved Kaiser Wilhelm promised the soldiers: You will be home before the leaves have fallen from the trees.

Erich Leyens, left, with sister, Grete, and brother, Walter, 1915

Nature provides every healthy teenager with the stuff that makes a good soldier, and for more than four years I wasn't an exception. It is foolish to project the wisdom of age—and the most natural ethical principles—onto the past. Recollecting episodes from "my" war, I must offer this caveat: "I did it," says my memory. "I did not do it," say my pride and my conscience, and remains inexorable. I refuse to be the same human being I was as a boy in uniform more than eighty years ago. And I am afraid that every soldier who suffered in misery and real combat, in any war, may share my painful feelings.

May 1915: My saddle is stolen while I am asleep in the stable with my two horses. I was at that time one rider of the six horses pulling a cannon. So I steal another saddle from a neighboring battery. It is the first time that I experience the thrill of a criminal and bask in the approval of his peers.

September 1915: The first gas attack of the war. We survive by pressing pieces of cotton, drenched in our urine, against our noses. While we fire wildly from an advanced position, the terrific noise usual in a major battle recedes to eerie silence. The enemy has broken through at our flanks. We are isolated. Running back, afraid of being captured, we are three days erring around. Eventually we find our battery far behind the front. Fortunately, I bring with me a calf which I had stolen at dawn. The "heroes" of our *Gulaschkanone*, the kitchen on wheels pulled by horses which was used to bring hot soup to the front lines at night, are delighted—and they are influential enough to save me from a court-martial as a suspected deserter! This is the first time—and not the last—that I am reported to my parents, officially, as missing in action.

November 1916, at Verdun: Helmut van den Bruck, a friend and neighbor from my hometown, repairs with me a telephone wire that we had laid to the trenches hours earlier but that has already been destroyed by enemy fire. In open view we are an easy target. One of the feared "fucking fires"— brisance shells—explodes right behind us. Helmut falls over me, perforated. I am without a scratch. I carry him back, but he dies within an hour.

Two days later, I stumble through an endless morass. I feel the need to be at Helmut's burial, miles away, far from the front. The mud is so sticky that often my boots don't come up with my feet. For many hours, deep in the night, I march on, scared, demoralized, hitting the mud with every nearby explosion. At dawn, exhausted, I arrive, to be shouted at by the officer in charge about my appearance. I faint. The now eighteen-year-old boy is not the hardened soldier he pretends to be. Helmut's brother, who is on the regiment's staff, is present. He is more of a comfort to me than I am to him.

1917, still at Verdun: We keep an English trench under steady fire before a planned attack. Then it becomes strangely calm. I am an observer in the trench closest to the English position. I have the idea to crawl through the barbed wire into that silent trench. There I am amazed to discover that it is abandoned. It is as miserable a place as our own, with one difference: I can pocket some marvelous stuff—unforgettable cans of smoked eel, genuine silk shirts, which we believe will protect us against the terrible plague of lice. I even bring a curved Sikh sword back. For my report that we wouldn't find any resistance I am promoted with the regiment's solemn citation for "bravery before the enemy."

September 27, 1917, Pinon woods: For the first time in the war, tanks appear. I have the responsibility for a cannon right behind the infantry line, with strict orders to remain undetected and to open fire only when the tanks are visible. I am successful. I hit two tanks in direct fire. But on both sides the enemy breaks through and we run back for some miles to the main position of our battery. There we find dead horses, dead comrades, all the indications of a sudden rout. In one of the shelters, the only one alive but gravely wounded is my brother Walter. He stumbles back with me, mostly on my shoulder. With unbelievable luck, we meet a medical group just about to retreat. The physician in charge is from Düsseldorf. He knows our name! He applies gruesome bandages, obviously the best thing to do to assure an emergency transport to Germany instead of to the next field lazarette. My brother survives, but some splinters not possible to remove bother him all his life.

After heavy losses in another major battle, my superiors have the well-meant idea to reward me with a kind of sinecure: for some months, I am to be an observer in a balloon for our section of the front, to report the enemy's movements.

Something newfangled just then makes an appearance: the parachute. After daily experiments with it, we realize that it is not yet reliable; an av-

Erich Leyens with parachute, "after being shot down," 1917

erage of eight of ten parachutes, filled with sandbags to approximate a man's weight, crash. There isn't an alternative, however, when an English flier shoots the balloon I'm in. It bursts into flame. I have to jump overboard. I don't think that I have ever had a happier feeling than to feel the hard jolt of the parachute opening! I land safely on top of a tree, and an infantry patrol is sent out to rescue me.

Early spring, 1918: Victory seems certain. Morale is high. Some months before, we dictated a peace treaty to Russia. Our government was so smart to have provided safe transport by sealed railway car from Switzerland to Lenin to take over the leadership of Russia in her revolution. For us, at long last, the bloody trench war seems at an end, and the war of movement will begin.

In our battery, I am leading two cannons. One sunny day, riding alone in search of a good position, I come upon about forty French soldiers. They stretch out their hands from a deserted trench. *La guerre est finie!* they shout. Instead of killing me, they surrender. They follow me obediently. I leave them with the first infantry unit that I meet. (I still feel ashamed that I took from their leading officer his fine binoculars.) Riding on, a single shell explodes, killing my horse, a beautiful little Russian Tiger-schimmel, throwing me against a rock. I suffer no more than a fractured knee.

After a short time in a field hospital, I recover in a peaceful forest at the logistic location for the reserve of my battery. There I have the surprise of a visit by the battery's captain, who wishes to emphasize that the Iron Cross, First Class, he brings to me rarely is bestowed on a non-officer. In a confidential talk, that decent man tells me that a remark I had made once—"A human being in our army would begin only with the grade of a lieutenant"—has been much quoted. He feels the obligation to tell me, in strict confidence, that he has to give up with his recommendation for my appointment as an officer. He has been rejected not less than five times, he says. And just yesterday the regimental commander has shouted at him to stop with it. He should know that, in his Prussian regiment, contrary to the Bavarian or Baden's military, a Jew could never be an officer even if he'd won a battle single-handed. He advises me to leave the regiment. He'll give me furlough for recovery. Then, he says, I should follow the request from a former commander who is forming a battery in Turkey and badly needs a seasoned officer.

This proves to be my good fortune. Safely taken care of in Wesel's hospital, I lick my wounds while the front collapses and revolution breaks out.

—ERICH LEYENS

The academic year 1916–17 was not a very good year for the pursuit of learning. A great war was raging in Europe and a great debate took place among the American people: Should the United States become involved? Young men are fascinated by war. Each secretly wonders whether he has the courage to expose himself to death or mutilation on a battlefield.

At Harvard, in the spring of 1917, a Reserve Officers Training Corps was speedily organized. As one of its members I soon found practical employment digging trenches along the shore of nearby Fresh Pond. A less fatiguing task was making a crude map of the golf course of Winchester Country Club. Then I found an opportunity to enlist as a flying cadet in what was then the Aviation Section of the Signal Corps.

My close friend and roommate, Dave Hoffman, also chose a clean and glamorous branch of the service, the Navy, as did his younger brother, Bob. In Bob's case a bout with influenza, followed by an abdominal infection, precluded sea duty. We all parted company, no doubt with assurances of a post-war reunion after the forces of democracy had triumphed over German militarism. It was not to be. In September 1918, the *Tampa*, on which Dave served as an ensign, was sunk by a German submarine off the coast of Spain and its entire complement of officers and men was lost. He was one of twenty-seven classmates sacrificed in the war "to make the world safe for democracy."

For a twenty-year-old who was physically lazy, the fledgling air force had much greater appeal than the artillery or infantry. The physical exam was quite an interesting affair. They stuck you in a chair, like a dentist's chair, and spun it around. And how your body reacted to that had something to do with whether you were qualified or not. It was very primitive. But I passed and was sent for six weeks of theoretical training at the Massachusetts Institute of Technology.

The airplane was a relatively new invention and even the engineers and physicists of M.I.T. knew little about aerodynamics. Most of what they taught us was a hundred percent wrong. For instance, they taught that if your plane went into a spin there was no known way of getting out of it and you just crashed. A few months later at flying school, posted typewritten instructions for various aerobatic maneuvers included the procedures for getting into a spin, and getting out again. I soon found that I rather enjoyed doing spins, loops, and so-called Immelmann turns.

Finally, in November 1917, I was ready for the trip overseas to flying school in France. The Atlantic crossing was uneventful. All ships were blacked out as a precaution against enemy submarines. Guards were posted on deck to see that blackout discipline was enforced. While I was on guard duty one night a figure emerged with a lighted cigarette in his mouth. I grabbed him by the arm: You're under arrest! The culprit proved to be the commanding officer of our detachment. He commended my alertness, complained of my unnecessary roughness.

I was selected for training as a pursuit pilot. We flew Nieuports, which had just been superseded as a front-line pursuit plane by the heavier, slightly faster Spad. The planes were very primitive. You flew along with your ear cocked to kind of listen to the engine to see when it was going to conk out, because for an engine to go for two hours without quitting was pretty good. So you had to be attuned to the possibility of a forced landing, and I had several of them. With a landing speed of fifty or sixty miles an hour, a forced landing in any reasonably-sized, fairly flat open space was no great problem. One time I landed in a large wheat field, destroying a considerable amount of grain. The farm's owner appeared shortly, unworried about any injury I might have sustained, but determined to get a receipt for the lost portion of his 1918 crop.

In another forced landing I came to rest about two feet from the trunk of an apple tree. This farmer was very hospitable, remarking that many planes flew over his house but I was the first pilot who had ever paid him a visit. He broke out a bottle of *eau de vie*, that potent brandy which seems like pure alcohol, and poured me a stiff drink. It burned my throat. He and Madame provided food and lodging. I also gained the impression that his daughter, aged eighteen or twenty, might be available as an added token of good will. With what politeness I could muster, I declined this particular favor.

The final step in training a pursuit pilot was a short course at gunnery school. For this we were sent to Cazaux, in the south of France. Gunnery school included practice in destroying clay pigeons with shotguns. Then we practiced for aerial combat by tossing small paper parachutes weighted with stones out of our planes and diving on them. To my consternation I found that after diving on a parachute and turning for another "attack," the parachute was a hundred feet above me. This meant that in turning I had inadvertently side-slipped. Obviously my flying skill needed considerable additional practice before I should really be ready for front-line duty. The exigencies of war permitted no such luxury. Early in September, I reported to a depot behind the front for assignment to a squadron.

Here my guardian angel intervened. The captain to whom I reported advised me that lousy weather during the impending winter would greatly hamper aerial operations. I might better employ my time, he suggested, acting as a ferry pilot, flying planes then stacked up in large numbers at a field near Troyes to fields just behind the front. Then, if I still longed to be a hero, I'd have ample opportunity in the great spring offensive that would end the war. The suggestion was persuasive and I soon found myself at Vinets-sur-Aube with a dozen compatriots. Here were Nieuports, Spads, Sopwith Camels, and de Havilland 4's. The latter were American-manufactured planes of English design. It is an extraordinary fact that four years after the outbreak of the war the United States, home of the Wright brothers, had not designed a single airplane fit for combat, and only built one copy of a British model.

—PHILIP L. CARRET

Here I am, a student at Harvard University, and it's about mid-year 1917. In the Yard—Harvard doesn't have a campus, it's the Yard—up there at the John Hancock monument there are two French officers dressed in their gorgeous colors. One hasn't got an arm and the other is missing a leg. My pal and I are standing with the rest of the dumb clucks. He says to me, Do you feel something?

Yeah, I says, I do. Something inside of me said: Enlist.

So I went to the recruiting office and they said, You qualify as a meteorologist. I said, That's me. I enlisted. My family said, What the hell is it with you? Why don't you wait till you're drafted?

Anyway, I get on the train and I get off at Washington, D. C., and there's someone in uniform and he's calling out my name. He said, They want you in the chemical division—I had majored in chemistry—but because you enlisted, it's your choice. I said, I'm sticking to what I enlisted for.

We line up the first day on the parade ground, and I see this real military man advancing, a captain. He starts at one end: What's your name, soldier? Passes him. What's your name, soldier? And what's your name? Comes down toward where I'm standing. There's a little runt near me, he gets to him first. What's your name, soldier? The kid says, Me name's O'Leary, that's me name.

He passes him; now he comes to me. What's your name, soldier? I stiffen up. I salute, and I say, Private Goldstein, Sir! He says, Get the hell over there! Soon he has five of us lined up at quite a distance. He cups his mouth. I want you to yell, he shouts. I don't give a damn what the hell you yell, but I want you to yell as loud as you can! When he pointed to me, I gave a yell: Squads left, squads right, left front of the line! And he says, You're a sergeant.

That's almost unbelievable! A very quick promotion. In a little while, I was a sergeant first class.

Sergeant first class Joseph Goldstein, 1918

I was assigned to SRS #4—SRS is Sound Ranging Section—locating enemy guns and aiding our artillery. Three of them were already in the field by the time I got to France. The way it was done, we used French milk cans about three feet high. The stoppers were thrown away and platinum grid wires were soldered into the top. Those were microphones. They were placed on the arc of a circle, tied by wire to a center, and the center had maps of the region. A firing piece over there would reach this microphone first, and that microphone a little later, and that one much later, and so on. All that was "photographed" on these tapes and superimposed on the map of that region. Information was phoned to our artillery, and when our artillery was firing, we could tell if they were over the target, under the target, left or right. I was there, doing this, for a year and a half. I was in combat all the time.

—JOSEPH GOLDSTEIN

My younger brother was about to be drafted into the Army. He had a job and I didn't. He was supporting the family then and I couldn't. I ran over to the Selective Service board. I knew them. And I says, I'll give you a proposition. I'll join immediately if you promise to leave my brother alone. The agreement was made. He was not drafted. I joined the Navy.

In the Navy, they asked me what I was doing. I said I was an artist. So they sent me over to a submarine base in New London. They had an old submarine to be repainted. A submarine in those days had openings two, maybe three feet wide to feed the ballast tanks with water. They began to rust. I was slim enough to fit in the openings, to get into the ballast tank, to chip off the corrosion inside and to paint it. As an artist. I spent the war painting and chipping in New London, Connecticut.

—ALFRED LEVITT

Wherever there was a motorcycle race, I went. One race was in Canton, Ohio. This fellow settin' up in the grandstand saw me ride. Turns out he was a colonel in the division they shipped me to in Chillicothe, Ohio, when I got in the Army. Well, he knew who was comin' in. Soon's I got off of that train, he grabbed me. Do you ride a motorcycle? he says.

No, Sir, I don't know anything about motorcycles.

Well, he says, you come with me. He took me down to headquarters. There's a brand-new Harley-Davidson sidecar outfit in that lean-to out there, and we don't have nobody to run it.

I don't know nothin' about it.

Well, you try and start it.

So I says, What do you do to start it?

You have to kick that lever down.

So I kicked it down a couple of times. There must be something wrong with it, I says. It won't start.

Well, you stay out here and try.

He went in his office and he'd look out the window every once and a while. And as I was playing around with that outfit, I got to thinking, Why'd I want to be so bullheaded for? This'd make a pretty nice job for me. So I started it. And the colonel, he come right out.

I see you got it started.

Yes, I says. See that little key? I accidentally bumped that, and when I kicked it, it started.

He laughed. Let me tell you something, Davis. If you want me to, I can tell you the last place you rode and what you rode there and how you finished.

Well, why didn't you tell me that in the first place?

Oh, I just wanted to see how far you was gonna go.

And geez, did that help. In three days I was a sergeant. One of the guys I was workin' with, he says, You must know somebody that knows somebody.

Yeah, I says, I do.

That was how I spent the war, stationed in Chillicothe, Ohio. But it wasn't all easy runnin'. When I first got in, they sent me over to the quartermaster where they take your civvies away and give you your uniform. The guy there asks me what size shoe I wear, and I tell him a ten. He gives me what they call a ten-benny: almost a twelve. He says, What size shirt you wear? I says, a fourteen. A seventeen I got. I took 'em back. Trade with somebody, the guy says. He wouldn't give me anything else. That's when I told him, I says, You treat us like cattle. I got mad.

One day I got so mad I went home, without permission. I thought, ah, the hell with the Army. I just went home. Next mornin' the MPs pick me up and take me back. The colonel says, What made you go home?

I says, I didn't like the way things were going.

Jimmy, he says, you can't just go home! You have to work it out here.

But I was home in my own bed more nights than I was at camp. So I wasn't hurtin' any at all. I really had just a nice long vacation.

—JAMES M. DAVIS

*Yeoman third class Frieda Greene
(Frieda Greene Hardin), 1918*

I was twenty-one when I joined the Navy. I was working as a sales clerk in a dime store—Kresge's—in Portsmouth, Ohio. One evening, my father said that a Navy recruiter was in town. I thought it would be interesting, and I wanted a career. The following Monday, I went down and signed up.

I called home. Momma, I said, I've just joined the Navy.

Frieda, she said, you come right home right now!

I rushed home and, oh, she gave me an awful going-over. My mother was terribly opposed to it. By that time, her sister had arrived for a visit, and they both landed on me roughshod.

Well, Momma, I said, you go with me this afternoon, and if you can get me released from my obligation, all right. So she marched me down to the recruiting station. When they called my name she said, This girl's not going.

The recruiter asked her, Why? And she said, Well, she hasn't talked to her father about it yet.

So he said to me, Go home and talk to your father and come back tomorrow.

Well, the first thing my father said when I told him was, Let her go. And that settled it.

I wasn't in very long, a little less than six

months. The Navy was enlisting women to do office work. I was a yeoman third class—"yeomanettes," they called us. My job was checking dock receipts in the freight office at the Norfolk Navy Yard in Portsmouth, Virginia. But they didn't have barracks then for women—they didn't even have uniforms for women. They gave us two dollars a day quarters' allowance and we boarded in private homes in town. I lived like a queen: two dollars a day was a lot of money then.

That was one of the best times of my life. If there was any prejudice against us women serving, I didn't encounter any.

—FRIEDA GREENE HARDIN

Orlando F. Morley

I enlisted for the duration. They asked me what branch of the service did I want. I told them I just wanted to join the Army. They said, What kind of work do you do? I said, I'm working as assistant payroll clerk at Westmoreland Coal Company. They said, We need men in the Quartermaster Corps in the accounting department. I said, Well, that's okay, that's what I been doin'.

So they sent me up to Fort Thomas, Kentucky, which is strictly a doughboy outfit—an infantry outfit. I didn't stay up there but a month when they'd run out of OD [olive drab] uniforms. They issued us khaki uniforms. That was the worst winter hit that area in history. It'd get around twenty-seven, twenty-eight below zero at night routine, one night after the other. It'd be twenty-four below and we'd be standin' out there for an hour to get fed, freezin' to death in our khakis. Then they shipped me to Florida. And way down in balmy Florida they took my khakis and give me an OD woolen uniform.

They drilled the heck out of us for four, five months. We was all outfitted for combat duty, got a 30.06 Enfield rifle and a pistol belt, trench shovel, all the business. At formation one night before retreat, they told us we was shippin' out the next day. Next morning at reveille, they changed it; we wasn't goin' anywhere. But they formed the Motor Transport Corps, and they's needin' some students for it. They took me and sent me to take a crash course in combustion engineering. I got my certificate in six weeks' time. Then they pulled me and told me I was chauffeurin'. And I'd never even driven a truck.

After that, they finally shipped me over to France, the tenth day of June, 19 and 18, with that same rifle. After I'd been overseas about three months, they organized the MTC as a new branch of the Army. They operated kind of like the railroad. We'd go down to the dispatcher's office every mornin' to see what we was goin' to take out, a three-ton Packard truck, a five-ton Mack truck, whatever.

They gave me a regular job after I'd been over there a couple months. I had to furnish four base hospitals across this part of France with beef quarters and bakery bread. I'd have to make two trips every day, one trip haulin' a load of bread, one trip haulin' a load of beef. That's all I did, just drive, drive, drive. It did get pretty rough, on the Meuse–Argonne campaign, especially, when we had so many casualties; it was more than we could handle, really. We'd do a day's work, come in for chow at night, then work all night haulin' the wounded from the trains to the hospital. We'd stop that at nine o'clock the next mornin', still had the day's work ahead of us, loadin' and unloadin' the beef and the bread, with me behind the wheel. Then we'd rest one night and start all over.

—ORLANDO F. MORLEY

I was a trooper in the First Division, Third Army. When the United States entered the war, they sent us over. We went to New York, got on the

boat, landed in Brest. My lieutenant saw how good I worked
on the ship, I wasn't seasick or
nothing. He told me I had to
shovel coal.

What? I said, I don't know how
to shovel coal.

We'll teach you.

I spent the next sixteen days
shoveling coal down in the engine room: one hour shoveling
and two hours outside getting the
fresh air. I got a dollar a day extra. Then they sent me out to
headquarters with my unit. The
captain there saw that I could understand what the French people
were saying—I was Italian, and I
understood French—so he made

Ralph Montecalvo, 1918

me interpreter. I had a room for myself; I didn't have to sleep with the rest
of the troops with the horses on the hay in the barn.

After a while I went up in the front lines. We were relieving the Marines.
I got gassed. We were fighting, see. The shell come in. It exploded. The gas
masks we had were no good. I guess I passed out. Guys were wounded;
guys got killed. When I woke up, my head was asleep on top of a dead
person. I didn't even know who the hell he was, just he was dead.

After they fixed me up, I was sent as a replacement to a National Guard
unit. Again they made me an interpreter at battalion headquarters. One
night, the German artillery bombarded us for three hours. My mission was
to try and find where the enemy was. I went out past our lines. I heard
talk. It was German. I spotted a machine gun dug in deep, with three soldiers around it. I came right back. When I got back, my men, they was
gonna shoot me. I had to give them the password. I caught up to the artillery and told them where the machine gun was.

—RALPH MONTECALVO

One of my brothers was one of the first to go over to Europe. He was in
the engineers. Well, they sent sixteen of them out to build a bridge across

some river, and he was the only one to survive. Fifteen were killed, and he was so badly wounded that they found him unconscious. He was in the hospital for a long time.

Back home, we were worried sick. It had been so long we didn't hear from him. We didn't know what was going on. We sent letters to Fred, and he could write and say that he was all right; there was only certain information that he could give us. But those letters were all censored, and the letters that we sent him I guess were censored, too.

—ADA TABOR

When Congress issued a declaration of war against Germany, I was in my early twenties. So many of our young men, my friends and contemporaries, were leaving. There was a terrible feeling of excitement and confusion, apprehension and fear.

I was working in town then, as deputy county auditor. One day we went down to the railroad station to send off a contingent of young men. A captain was brought in to put them through some very basic training and then they took them to the railroad station. We didn't have communications then like we have now, but we did have a paper in town and reports came in on Western Union telegraph. It was a frightening time because there were reports of fatalities, of known casualties, and the missing in action. And in a small town like Dunseith, North Dakota, where everybody knew everybody else, there were no secrets. If a message came to one family, it was shared by all. That was the way the community took care of it. My mother's youngest brother, Robert, was a casualty. So was her cousin, Colonel John McCrae, who wrote *In Flanders Field.*

When the harvest time came, there weren't enough young men left to work the fields. So an old bachelor organized a bunch of us, about a dozen young women, and came with a wagon and took us out to the fields to shuck grain. He told us we were helping the war effort.

There were also shortages of staples, like sugar and flour. Mother would try to make bread with rice flour. She was not very successful. Ladies' shoes were in short supply, as leather was needed for soldiers' boots. Having been raised on a farm where produce shortages were unknown, I realized how fortunate I had been. And that helped me to accept the shortages and make the best of what we had.

ELLA MAY STUMPE

Back in the thirties, the Second Division put up a monument down in Washington, and I went down. I ran into this chap, Montgomery Budd, his name was. He had been a cannoneer, an eighteen-year-old buck private, who served under me. We got reacquainted and became quite friendly. After the war, he went to college, worked for the DuPont Company down in Delaware—he was in charge of advertising—and retired to Mexico.

He wrote me a letter around 1987. He thought a great deal of me, he said. But you were not Mr. Roberts the night we were going up into Soissons when you used a searchlight and chased us off the caissons and made us walk through the mud. Well, that night, there were so many things going on, but I wasn't even in C Battery.

So I wrote back, Either this is a case of mistaken identity, or else you're off your nut. And I decided, What the hell? I'll write the whole thing down. I wrote about a chapter a month for about a year and told the story, not only of Soissons, but of my whole war (excerpts of which follow).

. . . At the time we entered the war, the United States had almost no field artillery, either guns or men. The French supplied the guns and the Army had to train officers and men quickly to back up our infantry when they went into battle.

John Dodge Clark

I imagined that if all went well I would be sent to a training camp to qualify for a commission. Consider my surprise when I received a beautifully engraved document stating that the President of the United States, reposing special trust and confidence in me, had appointed me a second lieutenant in the Field Artillery Reserve Corps, effective November 19, 1917. I was to report for duty at le Valdahon on Thanksgiving Day . . .

In Base Hospital 15 at Chaumont, where General Pershing had established the headquarters of the A.E.F—the American Expeditionary Force—we hardly knew we were in the Army. Once, we put up a few engineers overnight, and in the course of conversation, they asked if we knew our ten general orders. Not only did we not know them, we did not even know that they existed. Every soldier is supposed to know them by heart. One day, I passed an elderly soldier who had broad black bands on the sleeves of his overcoat. I took these to be signs of mourning and I felt sorry for him. Later I learned that the black bands indicated that he was a general.

The first time we went into the field after horses were issued to us at le Valdahon, I was sitting down eating the lunch which my orderly had brought me when Major Bailey, our battalion commander, rode up and asked me if all the men had been fed yet. I said I didn't know. In this Army, he said, the horses are fed first; after them, the men are fed; only after all the men are fed do the officers eat. I folded up my mess kit and went down to the chow line to check up. So I gradually got educated.

Some time in February, all of us new second lieutenants were called in and asked by the colonel whether we would like to go back to the States to become instructors at training camps. I told the colonel that I had come over to France for some excitement and I certainly did not want to go home before we had even got to the front. Among those who did go back was Brad Boardman, one of the two Amherst men I'd met in Paris who had put me on the track of the field artillery. He died of the flu in October. During the influenza epidemic, which killed thousands in camps in both America and France, the safest place to be was at the front, where each man lived and slept by himself in the great outdoors . . .

I was placed in charge of the B Battery echelon. This included the approximately 150 horses, the major part of the two hundred men, the kitchen, wagons, caissons, supplies, office. Food would be taken up to the forward gun crews daily and every other night I would ride up to the gun positions with a group of caissons and wagons loaded with ammunition. Our echelon was located in an old camp which the French artillery had used before we relieved them. The camp was in a ravine and relied on abundant trees for camouflage. It rained twenty-eight days in April 1918, so that we were wading in mud almost halfway to our knees. Luckily, we had rubber boots; unluckily, after a few days, orders from division headquarters forbade the use of the boots: they were to be saved for an emergency, which never came.

I had a little hut to myself and a pet rat. When I awoke in the morning, he usually would be sitting on a two-by-four beam above and alongside of my chicken-wire bed. He ducked behind the tar-paper wall at the slightest movement on my part. I would cut through the wall with a hatchet, but I never caught him. Actually, I think we got to be friends . . .

About the middle of May, the Second Division had moved to Chaumont-en-Vexin, north of Paris, for training in open warfare. General Pershing had resolved that the American Army would not settle for the stationary trench warfare in which the French and British had been engaged for four years.

On May 27, the Germans launched a surprise attack, had advanced thirty-three miles in four days, and had reached the vicinity of Château-Thierry, only forty miles from Paris. The French were badly demoralized and the situation was desperate. General Pershing offered to send them the Second Division. The French sent motor trucks to transport the infantry. Artillery were to travel by train.

We were to entrain at a small railroad station which was located somewhat lower than the road. I was stationed near the top of the approximately hundred-foot downgrade to the loading ramp, signaling each gun, caisson, or wagon as the way was clear for it to descend. Down near the ramp was our regimental commander, Colonel Davis, and General Chamberlaine, commander of the Second Artillery Brigade.

All had been going well until it was the turn of one of the big "chariot" wagons pulled by three husky horses to descend. I waved to the driver and started to walk down myself. I glanced back just in time to see one of the reins break, so that the near horse was loose. I ran back and grabbed the horse's bridle. He started to trot and the other two horses followed suit. I couldn't stop them. They were headed for the colonel's car. They were running, and so was I. I pulled as hard as I could and managed to swerve the horses to the left. But then they were headed for the general's car. So I leaned my shoulder as hard as I could against the near horse so that the team went between the two cars and ended up in the rolling kitchen as I let go. The driver vaulted down and gained control of the horses. The harness-maker was later court-martialed for cutting the leather reins too thin.

As we advanced on the right side of roads to the front, we passed hordes of old men, women, and children fleeing the German invaders with whatever household goods they could carry themselves or load on farm animals. Also retreating were French troops. We discovered that there was no established front line. A couple of our lieutenants, doing some reconnoitering, suddenly ran into a couple of Germans, who were just as surprised as they were. Both Americans and Germans turned tail and ran to their own lines. Our two officers were arrested by some infantrymen. In those early days before the front lines in this sector were clearly defined, some German soldiers in American uniforms infiltrated our lines and at night sent up flares, indicating target locations for German artillery. One night I went out with a corporal on a spy hunt. There was a large haystack which I figured would afford a good spot from which to observe anyone in the surrounding open area. So we crawled up and sat in the top of the haystack with just our heads visible. We had not detected anyone for half an hour when suddenly a circle of bayonets surrounded us. A squad of infantrymen imagined that they had captured a couple of spies; it was necessary for Major Bailey to come and identify us before we were released . . .

Our guns were located in a small patch of woods looking out over a clear field of fire. We were shelled from time to time and suffered some casualties, but we maintained the same positions. By this time we were pretty well able to judge the threat of an oncoming shell. In the case of German 77-millimeter shells, we could hear close ones for possibly two seconds before they landed—just enough time to throw ourselves flat on the ground. With larger-caliber shells, we had a little longer. The ones we hated the most came from Austrian 88-millimeter guns, which some of the German batteries were equipped with. These guns had extremely fast muzzle velocity and flat trajectory, so that we could not hear the shells before they hit.

One day we were doing some harassing fire when I noticed a German observation plane approaching. Not wishing it to spot our exact position, I said to the gunner, Hold your fire! and with the sergeant went out in front to see when the plane flew out of sight. Each gun has a shield which protects the gunner from enemy fire. At the same time, it prevents him from seeing what's in front of the gun. On this occasion, I was standing with my head about three inches from the muzzle of the gun when it went off. As I staggered back, I said to the gunner, I told you to hold your fire. Temporarily deafened by the firing himself, he thought I had said, *Load* and fire.

I didn't hear anything for three days . . .

After we were relieved on July 10, we took up support positions. Our battery had quarters with a farm family in the neighborhood and I had been elected mess officer. So I took it upon myself to teach the farmer's wife how to make French toast for breakfast.

Developments of a more serious nature were not long in coming. About ten o'clock in the evening of July 14, we received orders to pack up and be on the road by midnight. It was raining. We sat down in the wet fields alongside the road until dawn, when we started to march in a northerly direction. We heard heavy artillery fire in back of us. Around noon, we stopped, turned around, and started marching back. The noise we heard was the German attack in the Second Battle of the Marne, their last attack of the war. After a while, however, we turned around again and resumed our northerly march.

A couple of years after the war, I found out the reason for our erratic marching. My father, who was a member of the University Club in Brooklyn, my hometown, invited me to accompany him to a meeting at which General (Ret'd.) James G. Harbord, the president of RCA, was to be the guest speaker . . . He had been in Paris when he was notified to report immediately to General Mangin, commander of the French Tenth Army, at Villers-Cotterêts, the twelve-mile-square forest west of Soissons. He was informed that the Second Division would participate in an attack at 4:35 a.m. on July 18, for which he had to prepare an attack order. But he had no idea of the whereabouts of the various elements of his division and the French would not tell him, only that they would be in position on time. The reason for this arbitrary behavior was that the success of the attack depended on its being a surprise, and the French—not without some reason—had no confidence in the ability of the Americans to keep a secret . . .

We marched all day on the fifteenth, and did not get much sleep that night. I had to get up early on the sixteenth in order to take all of B Battery's horses to water at the nearest stream. Then we continued our march and arrived at our destination in the forest late in the afternoon. Everyone was exhausted. But before I had a chance to sit down I was notified that I had been detailed to duty with brigade headquarters. There I discovered an old chicken-wire bed, on which I promptly dozed off. Toward midnight, I was awakened in order to deliver the regimental ammunition orders for the attack. When I located the ammunition officer, he was sound asleep. Speaking to him had no effect; neither did slapping his face. Finally I closed the fingers of one of his hands on the papers. I guess he found the orders when he woke up in the morning.

Just to be sure, I rode over to the Fifteenth Field Artillery headquarters the next morning. To my consternation, there was not the slightest trace of the regiment. The result was the most frustrating day of my life. It was imperative that I locate the regiment, because later I would have to deliver the barrage orders for the attack the next morning. I spent practically all day exploring the Villers-Cotterêts forest. I found some First Division elements, the First Moroccan Division, including a regiment of the famed French Foreign Legion, but no Fifteenth Field Artillery. Finally I spied a water cart with

"15 F.A." painted on its side. Its driver gave me directions. When I found it, I established its location in my mind and returned to brigade.

It was after eleven o'clock before the barrage data became available and I started the trip to deliver them. It had rained. It was dark. I raised my hand in front of my face; I couldn't see it. The road was clogged with artillery, tanks, ambulances. For long periods, nothing moved. I rode a large rangy horse who seemed to possess a sixth sense when it came to finding an opening in the traffic. At one point he squeezed between two vehicles I could not see, and I pulled my foot out of the left wooden stirrup just as it was being crushed. Part of the time, he traveled in the ditch alongside the road. I got to regimental headquarters just before midnight.

As I was riding back to brigade, there seemed to be an open stretch of road just ahead and I started to trot. Then there appeared to be a darker shadow approaching and I reined in the horse just in time to avoid running into a column of infantrymen dogtrotting in the mud, each man holding on to the shoulder of the man in front of him. They were to reach the front just in time to shed their packs and go over the top. These were some of the men General Harbord was relying on to make the attack but of whose whereabouts he had not the slightest idea.

The attack was indeed a surprise. There had been no preliminary cannonade before the 4:35 a.m. jump-off, when the creeping barrage provided a curtain of fire in front of the advancing infantrymen, extending the range a hundred yards every three minutes. The ground gained exceeded the original objectives, but at a heavy cost. Adequate provisions had not been made for the avalanche of wounded. Quite a few who had been brought back as far as brigade headquarters died of exposure during the cold night. About midnight, as I was circulating around them, giving water and trying to help when I could, a young soldier, he seemed just a boy, wandered around crying. Everybody's been killed, he was saying, and I'm lost.

July 19, the second day of the attack, was my twenty-second birthday, and I thought it might be my last. I wrote a farewell letter to my parents. The fighting continued with the same intensity, and by the end of the day the infantry had suffered fifty percent casualties. In some companies all the officers had been killed or wounded, leaving a sergeant in command. At the end of the day, the division was relieved and I went back to regular duty, but now with C Battery.

When we stopped by the side of the road for evening chow, I figured that at last I was going to have a peaceful night's sleep. But surprise! The artillery was ordered back into the lines. We got into position late in the evening and dug a shallow trench to protect us against direct hits. When I awoke in the morning, I remarked that last night I had not noticed the shell hole a few feet from our trench. The others looked at me. Who are you trying to kid?

Nobody, I replied. I just said I had not noticed this hole.

Do you mean to tell us you didn't hear the German planes that dropped bombs on us last night?

I told them truthfully that I had slept so soundly that I had heard neither the planes nor the bombs.

The Germans continued to fire on us. One shell landed about ten feet from us. Lieutenant Larry Divine, Yale '17, who was sharing the trench with me, thought it was from a large-caliber gun. I bet him that it was from a 77 and I got out of the trench to check it. You could tell from the diameter of the hole. I was right. Then I heard the sister of that shell coming to hit the same spot. I didn't have time to run back. I just made a flying leap, twisting in the air, so that I landed on my ear in the trench at the same time the shell hit.

That morning, the Algerians were attacking the Germans and we were firing a three-hour rolling barrage, at the end of which we were to advance five kilometers (about three miles). We proceeded according to plan and had just pulled out on the road when Major Bailey galloped back and yelled, Get back in there and resume firing. Those goddamned sons o' bitches are retreating!

The fact that we got the word as we did was due to the good work of Lieutenant Bob Kean, Harvard '15 [the father of former New Jersey Governor Tom Kean], who was on liaison duty with the infantry. The second battalion of our regiment and C Battery of the Twelfth Field Artillery were not so fortunate. They advanced in accordance with the original orders and rode through the front lines in plain view of the Germans. Both men and horses suffered heavy casualties and several guns were lost.

That day, each of our guns fired a thousand rounds. The gun barrels got so hot that we were firing three of them and pouring water over the other one. Normally, an ammunition train would deliver supplies to a so-called ammunition dump a mile or so behind the battery positions and our caisson drivers would pick it up there and haul it to the guns. But with the incessant firing we were in danger of running short and the ammunition train was ordered to deliver the shells direct to the battery. Our guns were lined up in an open field in full view of several German observation balloons and we were under constant fire. Members of the ammunition train were not accustomed to such operating conditions. They arrived at a full gallop and I don't think they would have stopped to unload if we had not forced them to. I told them that they could not leave until they had unloaded every single shell. I saw one poor kid actually pull some of his fingernails loose in his frantic efforts to pull the shells out of the caisson. When they were all unloaded, the drivers left as they had arrived, at a dead gallop . . .

Soissons marked the turning point of the war. Our First and Second Divisions and the French First Moroccan Division turned the tide of war definitely in favor of the Allies. Although the Germans fought stubbornly to the end, they were henceforth always on the defensive . . .

During the month of August, the division recuperated in quiet sectors in the vicinity of Nancy. Casualties at Soissons had been 154 officers and 3,788 men killed, wounded, and missing. Replacements had brought the division up to full strength in time for the St.-Mihiel offensive, which was to begin September 12 . . .

At last, General Pershing had a complete American Army. The St.-Mihiel offensive for the first time brought the Second Division into action under American corps and Army commanders and alongside only American troops.

The St.-Mihiel salient was a big dent in the Allied line which had existed ever since the original German invasion in 1914, in spite of several French attempts to dislodge the enemy. The Second Division was stationed at the apex, so that it had the longest distance to travel in order to straighten out the line.

On the afternoon and going into the evening of September 11, the day before the attack, I was taking the gun limbers and caissons up to the gun positions so that we would be prepared to follow the infantry closely in what was expected to be a rapid advance. The narrow two-lane road was a duplicate of the one leading to the front the night before the Soissons attack—jammed in rain and darkness with tanks and vehicles of all descriptions. Somehow we reached our guns before the start of the 5 a.m. barrage.

Most of the new American divisions consisted only of infantry, so the French provided extra artillery, making a total for the initial bombardment of three thousand light and heavy guns which commenced at 1 a.m. and continued until the infantry jump-off. At 5 a.m. we started the creeping barrage, moving at the rate of a hundred meters every four minutes. With the rapid infantry advance, our batteries leapfrogged so that a continuous barrage could be maintained.

Toward noon we pulled off the road to take up a new position a couple of hundred yards from a crossroad which had to be traveled by any traffic going toward the front. The Germans were shelling it fairly consistently and the fact that they were accurate saved us from any danger . . .

Of all our major battles, St.-Mihiel was the least costly in casualties and hardship . . . Emboldened by the St.-Mihiel victory, the Allied Command assigned the American Army to a front extending fifty-five miles from that point on the Meuse River to the western edge of the Argonne Forest. To the west of the Argonne would be the French Fourth Army and, to guarantee that it would keep pace with the American left flank, the Second Division was loaned to it for the forthcoming attack.

The principal obstacle in this sector was a large hill which the Germans were defending heavily and which the French considered impregnable. However, our commanding officer, General Lejeune, was confident that the Second Division alone could capture Blanc Mont Ridge.

The attack began at 5:50 a.m. on October 3 with a rolling barrage progressing one hundred yards every four minutes. To achieve the advantage of the barrage, the infantrymen must "lean against it"—walk as close to it as possible without being hit by it themselves. And to do this, they must trust the timing and accuracy of their supporting artillery, to whom they are actually entrusting their lives. That is why, if at all possible, each artillery battalion supports the same infantry regiment in all its attacks. We always supported the Ninth Infantry as they attacked successive enemy defense lines . . .

Every officer had his own orderly—popularly referred to as a "striker" or "dog robber"—who took care of his horse and performed other personal duties. It was always a voluntary assignment, which carried some extra income provided by the officer. At the time we went into the Blanc Mont offensive, I had a fine young lad named Martin Roy, who hailed from the Pennsylvania coalfields. One day he spoke to me and said that inasmuch as the echelon was so far behind the gun positions, it might seem that he was shirking danger; therefore, he requested assignment with the guns. Although I explained that the echelon assignment was only temporary, he persisted in his request. I had him transferred. The next day he was killed.

My new striker was a Bostonian named Quigley, definitely not a product of Harvard, but a voracious reader of books. When I was in Paris on leave, I had stopped in at Brentano's store; later I sent them a check to cover the cost of a book titled *The Glory of the Trenches*, by an Englishman, and another volume of their selection. This turned out to be a description of English gardens. After trying in vain to find any interest in it, I gave it to Quigley. He returned it the next day with his apologies. He had thought he could read a book on any subject, he said, but this one proved to be the exception. Quigley endeavored to be very punctilious in addressing officers in the third person. But sometimes he got his persona confused, as when he used to address me: Sir, will the lieutenant want your horse today? . . .

When it was all totaled up, the losses for the Second Division during the period from October 2 to the tenth had been forty-one officers and 685 men killed, 162 officers and 3,500 men wounded, six officers and 579 men missing. It was the most costly of our battles . . .

On October 30 we received orders to pack up and march to the Meuse–Argonne sector. The Second Division was to relieve the Forty-second Rainbow Division—so-called because it consisted of National Guard elements from several states—at a point where they were held up. Our infantry commanders insisted that, if they were to attack, they wanted to be supported by their own artillery. Hence our forced march to be on hand for the attack at 5:30 a.m. on November 1. When Captain Fairchild heard the news, he conveniently developed ill health and was evacuated. Everybody was happy when Captain "Mike" Walsh took command of C Battery . . .

In successive jumps after the initial barrage, we had two or three positions daily. On November 3, as the battalion neared a small village, we could see that the Germans were concentrating their fire on it. Crash followed crash and clouds of smoke and dust hovered over the roofs, most of which showed gaping holes. As the only possible route of march led through the center of the town, word was passed back along the column to allow intervals of ten paces between guns and caissons in order to minimize the casualties which were bound to come. I timed the shells and found that they were dropping in at the rate of one every twenty seconds.

Down the hill into the outskirts of the town went the column. Then came a sudden slowing up. I rode ahead to investigate the delay and found that another road forked into the main road just at the entrance to the village. Along this road was the brigade's other regiment of 75s. It would have been suicide for either column to halt at this point, so the other regiment was dovetailing its pieces into our ten-pace intervals. The result was a solid column that moved along at a snail's pace.

As my platoon came into the center of town, the bombardment became terrific. Walls were toppling, bricks falling, and shell splinters whistling through the air. Doughboys dodged in and out of doorways; engineers, who were already repairing a damaged bridge, flopped in the ditches when a shell came especially close. The artillerymen on their horses could only duck their heads. All in all, the column stretched a couple of miles and no portion of it could increase its gait or leave its place. I felt as if my horse was Pikes Peak and I was a target for the world to shoot at.

After what seemed like an eternity, we passed through the far end of the town, where the thatched roofs of the houses had caught fire and were belching a black cloud to heaven. A hurried check revealed that the platoon had come through practically untouched, but B Battery immediately behind us had lost eight men when a shell made a direct hit on one section.

A kilometer beyond, just below the crest of a gentle slope, the battalion pulled off to the right of the road and into position in an open field. The attacking infantry were only five hundred yards ahead, facing the Germans, who were holding on to the fringe of a deep woods. Within ten minutes, the battery was pouring a hail of shrapnel and high explosive into the woods.

Across the left side of the road, a company of Marines were interested spectators. They were the second attack wave, resting on the reverse slope of the hill until called upon to do their part. High above circled a lone Boche plane. The significance of his presence was not long in doubt. With an angry whine, a salvo of shells dropped in the very midst of the resting Marines. While stretcher bearers carried away the wounded, the reclining men yanked out trench shovels and bayonets and began feverishly digging foxholes. They resembled nothing so much as terriers making the dirt fly in the hunt for a woodchuck. The humorous aspect of this sudden transformation appealed to our gunners. A chorus of laughter and good-natured gibes floated across the road.

But the tables were soon turned. The doughboys had scarcely dug themselves in before there came another salvo. This time the shells landed in the artillery positions. The Boche airplane observer overhead was evidently directing the aim of the German batteries, and it was no less than apparent that the object was to exterminate or drive out the American artillery.

The smoke of our barking 75s was mingled with the smoke of exploding enemy shells. The air seemed full of lead and steel. Extra cannoneers began digging in excellent imitation of the doughboys across the road. Captain Walsh and Lieutenant Shepler, who were figuring firing data on new targets, found time to scoop out a shallow trench. I was directing the fire and had to content myself with sticking my head behind a duffel bag whenever I heard the screech of a shell which seemed to be aimed especially at me.

On the left side of the road, the Marines might have been in a grandstand watching an exciting game of ball. It was their chance to laugh last and they made the most of it. It was a huge joke but a grim one, and they showed that they recognized it as such by changing their initial yells of derision into hearty cheers.

One shell struck the trail of the first piece, severing the spade of the gun, which weighed a hundred pounds, and hurling it twenty yards over the heads of the gunners. Every member of the gun crew was hit. Corporal

Burns of the adjacent gun crew had his left arm pierced by a jagged shell fragment. But he reached over, closed the breech with his right hand, and continued pulling the lanyard so that the piece did not miss a shot.

C Battery had been the first battery to start firing, although it was the last to pull off the road into position. In view of that, we would be accorded the honor of sending a gun and two caissons down to the infantry to lead a night march through the woods, which were held by the Germans. One of the battery officers was to be in charge, and inasmuch as the captain would naturally remain with the battery and Shepler had a swollen jaw from a sore tooth, I was the obvious volunteer.

With a couple of runners I went down toward the Ninth Infantry post of command. This was by now late in the afternoon, and Colonel Van Horn wanted to know where the gun was. I told him that we would bring it down at dusk when they were ready to make their march. Go and get it now, he ordered. I went back to our battalion positions to Major Brainard, our battalion commander, who instructed me to tell the goddamned fool that the gun would be there when the time came but not before, inasmuch as we were not going to take it over the rise of ground during daylight in full view of the Germans.

The maneuver was very successful—without our gun. I told the colonel that it would not be a silent march with a gun drawn by six horses and a couple of caissons drawn by a dozen more. This certainly would be inconsistent if silence was an essential ingredient to the success of the operation. The colonel finally saw the light and abandoned the idea of having artillery lead the procession through the woods. The infantry captured the Germans guarding the entrance to the road. Marching silently single-file, they came out of the woods five miles behind the German lines and captured the whole headquarters staff. It was written up in several histories as the most brilliant tactical feat of the war. In a strictly negative sense, I have always felt that I was responsible for the success of this brilliant achievement . . .

The next morning, we advanced again. It took us until noon to go a mile, hooking ten horses to one gun or caisson to get it through the deep mud. Going through the woods that afternoon, we encountered a considerable number of abandoned enemy artillery pieces. At one point, we were in a clearing and saw the red planes of Baron von Richthofen's Flying Circus passing overhead. Von Richthofen was the premier ace of the German Air Force and was popularly known as the Red Baron.

By November 10, we were outside the town of Beaumont on the west bank of the Meuse River, the Germans occupying the east bank, with headquarters in the town of Mouzon. We heard that an armistice was to go into effect the next day. But an armistice is a mere temporary stopping of warfare by mutual agreement as a truce preliminary to the signing of a peace treaty. Not knowing what the ultimate terms might be, both sides tried to insure that, when the armistice went into effect, their positions would be as favorable as possible.

Our target for the night was Mouzon. The battery was to fire one thousand high-explosive shells in a creeping barrage between 8:30 a.m. and 11 a.m. During the afternoon, Mike Walsh and I worked out on our plotting board a series of barrages. These had to be revised from time to time, due to the rapidity of our fire. We were compelled to take one gun out of action at intervals to cool it off, leaving the other three to cover the allotted area. Under cover of this shelling, the Second Engineers were to install pontoon bridges across the river, and an attempt to gain a foothold on the opposite bank was to be made by the Fifth Marines and the Ninth Infantry.

The German Air Force had prevented thorough reconnaissance by our planes, so that accurate location of German artillery batteries was not known. As a consequence, we sustained quite a lot of shell fire on our side of the river and the crossing resulted in very heavy casualties for all the troops engaged. The Germans had a clear field and a lot of machine-gun nests supplementing their artillery, which defeated attempts to secure bridges. Finally, a Ninth Infantryman tied around his waist a rope which was attached to a light pontoon bridge. He swam and floated across the river, landing a little downstream, then worked his way upstream under the bank and gradually pulled the bridge across. (He was awarded the Congressional Medal of Honor.) The First Battalion of the Fifth Marines worked its way across. The gunfire, the darkness, and the precarious footing—the bridge was a mere footway supported on floating logs, like a railway track turned upside down—scattered the battalion badly, and a strong machine gun nest encountered as it started forward from the bank completed the carnage. Only about a hundred men could be assembled before daylight.

Shepler was on liaison duty at this time and crossed the river with the Marines. Mike and I had been kept busy figuring firing data in a little hut, which gave us at least a small degree of comfort from the cold in preference to fairly safe trenches by the guns. In the morning, I checked on a close hit and found that the hole was about twenty feet wide and ten feet deep.

At eleven o'clock on the morning of November 11, 1918, there was a strange silence. For the first time in over four years in France, there was no background noise of guns. It didn't seem natural . . .

—JOHN DODGE CLARK

It's November the eleventh. The artillery battery started at nine o'clock. They kept shooting. Eleven o'clock. Twelve o'clock, one, two, three. They didn't stop. Everybody's saying the Armistice is started. What the hell's going on? We're supposed to stop, but we don't. Then I go up to the front line. There's no shootin' there. The captain sees me. Where the hell were you, you sonofabitch?

I said, Sir, too many shells was firin' and too many of my men are dead.

—RALPH MONTECALVO

I was coming back toward what had recently been the front. Everybody who had anything at all was shooting it off. Artillery, rifles, side arms, everybody was shooting into the air. There's going to be an armistice! There's going to be an armistice!

What latrine did that come out of? We had had so many false alarms. Then, one minute past eleven, there was a deathly silence. It was scary, it was so silent. And I said, Lord, thank you, I'll never forget this day.

—JOSEPH GOLDSTEIN

When it ended, everybody was out in the street hugging and kissing each other. Bells were ringing, fire trucks were going up and down the streets clanging. Oh, it was beautiful! Someone would come up and hug you. There was no shame about it, they'd just come up and hug you.

—THERESA NIGRELLI

The popular song of the day was "When Johnny Comes Marching Home," a song from the Civil War. We all sang it. And when we got word that the Armistice had been signed, it was a day of celebration. Businesses shut down. Schools closed. People took to the streets. A parade was formed and a march began and lasted until everybody was exhausted.

Over the next several months, the soldiers trickled home. There was no big welcoming. You were just glad they got home. Some brought messages of fallen comrades to relatives. Some came back to wives and sweethearts. Some returned to disappointment and lives filled with bitterness.

—ELLA MAY STUMPE

My brother was a farmer. He was called away to the Army to fight in the First World War. My daddy then had to hire somebody to work the farm.

When he come home, my brother never would tell much about it. He was a brave man. He killed his own self, my oldest brother.

—SALLIE JORDAN

After the war was over, they were giving a lot of the military equipment that was in Belgium and France to the different countries, and all that paperwork had to be done. I was an officer in the Quartermaster Corps, so I was kept over. To keep me satisfied, they would give me these furloughs. I got to visit Italy and Spain and Lourdes. And the Palace of Versailles.

One day I told the captain that I wanted to see the signing of the peace treaty and could he do anything for me? Well, he said, I don't know why we can't give you the day off to visit Versailles. So I went there.

I had learned to speak as well as a Frenchman. I knocked on these big doors. I told the soldier guarding the doors that I wanted to see the signing of the treaty. He was all beside himself. *Ah, mon ami*, he said, come on in. And I did.

Inside, there was a hall, just about thirty feet wide, and on the bottom of the walls was a glass footing that they put these mirrors on. Each one was just about ten feet wide on up to the ceiling. That's why they called it the Hall of Mirrors.

And there was Woodrow Wilson. I guess I was just about ten feet from him, that's all. And so I watched the signing. Then he started heading toward me. I got up and I met him halfway. We began talking. He said that there were two things he'd always remember: the signing of the peace treaty and that America was against it. He said, the first thing is that we will have no more wars. This has been enough. And the second thing is, seeing the first American soldier watching the signing of the peace treaty, he said, I did what I thought was right. But back home, he said, they don't feel that way. I said, More than likely they will when you get back there because they'll be so glad it's over.

But they didn't. Many Americans said they did not want any President that would let our country go into war. They felt that we should deal with our own problems and not get involved in the problems of other countries. And when President Wilson got back he didn't get a cordial welcome. And I'll say this: That was the making of the end of Woodrow Wilson. He took it so hard that the people would turn on him that way, it brought on his stroke. A month after he had the stroke, he died.

—ERNEST C. DEETJEN

My oldest brother, John, enlisted in the Army as soon as there was the announcement of our engagement in World War I. He was among the first to land in France and one of the last to leave.

When he returned home, he said, I get back here and people are talking about this being "The War to End Wars." But this war isn't over. I know. I was billeted among those German people, and they told me right out that that's not the end of the war. We're going to be in it again.

—MILTON W. GARLAND

From my sixteenth to my twentieth year, I was in constant danger. I was shell-shocked, traumatized by the loss of close friends at my side. But I wasn't sick a single day. Nor did I even get my peacetime cold when I slept in utter exhaustion once in a cold, water-filled shell hole aside a firing gun.

Today it's hard to believe that, until the bitter end, we adored our Kaiser, learning only many years later that in his hubris he had renounced Bismarck's reassurance pact with Russia and had rejected no less than three times England's feelers for an alliance, thus making inevitable the Triple Entente against Germany.

After the war, my father showed me a scribbled note which I had mailed to him during the battle of Verdun, when nobody thought it possible to survive. It was kind of a "last will." In it I wrote, obviously in deep depression, that my carefree upbringing had not prepared me to face a terrible fact in Germany: that, contrary to our convictions, there was, even in the Army, an all-pervading anti-Semitism. Its basis with the common people seemed to me to be religious; with the officer corps, social. Nobody had heard about a "racial" thesis which would become the deadly philosophy of the Nazi regime.

In my miserable note to my father I asked him, after my death, to find an organization to publish exactly the number of Jews fighting at the front, and how many fell "on the field of honor." And also, by name, the famous scientists and artists and writers. And the contributions made by Jewish industrialists and merchants to the successful German economy. How naïve the eighteen-year-old boy was with his "testament." How was he to know that, just twenty years later, the anti-Semitic virus would become a plague: the Holocaust.

—ERICH LEYENS

The Influenza Pandemic

I saw so many people dead.

They were layin' all over the grass.

The railroad cars were loaded

up to the sky, full of deads.

—JOSEPH LICCARDO

Born February 12, 1897

Naples, Italy

Just before the signing of the Armistice, the influenza epidemic attacked the nation. It was furious, it worked fast, showing no favoritism, and it was ferocious. We all knew people who died. I came home one day and they said, Leah died. She was twenty-two. She was my best friend. I was in a daze. It was such a drastic time.

I missed our Armistice parade. That day, I was isolated from family and quarantined from visitors. I lay on my bed in a screened-in porch with the flu.

Ella May Stumpe

I did not know the seriousness of my illness. My sister had called my father and mother at the suggestion of the doctor. With his very busy schedule, he was stopping in to see me every morning and evening. But I wasn't very nice to him. I knew he had a reputation for "trifling with the ladies' affections" and, at age twenty-three, I was conceited enough to think he was using my illness to impress me with his charming manner. I learned later that this dedicated doctor had been traveling day and night, ministering to all who were in need. He had hired a driver with a buggy and team of

◄ *American Red Cross workers remove a victim of the Spanish influenza during the pandemic, 1918 (Culver Pictures)*

horses—he changed over to a sled during the winter months—to drive him from one patient to another. With heated stones for warmth, he slept when he could and stopped to eat when hunger overtook him. He lived this way for months—and he didn't get the flu, despite having been exposed to it countless times.

—ELLA MAY STUMPE

All through the war, we did a lot of entertaining of the soldiers. Camp Grant was right there at Rockford, Illinois, just a few miles out in the country. We used to have lots of parties for the soldiers; we did what we could to make them happy. But when the flu struck, it was a sad time at Camp Grant. Schools were closed, and because they couldn't get enough nurses, many of the teachers, myself included, went to the camp every day and did what we could. Of course, we couldn't actually nurse them, but we could see that they had cold drinks and were comfortable, and we could meet their relatives when they came to see them.

They put out a daily newspaper at Camp Grant. One day, the paper said we had only ninety-nine deaths yesterday and the people, oh, they were so happy to think that they were under the hundred mark. The man who was in charge of Camp Grant, Colonel Hagedorn, committed suicide because he was losing so many of his men. There was one man, the father of one of the soldiers, who came to the camp. I felt so sorry for him. He had three sons all in the service in different camps. He got to the first camp just after his son died, and he went immediately to the next camp and his son there had just died. And he got to Camp Grant just after his third son died.

The strange thing to me was that most of us who went down to the camp never got the flu. Sure, we were careful and all, but it didn't worry us. And people who didn't leave their house because they were scared to go outside, the woman living next door to us, for instance, got the flu and died of it.

—ANNETTA GIBSON

I don't even like to think about it, it was so awful. We were living in Logan, West Virginia, then. Every time we got news from anybody, somebody else was dead. My mother took the flu, and the doctors said, frankly, they didn't know what to do; this was something new. My mother took a notion that it might help her if she put an onion poultice to her chest. This was an old-fashioned remedy.

Annetta Gibson

Well, she tried that, and we didn't know whether it helped or not, but my mother began to get better. Then my daddy took the flu. He never did get real bad with it, but he was bad enough. He couldn't work for a few days. And my brother, who lived up in another section of town, came down to see Mom and Dad, and while he was there he just slumped over with it. He must have been taken with it when he came down. Anyway, he got awfully bad with it, and they didn't think he'd live.

There was a family living near us, I guess it was a block away, by the name of Bates. We got word that Mr. Bates had the flu. One of their children had already died of the flu. Two or three hours later, we got word that Mr. Bates had died. Mrs. Bates went to his funeral, and that night she took the flu. The next day, she died. And two days later, one of the other children died with it.

But there were so many deaths. And anybody that was able, even youngsters, would go and sit up with the family, or try to help them any way they could. I went over to the Bateses' because one of the other children was awfully sick with it. And with my brother so bad, they was expecting him to die at any minute. So the signal was, if Mama put a light in the window, I would know that my brother was dead, and I was to come home.

All night I watched for that light, but it didn't appear. Then he had a great big lump come in under his shoulder blade, and the doctor said he would have to lance it. Another doctor said not to. Finally, my brother said, I can't stand this; just go ahead and lance it. And that was so full of poison, when they lanced it, the pus flew clear over his shirt onto the wall. But he lived. He lived a long time after that.

But, oh, it was bad. It killed so many people. Everywhere, people were dying. Back in them days, though, they didn't call it the flu. It was always the Spanish influenza. They always pronounced the whole thing.

—ADA TABOR

A lot of people would die. But some, when they got them to the cemetery, they'd come to; they weren't dead yet. People were dying so fast they didn't even check them good. If you passed out, they buried you.

—PAUL ONESI

My father was a doctor, and his work was in the valley where they had the mines. The mines paid him to take care of their workers and took money out of their wages to pay him.

When that terrible flu epidemic struck, he closed his office and went from house to house helping people and advising them what to do. My husband's sister lived in Harriman, Tennessee, and some people that were close to her moved there. And this woman had the flu. She was pretty sick. Her husband wasn't satisfied with what her doctor was telling her. So he called and said to my mother, Mrs. Hill, what are you feeding your children? And she said, Well, I have a daughter here, she's just made some rice and I'll be glad to send some over.

So I went over. Now, this Mrs. Crane, she was lying in bed just burning up with fever. And she says, My doctor told me not to take any water.

Now, can you imagine? I said, Well, I won't give you any water, but I'll be glad to get some ice and moisten your lips. So I did that and I said, Your house is so hot, and you with this fever, I don't see how you can stand it.

Well, the doctor says not to open the windows.

So I go in the other room and I open the windows a little, you know. Everything I did was against what her doctor had said. I left and went home.

When that woman's doctor came again, her husband told him, I'm turning my wife over to Dr. Hill.

So Daddy went in to see her and the first thing he said was, You can have all the water you want.

She said, I never heard anything as wonderful.

I took over some juice and she drank some of it and she retained it. When Daddy come home, he said, She's the sickest person I've ever seen, I don't believe she'll live. Let's get her mother here to take care of her.

And you know, everything turned out. That woman got well.

—PAULINE HILL MASSEY

It was sad. In Norfolk, Virginia, there was so many dyin' they couldn't get enough coffins to bury 'em in. They had to ship 'em on the freight train to different places to bury 'em, white and colored. I was livin' in Seaboard, close to the railroad, and I could see the boxcars loaded with caskets.

People were scared to go where the influenza was 'cause it was killin' a lotta, lotta people. Me and my husband helped bury many a one that died. One woman died and left a little-bitty baby, and her man was scared to go and bury his woman, afraid he'd catch the flu. My husband weren't afraid of no kind of disease—he had the swamp pox when he was a young boy—and he'd go and help bury folks that died and couldn't have no funeral in the churches.

—SALLIE JORDAN

I had a girlfriend that I grew up with. She and I were always together. She had a sister who lived near Helix and she stayed quite a bit of time with her. I used to go over and we'd all get together.

Anyway, she met this farmer, Max, and married him. And then, when they were expecting their first child, she stayed with me for the week or so before she had to go over to the hospital. A year and a half later, she had another child. But that was the year of the big flu epidemic. She lost her life when that baby was born. Max also had the flu and he couldn't even go to the service when his wife passed away.

I was teaching school out at Max's brother's place. Max would come down from Lacrosse, Washington, where he was farming, and we started going together. We got married in the fall of 1922.

—JUANITA DUDLEY

People would die left and right. We had a three-tenement house, we lived on the second floor, and this fellow and his wife lived on the first floor. I was going up on Pier Street one day and I saw him. Aren't you working today? I said.

No, I'm not feeling too good.

Oh, I said, you must be coming down with the flu.

By the time I got home, he had died. His wife had gone to visit her mother in New York. I called her up on the phone. I said, Make it as snappy as you can 'cause your husband is very, very sick. By the time she got back to Westerly, of course, he was gone. The poor thing. They had no children, and they were not young, either.

A lot of our neighbors died. One of my neighbors ran a butcher shop. She had a little baby. My son, Clarence, was a baby, too, then. She came down with the flu. And I said, My Lord, what am I going to do, make that lady die with a baby now? My mother was mad, though. She said, Listen, *you've* got a baby. Something should happen, what's going to happen to the baby? But Ma, I said, if I get it and if I'm meant to die, I'm gonna die, but I can't make that girl die like that. People thought I was crazy, but I wasn't. I was just nice.

Her daughter is still living.

—THERESA NIGRELLI

Juanita Dudley

Prohibition

Just 'cause they banned liquor,

it didn't mean

you couldn't get any.

—LENA STANLEY

Born May 18, 1895

Hillsboro, North Dakota

I have never smoked a cigarette. I have never tasted wine or beer or any alcoholic drink. I have always been a total abstainer. I signed a pledge when I was eight years old: *I pledge that I may give my best to home and country. I promise, God help me, not to buy, drink, sell, or give alcoholic liquor while I live. From all tobacco and other harmful things I'll abstain and never take God's name in vain.* And I have kept that pledge all these years.

Mother was the first president of the Woman's Christian Temperance Union in Saluda. That was organized in 1905, and I organized the Loyal Temperance Legion. That's for children, to get them to sign the pledge when they're little; then they don't have any chance, you see, of becoming alcoholic. You didn't ever have to be drunk to be an alcoholic. You can become an alcoholic just by drinking a little bit of beer or a little bit of wine every day. That's the nature of alcohol: it sneaks up on you.

Let me tell you: The grandest moment in this century was when Prohibition came. The lowest was when it was voted out. It was a howling success. And that's why seven millionaires pooled their resources and sent a million dollars, in 1932, to the South Carolina legislature and paid them to vote to repeal Prohibition. They claimed that beer and wine were not intoxicating, and that Prohibition was a failure. Not a bigger lie has ever been told in Columbia.

Lois Crouch Addy in her senior year at Winthrop College, 1914

We had a neighbor, Mr. Stevenson, who never liked anything but beer. He used to say he never brought a bottle home. He drank his beer uptown and would come home and go to bed and stay in bed until he sobered up. He never liked anything but beer. And yet they said just give us beer and wine. Well, that was just getting a foot in the door.

Of course, some few made home brew. There's some people that are gonna do what they're gonna do, regardless. But Prohibition was not a failure. Those years were the golden years of our lives. You could go anywhere, you didn't have to lock your doors, you could believe anything anybody told you, and you had money to buy things that people that drank didn't have.

—LOIS CROUCH ADDY

Prohibition was very unpopular in the Delta. Although the women thought it was a great protection to them, Delta men liked to drink and didn't want to have to snoop around the corner to get their drink. There used to be a saloon on nearly every corner, and to get them closed down was quite an effort.

They called a meeting one time to get women signed up to work for the Prohibition amendment. My mother, who was very strong against drinking the alcoholic drink, spoke, and then there was a general discussion. Somebody said something about we should help Mrs. Somerville to push this, and one person got up and said, Well, our father had a saloon and that's the way we were educated and brought up. Then this other lady said, But we have to remember that the people who were trying to abolish liquor sales were trying to do good for the community. That impressed me.

Of course, bootlegging went on all over. Mississippi was never enthusiastically supporting Prohibition. They had it, and the state did the best they could in enforcing it. But the community—the men—always wanted to be able to get a drink. And I wouldn't hesitate to say that I feel sure that some of the women wanted a drink. But they didn't hang around on corners at saloons. They were more discreet. If a woman knew you well enough, she'd offer you a drink.

—LUCY SOMERVILLE HOWORTH

Yeah, bootlegging started people drinking that never drank before. Because people couldn't have something, all of a sudden they wanted it.

I was working in the bank at that time. A lot of my friends were making booze. In fact, one lady that ran the bootleg joint between Columbus and Beaver Dam would bring the money in and I'd help her put it in a safe-deposit box. When she needed some, she'd come and get it. I knew where it was; nobody else did.

I was not a drinking man, though. But I liked a good glass of beer and I knew where to get one. Of course, there was a lot of homemade stuff out there that wasn't fit to drink, but people drank it anyway.

Oh, the authorities would go after the bootleggers, but I don't think they were too serious about it.

—AL KRAUS

Before Prohibition came, my father's grocery store was a liquor store, too. The liquor was sold in the back, and everything else in the front. He sold liquor until the law changed.

Prohibition was enforced in North Carolina. They'd catch you making white lightning and they'd put you in jail for five to ten years. But people wanted the liquor. And the people who could make the liquor wanted to make the liquor, and in Virginia they didn't have restrictions like they had in North Carolina. Finally, when North Carolina broke down and went legal, that was because all that money people'd been spending in Virginia could come back to North Carolina. See, people who liked to drink, that's what they wanted and they would get it one way or the other.

The only place you could get alcohol legally in North Carolina during Prohibition was in the pharmacies. Most of medicines then were made with alcohol—like ninety percent pure alcohol. And what a lot of the drugstores did was to buy this alcohol from the government in gallons of ninety proof and put some good stuff in it to make it look better and taste a little better. They made more money selling liquor than they did filling prescriptions.

—YORK GARRETT

In every hollow out in the country there was a still. There was shoot-outs 'n' all between the moonshiners and the revenuers. The revenuers, they'd chop up a still everywhere they could find 'em, then the bootleggers'd make two more. Bootleggin' was everywhere. The law didn't work at all.

People wanted to drink that old mean stuff. It killed a lot of people. They put everything in it: tobacco stems, rubbin' alcohol. I drunk some of that, not very much, though. Don't remember a time when I didn't take a drink. Still want one before I eat.

—ORLANDO F. MORLEY

Jack, my husband, he could drink just about anybody under the table. But you couldn't see it on him. He was just straight, just ordinary, but he'd lap 'er up. There was no harm in him, you know; he was just plain Jack.

I was waitressing, working nights right here in Williston, and one evening these two guys came in. They were either gamblers or bootleggers or both. They were well dressed: black suits, white shirts, black bow ties. They sat down and I went to wait on 'em and the one looked right up at me and started talking Norwegian. I didn't pay no attention to him, I just let him talk. And the other guy says to me, He doesn't talk American. I still didn't say anything, you know, I just worked around and waited on 'em. This went on through supper, and when it come to pay, he said, The joke's on you. I can talk as good American as you can. I answered him in Norwegian. The other guy laughed. Yes, I wonder who the joke is on, he said.

So that's just the kind of a hasher I was.

—LENA STANLEY

Oscar C. Weber, Mount Rainier, 1920s

Washington State went dry one year before the national Prohibition. Of course, Prohibition was supposed to be strictly enforced, but it wasn't. I think the people who did the enforcing were just as guilty of bootlegging as anybody else. Some people were arrested, sure. But it seemed as if everybody was making beer and wine and whiskey. Some of the big bootleggers went up to Canada and loaded up ships and cars to haul the booze in. One year at Christmastime, I wanted to buy a bottle of liquor for a party, and the price got up to twenty-nine dollars a fifth. So it really got pretty expensive if anybody wanted to keep on drinking any quantity at all. And I'm not talkin' about boot liquor; I'm talkin' about good, honest-to-God brands of liquor.

—OSCAR C. WEBER

Long before the so-called Gilded Age in Newport, when all those big mansions, the Breakers and the Elms and the others, were built by the Auchinclosses and the Vanderbilts and the other wealthy people who came here and were vying with each other socially, Newport was involved in the rumrunning trade. This was back in the 1700s. Then they traded the rum for slaves. That was particularly true not so much in the North as in the South.

Rumrunning started again during Prohibition. Prohibition, you know, was a great example of hypocrisy. There was really no such thing as absolute Prohibition. They tried to enforce it, but they couldn't. The problem for the government was, people liked to drink, they liked to go to the pubs. In those days, because of Prohibition, they had to find places where they could get the drink. I was not a heavy drinker, I didn't frequent those places, those speakeasies, very much. Good liquor, of course, was very expensive. But there was a lot of bad liquor—bathtub gin—sold, too.

Anyone that drank wasn't looked down on merely because they were violating the Prohibition law. Life went on about the same. You can't legislate morals into a people. You can't do it.

—EDWARD J. CORCORAN

The Great Depression

In the summer of 1929 . . . there

seemed no reason why prosperity

shouldn't continue, if not forever,

at least for a long time.

—PHILIP L. CARRET

Born November 29, 1896

Lynn, Massachusetts

Through the 1920s, the action on Wall Street was mostly on the floor of the New York Stock Exchange. There was a certain amount of over-the-counter market, but not much. I don't know how many stocks were listed on the Big Board, but probably not more than a few hundred on the outside. And the curb market was literally a curb: They used to trade on the street, out on Broad Street. Brokers would sit in the windows and signal back and forth to each other to make the trades. The over-the-counter market literally started that way. Somebody would have a block of bonds to sell, he'd put them in his pocket and go from office to office until he found somebody who'd buy them.

The New York Stock Exchange was a quasi-gambling institution. Most of the action was people trying to make quick profits. There was a lot of so-called pool operations, where wealthy operators would gang up and form a pool. Their most famous pool, I think, was in Radio Corporation of America, which was sort of a gambling counter. They'd run the stock up, take a profit, knock it in the head and run it down again.

There was no Securities and Exchange Commission, and the stock trading was dominated by the pools. All the manipulating they used to do. One scam was called "paint the tape." Two brokers—one would sell and the other would buy—would want a stock to have a big volume. So they'd sell back and forth to one another. And everybody else would say, Geez, there must be something going on, there's a big merger pending or something like that. So a bunch of suckers would rush in and buy the stock. And then the people who were in on that pool would unload it, take their profit and run. The ratio of speculative trades was probably ten times as much as the volume of actual investment purchases and sales.

In the summer of 1929, almost no American, from the executives of Wall Street banks to the steel workers in Gary, Indiana, saw any clouds on the horizon. America was rich and increasingly prosperous. The country was growing. Its people were energetic. There was such a phenomenon as the business cycle, however, and the partners of Blyth, Witter & Company, the investment firm where I had been working since 1927, were dimly aware of it.

◄ *At a demonstration in Times Square, New York City, in 1933, the unemployed protest the lack of jobs (Culver Pictures)*

Technically, the stock market in September 1929 was in a precarious condition. Many who considered themselves investors were really gambling, trading on thin margins. Many firms permitted customers to buy $10,000 worth of stock with a $1,000 payment! This was great if the stock went up, say, from twenty dollars to twenty-two; then the lucky customer had doubled his money. But if the stock went down, he was required to put up more money immediately or his broker would sell the stock and bill him for any additional loss. The casinos of Atlantic City and Las Vegas did not then exist, nor were there state lotteries, and Americans in unprecedented numbers were attracted to the stock market. The Blyth, Witter partners had yielded to the prevailing mania, bought a seat on the New York Stock Exchange, and rented additional space. No expense was spared to make these quarters attractive. Similar quarters for the new activity were opened all over the country.

Margin calls had a domino effect. As large numbers of amateur speculators were sold out, stock prices declined. This triggered another wave of margin calls and prices declined further. The dream of unending prosperity quickly faded away. The misery of the unfortunate speculators whose accounts had been so brutally eliminated spread unease, then panic, even among investors whose securities were not pledged as collateral to any bank or broker. In a short three months the public mood changed from euphoria to despair.

"Black Tuesday," at the time, was merely an exciting event which nobody considered of vital importance. There had been panics before, in 1907, in 1893, 1873. These things happened every once in a while. But I don't think anybody thought at the time that it meant a great effect on business. I think it was realized a year after the panic, and from then on.

Richard Whitney, who was selected by the bankers' pool to buy up millions of dollars of stock in an attempt to avert disaster, was the brother of George Whitney, a Morgan partner. That's how he got to be president of the Stock Exchange. He was, I think, a gentleman of limited financial sense. He was involved in the company that made Applejack when Prohibition was ended; this was not a very glamorous drink and was a failure as far as finances went.

Richard Whitney went to jail. My partners and I did business with an aristocratic gentleman who had a number of wealthy clients who had entrusted their affairs to him. Unfortunately, the fees that he got from his clients were somewhat less than he needed to maintain his lifestyle. So he dipped into their accounts, I think, to a minor extent. Most of them were willing to forget about it, but one of them insisted he go to jail. He and

Richard Whitney were both graduates of Harvard, and of the Groton School, a very aristocratic prep school. I was fascinated when he got out of Sing Sing and he came into the office. Before his fall he'd been arrogant; he'd been born to the purple, as it were. He was just as arrogant after he got out.

During the early 1930s, commuter trains carried thousands of weary executives home to the suburbs from a never-ending battle. In war, with all its misery, boredom, danger and death, there is at least occasional excitement and a tangible enemy. The Depression was a different kind of battle. The enemy could not be identified. It was an amorphous force. Its agents were the bankers who called loans, the margin clerks who demanded more money to bolster accounts which had once seemed impregnably secure, and the landlords and other providers of overhead whose demands exceeded the revenues of their tenants. The commuter who was a partner, sole proprietor or executive in many cases watched the slow erosion of his capital and wondered whether it would last until the economy recovered. Prosperity was just around the corner, it was said, but would we ever reach the corner?

The little firm of Carret, Gammons and Company was established in 1932. Two of the three partners, Clifton N. Bradley and I, had just been eliminated from the payroll of Blyth, Witter. That firm was suffering severely from the Depression and was cutting overhead drastically. Economic Research, Inc., the service organization which Clif and I had managed, had no further utility for Blyth. We were excess baggage. When I lost my job, I didn't even look for another job. It would have been useless. The firm sold Economic Research to me for one dollar plus the cash in the bank. We thus had a shell on which to build a business. This was the sort of "golden parachute" available to dismissed executives during the Great Depression.

We started with very limited capital, and we were very cautious, too damn cautious, as it turned out. The first year, 1933, I think I made maybe $2,000, so I lived partly on my savings—and lived very frugally. And the next year I made a bare living. And after that, everything was okay.

But for others, things didn't quite work out. There were a few suicides. My office was in 120 Broadway. One day a rumor went around the building that somebody had jumped out the window. We had an acquaintance who had a little shop, himself and an assistant, trading securities. One of my partners called him up. The assistant answered. Clif said to him, I understand somebody just jumped out the window. It wasn't So-and-So, was it?

It was.

It was all very well for Roosevelt to say that Americans had nothing to fear but fear itself. Most Americans had plenty to fear. They were afraid of losing their jobs. They feared that a bank failure might wipe out their savings. If they owned their home, they owed some bank interest on the principal of a mortgage. Default in payment would mean foreclosure, the loss of the home. Worse yet, in the unenlightened early 1930s, the mortgage institution would sell the house at auction. It would probably go at a bargain price, far less than the face amount of the mortgage. The hapless homeowner then owed a "deficiency judgment," the difference between the auction price and the mortgage. One of the better inspirations of the New Deal was creation of the Federal Housing Administration, which provided or guaranteed long-term loans, up to thirty years, amortized by regular, affordable monthly payments of interest and principal. Before this reform took effect, the suffering inflicted on thrifty Americans by the old system was horrendous.

—PHILIP L. CARRET

I was a young man going places, businesswise, for ten years. After the stock market crashed, I was stuck with half a dozen houses I couldn't sell. I turned into a landlord. A postal clerk told me he couldn't pay the rent, and he wasn't the only one. I found myself supporting people who were out of jobs. So for that ten years I was "going places" I just might as well have been standing still, because I didn't have any more than I had at the beginning.

There was this one man, a Harvard graduate, smarter than me, a rich man in the stock market. He gave me a little lecture when he took my homes. Then one time I picked up the Trenton *Times*. The headline was about the guy that took my homes. He'd committed suicide. What had happened was, he lost his paper fortune, then *zip!* he shot himself.

God knows how I got through the Depression. I got married.

—ARTHUR W. HAMER, SR.

When the stock market crashed, there was a run on the banks. So they shut the doors. We were a pretty good customer, so our bank let me in.

I walked in and I said, What does this mean?

We don't know.

Well, what's going to result?

We don't know.

—JOSEPH GOLDSTEIN

I was working for the Frick Company and I had charge of these people in the field. I had three jobs going on in the New York City area. One was up in the Bronx, two of them were out in Brooklyn. We traveled mostly by train. Railroad fare was two cents a mile, and you could buy a book that had these little coupons and you could pay for a ticket with those coupons. We were told not to carry too much cash, which I didn't do, because at the branch offices they would cash our checks.

There was this talk about the coming depression, but there really was nothing that would tell you it was going to happen now or a week from now. And the crash happened that day I'm in New York. As soon as I heard about it, I immediately got on the subway and went to our office on Cortland Street. The office was closed. When those people heard about it, they rushed out to get money out of the bank and went home.

So I'm in New York City with no money. What'll I do? I go to the Pennsylvania Railroad Station, to a ticket window. I tell the man, Look, I want to get to Waynesboro, Pennsylvania. I only have a dollar here, enough to buy a meal. Hopefully, you'll accept my gold watch and chain. It is worth considerable money as compared to the train fare. And the fellow said, Well, I'll take you up on that. I said, I'll be back here, I've got to be back here next week, and I'll give you the money, even pay you interest on it, and you give me back my watch and chain. And that's the way it worked out.

When I got to Waynesboro, the bank was closed. We had just whatever money my wife happened to have here in the house at the time, until the banks were finally opened and we could get some money.

But that's only part of the story.

I had made a pledge to our church that I would pay so much money. Okay, this pledge is due right at that time. I said, Look, I don't have money now to pay that. I'll pay it, but you're going to have to wait. But the treasurer at that time was just that kind of a guy. Oh, no, he said, this pledge is as good as a note and we're going to foreclose it on you. I had to borrow from relatives and friends.

Now, my brother John and I had started an ice plant in Carlisle, Pennsylvania, in 1925. We had a mortgage of about $10,000 that we'd been paying off regularly. The bank in Carlisle said, We're foreclosing. I asked them why. Here's this lumberyard over here, they've gone broke. But we're the only ones that are really paying you, I said. Yes, the banker said, you're the only ones that have the money and we need the money. So they foreclosed. But I was fortunate to scrape up the money and pay off the mortgage and we were able to save the plant, thanks to friends.

Within a year or so, though, most everybody had gotten adjusted one way or another. In New York City, there were people standing on the street corners selling apples and oranges. Whether you wanted one or not, you always bought one. People who had, well, they pitched in and helped out.

—MILTON W. GARLAND

After the stock market crashed, we gave up our farm near Colfax, Washington, and moved up to northern Idaho, to the Kootenai River Valley that was such a rich valley. We held our wheat, but the prices kept going down and down and down and we lost everything.

Max was able to get work up there for WPA for thirty cents an hour. They did all kinds of things—repairing roads, digging out roads. He was a foreman, but he got in trouble when he told a fellow whose mother had died to take two days off and work two other days instead. He had a friend who ran a pool hall, so he worked there for a while. Another friend owned an implement company, and when times were really rough, we went to the door one day and there was an envelope with twenty dollars in it, and that meant a lot.

Times were rough. To this day, I can just see Max, sitting and holding his head in his hands: four kids to support. But we had our vegetable garden, and a cow in the back yard. The girls used to get so embarrassed with that cow in the yard. We lived in town then, in Bonners Ferry, Idaho. We had a lady who was an extension agent, and she'd go around and tell you how to make cheese and preserve vegetables and make things go farther. She'd get all the ladies in the neighborhood together and they called it the ETC Club: Eat, Tat, and Chat. They did a lot of good. So we got by.

It was worse for others. In 1939, we moved to Seattle. Downtown, just off First Avenue, there was a Hooverville. People were living in little old shacks, cardboard shacks. They would take these big cardboard boxes they'd probably get from furniture and make them into a home there. They even elected their own mayor.

—JUANITA DUDLEY

A fellow that had been a classmate of mine at the University of Washington came down, and I was talking to him, fairly muttering about the fact that we'd had a ten percent salary cut. He worked for one of the tire companies. They'd had a sixty percent cut. So you can imagine how he felt about my moaning over ten percent.

But at Procter and Gamble they'd turn handsprings to keep all their employees. At that time, if you'd been there for six months and hadn't made any serious errors, you really had a lifetime job. Skilled mechanics would be out chipping paint off of an iron fence and repainting it. They weren't paid the salary they'd earned before, though; they were paid what P&G could hire a painter for.

—VICTOR MILLS

The owners of the Westmoreland Coal Company, where I was a paymaster, were very conscious of their people's needs. During the Depression, I took a hell of a cut; I think they cut my salary fifty dollars a month. And that was a lot of money back then, when I was earning $175 a month.

The company had their own retail stores, and we issued scrip to the employees to buy groceries. But if a fellow needed some credit, I couldn't extend any till it was authorized by the superintendent. So one day the superintendent come to me and he said, Orlando, you know all these people. We don't want their families to suffer, so we're going to turn the credit over to you. You just go ahead and credit them on the basis of a dollar a day for a single person, two dollars for a married couple, and extra for a child. Back then, a dollar a day bought a lot of groceries. And we did that. My debit/dollar ledger got so heavy I couldn't carry it. I organized me another system, so that payroll kept the monthly charges for each employee till the end of the month, then I balanced it and cross-balanced it, drew my total and transferred it to my daily ledger.

But I'll tell you, if the company hadn't taken care of their employees, they'd a starved to death, no question about it.

—ORLANDO F. MORLEY

We never gave credit to anybody in the A&P. But I saw how the Depression was hurting people, and I told my wife, If I see Henry Brown needing any advance money, I'm going to give it to him. Because I was still making big money.

So Henry'd go to the register and I'd see him. When I saw the clerk pushing back some of his groceries, I went up to the aisle they were checking out and I said, Good morning, Henry, how are you?

Now, he'd have maybe $5.90 worth of groceries that he'd be short. So I'd put my hands in my pocket and get out $5.90 and I would hand it over to him. I said, Here's what you're short. You go ahead and put that with yours. You're not borrowing from the A&P, forget it. Whenever you have it to pay me back, you see Ernest Deetjen.

I had I would say two dozen I was doing this for. They were good people. And my wife would say, We're making more than we ever made. And you know, it wasn't long before they had paid back every bit of it, every cent.

—ERNEST C. DEETJEN

Back in those days, banking meant your customer was part of your duty. If there was a death in the family, you lent your services. The old farmers, some of them, they did all the business, the wife didn't know anything that was going on. Then the husband would die. Our president would say, Al, you go out for a couple of days and help the lady get adjusted. And I would do that. Nowadays, they don't hardly know their customer when he comes in. He's just a number. Unless he's a very big customer, of course.

In 1934 I went to St. Paul with the Farm Credit Administration. We would go out and help a man that was belly-up. Of course, we would put restrictions, and they would live within those restrictions.

Our manager would say, Kraus, So-and-So is in trouble. I would go out to his farm. And you could tell when you drove up there that he was. Two, three cars lay in the front yard. His crops was not doing as well as his neighbors', and so on down the line. First thing I would say, Where's your wife?

In the house.

Well, let's go in.

What's she got to do with it?

Quite a lot.

So I'd get in the house. She probably had the dishes all piled up on the table or in the sink. She'd say, I can't do things, my washing machine is broken.

Lady, I'd say, I can remember when we used a tub and a washboard. Perhaps you're going to have to use that for a little while.

Of course, this didn't go across too well, but it went across. Then I would talk to the farmer the same way. The wife was probably harder to handle than he was. I would find out from all the people that he owed what he owed them, try to consolidate that debt, loan him the money to get him going, with the understanding that so much went to pay off the debt. And they conformed. They adjusted.

It wasn't easy for the farmers. Kansas and even some parts of Minnesota had those dust storms. We were blessed pretty well, though, with weather. Of course, I'd go to this farmer that was kind of behind. Oh, the weather's been bad, he'd say.

Well, my good friend, I'd say, your neighbor had the same weather and he's got a good-looking crop. What happened? You didn't get it planted in time. Or you didn't take care of it, see. There's the answer.

—AL KRAUS

We just had to learn to get along with less. But I had my job all that time. Everyone knew that the teachers' salaries were being held up and everyone was very good about it. The stores charged anything we wanted, and we'd pay them when we got paid, so it wasn't too bad.

The one thing that was bad was that we had worked hard at school to get the children to save. One day every week we had banking at school, and the children would bring, oh, maybe just a few pennies that they would put in their banks. Some of them had nice little bank accounts when the Depression hit, and some of them never got their money back. It wasn't too good a lesson for them because they thought they might as well spend their money as save it and then have it gone.

—ANNETTA GIBSON

My husband and my brother got together and bought the newspaper in Harriman, Tennessee, just at the time of the Depression. Well, of course, papers make a living by selling ads. But nobody had any money. So when a grocery store would take an ad, they'd let us just come in and take groceries for the price of the ad. And there was a hotel there, and the woman who ran the dining room, every Sunday she would take an ad telling what she was serving. Well, you know how she paid for it: we went and ate there on Sunday.

—PAULINE HILL MASSEY

We were a little better off than a good many other people in Westerly. But some poor people, it was tough on them. We used to sell rags. We used to sell paper. I'd get a dollar and a half for paper and I thought I'd become a millionaire.

One of my friends died. They were very poor and she didn't have a nice dress. And I said, We're going to bury her with one.

What are we going to do? There's no money.

I said, I'm going to give her my wedding dress. She's going to wear that. She was a friend of mine, she was a nice girl and she's putting on my dress.

Then everybody says, You're going to have bad luck. If I have bad luck, it's me, it's not you, I told 'em.

So I said, Ma, go get the dress. My wedding dress is underground for years and years and years. And I still got good luck.

—THERESA NIGRELLI

Jessie Turner with her husband, Simon, on their farm in Henry County, Georgia

It was bad on us poor folks. We didn't have nothin', and we couldn't even make the five bales of cotton rent to Miss Cora Wise. The boll weevils ate the crop, so we could only make three. But she was a rich woman and a fine person. We just had to pay for the food we ate. And that's how we got by one year.

—JESSIE TURNER

The Depression didn't affect us at all. We were poor, and my husband had a job and we had enough money to get along. When poor people like us were trying to find their way home after they were discharged and had nothing, and they had to beg their way, we used to feed everybody that came along. We'd share what we had with them. If I had nothing in the house but some eggs and some bacon fat—and we always had eggs because we always had chickens—I'd cook up a batch of eggs, give them coffee or tea, whatever we had, and some bread. And if there was enough, I'd give them a sandwich or two to take along with them.

—JULIA TYLER

Oh, it was bad. I'd send one of my kids down to the corner store to get a chicken; it was about a quarter. They'd have the chickens in the coop and you'd point out which chicken you wanted and then you'd take that chicken home and I would break its neck and pluck it. Or you could get five pounds of fish—croaker—for a dime. And the kids would clean it.

My husband was always able to get some land from somebody had a great big yard. And what he would do is plant theirs and take care of it in order to get the chance to plant his. So we always had vegetables—green beans and black-eyed peas and corn and tomatoes—and I'd store them up in jars and we'd have them all year round.

Most of the time, there wasn't any work in the steel mills. And when there was work, they had so many strikes. When they went on strike, my husband went home. He wasn't gonna be run over, 'cause at that time they would bring in the horses to trample on the strikers. Mrs. Darko's little boy got trampled by one of the horses. And people who'd really want to work, scabs, they'd break the strike line.

Things got really bad when the company homes were sold to realtors and they would come knockin' on the door to collect whatever the rent was because nobody was deductin' your rent from your pay anymore. I mean, it was bad. Then when President Franklin Delano Roosevelt came in, some of my boys went to work under the New Deal and they could bring some money in.

One time, President Roosevelt came through the town with the heavy-weight boxer Joe Louis. I think he was campaigning. So naturally that brought the crowd out: everybody wanted to see the champ. But I wanted to see the President. I was bold enough to walk up to him and thank him and shake his hand for what he had done for the people. He was very pleased that this black lady would come up to him and shake his hand and say to him, If I could, I would kiss you. Because he had put a chicken in my pot. Poor people really fared better after he was elected.

—CHARLIE LUE MOSLEY

The Depression hit very deeply into the middle class—the educated, the articulate. I think we were pretty close to a revolution when Roosevelt came in with the National Recovery Act. Welfare, Social Security—all of these social programs—grew out of those days. It's hard to realize that before then there was nothing. Today we're so accustomed to having pensions, we take them for granted. It was not that way for my father; when he was injured, they literally threw him overboard; there was nothing for his widow or his children. All this came in with Roosevelt.

The government set up work projects tailored to artists, musicians, teachers, construction workers, clerical workers, and many professionals. Artists painted murals in public buildings; musicians toured with orchestras, bringing their art to remote parts of the country. Untranslated documents in university archives were translated. Bridges were built along Highway 1 in the West, replacing the time-consuming ferries. Here in Seattle, the library was constructed at the University of Washington. Classes were set up to teach the illiterate to read and write—and there were quite a lot of people who were illiterate. I knew one young man who could not read. He got a job as a waiter. His wife would acompany him to work to read the changes in the menu, which he would memorize.

I worked for WPA for a while. I worked in an auditor's office where they were reevaluating property for tax purposes. And I worked for the teachers. They had educational classes for adults and unemployed teachers, and I did research on how to help them learn in a classroom. I was also on welfare then, and one day I met a man with a petition for unemployment insurance, which I supported. I went to a meeting and then I joined the Communist Party. Eventually, I drifted away.

—HAZEL WOLF

The Depression really didn't affect us very much. I don't think it affected our law practice. Lawyers do well in good times and in bad.

—EDWARD J. CORCORAN

When the Depression hit, my husband was treasurer of the International Harvester factory in Rock Island, Illinois. That was a pretty prestigious job. But it wasn't long before many workers had to be laid off. All of the executives had to take a salary cut. It was only maybe ten percent, but that took the gravy out of our living.

Rock Island was a railroad division point where crews changed trains and trains changed tracks. So a train would be there a couple of hours or more—bringing with it the homeless and the unemployed, who rode for free in extra boxcars. While the train was changing crews, those people would just fan out through the community. There was a Catholic girls' academy where there was usually food left over from the noon meal, and anybody wanted to walk the mile up the hill from the railroad yard could have what was left over. Well, it was never enough. And we lived one block from the academy, so we were never missed by the streams of people coming up the hill. They had to go by our door. The first ones would get fed, but there were so many more people than there was food, and every day there was somebody at my back door asking for something to eat.

One day, my husband was home and he fixed a sandwich and coffee and went out and sat on the back porch with this man while he ate. Turned out that he had been a bank president from somewhere in the East. He had just lost his job. His situation was not uncommon.

I had a personal experience with the manager of the bank where I worked at one time. This was when I had gone out to work as head cashier in a department store in Hammond, Indiana. All the gripes had to come to my window and I had to settle them. One day, who comes to my window but the manager of the bank where I used to work! Now, this was during the very hard Depression days. And he said, Ella May, could I borrow a hundred dollars? I don't think I gave him a hundred, but I did give him some money. He disappeared. A couple of weeks later he was back again, asking to borrow another hundred. He said, I haven't been able to pay you back, but I will. Now, I didn't have very much money, but I did have a salary, so I gave him what I could. I never saw him again.

Ella May Stumpe

He was somebody I knew, or thought I did. I had met his wife. They'd had me to dinner. She was very friendly and I liked her. She was an artist. She went to the Art Institute in Chicago every week for lessons and she did portraits. Theirs had been a late marriage for both of them. She confided to me that she had been a very successful business lady at one time, but now she was an artist, using her talents to create these lovely pictures.

Well, after he disappeared, I heard that she went to the bank, and their safe-deposit box was empty: He had taken her money and her bonds. I don't know if he'd tried to invest them or if he liked to gamble. It was all a big gamble then, anyway. And she had nothing except a brother who lived out in the country that came and got her.

Those years were very, very difficult. But we adjusted to them. We had to.

An elderly couple lived next door to us with whom I was not too neighborly. My son was a year old and demanding of my time, and they were *old*. A friend stopped by one day and said, Do you know your next-door neighbors haven't eaten in three days? I was aghast that this could happen. So we all shared a little.

I was involved in my church work. Guy, my husband, was an elder and I was active in the Friendly Married Folks Sunday-school class. To meet our minister's salary, the class cooked and served dinner once a month on a Saturday night to the downtown workers who kept the stores open. Our church was two blocks from the shopping area, and those workers had to eat. I prepared the menu and bought the food, enough for a hundred people. Helpers canvassed the stores, selling tickets at fifty cents apiece. I cooked the meat. Others peeled and mashed the potatoes, prepared the vegetables, made Jell-O salads, baked dinner rolls, made ice cream and angel-food cakes. We were able to pay for our supplies and net twenty-five dollars a night for the general fund, which helped pay the minister's salary for six months.

We started quilting projects. Our mothers and grandmothers had made quilts, so here was our chance. I bought fabric at twenty-nine cents a yard and cut it up into quilt blocks. After we finished our quilts, we would meet at the church and have shows. We'd gather up a dozen or two and bring them down to the church so everybody could see them and admire them and we'd serve tea and have some cookies. That was our social life.

And that's what the Depression was.

—ELLA MAY STUMPE

The Second World War

You never can believe it,

what happened then.

—JACOB GEWIRTZMAN

Born February 2, 1896

Losice, Poland

The city where I was born, Tachau, was more than six hundred years old, and Jews were there at least three hundred years. There were at least ten little villages around the town with Jews which were longer there than in Tachau.

Emil Glauber, standing second from right, with his parents, who were murdered in Treblinka, and brothers, one of whom, Walter, second from left, was killed in Birkenau, 1916 or 1917

As boys, we had all kind of friends. Sometimes you'd be called a *Juden* boy and stones were thrown at us when we went to *shul*. But it wasn't real anti-Semitism. See, my father was a cattle dealer that bought from the farmers all the cattle he needed. We had a big farm and two big stables. We had respect. Before 1920, 1930 even, we didn't feel any real hatred.

Then the Germans came. They threw the Jews out from the cities and villages in the so-called Sudetenland. They took away whatever land and houses they had. The Jews had to go to Czech villages and to Prague to live.

I have four brothers and we saw what was going on. We knew Jews were being rounded up and killed. So in the fall of 1938 my wife and I, we

◄ *His father, mother, and sister bid a tearful goodbye to a young Army private off to training, 1940 (UPI/Corbis-Bettmann)*

took the children and went to Antwerp to emigrate to the United States. Because my close friends there wrote and wrote and wrote: Come now, it is time to get out. Gusti, my wife, called me up one day and said, You either come home within two hours, or I'll leave alone with the kids to Antwerp. So I came home and we went.

In Vienna, I had been working as an engineer for a company making rayon, which was very new then. But when I left Vienna, I didn't see my parents. So I went in December 1938 to Prague. I chased my brothers out to Palestine. But my parents couldn't go; they were very, very sick, and they didn't want to go. Then the Germans marched into Prague, and they couldn't go.

So I had to get out. I bought a ticket to the train. After three stations, the SS came in and threw all the Jews out. But then, after about four days, I was told the SS has not established any power in Prague. The power of the Germans in Prague was still the Army. And I was told maybe I could get an exit visa.

Well, two days before, my wife sent me a cable that one of the children will be operated on. I thought that maybe this is something I can use. And this cable I had when I went in the morning up to the castle where the authorities were. After an hour of waiting I came to an officer, and I showed him the cable. I told him, I have to go home to Antwerp; if I have to stay here, my life is gone.

He said, Have you been in the First World War?

Yes. I was four years in the war. I was wounded in the elbow on the front in Russia.

Have you been a reserve officer?

Yes.

Give me your word of honor as a former reserve officer in the Austrian–Hungarian monarchy that this cable is correct.

So I told him, Listen, I can swear I think it is correct; but to give you my word of honor is impossible.

Then he says, Do you want to stay here?

No.

Okay. Here is your visa. Congratulations.

And then he said, I wish I could come with you.

I was so flabbergasted, I forgot to ask for his name. He saved my life.

— EMIL GLAUBER

Part of the allure of the Nazis was this oft-repeated assertion: "We were not defeated by the French, English, or American armies; we were stabbed in the back by the socialists and the Jews. Revenge against the Treaty of Shame—Versailles—is the supreme national duty." Not all were united yet behind Hitler, but certainly the majority of the people agreed with such parols and a major thesis in *Mein Kampf*: the inexorable enemy of the German people is and always will remain France.

The spiritual preparation for war was under way.

I thought at the time about how the dangerous nationalistic mentality in Germany might be changed. An idea came to me: At the long German–French front of the war, festive tents should be erected, there where the bloody battles were fought and so many had died: Verdun. Soissons. Flanders. Chemin des Dames. La Bassée. The former soldiers of the combatant nations should be invited, with their families, to meet their opposites. There where nobody believed it possible to survive, where they killed and were ready to die, where red and green flares would remind of the horrors they lived through, the former enemies would meet. There would be common meals, performances of artists, and then, the inevitable shock, the former enemies would understand: Those men and women on the other side are as we are. We cannot hate them.

Of course, the political developments in Germany made this an illusion.

On April 13, 1930, my father died. In spite of the political climate, the Wesel newspapers had their first page framed in black and reserved for extensive obituaries recognizing the great contributions Hermann Leyens had made to the life of his town. Indeed, life in the city practically came to a standstill on the day of the funeral. Such contradictions were still possible in Germany.

Just three years later, on April 1, 1933, I stood in the street, next to a group of SA—Sturm Abteilungen—men, and distributed leaflets to passersby. The SA were the storm troopers, organized along military lines, of the Nazi Party. A short time before, the party had obtained key ministries in a newly formed government; as a consequence, the SA were able to rule the streets. Even the regular police had to follow their orders. They didn't interfere when people, particularly Jewish citizens, were trampled to death for whatever reason. It was the time when Goering, who as Prime Minister of Prussia and also head of the SA, could be heard over the radio to say: Each shot fired by the SA is as fired by me.

The previous evening, I had been alerted that the SA were being mobilized for a boycott throughout the country of any enterprise owned by Jews. The next day, SA men blocked buildings decried as "Jewish." Pickets carrying hate banners were planted in front of "Jewish" stores as well as the offices of Jewish doctors and lawyers. It was an action felt by countless numbers of Jews as a personal humiliation to such a degree that they considered their lives robbed of all meaning. On this day began the ever-rising incidence of suicides.

I felt different. I wanted to fight. My first reaction was to quickly design a leaflet which I wished to distribute in the street myself.

Unser Herr Reichskanzler Hitler

die Herren Reichsminister Frick und Göring haben mehrfach folgende Erklärungen abgegeben:

"Wer im 3. Reich einen Frontsoldaten beleidigt, wird mit Zuchthaus bestraft!"

Die 3 Brüder Leyens waren als Kriegsfreiwillige an der Front, sie sind verwundet worden und haben Auszeichnungen für tapferes Verhalten erhalten. Der Vater Leyens stand in freiwilliger Wehr gegen die Spartakisten. Sein Großvater ist in den Freiheitskämpfen an der Katzbach verwundet worden.

Müssen wir uns nach dieser Vergangenheit in nationalem Dienst jetzt öffentlich beschimpfen lassen? Soll das heute der Dank des Vaterlandes sein, wenn vor unserer Tür durch große Plakate aufgefordert wird, nicht in unserm Haus zu kaufen? Wir fassen diese Aktion, die Hand in Hand mit verleumderischen Behauptungen in der Stadt geht, als Angriff auf unsere nationale und bürgerliche Ehre auf, und als eine Schändung des Andenkens von 12000 gefallenen deutschen Frontsoldaten jüdischen Glaubens. Wir sehen darüber hinaus in dieser Aufforderung eine Beleidigung für jeden anständigen Bürger. Es ist uns nicht bange darum, daß es in Wesel auch heute noch die Zivilcourage gibt, die Bismarck einstmals forderte, und deutsche Treue, die gerade jetzt zu uns steht.

Heinrich und Erich Leyens
zugleich als Verfasser und Herausgeber.

It read, in translation:

Our Reich Chancellor Hitler, the Reich Ministers Frick and Goering have repeatedly made the following declaration: Anyone who insults a combat veteran in the Third Reich will be punished with imprisonment.

All three Leyens brothers served as volunteers on the front. They were wounded and were decorated for courageous action. Their father, Hermann Leyens, had been a volunteer in the fight against the Spartacists [a radical group of militants, precursors of the Communist Party in 1919]. His grandfather was wounded at the Katzbach during the Wars of Liberation [1812–14]. With such a record of past national service, do we now have to be subjected to public humiliation? Is this how the fatherland today expresses its gratitude, by placing huge pickets in front of our door with the demand not to buy from our house? We regard this action, which goes hand in hand with the dissemination of slanderous accusations all over town, as an attack on our national and civic honor as well as a desecration of the memory of 12,000 German front soldiers of the Jewish faith who gave their lives in action. Furthermore, we regard this provocation as an affront against every decent citizen. We have no doubt that, even today, there are citizens in Wesel who have the courage of their convictions, which Bismarck once called for, and show German integrity, which, especially now, stands steadfastly by our side.

That very night I found a printer who had the courage to print the copies and have them ready by morning. I had no doubt that I might be killed in the course of distributing these leaflets. But I was convinced that only an open stand, before their very eyes, would cure my fellow citizens of their misguided faith in the new race ideology. In the profound agitation in which I spent the night, my deep conviction became strongly associated with a desire to die.

At ten o'clock in the morning, two SA men were posted at the front entrance to our department store, Leyens and Leverbach. And there I was with my leaflets, right at their side. I had put on my old field uniform with my war medals, next to which was sewn the yellow "Jew patch" the Nazi press had been demanding all Jews wear. What happened then proved how wrong my assumptions about my fellow citizens had been.

At first, a few people stopped and observed the strange spectacle in disbelief. They read my leaflet with obvious shock. Soon several youngsters came running up to me and asked for leaflets to hand out in other parts of the town. More and more people gathered around, until they were so many that the street traffic was disrupted. Voices were raised, loud and clear, in support of the statement in the leaflet. Men gave vent to their indignation. Women, crying, came up and hugged me. The famous composer Blankenburg pushed his way through the meanwhile enlarged line of SA men, purchased a small item, and insisted to have it packed in the largest box, with the name of the firm clearly visible. He demonstratively walked about town with that package.

The SA men remained in front of the main door but made no move. Only once was a bundle of leaflets knocked out of my hands. I returned immediately with a new stack, and this time they left me alone. The tense standoff was finally resolved when they received an order to withdraw. The next day, all three local newspapers still had the courage to run stories that condoned my actions.

About a week before the boycott day, the chief police inspector of Wesel sent an officer to me and asked for my visit. He received me with outstretched arms. My dear Mr. Leyens, he said, I wanted to see you because I wish to be sure that you aren't without a weapon in these perilous times.

When I said I did not have one, he offered me his own service gun and the use of the police range for retraining. I declined, of course, explaining that I never would shoot at a fellow citizen, whatever the provocation. I didn't believe that it was a frame-up, although this powerful man later on became a member of the Nazi Party.

In retrospect, I can understand and explain my own life and my decisions only when I try to describe the most typical changes that occurred in these years. The masses of the people were seduced through the elaborate, glittering pageantry of demonstrations and military parades. In the atmosphere thus created, gullible human beings were convinced that they were following new national values.

A new archenemy was created by brilliant party demagogues. This time it was not France, which according to Hitler would always remain hostile, no matter which party happened to be in power. The old canard of the "International Jewish Conspiracy" became the central message of Nazism: In the East, there was "Jewish" Bolshevism; in the West, the "Jewish" democracies, a degenerate type of government created and dominated by Jews. To combat Germany's enemies East and West, providence had dispatched to the German people a Führer, a leader who appears only once in a thousand years.

Many of the newly faithful saw in Hitler the incarnation of the German soul and the Nazi movement a form of national religion. In shrines that frequently lined rural roads, I saw, with my own eyes, pictures of Hitler replacing traditional images of the Madonna. There can be no doubt that the majority of Christians disapproved of blasphemous excesses of this kind. But nobody, no cardinals, no bishops, no Protestant leaders, dared to speak out publicly. And when the virus spread and became virulent, not one of the highly regarded leaders of the Catholic or Protestant faiths said a word about the fate of the Jews. Nor did they object that the required new greeting—*Heil Hitler!*—replaced the traditional *Grüss Gott* (God be greeted).

The lives of Jews became even more restricted by a series of exclusionary laws. First, all Jews were denied equality under the law. Then, as the noose tightened, they were deprived of their livelihoods. The German *Rechtsstaat*, the constitutional state, came to an end.

A theory, proclaimed as science, was taught at all schools, and hammered incessantly into the national consciousness by the media: the "enemy of the people," the non-Aryan element within the national body, had to be destroyed. The notion of "collective guilt" came into being. The reigning majesty of law among civilized nations, that only individual guilt can be punished, no longer applied to Jews. Hitler, asked during the Olympiad in Berlin in 1936 about black people, said, You can teach tricks also to dogs.

On the fateful day of April 1, 1933, I made a resolution: If after one year the Nazi government's anti-Semitic persecution will continue, I shall leave Germany. During that year, my fight was ludicrous, brave, foolhardy. But it wasn't wrong. In the beginning, I felt the moral support of the town's majority, which wasn't intimidated and even gloried in a defying attitude as they were photographed or insulted when entering our store. That changed after the death of the venerated President, Hindenburg, and Hitler became the one and only head of the nation. To the Führer personally was pledged the oath of obedience—not only by the now millions of the party's paramilitary forces but by the ever-growing military as well. Wesel's newspapers, of which we were for many decades the largest advertisers, were no longer permitted to deal with us. They were forced to reprint the violent anti-Semitic articles from the official Nazi press. It may seem amusing, now, how I fought back, but I certainly was not a happy warrior.

I had my own newspaper printed with irresistible offers. Delivery vans distributed them in Wesel and in surrounding towns. Some of these vans I had converted into buses that brought potential customers to our store without charge. Free refreshments were provided in a large room. There was the attraction of a permanent fashion show. Frequent sales made people resist the political pressure. No doubt about it: people understood that something of a battle was going on between our department store and the organizers of the boycott, and they followed the developments with curious pleasure. Once a week I called a meeting of all employees after business hours to discuss how to deal with problems that came up and how improvements could be made.

It was during such a meeting that I made a remark that was potentially a dangerous mistake. It would be unbearable for me, I told the employees, that somebody could work with me who accepts the anti-Semitic program of the Nazi Party. I made the odious comparison with lice and bugs, from which I frequently suffered more during the war than from the fire of the enemy. Please, I said, whoever belongs to the party or supports its pro gram, have the decency to resign. I will gladly give you a half year's salary with my good wishes.

The next morning, a young woman came into my office, with an embarrassed though friendly expression on her face. She had heard about my speech in the workshop where she was employed. She herself didn't belong to the party, she said, and she wanted to stay with us. But at home there was a lot of politicking every night, and her fiancé was active in the party. She therefore thought it best to accept my offer—but she would make sure that nobody ever would say anything against me or my family. She was choking back tears when she shook my hand to say goodbye.

Surprisingly, my foolish outburst was not reported.

But this was only 1933, the first year of the Nazi regime. In the following twelve years, far less would suffice for one to be deported to the death camps in the East.

Twice during this year of upheaval I was summoned to appear in court. In normal times I would have laughed off the absurd accusations brought against me. But I would have been ill-advised had I not taken these accusations as deadly serious.

In the first case, a young "Aryan" woman filed a suit charging that I had fathered her child. When she was confronted with me in court, however, she declared: But this man I never have seen. As the courtroom erupted in laughter, the charges were dropped and I was allowed to go free.

The second charge against me was more dangerous. The circumstantial evidence that could have convicted me of *Rassenschande*—racial defilement—seemed irrefutable. I could not deny that I drove with a young lady, a former model of the firm, in my car to Cologne and came back with her the next day. Would they believe me—and her—that I had given her a ride, at her request, since she knew I was going to Cologne for a business meeting? If not, the very least I could expect was to be sent to a concentration camp. Her boyfriend's courage saved me. He stated under oath that the young woman had spent the night with him.

During the remaining months of my self-imposed deadline, the intensity of work plus endless negotiations with a potential successor kept me from getting demoralized. I recall, almost with pleasure, a well-planned special sales event I called *Wettbewerb der Freundlichkeit*—a Contest of Friendliness. Our painter went out of his way to create the background of all windows in the store. Hundreds of framed wooden posters hung throughout the store. The decorations were an artistic sensation. Four-leaf-clover ornaments adorned the white dresses of our female employees. These same ornaments and a children's book were given as gifts to all customers who were tempted to fill out the questionnaire for our contest. It was a tremendous success—until the third day, when the SA men stormed the store. They smashed windows. They took the posters, good material for the bonfire they set in the big square in front of the store. A police officer appeared and asked me to accompany him to the chief of the police.

Fortunately, the office was still held by Herr Moebus. He received me in his customary friendly manner. He explained that, to his regret, he no longer had the right or the power to intervene in the excesses of the SA. I replied with a straight face that I completely understood the difficulty of his position. Neither of us mentioned that not long ago he had offered me his own gun for my protection. Our friendly conversation lasted about an hour. Then I walked back unhindered to the store, past the still burning bonfire and within easy reach of the heroes singing: *Wenn's Judenblut vom Messer spritzt, geht's uns nochmal so gut (We feel best in our lives with Jewish blood on our knives)*. But nobody laid a hand on me. As long as I was in my hometown, I never felt to be in danger.

The next day, all three newspapers reported, in identical words, that I had been taken into protective custody—*Schutzhaft*—for disturbing the peace.

I decided then to give up the unevenly matched bout. After nerve-racking negotiations, I leased the firm. The sizable amount I received for the inventory, as well as the yearly payments, however, were blocked. And I never saw a penny after the war.

I spent the next five years in Italy. But this was not Goethe's land "where the lemons bloom." This lemon, Goebbels proclaimed over the radio, was the "lewd fruit of the South." Mussolini, who was not then a friend to Hitler, no longer wanted "German boots to trample through Italy's museums."

I was fortunate. In no time, I was wonderfully busy working with an acquaintance from Berlin on a new enterprise: a mail order business, heretofore unknown in Italy. I entered into a partnership with the Italian Senator Silvio Crespi, who was a former Minister of Agriculture, to initiate a new business venture for transporting raw milk, based upon a German pharmacist's invention of a process for maintaining the freshness of raw milk for a lengthy period of time. The anti-Semitism of the Nazis was not replicated in Fascist Italy. Ministers in the government were Jews; so was Mussolini's mistress, who also was his biographer.

As part of my responsibilities to help in the development of the promising patent to industrial reality, I had to return several times to Germany. No longer could I stay at the hotels which I and my father had frequented for decades; they no longer admitted "Jews and dogs." I stayed instead at a small boarding house. On one of my trips to Berlin, my passport was confiscated at the border by the SS. Fortunately, I knew the Italian ambassador to Germany—because of my work with Senator Crespi on the milk-production business—and was able to secure his assistance in retrieving my passport. Without the ambassador's intervention, I would have surely ended up in a concentration camp.

On my last visit to Germany, in 1937, I saw my mother. Where did she get the strength, after all these years of complete isolation, when not one of so many friends who had enjoyed her hospitality before the Nazi time had the courage to visit this lonely woman? Yet she rejected out of hand my plea to come with me to Milano. Not only because I had not established myself there—I was living from hand to mouth, she said—but, most of all, because of her unshakable faith that God would not permit this injustice and evil to prevail. No, she wanted to remain in Wesel, in the town where she had been loved and respected, where she had raised five children, where she could visit her husband's grave.

I never saw her again.

Only after the war was I informed about what happened to my poor mother. Less than a year after my visit, Kristallnacht happened. SA men destroyed whatever could be destroyed in our house and threatened my mother and my older sister. They fled in lamentable condition to St. Mary's Hospital, my mother bruised from a fall and under shock. After two nights they were forced out of the same hospital that, before the Nazi regime, looked up to her as a major benefactress.

She went with just a small suitcase in hand to "neutral" Holland, where Leni, my younger sister, could take care of her. But when the German Army invaded, they had to be hidden, they had to go underground. They were able to bring Anneke, Leni's baby, to trustworthy peasants in Hilversum, with whom they left all their possessions. After the war, I received official information that they had been betrayed: my mother, my sister, her husband, and his mother were deported, first to a Camp Westerbork, then to Auschwitz. There they were murdered by gas, as were more than one hundred thousand other Jews from Holland, the little country where they believed they were safe.

Anneke survived at first with a family in Hilversum, then was taken to an orphanage in Amsterdam. There she was found after the war by Anne Frank's father, who had miraculously survived the concentration camps. I was informed and could claim her. She is now my beloved daughter, who lives in Nashville, Tennessee.

—ERICH LEYENS

In 1939, that's when the problems started. We had been living in a city, Munk'acs, where the children could get a better education. Then Hitler gave the Hungarians a gift, and Munk'acs was part of it. So we had to move back to Polena, the town where I was born.

There were only about sixty Jewish families in Polena, and maybe three hundred other families. My husband was the town shoemaker. My father cut the trees in the woods and shipped them down from the mountains and delivered them to the cities and they made boards. He employed Christians, peasants. Through the Jews, see, they made a living, whether they liked us or didn't.

But the Hungarians had what was the equivalent to the Nazis. They were very willing helpers. First, around 1940, we started having to wear yellow stars. It was mandatory. There was a curfew. They started rationing the food, and Jews got less than non-Jews. Jews were not allowed to have businesses. My husband had his workbench by the window, fixing shoes. One of the gendarmes came and said to Idy, my daughter, What is your father doing?

She said, What do you mean? He's working.

You know he's not supposed to do that. I'm going to report him.

My daughter, she begged him not to. We were very friendly with most of the local police, the gendarmes; they were Ukrainian. My daughters would spend time with them. They would come in to a Jewish home to spend a social evening because the peasants did not speak Ukrainian. It was against the law, but they did it.

Then in 1944, the last day of Passover, there were soldiers in town, Hungarian boys. They were very nice boys, and they wanted to spend their time, too, with Jewish girls. So they came, three of them, and they were sitting with the girls, talking and talking. When they were getting ready to go away, they said to me, Would you please walk with us. I got afraid. We went a half a block. We stopped. One of them said to me, Look, I have a very big secret. But I must tell you. They are going to take you away. Tomorrow morning. You should give us your two girls, they'll be safe with us.

My husband came home from *shul*, and I said to him, They're going to take us away tomorrow morning. And he says, Uh, uh, I know what it is, what they want to do with the girls.

So, early the next morning, it's a little bit light, he goes out. He comes back. He says to me, You know what? Every Jewish house is surrounded. And then they started to take us away. We had neighbors, we always were very friendly with them. He was a policeman. They sent him to take us away. And he felt terrible. He cried. He said, I don't want to do it. I have no choice.

We packed what we could carry, and they brought us to the school. We got everybody together, and the policeman's wife brought us breakfast. They kept us there a few days. They asked us questions about what we had. They frisked us. They took away all our jewelry. Then they shipped us to Munk'acs, to a brick factory. They came and they shaved off the beard from my father and all the Jewish men. He lay down and never got up. He died, in Munk'acs, in that place. When the funeral was, they wouldn't even let us go to the cemetery. Just to the gate. There was a rabbi. And he said to us we shouldn't cry because we were going to envy him. He's going to have a grave, but we won't know where we will be.

We were brought on a train to Auschwitz. When we got off, right away it was with the dogs and the nightsticks. There were inmates who were helping organize and they would say to us—they weren't supposed to talk to us—but they would tell us, Young women, give your children to your mothers. They made the selections: who will work and who will be killed. Only we didn't know what was going on. I wanted to go with my mother. They wouldn't let me. You are too young, they said. You are going to work. We didn't know where my mother went.

So then we were standing for endless hours every morning until we were sent to work. In the morning was frost. In the daytime was hot. About a week or so later, we were very noisy in the barracks. There were Jewish girls that were over us, the ones who had been there a long time, and one of them said, What are you so happy about? Why can't you settle down? Don't you know, your mothers, your fathers, your sisters, your babies are burning over there? I mean, we saw the flames, but we didn't know. They said they were baking bread for us.

So that's when we found out what was going on.

They dressed us in blue-and-white-striped dresses and white kerchiefs and we went to work sorting clothes from the suitcases. We were shaved. We looked at each other and we didn't recognize each other. There were four crematoriums, and in the middle were barracks where they brought in the suitcases, the backpacks, the bundles tied up in a sheet. That's what we sorted. There we saved a lot of jewelry, diamonds that people had hidden in the seams. The Jewish men that were our "foremen," we gave the jewelry to them. They were in touch with the underground, the partisans, and they gave them what they could.

We worked there from the beginning of May 1944 until the end of the summer. We would see everything that was going on. We would sit twelve hours and we would see the people going in and then the smoke and flame and stench of burning flesh and bone. So we knew exactly what was going on.

How did we survive? We were strong. There is no other answer. They drugged our so-called soup. Women didn't menstruate. Men had no sexual desire. Somehow or other, we took everything in stride. We were always hungry. Our main concern was food. When we were sitting and working and talking, what did we talk about? Food. Because we didn't have any. We were ninety-nine and nine-tenths percent sure that we will not survive. We

Sari Muller, with her daughter, Idy Farber, her son, Bill, and a niece in a displaced-persons camp near Munich, Germany, shortly after the war ended

knew we were only alive as long as we can work, or until the end of the war. If the Germans win, definitely we wouldn't live. And if they'll lose, they'll kill us before anything happens.

Toward the end, we were marching from work to our barracks. They brought in a transport from Hungary—the last transport to Auschwitz. We see the little old ladies and little old men. In those days, the women wore print dresses and light gloves and straw hats and patent-leather shoes. They ask us, Where are they taking us? We answer, To a good place. I mean, what do you say? By the time we got back to our barracks and were standing roll call, we saw the flames.

—SARI MULLER

The Germans came to Losice on the thirteenth of September 1939. And then, not only the Germans, but the Poles from the villages, they come and they grab everything, all the merchandise from the Jewish businesses. In one of the mills, they threw out the owner and gave it to some Polish people. Only they didn't know how to work it. So they took me as a partner to operate the mill, because I knew how to do it.

Every day was something. They took out Jews to kill right away. They killed men. They killed women. A farmer brings a wagon of potatoes. They won't buy from him. They kill him instead. You can't understand it unless you lived through it. The Germans took over a church. It was near a field. They dug a hole four meters deep. They put four wild dogs into the hole. Then they took my father and three other old men. They made them jump over the hole. They took my father first. He was seventy-seven. He ran and jumped over. He made it. They laughed. They sent him home. The other three didn't. They were torn apart.

Each day was the worst. The Germans went around with whips and beat the Jews for the least offense: if you didn't take off your hat, or if they didn't like your looks. One Saturday—my house was on the town square; my bed was by the window—I woke up in the morning and my daughter, Renée, looked out the window and saw my son, David, he was thirteen years old, lined up outside with other men and boys for a selection to take supposedly to work. But sometimes those they took, we never saw them again. I ran down and there were gendarmes and SS, picking out people. So I was pulling David one way, and a Polish policeman was pulling him the other. All I remember is pulling him out and the two of us running home. It was a miracle that nobody shot us. What I did, nobody else did.

In June 1941, they had moved all the Jews into a ghetto. About eight thousand Jews were crammed into a few blocks. And from there they would have selections and liquidations. They would round up the Jews and take them away to the camps. But lots they killed right away. Life in the ghetto was miserable. People died of hunger and disease. There was typhus. My little boy, Itzek, had typhus, but he recovered.

The big liquidation occurred on August 22, 1942. All Jews were ordered out into the town square. They were crying and calling for their loved ones while the Germans with their dogs searched the houses. We hid in the attic, twenty-seven of us under a hot roof with no water or food. I wanted to go with the crowd outside, but my nephew said, Better to die here than to walk to your death. The wailing outside was terrible. We crouched, terrified, in our attic, listening to the waning cries of our relatives and neighbors as they were hauled away to be murdered.

How we survived is a miracle. My two older children were caught by a Polish policeman. They were jailed to be shot, but the Germans made a mistake and shot two Polish Gentile children who were on the first floor in the same jail. My little David and Renée were taken to clean up the houses of the emptied ghetto. I found them later.

My family was lucky. Before the Germans came, I was a big business-man. I was selling grain. I made money. And I hid some money away—gold Russian rubles that later a poor Polish farmer accepted in exchange for hiding us in his animal shed in an underground pit. We were lucky to find hiding places before the second and final liquidation. Renée—she was only about eleven—was staying at first in the home of a policeman, hiding in a closet, a wardrobe, for five months. Later she joined us in the pit. My youngest, Itzek, was with the *soltys*, the village administrator, who accepted him also for money. He kept him in his house or in a haystack outside in the fields. My oldest son, David, remained with us under the floor of the shed for the whole two years. With us in that pit were also four members of my sister-in-law's family.

On November 27, 1942, the final liquidation took place. Only about 150 Jews were left in the ghetto. It was then that my daughter, Renée, hiding in the Polish policeman's house, watched in horror as people were crawling over the ghetto fence, trying to escape, and a German gendarme with a pis-tol was picking them off, one by one. During this second and last liquida-tion, by luck or fate, I am out of the ghetto buying cigarettes and changing small money for larger money. I am able to escape, to join with my nephew and others from the family who are hiding on a farm.

For two years, eight of us, we lived, if you can call it living, in a dugout pit under manure piles in a pigsty of the farmer Karbicki [a pseudonym] in the village of Koszelowka. For two years. I can't tell you how we survived. We had hope. Hope for the children. The will to survive was for the children.

The pit was about seven feet long, five feet wide, and perhaps four feet high. We slept on hard boards, which during the day were adjusted to make two benches and a table. Parts of the walls and the ceiling were propped up with wooden boards, but water and manure seepage was com-mon. There was a small opening into the pit, a square, movable door of sorts, just wide enough for one person at a time to slip through. It was propped up with a stick, which was quickly pulled to close the opening when there was danger. The pit was covered with caked manure and straw. Sheep and lambs walked around above us.

In our hiding place it was damp and hot. We had lice and bedbugs and sometimes we had to fight off rats. We were hungry. Most of our diet con-sisted of two pieces of bread, some soup—we were lucky to find a piece of potato once in a while in the soup—and "coffee" made from burned grain kernels.

Karbicki was no "righteous Gentile." He was like a bandit. We paid him and he starved us. He would not have taken us if not for the money. He threatened many times to kill us or throw us out if he doesn't get more money. He was often drunk. When he took us in, he said, Either I will have an elegant coat or I will be dead. Meaning, Either I'll get wealthy or I'll get killed.

When we did run out of money, he ordered us out. We humored him and promised him all kinds of goodies after the war was over. One day he just came and said, I can't throw you out. You're just like my animals. And I love my animals.

On July 30, 1944, the Soviet Red Army arrived in our region. We were free. Of the original six thousand Jews who lived in Losice before the war, sixteen survived: five Gewirtzmans, four Pinkuses, and seven others, two of which, a father and his son, escaped from Treblinka. They were the ones who came back to the ghetto and told everybody about the gassing.

I had six brothers with large families, my father and stepmother. The Germans killed all of them, except for one brother that emigrated to the United States in 1938. My youngest brother, Chaim, died while fighting the Germans in France during the Normandy invasion. My wife had seven brothers and sisters with large families. Only one sister, her husband, and two children survived. Two other brothers survived alone in the Soviet Union. All of the others perished.

—JACOB GEWIRTZMAN

My son and another boy, Walter Parks, were in his apartment up in the top of our house. He was in high school then. And he hollered downstairs, Hey, Mama, where's Pearl Harbor? The Japs just bombed it.

I says, Search me, I don't know nothin' about Pearl Harbor. Who is Pearl Harbor?

Then Hunter went into the Navy. See, the boys, they all went in right out of high school. The only choice was, Army or Navy. He didn't see any combat, though. Oh, he was so mad. Four years in the Navy. He went in at eighteen and came out married.

—SARAH HUNTER JACKSON

I had a first cousin who had fifteen children one year apart. She did not lose a child until her son, Carroll. He was twenty-one years old. The government had spent $10,000 to train him to fly an airplane, and he was killed at Pearl Harbor.

We heard about it on the radio. On the seventh of December, my nephew who was going to study to be a doctor happened to be here in our living room and we were listening when it came over the radio. It meant that we were in trouble. And he was at war.

—LOIS CROUCH ADDY

In 1941, we were renting a house near the Buddhist temple and very close to the big commercial laundry my husband worked for as a driver. Next door, in fact, was the dining room for all of the laundry workers. When the whistle would blow at twelve o'clock and at five o'clock, all the workers would come streaming into the dining room to eat.

Then came the attack on Pearl Harbor.

First thing, the F.B.I. came and confiscated all the radios and anything like swords and guns. Kenichiro, my husband, had a few mementos that he had brought back from Japan. They confiscated everything. Then they took him away, to a camp in Montana where "enemy aliens" were sent. This happened immediately. It was really surprising. My daughter, Miyoko, and her husband were on their way to Camp Washington in the country to visit some friends. They heard all these derogatory comments about "Japs." People threw things at them.

In Seattle, we were not supposed to move out of wherever we were. They set a five-mile radius and we couldn't travel beyond it. My daughter and her husband had to spend their honeymoon in a downtown hotel owned by another Japanese. Most of the Chinese people would put signs in the windows of their little shops: "We are Chinese, not Japs," or something like that. It was not a very happy time for any of us.

Then they sent us away, too, first to the fairgrounds at Puyallup, where all the horses' stalls were turned into little compartments for us to live in; we had to fill our mattresses with straw. After a few months there, we were trained up to Idaho, to the Minidoka Relocation Center, they called it, near Twin Falls. My husband was still in Missoula; they didn't let him join us until 1943. All they permitted us to carry was one valise, or suitcase, per person. We had to sell all of our furniture or other personal belongings, or get them stored.

They said that they were putting us there because of the danger of sabotage. And they said they didn't know how to keep us protected if they didn't group us up. In a way, it might have been a blessing. You never know what some of the people might have done. Yes, some people protested. One man protested loudly, and he was jailed. Afterwards, of course, they found out that none of us did anything to harm the government, or to be disloyal to our country.

All the Japanese-Americans in the coast states closest to the Pacific Ocean—closest to Japan—were all sent to camps. The people out East were not. Many people felt that the government put us here, and when they're ready they'll take us out and give us our living back. Some were angry at the government. For me, it was something we had to accept. It was part of living here, I guess.

At Minidoka, we lived in barracks. We were divided into blocks. Each block had a dining hall and a shower and laundry room. We had to go there to eat, and to get our showers, and do our laundry. There was nothing much to do in the way of enjoying yourself in camp, other than to read. Some of the ladies took up knitting. They would send for yarn from Montgomery Ward. Some gardened in patches around the barracks.

The center was surrounded by a barbed-wire fence. I never heard of anybody trying to escape, although a couple of them got lost out in the

Asano and Kenichiro Kanzaki with their youngest son, Hitoshi, in their barracks at the Minidoka Relocation Center, near Twin Falls, Idaho, circa 1943. On the table is a photo of their oldest son, Akira, who was killed in action in 1943

sagebrush and perished from the cold. The ones who "escaped" were the boys who joined the service. My oldest son, Akira, was the first to enlist. He joined the soon-to-be-famous 442nd Regimental Combat Team, the Japanese-American outfit that distinguished itself fighting in Europe. He died there, killed in the Arno River campaign following the Allied invasion of Anzio in 1943.

Akira was a very passionate person. He did everything—studying, taking care of us—with passion. I depended on him a lot. For the longest time, I believed he didn't die, but that he was coming back. Then one night I saw him in a dream. He was on a white horse. Then I knew he wasn't coming back.

My other three sons—Satoru, Tsutomu, and Hitoshi—also served. The second oldest was in military intelligence because he could read a little Japanese and speak a little Japanese. The youngest was in military intelligence also. He was in the Philippines, and then on Okinawa, which is where his cousin died, fighting for the Japanese. Another nephew who was a doctor was my sister's only child. She had emigrated to Manchuria, and he fought for the Japanese and became a prisoner of Russia.

—ASANO KANZAKI

My son, Arthur, enlisted immediately. He was wounded in the Battle of the Bulge. My other son, Jimmy, when he came out of high school, everybody he knew went into the service. He tried to join the Navy. They wouldn't take him. The medical officers said he had a murmur in his heart. Mrs. Hamer and I went to the foremost heart specialist in this area who said to us, Oh, he's fine, Arthur, he's fine. I wish I had his heart.

That war meant blood money. Well, all war money is blood money. There's plenty of work to go around if somebody's dying. We weren't out of work anymore.

—ARTHUR W. HAMER, SR.

There was no real reason for Japan to want to fight us. Roosevelt had warned the Japs not to go in and try to take over the colonies of the British and the Dutch in the Far East. Don't do it, or else, he told them. Well, Japan wanted to expand; they decided "or else."

But the thing of it is this: we were caught by surprise—big surprise. At the time, I subscribed to some magazine. On Monday, the day after Pearl Harbor, I got in the mail a copy that had been printed and mailed before the attack. In it an article said: It looks as if we will be at war within two weeks—with Japan. And yet we took no precautions. General Marshall was out riding his horse on Sunday morning. Our communications with the island were not good, and Washington had to send its first message by Western Union. The Western Union boy was on his bicycle when the planes started to drop the bombs.

Both of my boys served. My younger son, Bob, tried to enlist but they wouldn't take him. He'd had a mastoid operation when he was a kid; he was in a bad way. He finally signed up with the American Ambulance Field Service. He was in the Italian campaign with the British Eighth Army—he had some narrow escapes there in Italy—and then they sent him over to India. He was in action although he wasn't in the U.S. Army. After the war was over, after he had served, *then* he was drafted. At the end, they were drafting old people and babies and everything in between. The damn fools sent him down to Fort Dix, and he got pneumonia. He had a hell of a time before finally he was discharged.

My older son, John, was a lieutenant. He was hit on Iwo Jima. Before they assaulted, the Navy shelled the place for three days. The Marines wanted them to do more, but the admiral in charge said he had to save the rest of his ammunition for the next battle. The Marines went over the side of the ships and took the beach in landing craft. John's captain was hit, so John, who was senior lieutenant, was in command. He exposed himself in order to check on where his men were, and he got several bullets in him.

I'll tell you how I found out: I came back from the office and a friend of my wife's who lived down the next street was just leaving. When I came in, Emma said, You'd better sit down before you fall down. She had this telegram saying that John had been hit very bad, and his chances were not very good.

He was brought out on a hospital ship to Hawaii, and from there to the Coast. A classmate of mine from Amherst, who lived out there, went to see him. I talked to him on the telephone every night. It was still very problematical whether he'd make it or not, and he almost didn't.

Then they were going to dump him down at a hospital in Virginia. But I was in touch with a doctor over at the naval hospital out on Long Island, and he said of course John should come up there, with the type of wound that he had.

Well, this chap I was in business with, he'd gone to Princeton with James Forrestal, who was then in charge of the Navy. And he got word to Forrestal, who sent a message out to San Francisco and told them that John was to be brought to St. Alban's. He was. He spent over four years there, where he was promoted to captain. Then he finally came home. But he had to get along in a wheelchair until he died.

At one of our reunions years after the war, I was talking with this Marine general who had been in charge of the Fourth Marines over on Iwo Jima. He said Iwo Jima was not only the worst battle of that war, it was the worst battle of *any* war.

—JOHN D. CLARK

With the war on, we couldn't get meat. Maybe once a week the butchers would report they'd have meat the next day. One morning I was third in line at the market; I might have been there two hours before the door opened. There was this gentleman on crutches behind me and he beat me to the meat counter. I don't know that I even got meat that day. The frenzy was terrible. As soon as the door opened, the people just went for it. And those were my more agile days, too.

Gasoline was also rationed, according to need. Housewives were allowed only enough for bare necessities. Everyone traveled with a book of coupons. The little house in Wheaton, Illinois, that I lived in then with my son, Ralph, was about a mile out from the town center. I had three nephews in the service and they would write home to please send cookies. And we did try to send packages to the young men we had connection with. So I would walk that mile to the post office in the center of town to mail these boxes and walk home again to save gas so I could have it to go maybe to church on Sunday.

I had these friends about fifteen miles away that owned a gas station. About once a month they would call. Ella May, they'd say, if you have enough gas to get here, we'll give you Sunday dinner—the butcher was giving them meat in exchange for gas—and enough gas to get home.

That's what rationing was about.

—ELLA MAY STUMPE

After Pearl Harbor, I went over to sign up. The man, he says to me, Ralph, go back home. You got nine kids. The government don't wanna feed nine kids.

Three of my sons was in the Navy. I had one daughter home for my wife. I go to the factory in the morning at seven o'clock. I get through at four o'clock. I go home, have a cup of coffee, go upstairs, go to sleep. I get up half past ten. My wife, she makes me dinner. I eat. I go to the bakery. Then I go back to the factory. And my wife, she don't see me until four o'clock the next day. I never loafed. That's why they used to call me the Iron Man.

I used to work on 550 pairs of boots a day at Converse Rubber for the Army. It was a sonofabitch. I was the starter. Every seventeen seconds, one boot is gone. I grab the list, I put them on the machine, grab the stock, put them in. I had a callus on my hands. My kids say my hands were like a rock. We put in steel toe caps. People said, Why with steel? So they don't get hurt when somethin' heavy falls on their feet. Fifty-seven pieces I put in every boot. My boss, he says, How the hell you remember what to do? He says, You can't read.

But I knew what I was doin'. That's also why they called me the Iron Man.

—RALPH MONTECALVO

We ran day and night for five years. We made LSTs, we made railroad car frames to be shipped to Russia. We made bolts, about ten inches long, an inch in diameter, and we had to thread 'em, drill a cotter keyhole in 'em. We were gettin' fifteen bucks apiece for them things. Lord knows what the guy got before we got it. And, geez, we made them things by the thousands.

See, I looked for the work. I told my dad, The stone business is not gonna be much good in a war 'cause there ain't much call for stone. So we have to make stuff for the war. And we did.

—JAMES M. DAVIS

In 1940, I knew war was coming on. So I bought me a new Studebaker President, 1941 model. The last one built. I drove it 187,000 miles during the war. Air travel was limited mostly to the military people. Train travel was terrible. I was on the road all the time, driving to the various shipyards and other installations. I was given the necessary gas-ration tickets because of the work I was doing.

We were already doing so much work for the Army and the Navy. The Army had put out specifications covering a gun-firing room. Now, a refrigerated gun-firing room is capable of holding whatever they wanted; in this case, it was a tank. The Sherman tank. They would put the tank and the ammunition in there, and there was a slot through the ceiling so they could shoot from a refrigerated gun with refrigerated ammunition to test how they would perform in cold conditions. The first room we built was at minus ten degrees; the next one was at minus twenty.

We also built a lot of special stratospheric chambers. They wanted to test equipment that would be in an aircraft at a high altitude in extreme low temperature and low pressure. One chamber we built could hold a whole Army truck or anything they wanted to put in there.

Back in those days, we got our performance data for a given design of equipment by virtue of the test results. That's why those tests were so important. A company might say, We need to cool so much of something.

Now, what did the test results show? Maybe that they'd oversized the design. In that era, you might say, our test laboratory was the field, because we were building things and designing things that had never been used before.

We did all kinds of work. The Frick Company was supplying machines by the hundreds to the different Army installations and Navy bases and shipyards all over the country. All of them required refrigeration and cold storage. Because we were supplying refrigeration to the atomic-energy plants—we had the Oak Ridge plant and one out in Paducah, Kentucky—I had to go through a whole day of lie-detector tests to get a "Q" security clearance.

We had dozens of installations going on at the time. For example, the four big battleships, the *Missouri*, the *Iowa*, the *New Jersey*, and the *North Carolina*, we had thirty-four units that were air conditioning the ammunition holds in those vessels. The minesweepers that were built along the East River in Brooklyn, we had equipment on them. Bethlehem Steel was building cargo ships and we had equipment going on them. I rode the trial runs of the battleships and I sat on the capstan where the peace treaty was finally signed on the *Missouri*.

One of the other very important and difficult jobs was engine testing. They wanted to test engines at −75 degrees Fahrenheit. Well, not only do you have to have a room to have the engine in at −75, but you also have to cool the air that's being fed into that engine at −75. Now, how do you do that and not have to shut down to defrost the coils? Well, again we were able to come up with the design. All those things I was involved in.

That was an era when everything was special. For example, our supply of natural rubber was cut off immediately. And immediately the government started the Rubber Reserve Corporation. They designed and had built five plants for making artificial rubber here in this country, and one in Canada. They no sooner started them than every batch of latex they ran was spoiled. In artificial rubber making, they have a big reactor, a tank about sixteen feet in diameter and twelve feet high, and it's supposed to be refrigerated because when they put this mixture in and start the reaction there's tremendous heat generated that must be controlled, that must be held at a certain constant temperature.

Well, the government came to each of the big refrigeration manufacturers—there were three of us—and they said, We're gonna give you a reactor down at American Rubber in Louisville, Kentucky. We want you to come up with a design for cooling it. You see, they'd already had a double shell and they were just trying to refrigerate this double shell. Well, that wasn't anywhere near enough surface to take care of the work. All the equipment we had to design had to be sized such as it would fit through the standard manhole-sized cover used to get in and out of the tank. Everything then had to be assembled internally. We were the only successful designers, and we proceeded to patent that design. And for the next seventeen years anybody that wanted to make artificial rubber had to come to us for reaction control.

—MILTON W. GARLAND

Before World War II started, Bell Labs and AT&T were very busy turning out war-related equipment. One of the things they wanted to produce was a two-way telephone for tanks. It contained a tremendous number of frequencies. If two tanks were communicating and the enemy succeeded in jamming them, they knew which number they should refer to, which frequency they should start transmitting on. And if that was jammed, they knew what the next one was. The sequence that was to be used was changed every day, so if the enemy got ahold of the sequence, it was only good for that day.

I didn't know anything about radio. When I was transferred onto this project, my supervisor said to me: You can learn. Boy, did we work hard on that! I think AT&T told the government that for every tank that was turned out we would have a set ready. And we did. Ordinarily, Bell Laboratories would not send a man out to Chicago to the Western Electric factory there to help on the job. But in this case they did. They sent an electrical-engineer man, and they sent a mechanical man: me. And we turned them out like hotcakes, these tank sets.

One of the things I'll never forget on that job was the conveyor belt. Workers—they were mostly women—were putting telephone sets together, ordinary telephone sets. And I noticed the speed of this conveyor belt. I was very friendly with the supervisor. He said, If we make that belt go too fast, we'll turn out a lot of telephones, but the women will be played out by 2 p.m. So we make it so the women can chat with each other. If they can chat, they last all day, no trouble at all.

—JOHN SAILLIARD

The war ended in Europe on the fifth of May 1945. The main feeling that I had was for my brother. He was arrested by the Germans in the Netherlands, and was in a concentration camp, and so we hoped that he would return. In the days after the fifth of May, I was very worried about what happened to my brother.

He never returned.

He had been arrested because he was a Communist. He was in the Resistance. He ended up in a concentration camp near Hamburg, and the story, as I have been able to find out, is this: At the end of the war, in April, the Gestapo tried to empty the camps because they didn't want to leave too many traces of them. Many prisoners were driven up north in the hope that some of these Germans could make a stand in Norway.

So my brother belongs to those that were driven out of the camps to the Baltic Sea, where there were boats to bring them to Norway, among them the steamer *Cap Arscona*. There were hundreds of prisoners. These boats were bombed by the RAF. Eight thousand people drowned. This is an incident in the last days of the war, on the third of May, which has been not very much publicized because so many other things were happening.

He lost his life there, on the third of May 1945, in this catastrophe as horrible as the bombing of Dresden or Hiroshima. But we didn't know that at that time.

— DIRK STRUIK

The atom bomb, of course, ended the war with Japan. Back then, we weren't opposed to it. Nor were we in favor of it, particularly. No one had ever heard of it before.

— JOHN D. CLARK

Right after the war ended, we applied to go to Spokane, where my husband had friends. The government would not let us come back unless we had a sponsor, a place to live, a means of earning a living. Spokane people were not affected by the internment camps because they were on the other side of the mountains. And then my third son, he was the first to be discharged from the Army, and he brought us back to these barracks they had built along what is now Martin Luther King Way. That's where we first stayed when we came back to Seattle.

We were not really welcomed. Other Americans pitied us, I suppose. Some might have been sympathetic. Most were probably more curious than hostile.

— ASANO KANZAKI

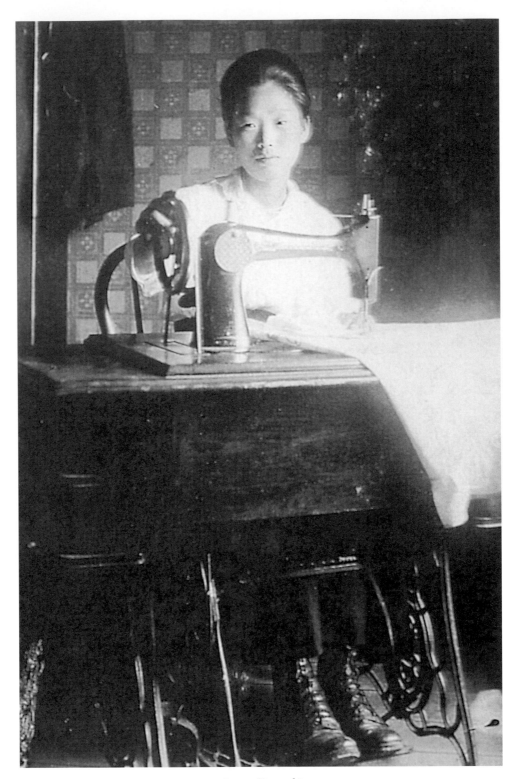

Asano Kanzaki

The Red Menace

A quarter of a century of alarmist propaganda

from 1917 to 1941 left a foundation of suspicion.

The "menace" of Communism outside

the United States had only to be matched

by fabricating

a threat of internal Communism.

—PROFESSOR DIRK STRUIK

Born September 30, 1894

Rotterdam, the Netherlands

I made a mistake, I suppose, one time. I was asked by a good family friend, what did I think of Communism? I said, if Communism in Russia is putting shoes on children who never had shoes, if Communism in Russia is putting children in school that had no hope for schooling, if Communism in Russia is bettering the living conditions for the masses of the people, I said, that's their business. I'm not for it here, but it's their business over there, as long as they keep it in Russia.

—ARTHUR W. HAMER, SR.

The anti-Communist hysteria that gripped the country after the war, I was against it. I was living in Short Hills, New Jersey. One of the fellows I was in business with was active in civic affairs, he was on the board of education. Well, there was some woman in Short Hills who was a regular McCarthyite. We went to her house on one occasion, the two of us, and we tried to influence her. We weren't very successful.

One night, she had McCarthy out there. I saw the bastard, but I don't think I shook hands with him. We didn't consider that Communism was a real threat to the United States the way he was making it out. What I always said was, Look, the people of this country do not have the same reasons for it that they might have in Russia. There, possibly, it's all right. But nobody in this country is going to be a Communist. There's no point to it.

—JOHN D. CLARK

Being a Communist branded some people for the rest of their lives. It didn't affect me particularly because I wasn't a professional person. If I lost one job, I'd just move over and take another one.

But when I tried to become a citizen, I was turned down because of my membership in the Communist Party. They didn't try to deport me until 1949. I was arrested. It was an exciting day. I was in a cell with two other women. One of them said to me, What are you in here for? And I thought

◄ *Anti-Communist demonstrators, New York City, 1949 (UPI/Corbis-Bettmann)*

I'd make them laugh. Well, I said, I've been accused of trying to overthrow the government by force and violence.

But they didn't laugh. And one of them said, Well, the damn government ought to be overthrown! She never heard of such a noble cause.

After I got bailed out, I had to go through several administrative hearings. My case lingered for fifteen years. We even went up to the Supreme Court of the United States a couple of times.

Back then, if you said you were a Communist, that was too bad. If you said you weren't, well, they had a whole stable of stool pigeons that would come up and say you were. So you'd be facing perjury. The only safe thing was to say nothing.

Finally, the hysteria subsided somewhat, and people realized what had been going on. The turning point was when McCarthy accused the Army of being filled with Communists and the Army fought back. Important generals and other people in high positions in the Army were outraged. I watched some of these things over the television. I can still visualize this Army man shaking his finger at McCarthy and saying, Have you no shame, sir?

I was finally granted citizenship—in 1976.

—HAZEL WOLF

A few Scarsdalians were frightened by the specter of hidden Communists and Communist sympathizers in their midst. They organized a Committee of Ten to investigate the public schools for possible infiltration by Communists or "fellow travelers." If such infiltration was found, they were determined that it should be extirpated. Chairman of this committee was Otto Dohrenwend, partner of a New York Stock Exchange firm, a devout Roman Catholic, an unquestionably patriotic American. His committee included two Protestant clergymen, Lutheran and Episcopalian, respectively. Their search of the high school library soon uncovered some books by Howard Fast, a prolific writer of historical novels portraying the Founding Fathers in a less favorable light than is customary. Allegedly Howard Fast was a Communist sympathizer.

One allegation by the Committee of Ten bordered on the ludicrous. The Greenacres School P.T.A. had sponsored a dance recital by a young black named Pearl Primus. Out of the multimillion dollar school budget she was paid something like fifty dollars for her performance. President of the Greenacres P.T.A. was Will Garey, a senior editor on the staff of McGraw-

Hill, publishers of *Business Week* and various trade journals. According to the Committee of Ten, the children who watched Pearl Primus dance might have been contaminated by the mere sight of an alleged Communist. Worse, the lady had probably contributed her fee to the Communist Party. Hence, Scarsdale taxpayers had been coerced into supporting a Communist enterprise.

When this hue and cry developed I was a fairly recent "alumnus" of the board of education. My three children had all advanced through the Scarsdale schools from kindergarten through high school graduation. If they had been exposed to Communist influence, they were singularly unimpressed by it. All three were conservative Republicans. I had more recently been president of the Town Club, an organization which devoted a great deal of energy, year after year, to studying all aspects of the Scarsdale schools. I was a hardworking member of the Wall Street community, that bastion of economic and political conservatism. In World War I, I had been an early volunteer, among the first American troops to reach France, and served there for sixteen months. It seemed to me that my credentials as an anti-Communist were impeccable. If there were Communist infiltration in the schools, two men in particular bore some responsibility for it. They were the superintendent of schools and the principal of the high school. Both were personal friends, men of integrity and hitherto of unquestioned patriotism.

On the face of it, members of the Committee of Ten were suffering from delusions. No reasonable basis for their concern was apparent. Nevertheless, their charges could not be ignored. In the early stages of the battle I had asked the friend who was then president of the Town Club to appoint me chairman of the education and school budget committee. For once, this committee put the financial aspects of school affairs on the back burner, concentrating instead on the issue of Communism.

Of the many meetings of our committee, the climactic one was a joint discussion, held in the Carret living room, attended by most of the members of the two groups. Members of the Town Club committee tried to enter the meeting with open minds. If there were anything wrong in the Scarsdale schools, all of us were eager to know what it was. No new allegations and no substantiation of previous charges developed during the evening. Of course, Otto thought that the cards had been stacked against him, that my committee really had not listened attentively to his presentation. There was nothing more to be said, however, and in a few months the hue and cry died down.

—PHILIP L. CARRET

You cannot imagine how people lived through that period, McCarthyism, what pressure there was, what uncertainty and pain, every time I saw the terrible headlines. You have a tear in your stomach. There was fear, there was disgust. It was a terrible time.

Professor Dirk Struik

But also there was resistance.

In September 1951, under the laws of the Commonwealth of Massachusetts, I was indicted. But I had to fight, even though I was scared to death, of course, sometimes. But dammit, I am a Dutchman. They can't beat me down! I felt the old blood of the fighters in the 80 Years' War in my blood. I was very upset. But, I said, I am going to fight it out. At the same time, I had my mathematical work to do here. And I had trips through the United States, which were, of course, in my defense.

Communism and its legion of "fellow travelers" were alleged to permeate trade unions, schools, churches, and the government. A flood of propaganda was released. The myth of the great "Communist conspiracy" was created, which supposedly manifested itself in the presence everywhere of unscrupulous persons who had "infiltrated" organizations (such persons never merely "joined") in order to overthrow the government and betray us to the Soviets.

In this atmosphere, half reminiscent of Nazi Germany, half of *Alice in Wonderland*, I was able for a time to continue my work at M.I.T., teaching, exploring mathematics, and preparing two books, one on the history of science in early New England, one on the history of mathematics. Ever since my naturalization in 1935 I had participated, as I had already done in the Netherlands, in the struggle for what I saw as social justice, in activities now mostly proclaimed to be heretical and "un-American." Such were the fight against war and Fascism in the 1930s, the support of Loyalist Spain against Franco, the quest for better understanding between the peoples of the U.S.S.R. and the United States, the support of militant trade unionism. I worked with members and friends in the Communist Party, as well as with trade unionists, academics, and church groups.

Thus, I was directly involved with some of the organizations placed on the Attorney General's List (that were designated as having "totalitarian, Fascist, Communist, or subversive" elements). This did not escape the attention of newspaper reporters, who mentioned me and many others in their attacks on heretics—supposedly in touch with spies for the Soviet Union, especially "A-spies."

I was called before one of those witch-hunting committees in Washington, together with my friend Harry Winner, who had been treasurer of the Samuel Adams School, one of the "progressive schools" which educated workers for good and progressive citizenship. We obtained good lawyers. That was not easy, finding lawyers in those days to serve "subversives." In New York, after sentencing the Communist leaders to jail in the first Foley Square trial, Judge Medina had also sent some of their lawyers to jail.

What the witch-hunters were mainly after was *names*. For me, that was to be avoided at all costs. So I used the only thing possible, the Fifth Amendment (against self-incrimination). Those who used the First Amendment, citing freedom of speech, faced contempt of Congress.

To tell the truth, I am not very proud that I took the Fifth instead of the First. But I did not want to go to jail, even for a principle. I liked my job, loved teaching, had three daughters in college, had to protect my wife's health, and had to avoid mentioning names, the main thing they were after. My colleague Chandler Davis, more principled than I, used the First Amendment and had to spend six months in jail. So did others.

My work at M.I.T. could continue, and in a not unfriendly talk with President Killian and other M.I.T. authorities I was able to define my attitude. Killian advised me to act "with all dignity"; I had called the informer Herbert Philbrick a stoolpigeon.

Now this Philbrick, he testified about me and said that as a Communist Party member I attended classes at the Samuel Adams School and was very active in teaching Marxism at this school. This was one of these petty exaggerations he indulged in, hoping to have it spread around by the newspapers. This Philbrick, who played such a role in fingering "Communists," had as a young man joined groups in Cambridge that were under Communist influence, and had for a while been accepted by the Communist Party in the Boston district. He claimed that, horrified by the extreme language he heard, he had reported what he had picked up to the F.B.I. Contrary to the usual informers for the F.B.I., who were mostly psychopaths, alcoholics, petty criminals, or liars, Philbrick presented himself as a clean, normal American whose sense of patriotic duty had led him to report to the F.B.I. He stuck more or less to the facts as he knew them, but liked to embroider them for their effect on his usefulness (and his purse: in a later controversy with a lawyer it became public that his testimonies and writings had been most lucrative).

But for me, worse was to come.

In September 1951, an ambitious district attorney in Middlesex County had me indicted under an old law of Massachusetts for advocating, "by force and violence," the overthrow of the Commonwealth and the U.S.A. Three others were indicted with me, including Harry Winner. I was never accused of any action, only of talking. The indictment stated that we conspired together "to advocate, advise, counsel, and incite the overthrow by force and violence of the Commonwealth of Massachusetts by speech, exhibition, and promulgation of certain written and printed documents, papers, and pictorial representation." A second part of the indictment made us out to be "conspirators" who were planning to overthrow the government of the United States. In a third I was accused of having given a speech on May 1, 1948, to "advocate, advise, counsel, and incite the overthrow by force and violence of the government of the Commonwealth of Massachusetts." Hence, two "conspiracies to advocate" and one direct "advocating." No action, only talk and conspiracy to talk.

There were again big headlines. Oliver Allen again stood by me as my lawyer. Bail was set at $10,000; in a few hours, friends and indignant citizens provided the money. Defense committees were set up. M.I.T. suspended me, but I kept my salary.

Since the indictment was national news, it brought I. F. Stone to Boston in October. He wrote in those days for *PM*, a well-known paper of progressive leanings. Izzy wrote articles . . . one on me, one on Winner, one on Philbrick and the whole case. They were published in a pamphlet and are worth reading even now: *A Plot Against the Commonwealth of Massachusetts*. Stone asked Winner how he had become a radical. "Shelley" was the answer. Asking me the same question, Stone was amused when I said it was Oscar Wilde's *The Soul of Man Under Socialism*. This shows, Stone wrote, in what strange corners the heresy hunters must probe when they get around to cleaning the libraries.

To heighten the *Alice in Wonderland* atmosphere, Governor Dever proclaimed November 27, 1951, "Herbert Philbrick Day." There were patriotic speeches and a grand dinner with a melodramatic speech by Philbrick himself. Will schoolchildren be asked to snitch on each other that day? some of us asked.

And now the long wait for the trial began. Since the reasons for the indictment were rather vague, the defense asked for a Bill of Particulars. The first bill came in January 1952 and was so unsatisfactory that the Supreme Court of Massachusetts requested a new one, which was duly received. It contained many big words on subversion but few facts.

But the district attorney kept postponing the trial. I can guess some reasons for it. First of all, he seemed to have only one witness to testify against me, the ubiquitous Philbrick. We heard of attempts to produce others which failed. An example was the story of a Boston progressive bookstore manager who was approached by a man from the D.A.'s office. Question: "As a good American, tell me what you know about Struik." Answer: "I am a good American. Therefore I shall not talk to you about Struik." Another reason may have been the strong support I had from the sponsors of my Defense Committee, with names the D.A. could not but respect. And a third reason may well have been the fact that the D.A. did not get much help from the F.B.I. The Feds have never liked local busybodies who barge in on a domain they consider their own.

The end came in 1955, from a rather unexpected source. In another case in Pittsburgh, Steve Nelson, a militant trade unionist and Communist, had been indicted, convicted, and sent to jail with a sentence of twenty years. He had been prosecuted under a Pennsylvania anti-sedition law. But the Supreme Court of the United States accepted one of the arguments presented by his lawyer on appeal that, because sedition was a federal offense, state anti-insurrectional laws were unconstitutional. My own indictment had to be quashed also, and all the indictments of others under the Massachusetts Anti-Anarchy Law.

I still had some trouble with the Massachusetts witch-hunters and had to face a committee of my peers at M.I.T. The confrontation with the committee was formal but not unfriendly. And in September 1955, I stood again before my class.

Thus, it was all over. Yes, but not quite. In 1960, at age sixty-five, I was going to lose my tenure. Under ordinary circumstances, I could continue teaching on a year-to-year appointment until I was seventy. But I did not get it. Attempts to get a position at other universities with no age limit for faculty failed. In 1959, I traveled around the country meeting colleagues: Texas, Illinois, Ohio. Invariably the mathematics faculty was glad to have me. Invariably the administration refused. My teaching days in the United States were clearly over.

Happily, I could survive easily on my pension and Social Security. Invitations to teach came from abroad. By this time, thanks to a lawsuit brought by the artist Rockwell Kent and a Los Angeles psychiatrist, the State Department could no longer refuse to issue passports to heretics. And in 1986, on the occasion of my ninety-second birthday, the House of Representatives of the Commonwealth of Massachusetts, in an impressive document, congratulated me. It was signed by Keverian, Speaker of the House, and Mary Jane Gibson, assistant majority whip and the representative from my own district. The Commonwealth had finally decided to forgive me for the injustice it had committed.

—DIRK STRUIK

Them years, they just

crawled up on me.

LENA STANLEY

Born May 18, 1895

Hillsboro, North Dakota

My partner has a place down in Florida, and he has a lot of neighbors who are retired. After they retire, he said, they get down there and they haven't anything to do except play golf and sit around and maybe play bridge. After six months, why, they're gone. They may have been very sharp businessmen in full possession of their faculties, but they've lost their wisdom.

—PHILIP L. CARRET

Why did I start to paint? I'll tell you. I lived with my wife for thirty-one years. She got cancer. She was sick for ten years. When she finally passed away, I figured, Why struggle? So I retired from my business.

I had quite a few friends. And some of them asked me how I'm getting along. I said, Well, I feel all right, but I'm very lonesome. One of my friends said, Lonesome? That's nothing. I'll give you a dog, a dog is a good companion, and you would not be lonesome. So, a dog is a problem. You gotta take care on it. I gave back the dog.

Then I was lonesome again. From Europe, I used to like birds. So I went out and I bought a few canaries. But this is the same thing. You gotta take care on it. I got rid of the birds.

But I gotta do something. So I figured, how about starting to paint? You paint, you keep your mind occupied. I made the first picture. Mine daughter came in to visit me and she saw that picture. Where did you get that? I said I made it myself. She said, You made it? How did you— Because I never painted. She said, Can I have it? I said, I want to throw it out.

So she took that picture and she saw the family and she said, You know, Daddy has no more dog, no more birds, now he's starting to paint. He paints? Yes, he gave me a picture. If you come into my house, you'll see it. So the family started to ask me for pictures. I was glad to give them. Then my friends started to ask me for pictures and I gave them. So I got busy.

Then, by my surprise, teachers that teach painting, they came over to my house. They asked me, Can we see your pictures? Sure, you can see them. They asked me if I can give them some pictures. I was surprised. I gave them. Then they came again. And I gave them. Then they start to make a

◄ *Alfred Levitt, in his eighties, climbing out of a cave in southwestern France after exploring for prehistoric art, 1976*

Aaron Birnbaum, Brooklyn, New York, 1988

show with my pictures. They invited me to come to the show. I invited family, I invited friends. And that's how I started to paint.

I don't do it for pleasure. I do it just to occupy my mind, that's all, to keep on. Because, you know, I was born a slave. What I mean is this: I was born always to work. I can't stay idle. So that's what it is.

Listen, the thing is this: How long you think I'm gonna last on this world? If I'll leave this world, hundreds of people will have my pictures in their homes. So I'll leave something. If you give somebody a present like a box of candy, how long does it last? But if you give a picture, sometimes it goes from one generation to another. I'm glad that I do painting.

So that's what life is.

—AARON BIRNBAUM

In 1944, I went back into the grocery business. I had that business for ten years when I had a heart attack and I had to sell it. From that time on, I had to give up anything that required a lot of physical labor. You might say I've been more or less forcibly retired.

I've spent most of the rest of my life just doing things for others. The last six or seven years, I've been building dollhouses and miniature houses for little railroads and so forth. I give these

Oscar C. Weber, Seattle, Washington

houses to outfits like the Kiwanis Club and the Habitat for Humanity. They raffle them off and make several thousands of dollars from them. And I give a lot of them to different families that I know that have little girls that would enjoy little dollhouses to play with. By trying to help people who need help, I'm enjoying my life.

—OSCAR C. WEBER

When we got to Atlanta, we lived about three and a half miles from downtown. It was so far in the country that people wouldn't rent houses out there. After I finished my internship and had my daughter, we bought a house that was even farther out in the country; nobody else would live out there. We lived there for seventeen years. Today, that part of Atlanta— Sandy Springs—is one of the most congested parts of the whole city.

But by then the people were so close to me they began to complain about the children crying. So one Sunday afternoon we were driving out twelve miles from Atlanta into the country, it was really in the sticks. We found a beautiful piece of land that they were selling for a hundred dollars an acre. We bought seventy-two acres and built my house. We moved out there, and we stayed there for forty-something years, until it got so crowded you couldn't get out of our driveway. There were three hospitals right in back of our house. Then they began to tax the land, so we decided we'd sell some of it. And the dealer said, We'll buy the land, but you've got to give us an option on your house.

Now, my office was always in the house. I never left home—I would never have left my child and my husband for medicine—but by then we were in our seventies, and we knew we wouldn't live much longer anyway. They gave us fourteen more years to live in that house, and then we'd have to give it up. Well, at the end of fourteen years we were still living, and we had nowhere to go, so Mr. Denmark bought some land that was *really* out in the country. There was an old log house out there on the land that we bought. My grandson fixed that up for my office, and that's where I am today.

—DR. LEILA DENMARK

After I left Bell Laboratories at age sixty-five, I became interested in Braille. I took a course and passed the exam to be what they call a Certified Braillist. When I took that exam, they asked, Do you speak or can you write any other language? And I said I could write French.

Eventually, I got a letter from a lady in Norfolk, Virginia. She had a daughter who was blind and who was about to take an examination in

French in high school. She asked me whether I could help. I made arrangements that they would send me her lessons and I would transcribe them in

John Sailliard, working on his lathe, Madison, New Jersey, 1966

Braille and send them back to her. It was quite a job. I even completed a Braille translation of an entire French textbook. She passed the course with a mark of "B."

I also translated from French the original records of Rochambeau's troops from when they marched through New Jersey two hundred years ago. And I used to have a beautiful machine shop downstairs, oh boy. I could spend a whole day running a lathe without getting tired. I'd make or fix just about everything that anybody asked for. I was always repairing something for our church.

Drew University wanted a harpsichord. Their organist was the organist of our church and he asked me and I said sure. The materials came in a kit that was delivered to our house. It was what you call a two-string harpsichord; it could produce fifty-eight sounds. It had two wires for each key, so when you pressed a key, you could, depending upon how you had it set, pluck either the higher wire or the lower wire or both. It made very beautiful sound. It was quite a project, drilling all the holes so precisely. And now they have it at Drew University and they bring it out every once in a while for weddings. I got along very well until my eyes finally gave out and I had to stop.

Incidentally, the Social Security recently sent an examiner around here. They wanted to know whether I was the real John Sailliard or an impostor. Because I'm going on 103 and I've been getting Social Security all these years and they thought maybe I was a faker. But the fellow left after a while.

—JOHN SAILLIARD

My husband, Harry, was in the typewriter line, retail typewriters and business machines. He was in wholesale. But when he died, he didn't leave me with Social Security. He was self-employed and I had to sell the business. I was fifty-nine. So I went to business school because I didn't have any experience in so many years. And a few years later I decided to work on account of one thing: Social Security.

I went to the Manhattan Life Insurance Company, and introduced myself and asked is there any vacancy. I could speak four other languages, plus Yiddish, you know. The manager liked that. It wasn't five days he called me. He put me three months on trial. Fifteen years I worked for them.

They never knew my age. I told them I was fifty. Why should I go and volunteer how old I am? It's not their business. I had to retire when they thought I was sixty-five. I was seventy-nine. You had to work there fifteen years to get a pension and that pension I still get. Plus the Social Security.

—ROSE FREEDMAN

I retired in 1963. I was seventy years old. My wife, she was sick, she had diabetes. They cut the leg off. I had to take care of her. Then she died. I go crazy.

I moved down to Florida in 1967. I lived with one woman down here. She had a room, see. Then I bought a trailer. I started going to the track, to Gulfstream. I used to go just about every day. Everybody knows me there. They even put my name on a nameplate in a box near the winners' circle.

I went back to work when I was eighty-seven. Baking bread down in Miami. Three hundred and fifty loaves a day. Go in at five o'clock in the morning, stay until five o'clock at night. I was getting eight dollars an hour.

I went in this restaurant one day. They had their dishwasher, he used to wash the floor and make the bread. I says to the owner, What the hell kind of bread is this? You have somebody in there wants to kill me?

Ralph Montecalvo with his wife, Jennie, Malden, Massachusetts

He says, Are you a baker?

Yeah, I'm a baker.

Why don't *you* work for me?

I'm a retired man, I says. But I work a couple of days for you.

Oh, no. You gotta work five days.

Work five days? I'm eighty-seven years old.

Then I says: I'll work two days. I want ten dollars an hour.

What happens if I don't pay it?

I don't work.

Well, Mr. Montecalvo, he says, I'll give you eight dollars an hour, but you gotta work five days.

So I work five days. But first thing you gotta do, I told him, is tell the colored guy I'm the boss.

And I'm doing good over there. I'm making good money and I liked the work.

Then another guy took over. They made him boss. He says to me, Ralph, I'm gonna cut on the expenses.

You ain't cutting me.

You gotta work for five an hour.

I says, You need me. I don't need you. I says, Pay me right now. You got bread in there, you take it out. And I left.

—RALPH MONTECALVO

One of my friends belonged to the Audubon Society—we often went camping together, and hiking—and she was trying to get me to join. But I didn't want to belong to that "bunch of bird-watchers." Well, she kept on, and so finally I went with her on a field trip. And for the first time I really looked at a bird. You know, they were flying around all my life, I liked them and all that, but I never really watched one of them.

On this particular trip, I saw a brown creeper. Creepers climb up trees. They live in the trees and they find their food in the trees. They always go up the tree. And when I watched this bird, I thought: This little bird works hard for its food, like I do. It has a life-style. And, come to think of it, I do, too. I get up in the morning, eat my breakfast, go to work, eat my lunch, go back to work, and go home again. I never got up at two o'clock in the morning to go to work. *I* always went up the tree, never down.

That bird became personal. So I began thinking about the Audubon Society, about what its mission was: to protect the birds. Of course, it's really broader than that, but that's what I thought. At that time, I was just about to retire—I had been a legal secretary—and I went to a couple of meetings of our local chapter, and the nominating committee wanted me to accept the nomination for secretary. I'll think it over, I said, and I did. I realized that pretty soon I'd be retired and it might be kind of fun. So I accepted the nomination and was elected—and I'm still secretary. That was more than thirty-three years ago; I retired in 1965.

Doing environmental work—doing any community service—there's a particular gratification. You're not worrying about your own problems;

you're concerned with somebody else's. You can't worry about two things at the same time, so you tend to forget your problems. Most of the things that you worry about never happen anyway. Doing community service is a kind of a healing process. And I guess you could say this set me on the course of environmental activism.

I was president in the late 1970s of the Federation of Western Outdoor Clubs. That's an organization of environmental clubs which also has a recreation program. When I was president, I got the idea that we had a lot in common with the Native Americans: our attitude toward Mother Earth and their concern for wildlife seemed so similar. So we had a joint conference. I traveled throughout Washington, visiting almost every tribe, also a couple in British Columbia. And we became acquainted in the three days that this conference lasted, learned each other's problems and perspectives. Many of them were shared. And we've never had to *have* another conference. We help them, and they help us. And together we make a difference.

Hazel Wolf with students at Brookhaven Middle School, Decatur, Alabama

I still do a lot of public speaking, from kindergarten students on up. I don't try to tell them what to do; I try to get them to relate to a bird the way I related to the brown creeper. I do that by illustrating the things we have in common. One winter I saw this robin. It landed on a very thin coat of ice and slid to one of the little holes in the ice. Then it flew up, went back, slid again to one of the holes. Well, that bird was just playing! So I carry that image through and show them how all young things are playing.

And I always end with the spider. I haven't been able to figure out how little spiders play. But I noticed their webs are very fragile. Could it be that baby spiders get on the end of these things like bungees? And the kids think, Yeah, that's the way they do it. So it starts to make sense.

That's the kind of approach I make to small children. It's our job to enlighten them, so that they'll be well versed in the need for environmental protection as they grow older.

—HAZEL WOLF

I play solitaire a couple of times in the morning, and if I don't have anything to do while I'm eating my lunch, I play it again. I play it in the evening. If I feel myself slipping—if I don't remember things—I play solitaire. And I remember.

If you keep those channels active, I think they'll stay with you a long time. But you have to work at it. So many of the older people I know in the nursing homes where I've been visiting seem to have nothing to do. They sit and they think, Oh, dear, I wish I was eighty again. They're dwelling on the past. They're not thinking about what they *can* do. And that's where they stagnate.

—ELLA MAY STUMPE

Milton W. Garland on the job

I took up flying in 1955 when I was sixty years old. I bought an airplane and learned to fly. The next fifteen years, my hobby was flying. But the insurance company had a rule at that time, that at age seventy-five and above they will not give you liability insurance. They would insure the plane, they knew what it was worth, but they didn't know how I might mess up. That's when I quit flying.

—MILTON W. GARLAND

Harley Potter on the links

I took up golf when I was ninety-two. I'd retired in 1974, when I was eighty, and we moved to De Soto, Missouri, where my daughter was, in 1982. I needed exercise, so I would walk around the high-school track. I was just going around in circles and I decided that that was too monotonous.

They had a nine-hole golf course there, so I drove out and went into the clubhouse and talked to the manager. He took me in a cart around the course, and when we came back to the clubhouse, I signed up for a membership. He was surprised, 'cause he'd never had anyone ninety-two years old playin' golf before.

And I'd never had a golf club in my hand before in my life. I taught myself to play. I try to do the best I can, but sometimes it's not so good. But I was doing pretty well on the fairways, and my putting wasn't too bad. For a while there, I was shooting my age. My only advice: Watch where you're hitting the ball, even if it doesn't go there anyway.

—HARLEY POTTER

I started bowling when I was sixty-four. To this day, I'll meet somebody that I really don't recognize and right away they'll say, Oh, we used to bowl together.

I kept busy. I stayed independent. Like one guy said, We can't even buy her a cup of coffee. And I think I did the right thing. Being with a bunch of people, I couldn't get serious with one, I never give anyone a chance. Because my Jack, he was the only one.

About twelve years ago, I had an operation on my knee. I laid there in the hospital for about two weeks with my leg straight out and it didn't hurt too bad; the hurt came when they took the stitches out and started bending it. When I went back for a checkup, I said to the doctor, How about bowling? He said, It'd be good for you. So I went right back and I bowled until I was ninety-four.

—LENA STANLEY

After I quit competitive racing, I still rode quite a bit, in endurance runs just for fun. And I was a flagman. I would come down to the beach and wave the flag to all these kids, and I tried a lot of machines out for kids who was tryin' to get goin' good.

I rode a bike every day till I was ninety-four. In fact, I just got rid of it. After a while, you just don't move fast enough anymore, and I didn't want to get hurt. It's just one of them things that you gotta be careful.

—JAMES M. DAVIS

My wife passed away in 1968. I could have married several times, but I never got married again. I was a ballroom dancer. Plenty of women I'd meet would be interested in getting married. But you might choose the right partner, or you might get the wrong partner. And if you get the wrong partner, and you get a divorce, they want to split this thing right down the middle. Well, I didn't want no woman spending my money. I got a fair bank account. I've owned this house since 1942. I didn't want to make no mistakes, so I stayed alone.

I'm staying here as long as I can. The community nurse sends over a lady that helps me keep the house clean. She does whatever I'm unable to do. And I get into this ham radio. I was eighty-two when I started. I happened to be lucky to meet somebody that would work with me and help me to get my ham-radio license. I passed the test for novice and I never cared about going any higher. I get kind of a bang out of it. It keeps my

Eddy Kincaide at his radio set in his home in Fairhaven, Massachusetts, December 1995

mind active. I can talk to people all over the world, when the weather conditions are good, and most all over the United States. I can sit my ass
down, work that key eighteen, twenty, twenty-five words a minute in
Morse Code. I don't brag about this, but when I became a radioman in the
United States Coast Guard, they classified me as one of the best.

EDDY KINCAIDE

I became an eclipse addict, resolved to view every total eclipse that I could
possibly reach. Eventually, this passionate preoccupation took me to central Africa, India, Siberia, Java, Australia, and Finland, as well as places
nearer home. I like to travel, to see different cultures, different kinds of
people, different economies, different life-styles, sample different cuisines.
I'm still very curious about the world.

In February 1979, my wife and I journeyed to Montana for another
eclipse. We stayed at the luxurious Big Sky Lodge as our base of operations. On the Northwest Airlines flight to Big Sky, we read the airline's
monthly magazine. It contained an article about the impending spectacle.
Included in the article was a statement of particular interest. "An eighty-
year-old man disembarking in Los Angeles from an eclipse-viewing voyage
on the ship *Fair Wind* was overheard to say, 'I like to look at snow-

covered mountains, waterfalls, pretty girls and total eclipses of the sun.' "

That was me. I've seen twenty eclipses. I've probably seen more eclipses than any other human being.

—PHILIP L. CARRET

I started off in Masonry in the 1920s. I joined because a lot of the boys I was palling around with were Masons, and they extended the invitation to me to join. A lot of those fellows had more money than I did, and they moved on up from Masonry and became Shriners. I didn't have money enough to go along until 1954, when my finances were a little better.

The girl that I had married had gone with a chap who was a Knight Templar, and many of our friends were Shriners. She said, Why don't you go into the Shrine? So I did. I'm not the oldest Shriner in terms of the number of years of membership, but I am by age the oldest Shriner in North America.

The Shrine is the playground of Masonry. We'd have picnics and excursions and a lot of social events with women and men getting together, which they did not do in Masonry.

When the Imperial Potentate was elected two years ago, he said his first desire was to meet the oldest Shriner in North America. This friend of mine invited my wife and me to go down to Tampa and have lunch with him. This was one of the greatest thrills in my life.

—ALBERT M. COLEMAN

You know I was on *Johnny Carson?* My youngest granddaughter saw some of the guests on that program and she said, Grandma can do better than that.

She wrote in and they interviewed me in March and we went in May. This was in 1986. When a local department store heard I was going on *Johnny Carson,* they wanted to give me a dress. My Avon district manager was with me. I picked out a dress, a jacket, a pair of shoes, and they gave me a purse, too, all free of charge.

There was a problem. I would not fly. We went by train from Minot. We had to get off at Chinook, Montana, because of a washout on the track. They put us on school buses and we had to ride about thirty-five miles to the train depot.

When we got to Los Angeles, a white limousine with red velvet interior was waiting to take us to our hotel. We stayed at the Sheraton Universal, on the nineteenth floor. In our rooms was a big bouquet of flowers from my Avon manager in Chicago. We ate supper and the district manager, who was with us, said, Don't look at the prices, just order. I had salmon.

While I was onstage with Johnny, I gave him some aftershave. I said, If you put that on, they'll follow you around. Then I gave him some roll-on deodorant. He said, Do I smell bad? I said, No, no.

Next, I gave him talcum powder. Then I gave him six bottles of perfume. One for each of your girlfriends, I said. He laughed. Finally, I had to get off the stage. I was on so long that one guest couldn't get on the show. When I left, they told me that he shook his head and said, Some woman, one out of a million.

After the show, my family walked out with me. All of a sudden someone grabbed me. It was Johnny. He had on a sweater and jeans. He gave me a hug and a kiss and walked off.

The return trip, I agreed to fly home. When we got to the junction near Goodrich, there was a caravan, twenty cars maybe. When we stopped I asked, Is there a funeral in town today? They laughed. Then they followed us along and drove by my place. The minister had a big yellow ribbon all around my house and a bow by the door and a sign that said, "Welcome Home."

Back in Goodrich, life was pretty much the same for me, except I got nearly one hundred cards after the *Tonight Show*. And sales of my Avon products went up sharply.

—ROSIE GRIES

I gave my car up when I was ninety. When I told my son that I wanted to sell my car, he laughed. You won't get anything for that old gas guzzler, he said. So I'll give it away, I told him.

I was living in Leisure World, a retirement community near Washington, D.C. This black lady was a practical nurse there, and I knew she was having difficulty making do. She lived about five miles out and had to come in by cab. She wasn't getting that much money that she could pay cab fare two ways. So I said to her, Annie, I want to give you my car. She said, I can't drive. I don't have good vision. But would you give it to Sylvester? He was her oldest son and he was trying to be a minister, one of these lay ministers in a black church. So I said, Yes, I'd give it to Sylvester. And that's what I did with my car.

I never saw a black person until I left North Dakota. There were none there. None. In my mother's church paper, we'd read about missionaries that went to Africa. Oh, I was afraid of those Africans. We called them Negroes. We knew that the Negroes had lived in the South as slaves; all I knew about that was that they were controlled by the plantation people. Even though I didn't approve of that, there was a feeling I heard expressed many times that they were less than human.

Of course, I met black people long before I met Annie. And I had some good relationships. But Annie was a special person. She had been taking care of two ladies in a two-room apartment at Leisure World, over near the clubhouse. Now, when I went into Leisure World, I bought a one-bedroom apartment. I had arthritis. I was getting old—I was seventy—and I settled for a small apartment. Then I got into art and I got to carrying my paintings and drawings home. I had them under the bed, behind the doors, in the closet. The place was filling up and I had to have more room. And I was lucky: the second of Annie's ladies had just died, and their apartment was available. I met Annie when she was clearing out the apartment. Well, I had been looking after someone and I was looking for help for her. And I said to Annie, Do you have a job? No, she said, I don't. I said, Well, if you're looking, I'd like to talk to you. So I arranged for her to meet my friend, Mrs. Savage, and she went to work there and took care of her for years. And we became friends.

Not long ago, Annie's youngest son, an alcoholic, had died and she was stuck with the funeral expenses. I sent her a check. And I got a call back from her. You know, she said, I've been praying for help and your check came and I just went to the Lord and I thanked Him and I asked Him to send you a special blessing.

Well, that was the time that I found out that I could get into this home for ladies here in Frederick. So, anyway, that's life for you. You don't know where your good fortunes are coming from.

—ELLA MAY STUMPE

I was a graduate of State College and we had a University Club here in Reading. I went to the club on Friday nights to play poker and bridge. That was one of the marriage laws: every Friday night was my night out.

After my father passed away in 1945, I was the owner of the office-supply store. I sold it in 1961, and got maybe $150,000 for it. I went to these three or four fellows I knew in the University Club who were stockbrokers. Each of them gave me advice. And, of course, I read *The Wall Street Journal* in those days, too. So I took that money and I bought stocks and bonds, a hundred shares of this, five hundred of that. One stock I bought, I bought two hundred shares of Sara Lee. Nobody ever heard of it then. In a year or two, it split. I had four hundred shares. Two more years, it split again. It kept on splitting until I have now more than three thousand shares. I didn't buy and sell; I bought and kept and it paid off. There's only one or two that went sour.

The income from my investments is what keeps us going. And that's my hobby today: checking the income from these stocks. At the end of every month, I tabulate the prices of, say, AT&T, how much it was a month or two ago, how much is it today. I have a list. I just play around with the figures.

— WILLIAM G. HINTZ, JR.

The thing I don't like about being a hundred is that I'm not busy. I've led an active life—going to college, going to war, in business, and socially. When I finally retired, there was a group of us who came down here to Lakehurst at the same time. We got together, we had lots of parties; we were doing something all the time. They've all left now, except us. You're a damn sight better off if you're busy than if you're not. That's the thing I miss: being busy at something useful.

— JOHN D. CLARK

I was in Scotland on a tour with my daughter, Gynath, and her friend, and we were in a pub. It's the only pub I've ever been in. The tour director had us all come in there because there was a band that was going to play for us while we drank them out of business.

A well-dressed gentleman and a lady come in and sit next to me. He turns to me and says, Aih, 'tis a grand day for Scotland!

I look at him, you know, I was having a good time in Scotland, and I said, Yes, I'm enjoying it, too.

Aih, he says, but Scotland's got a man on the moon.

What do you mean?

Armstrong, he says, belongs to our clan.

So that's how I found out that "they" had put a man on the moon.

My hairdresser's mother could not accept that a man had walked on the moon. She died believing that it was rigged. That's how hard it was for some people to accept progress. It's not hard now.

My generation, when that technology first came in, we were not going to have anything to do with it. We were so conditioned to our way of life, why did we want something most of us couldn't understand?

I'm not totally resistant to newfangled things. At first, I didn't want to get a computer. Just because I'm an old lady, I was determined to finish my life the way I had planned. I had wanted to write a book, the story of my life. But my hands were bothering me with arthritis, and I really couldn't work on a typewriter.

Well, my good friend Sue Ann's daughter-in-law—this was before she was the daughter-in-law—used to stay with me at night sometimes. I was living with my son and daughter-in-law at that time near Tiffany's place of work. And when they were away, Tiffany would stay with me. If I needed copies made, Tiffany would say, Oh, I can do those at work. I'll bring them tomorrow when I come for lunch. One day, I had maybe a dozen copies I needed, and Tiffany said, You need a computer so you can make your own copies. I just thought that was funny.

After I moved in with Sue Ann and her husband, Heinz, Tiffany began coming to this family because their son had found her. One day she said in front of everybody, Ella May needs a computer.

Mr. Wilms was working then. He had these long days, leaving at six o'clock in the morning and he wouldn't get home until six o'clock at night. We'd have dinner, and he'd go in and sit in his easy chair and talk and read the paper. One night, he said, Ella May, they've got a sale on computers down at Ward's. Let's go look at them.

I said, It's raining. And, It's been a long day for me. And, I don't want to look at computers. But he insisted. So I thought, I can go, but I don't have to buy.

Well, they got me down there and they pushed me up to this handsome guy. He had a well-prepared sales pitch. I was in a wheelchair and I couldn't get away, and Sue Ann—she always stands beside me, I thought; she'll get me through this—she disappeared and left me alone with this guy and Heinz. For two hours they worked on me. The salesman showed me the different parts of computers. He'd go off to wait on somebody else and then he'd come back to me. A lady came over, she was about fifty, and she said, I just learned how to use a computer. It will write for you, it will do your work for you. Another lady came by. Oh, you're going to buy a computer? I think that's wonderful!

Finally, I was getting tired and I said to Heinz, Please take me home. He said, Shall we sign up for it? I said, Yes. And he brought it home.

Heinz set up the computer in my room. For two weeks I just looked at my investment. I thought, I can't do it. Then I started opening the books and learning. I was six months into it before I realized the beginner's book

Ella May Stumpe at work on her second book, The Ladies of Record Street, *June 1998*

hadn't been included in the package and I was working with the more advanced books, familiarizing myself with words like windows, mouse, hard drive, applications, files. These were words I had learned at another time in my life and now I had to learn another definition for them, not understanding how to use them, or how they could possibly make life easier for me. Every day I'd get frustrated, but Sue Ann would cheer me up and I'd keep trying. She even called in a computer tutor who got me started on the right track. And I was able to start writing my book.

But the computer was disrupting the hard-earned tranquillity of my daily life. It was interrupting my concentration at the bridge table. It was causing sleepless nights.

One morning I came down at about eleven o'clock and I said to Sue Ann, I'm going to throw it out the window. She happened to be reading the Frederick Community College quarterly schedule of adult-education classes. She said, You need to go back to college. And, you know, that's a pretty ridiculous thing to say to a ninety-eight-year-old.

We kid one another quite often, and I thought, I'll let her think I'm interested. She said, Go call them up. She gave me the number. I called. The registrar said, I have one opening. You can have it if you're here by noon. I told Sue Ann. She said, Let's go. By then it was too late for me to back out, even though I thought, They'll never take me.

We got down to the college and finally found the registrar's office. She gave me a form, which I got completed with Sue Ann's help. When I returned it to the registrar, she looked at it and said, Is this your birth date? I thought that a strange question when I was the only one applying. Yes, I said, July the twelfth is my birthday. But her computer wouldn't register me, because it couldn't compute my age: this was 1993, and I was born in '95. As soon as we left the office, she sent the paperwork over to the main office. It had to be registered by hand. I made the front page of the Frederick paper because the computer wouldn't register me.

At my second Saturday class, the president of the college was there to welcome me. You are the oldest student this college has ever had, he said. I was not prepared for all the attention, congratulations, and humor that surrounded me.

But the really great event was the day I began writing my book: January 1, 1994. Writing—on the computer—filled my days. And I completed *100 Years, My Story* by the deadline I had set: my one hundredth birthday.

—ELLA MAY STUMPE

For a long time—after I was twenty-two—I thought of myself as growing old and being old. I don't know exactly when, but I became aware that I am ageless, I am absolutely ageless. I am able to lust after a handsome young man and it doesn't bother me that he doesn't know it.

The only shrouds of sadness are the loss of loved ones. Certainly part of us dies when a dear friend leaves, yet we must go on giving to the stream of life. Sometimes I think back to the remark Walter Arensberg made after the flood that took my house, that wallpaper is very important. The wallpaper of our lives—its distractions, ambitions, possessions—helps us escape from our emptiness when we find ourselves alone.

I regret that I haven't been a housewife making chocolate éclairs for my husband every Saturday night. I love chocolate éclairs—the way they used to make them in Paris. I think my dream, as a little girl raised on fairy stories, would have been to be a happy housewife, but my life didn't develop that way. I thought people loved and that everybody was faithful. But life is very different. And people don't read fairy stories anymore. They watch television.

—BEATRICE WOOD

We were married seventy-one years. I lost my dear wife six years ago, and I lost my legs about six years ago. Happily, she didn't see me in this condition. Seventy-one years with the same girl. I miss her. I sure miss her.

—JOSEPH GOLDSTEIN

Gossie and I, we were married fifty-one years. We had a beautiful relationship. We were blessed with three children, but I had to give them up to death, all three, in infancy. But I have had *plenty* of children all through my life, and I'm still collecting them. I still have people in here that call me "Ma." Some of the workers call me "Mother." Some of the people that serve us our meals call me "Momma Tyler."

I've had children all my life.

—JULIA TYLER

Our children grew up nice and good. My wife did ninety percent, but a little bit I did, too. I worked too much. A good education we got for them. I am proud how they came out.

The greatest joy that I have in the last years are the children's children. I have downstairs a lot of machinery and tools. And when two great-grandboys come, the first thing they want to do is to go downstairs.

I showed them how to drill, how to saw, how to put the nail in the board. I can't do it anymore, but I can pass something on to them.

—EMIL GLAUBER

I don't want to give up. Then my life is gone.

I had a wonderful doctor in Dr. Drake. He said, Rosie, don't quit working. Your body's used to it. You quit, you're gone.

He did his doctoring in Minneapolis, and that doctor was ninety years old himself. I got up there for a checkup. And he said, Rosie, I only want to live to see you on your birthday.

I said, Doctor, what will you do on my birthday? Are you going to waltz?

He grabbed me and we waltzed in the living room. He laughed. In a week, the man was dead. I sure miss him.

—ROSIE GRIES

At my age, I have no future. But I'm glad to be alive. I look forward to the next sunrise. Yes I do. I look forward to the dawn of each new day.

—MARION W. HARMAN

I'm lookin' forward to going to heaven. Every year I say I been a fool for making Him wait. But I'm talkin' to the good Lord, and He'll take care of me.

—FANNIE LOU DAVIS

My mother died in her thirties, and I didn't think that I was going to live any longer than she did. That was a thought I had with me. But after thirty years passed, God kept keeping me. And when I got to be fifty, Oh Lord! I thought I'd been here a lifetime, which is more than a lifetime for some people.

My mother's mother was eighty-something. I said, Well, I guess I'll be here a few more years. Not that I want to be. But it's part of God's plan and it's in His hands. Tell it like it is, I'll be very happy when that last day comes; of course, I won't know it, maybe, until the last breath is gone. I'll be happy when I leave this world: a hundred years, and the fighting is still going on to try to get along with all people. I've tried to live right, to be a good Christian, but it's a hard job. Sometimes something happens and I bubble over. I don't use any bad words, but I let it come out just like I feel about it. Those people in this nursing home that don't want to be bothered with you who are supposed to be trying to help you and you can't help yourself. There's very little now that I can do for myself, and I have to depend on somebody else.

—JULIA TYLER

If there's one thing I miss now, it is that I am not able to mingle with the folks, but instead they have to come to me. But making and keeping friends is paying terrific dividends. I never have time to sit in my room and stare at the wall. The daily mail is a joy. It usually brings a letter, a card, or a gift from among these many friends I've made and kept up with throughout my lifetime. These letters and notes require a reply of some kind. This means that every day an answer goes through the mail. This means that my attention is on others whom I love and respect and not on myself.

—F. ETHEL ANDREWS

I always was an outdoor girl. I just loved anything you could do outside, and I still do. Now I can't even walk in the garden. Isn't that awful?

But I always look forward to tomorrow. Let's see, today is Tuesday, so tomorrow I get to sleep, I don't have to be up at eight o'clock. Then Friday mornin' my granddaughter fixes my hair.

Sunday morning, Julia and Jimmy come by for me to go to church. Then we go out to lunch. And now we go to the nursing home on Sunday afternoons to be with her daddy. And then Monday morning my niece comes by and gets me at ten o'clock and we go to the nursing home. She gives a devotion out there, and then we very often eat there and visit the old people for two or three hours. Then we come home.

The rest of the week I flop. And I mean I flop.

—LOIS CROUCH ADDY

Usually, people my age kind of live in the past. But, you know, I forget the past. I'm always looking to the future. I'm looking toward the Lord coming, that's what I'm looking to.

Every day is a new day. And when I wake up I say, Thank you, Lord, for another day. And I say, Will you help me to keep from falling? You know, I have a fear of falling and getting crippled.

I've been very active all my life. When I was real young, I played tennis. When I finally got to the point where I felt like I couldn't do that anymore, I turned to golf. I played golf on my ninety-fifth birthday. Don't ask me what kind of game I played, but I played.

We have a therapist here. He decided that I could take these exercises. So I do them every morning. When I take a shower, see, I need to be very careful that I don't fall. So I exercise before I go into the shower, and that kind of limbers me up.

I'm thankful for my mind. I just thank the Lord every morning: I am so happy that I still can think and know what's going on. So I've got a lot of things to smile about. Yes, sir, I've got plenty of things to smile about.

—PAULINE HILL MASSEY

A Century of Progress

Our generation has experienced

the greatest changes

in the history of the world.

—RENATA BURT

Born December 24, 1895

Brown County, Wisconsin

The "good old days" were never so good. We had polluted water supplies and typhoid fever, a fairly common disease. We didn't have a Pure Food and Drug Act until 1906. The conditions in the slaughterhouses in Chicago were appalling. Kids got measles and scarlet fever and polio.

Tuberculosis was the great scourge. I had a lady friend who was a remarkable individual. Her husband died of TB. He had been in a sanatorium for a couple of years. And then she developed TB. The doctors gave her two choices: she could go to the sanatorium and rest for two or three years, or she could have one lung out. Take it out, she told them. She wasn't going to sit in a sanatorium, just sitting on a porch and gazing at the scenery for a couple of years. She showed me the scar, which very few of my lady friends would have done. A very impressive scar.

—PHILIP L. CARRET

Stop and think: What would you do without air-conditioning in the summertime? What would you do without all this heat in the wintertime? What would you do if you had to sit here without television? What would you do if you couldn't call somebody on the phone? What would you do if people didn't have some way to come and see you? Tell you what, I just enjoy them all so much.

—ADA TABOR

A good bathroom, I guess, is about the most important modern convenience I can think of. When I was a girl, we had to go outside to the toilet. One place we lived, we finally got running water outside, and Father would carry the water into the house. Mother would heat that water on her stove, and we would take a bath in a tub in the kitchen. Just think about that.

—PAULINE HILL MASSEY

◄ *Sarah Elizabeth Hunter at age eight; Sarah Hunter Jackson at age 101*

When the telephone was new, it was quite exciting, you know. In business, it saved so much time. Before we had telephones, if I wanted to send a message to someone downtown, I had to go there myself, or send somebody, or send a telegraph, or write a letter. With the telephone, I could be speaking to somebody instantly, without bothering anybody else.

Another thing that was amazing was speed in answering fire alarms. In the old days before the internal-combustion engine, the fire engine was simply a little steam boiler with a pump that could squirt water at a great distance. When the alarm rang, you had to hitch up the horses to the fire engine, get them out, light the fire, get up steam. And you had to get to the fire. What they had, they had horses that were trained. When the alarm rang, the door opened and the harness was up above, then the harness was lowered and all the fireman had to do was to hook it in place. He didn't even have to light the steam pump. That was lighted by a gas jet in the floor. When the fire engine was pulled over the gas jet, the inflammable material in the fire engine would light, and before long the fireman had up steam. And he could work that steam pump to squirt water the height of the building. Of course, back then the buildings usually weren't that high. I don't think they made them more than six stories tall.

—JOHN SAILLIARD

It's just like we're in a different world today from when I was young.

When my husband worked for the Southern Railroad, we lived in Chattanooga. My mother came down for a visit. And when she found out that they were going to vote on getting power from the Tennessee Valley Authority, she said, I've got to get home so I can vote yes.

We had the electricity in our house there in Chattanooga. I had an electric stove, and we'd be sitting around before my husband would come home from work, and my mother would say, We'd better start supper soon. And I'd say, No, we don't have to start it yet, it won't take long to fix us a meal. Well, of course, she found out then how easy it was. And she was cooking all those years with a coal stove.

—PAULINE HILL MASSEY

Electricity is the greatest.

Without electricity, we couldn't do so many things. We couldn't have an operating room. We just don't realize that it made our food safe; we can store food now that would have spoiled in the past. I just don't know how we could ever do without it, now that we've gotten used to it.

—DR. LEILA DENMARK

Electricity meant major changes for people. A lot of the big places wanted to get in on the ground floor and they installed their own power plants. Two department stores, Stewart & Company and Hochschild-Kohn, which were right across the street from one another, both had their own power plants. There was a hotel right around the corner had its own power plant; some of the office buildings installed their own power plants. It stayed like this for a long, long while, until the big power companies could go in and put in power lines. They could furnish electricity a whole lot cheaper than all these individual places could make it.

Electricity revolutionized people's lives. But people don't realize that domestic oil burners were a vast, vast advance. You didn't have to shovel coal into the house anymore and then shovel out the ashes.

—ALBERT M. COLEMAN

The icebox, the mechanical icebox, that was the most astounding invention. Until the mechanical icebox—the refrigerator—was developed, everybody had to buy a chunk of ice and store it.

—JOHN SAILLIARD

The first vacuum cleaner I had, I worked it with a sort of a plunger that went up and down to get the dirt out. Before that, we used to take the rugs up and put them out on the line and beat them with rug beaters. Vacuuming is no fun, but beating the rugs, now *that* was hard work.

—JUANITA DUDLEY

When they started these interstates, that's when people could begin to travel. Before then, we managed to get around, but the roads were pretty bad, and it was such slow going, especially with those early cars. They didn't have any power, and it was awful hard to get up hills sometimes.

—PAULINE HILL MASSEY

The national highway system has to be one of the greatest achievements of the century. It used to be all they had was wagon-track roads, grass-covered roads mostly in the country that we rode over in our wagons to get where we were going. My father thought they were desecrating the earth when they put pavement on it. Yep, they were destroying the wheat fields for parking and for highways. He died in '38, when a lot of roads had already been blacktopped, but it was nothing like what we have today. To come from that to the national highway system we have today is unbelievable. My father would have died.

And the airports today cover so much ground. You cannot believe many of them started in a cow pasture, when the planes would land in the fields.

—ELLA MAY STUMPE

The development of air transportation is one of the great phenomena of my life. The first commercial plane was the DC-3, which held fourteen passengers and later was expanded to hold twenty-one. The first time I flew to the Coast, you went from Newark Airport to a little field up in the Poconos. From there, you took a train and went to Columbus, and then you took a plane from Columbus to Kansas City, and then you took another train, and finally you took a plane again on the last leg of the journey. You got to California in, I guess, something like twenty-four hours. But the fastest train then would take five days, so that was an improvement.

You'd leave early in the evening, fly to Chicago, get off in Chicago, and change planes and go on from there, and get to L.A. early in the morning. And now, of course, you make it in five hours or thereabouts, and nobody thinks anything of it.

—PHILIP L. CARRET

I was admitted to the bar in 1919, which means I've been a practicing attorney over seventy-five years. In my practice, it was a simple thing, but the copy machine was one of the big innovations. Before you had that, you had to write out everything. You'd have to have one secretary that would make the copy, then another secretary would read it back to make sure it was a correct copy. And that wasn't all done in just five minutes, you know.

—EDWARD J. CORCORAN

Television has succeeded in giving us a lot of entertainment and knowledge. I certainly do enjoy watching football. But television also gives us too much knowledge. I'm not talking about the lousy stuff that you get on TV, most of which is immoral, really. But television gives us everything that's happening all over the world all the time. When I was a kid, we had to find out what was happening in the newspapers or in magazines. Now, every day, we know what's happening in South Africa, in Korea, in Bosnia, in every goddamn place in the whole world. It's too much. I think we were a lot better off when we didn't know so much so fast.

But the most important advances are the ones that put us out of business: computers. I mean, the two jobs I had, with the Monroe Calculating Machine Company and A. B. Dick: they don't have calculating machines anymore. The same with mimeograph machines—they're gone. And now you have this "information superhighway" . . .

—JOHN D. CLARK

The eight-hour day and the five-day week. The unions won that. I remember my father going to work until Saturday noon. I remember my father getting forty cents an hour. I remember the barbershop having to be open on Sunday morning sometimes to take care of the men that did nothing but work the whole blasted week.

—ARTHUR W. HAMER, SR.

Millions and millions of people used to work twelve, fourteen hours a day just to make a living. Today, with all of the consumption, we throw away so much. We waste so much. See, when I was a kid, you couldn't buy shoes almost nowhere. Today, who makes a second sole on his shoes any more? If the shoes are a little bit gone, *whissht,* you buy a new pair. I had five brothers. I was the oldest. I was the only one that got new clothing. My youngest brother was fifteen years old before he got a new suit.

—EMIL GLAUBER

The American public is going mad. They're absolutely mad about athletics, football and baseball and basketball. Payin' ballplayers $2 million a year to throw a baseball? And that's gettin' 'em cheap.

—ORLANDO F. MORLEY

After the big stock-market crash, you had to have some protection to offer to people so that they had faith in the banks again. The Federal Deposit Insurance Corporation was one of the big reforms that made a difference.

—AL KRAUS

There was the time when there were no "entitlements," none at all.

Social Security was introduced during the Depression when people were hungry. I really don't think I gave much thought to it until my husband, who was five years older than I was, was about to retire. He was of the first generation that got Social Security. Well, he began bugging me. He said, You've got to get your birth certificate so you can sign up. Now, he was born in St. Louis and he was able to get a birth certificate to establish his age, but I couldn't. I was not registered! I wrote to the vital statistics in Bismarck, North Dakota, and they wrote back saying, We have no record of you. For me to get Social Security, my older sister had to testify that she knew my age.

—ELLA MAY STUMPE

When I was young, older people had no security at all. If they had no savings, they had nothing. If they had anything, it was family. Which was a very precarious way to plan for your future. Social Security was a godsend.

—DELIA HARRISON-MARTIN

The treatment of the poor represented great progress. We finally developed a way of taking care of the poor people, with welfare. Before that, people went to the poorhouses. So that's been the big change. Has it been a change for the better? For the poor, yeah.

—EDWARD J. CORCORAN

The nation has awakened to the fact that you can't continually pollute our streams and our environment and not pay the price. I think we all recognize now that there's a limit on what industry can do.

—MARION W. HARMAN

We got doctors now and they're gainin' on all them diseases all the time. Cancer they can handle pretty good right now. There's still too much smokin'. They got to kill this tobacco market. It's killin' too many of 'em.

—W. F. JARNAGIN

When I started out, a person would come to me with a sick child with, let's say, meningitis or leukemia or Hodgkin's disease. And I'd say, Well, Mother, there's nothin' in the world we can do for this child.

But, today, nobody has to die. We've got treatments for diseases that used to be fatal. We can put in new livers, new kidneys, new hearts. We've got medicines we never had before. And we've got safer food and houses that can be heated in the cold.

But the greatest advance that has happened in medicine is immunization. It has saved more lives and done more good for the world than anything.

The next-greatest thing is baby food. Women quit chewing for their children back in the twenties. Back then, when I got into medicine, we had no baby food. We had a lot of scurvy and rickets, because all children had was evaporated milk. Now there's no reason for a little baby not to be taken care of. We can do everything except mother.

The other day I had a mother called about a child that was born with a cleft palate, six fingers, six toes, and a bad heart. Somebody said, Well, that poor child doesn't have a chance. And I said, Don't believe that. We'll take that baby to Egleston Hospital, fix it so people won't ever know he had a cleft palate, take the extra fingers off his hands and toes off his feet—they'll be as pretty as anybody's—and we'll put him in a new heart. He doesn't have to die. Nobody has to die now.

We've learned how to take better care of people. But people have to eat right and feed their children right. When you take your dog to the vet, the first thing he says is if you don't feed this dog right you're gonna have a sorry dog. Well, that's the hardest thing we have today with our little people. There's so much temptation out there, cookies and junk food; it's hard to get parents to feed their children right.

—DR. LEILA DENMARK

Listen, I want to tell you sometin'. You see, the life is this way: Your father had a better life than his father. And you have a better life than your father. And your children have a better life than you. That's how it's improving.

—AARON BIRNBAUM

Secrets of Longevity

I guess I was blessed

with the long genes.

—LUCY SOMERVILLE HOWORTH

Born July 1, 1895

Greenville, Mississippi

How come I'm still here at age 103? Somebody asked me that the other day when I was over at a party. He looked at me and said, You don't act like you're as old as you are. What's your secret?

I told him: The only thing about it is, I go to bed every night, I get up every morning.

But there are some things that I've never done. When I got out of school and opened my first drugstore, I knew I wanted to conduct it in a certain way. So I set this rule down: You can smoke anywhere you want, but not in here. You've got to smoke, go out. You have a habit of smoking you can't control, go somewhere else and get another job.

I never had a drink from the soda fountain in my drugstores. I never have, and I don't till yet, take any carbonated drink. No Coca-Cola, none of that stuff.

And I tried to do the right things. I married the right girl.

—YORK GARRETT

If you do right things in the world, the world won't hurt you. Ain't nothin' hurt me in these hundred and some years I been livin' 'cause I tried to do right. I tried to treat everybody right, I tried to live right. I try to treat you like I'd have you to treat me. So I ain't had no trouble.

—SALLIE JORDAN

I lived a simple life and a clean life. And I worked like heck.

—IVY FRISK

Now, that's the puzzling thing. Look how long I'm living and look how hard I worked, from age fourteen. I went to night school for years, and many times I lost sleep on account of my studies. I had a responsible job; I had twelve men I had to make sure weren't making mistakes. I never was

◄ *A birthday card for Arthur W. Hamer, Sr.*

one to go away on vacation, but I enjoyed my work and going to the opera and working in my shop. And I'm still here.

—JOHN SAILLIARD

Don't worry, don't smoke, drink in moderation or not at all. And make as many friends as you can.

—PHILIP L. CARRET

Well, you eat proper and you sleep proper and you keep good hours. And you don't drink too much. I never drink too much.

—CHESTER ("RED") HOFF

Beans and greens and two beers a day, one in the morning and one in the afternoon.

—PAUL ONESI

Eat a lotta garlic. Drink a lotta wine.

—JOSEPH LICCARDO

Meat, potatoes, and gravy. I don't like vegetables; I can't hardly eat any of them. The potatoes take care of all the vegetables. And very little fruit.

—LENA STANLEY

Gluttony is one of the worst things. You need three meals a day. You've got to have a protein in every meal to avoid hypoglycemia. If you get up and have a good meal in the morning with some protein, a good meal at lunch with protein, eat vegetables, drink nothing but water, you'll get along fine.

You can eat one egg a day the rest of your life and it won't hurt you. Red meat has never hurt anybody. Everything we have to eat is better than it's ever been. But you've got to exercise good judgment.

—DR. LEILA DENMARK

If you exercise, you'll get to be as old as Methuselah. Drink a lot of water, but don't drink coffee—that'll make you look old and ugly.

—GENEVA McDANIEL

I don't drink coffee, tea, or milk. I haven't drunk milk since I was five years old. The thing is: All mammals, when they're born, get milk from the mother, right? After they're weaned, they don't drink milk anymore. If you never drink milk, I think you're much better off.

I also quit smoking. I started smoking when I was at college. And I smoked during the war. And when I was in business, I smoked Camels all the time. But I used to have a trick: I'd give a pack to a guy up on the next floor, and every once in a while I'd go up and bum a cigarette from him. Then it got to the point where I figured I'd use a filter. Well, one day, I took this filter apart and I saw the stuff that was in it. And I said to myself, My God! To think that that's what I'm putting into my lungs. And I took the cigarettes that I had and I threw them out and I never had the least desire to smoke again.

—JOHN D. CLARK

During my first half century, starting with a grape-arbor leaf, I smoked like a chimney. Then I stopped. The first thing I managed to get rid of was the Chesterfields. But I was still smoking. We were building a couple of houses out in Mercerville at that time. I was working hard and puffing away on my pipe while I worked. Well, that pipe blocked up and I took it out of my mouth and broke it in half and threw it away. No, sir, I told myself, this is it. This has got to be it. I said, Arthur, you go buy another pipe you'll be quitting forever. So I never bought another pipe. I quit entirely.

—ARTHUR W. HAMER, SR.

My friend Tiffany told somebody one time: The secret is . . . Ella May eats her dessert first. I guess that's as good an answer as any.

But, actually, I would say it's my faith. I have tried to follow the Golden Rule: Do unto others as I want others to do unto me. And I followed my mother's program: Have a good attitude, make an honest effort, and be punctual. I think I've survived because I never let my problems be the main object that I was living for. I've not spent a lot of time worrying about things that were never going to happen.

—ELLA MAY STUMPE

The fact that I have lived as long as I have in the condition that I am in, I think I've been just about one of the most fortunate guys that ever walked on two feet. I don't allow myself to worry about how terrible life can be, and how badly I've been treated. I only think of the good things.

—OSCAR C. WEBER

I don't do anything but pray, that's all.

—ROSIE GRIES

I am a Christian. If I talk to a man and I find out he's an atheist, I'll put my hand on his shoulder and I'll say, Mister, if you're an atheist, that's your business. I am a Christian and that's my business. But I've got something to hope for. You don't. Jesus Christ is the hope of the world. I say this: Hope was born on Christmas day, and that hope was Jesus Christ. And He's coming again.

—EDDY KINCAIDE

God Almighty helped a little bit.

—ALBERT M. COLEMAN

I think the Lord has spared me. There were fourteen of us, all born from one daddy, and there ain't nobody here but me.

—FANNIE LOU DAVIS

My mother lived to be ninety-eight and a half. She never had to use a walker. And she had her mind. She was in the hospital about two weeks and just went to sleep. She didn't suffer any. I guess I'm my mother's daughter.

I think the only reason the Lord has left me here, see, is, I play piano. Played all my life. And I have four or five people up here that love to sing, and they don't know anything but "Amazing Grace." And they say to me, Can you play "Amazing Grace"? I thought, my Lord! I played it about ten thousand times! But they're cute old things. So I said, I'm not gonna play it another time unless you all sing. I think that's the only reason the Lord left me here. To play "Amazing Grace."

—SARAH HUNTER JACKSON

I'm just lucky. People always took good care of me: my family, my wives. And I always enjoyed what I was doing.

—KARL LONG

I used to say facetiously, A cold shower and a cup of hot water. But I think the answer is moderation. My father died when I was only about four years old. In my younger days, I never thought I'd live to be a hundred, I never anticipated that. I never abused myself.

—EDWARD J. CORCORAN

I do not like inactivity. I've always been very, very active. Before I'd go to sleep at night, I had my next day's work planned. And I've never felt like I've wasted an hour.

Keep busy, that's what Father would tell us: Keep busy with something that's uplifting, something that would help people. That's the secret. And have a happy outlook on life.

—LOIS CROUCH ADDY

You've got to have children. What do you think I've been living for?

Hey, because you're old, a lot of people think you don't know what you're doing. But I do know. That's why I don't want no one to stay with me. I want to be alone. I want to cry, I cry. I want to sing, I sing. I want to open up my door, I open it. I want to eat, I eat. No boss. I don't want no boss over me.

Alive is working hard. Nobody comes here and does my work.

—THERESA NIGRELLI

My formula for long life, of course, wasn't premeditated. I never made it an ambition to be a hundred, but when I got within sight of it, well, I thought it would really be a distinction. In retrospect, I think it was not overdrinking, overeating or indulgence in bodily functions, like going out with men and forgetting that I wasn't married to them. I never got into that.

I don't think I was prudish, and certainly I had a great many friends among the men, but I was a single woman for many years. Then, after I married, I wasn't going to forget that I *was* married and take up with any other man. Of course, I do know that the sex drive is very strong, and that's what keeps the human race populating the globe. But it's obvious, as you go through life, that some men and some women have more of that. Some can control it; some pretty well have to let it loose.

—LUCY SOMERVILLE HOWORTH

I attribute it, honestly, to the inheritance of good genes given down to me by God knows how many generations. And to the inner drive I had to build my life.

—ALFRED LEVITT

Try to take care of everything that comes up and down your street. And take care of your finances so you don't have to worry about anything as you get on in life.

—WILLIAM G. HINTZ, JR.

I'll tell you the way I look at it. You know, sometimes you go in conversation with somebody. Everybody wants to show that he's right. You know, I never want to be right.

I had once a conversation with a friend of mine. I told him, Well, I think you're right. Two weeks later, he said to me, Aaron, you remember we were talking this and this? And you said that I was right? Well, I was not right. I'm thinking that you was right. And I say, Now you're right again.

So you know what I mean? Don't argue with anybody. Let them have the right.

—AARON BIRNBAUM

Don't hate.

—EMIL GLAUBER

Work at something that is of value. But the main thing in life is to find what's good in every person you meet. And, by daggone, you can find it. I don't care who he is, or who she is, but you can find some nice thing about that person. I believe that's the secret of living: no hatred. And no ill feeling. Keeps your old body well.

—F. ETHEL ANDREWS

I never was sick in my life. I never took a pill in my life. I never smoked in my life. I never drank in my life. The doctor says that's why I'm in good condition.

I played two rounds of golf here not too long ago with one of my friends. Hell, I can hit the ball as good as I did twenty years ago. Some days I feel like I want to stay to 105, because that was my unit number in the state highway patrol in Ohio. I told them at the bank: I'm gonna be here till 105, just like that.

—JAMES M. DAVIS

As I went along in life, I used to say I hope to see ninety. Then ninety came. People asked me, Well, how do you keep going? And my only answer was, You just keep going, period.

I feel as though I can do the same things today that I did, say, when I was seventy. I feel that way, but I cannot do the same things. My eyesight is poor. I can't read without a magnifying glass. My hearing is going bad. When I get up and get dressed to go to work, it takes me longer than it used to. I work at golf, it's an exercise, but I feel as though I'm swinging the club just as hard as I ever did but that darn ball won't go near as far as it used to go.

So that's the way it is.

—MILTON W. GARLAND

I have no formula for longevity. I have never had any desire for long life. I've always faced my age. I've never tried to lessen my age. My age was my age. I take life as it comes, year after year, and I do what I'm capable of doing, or what I'm allowed to do.

—SR. URSULA INFANTE

I simply didn't have time to die. I was too busy. Every day I was too busy.

—SAMUEL D. SCHNEIER

I just gradually lived year after year, year after year. And the next thing I know, I'm a hundred years old. I never had any serious injuries, any serious illnesses. I can't say that I had a hard life. I think I got along fairly well, or so it seemed to me.

So my recipe is simple: Keep on breathing.

—FRED BENSON

I don't attribute my longevity to anything. I'm just thankful.

—HELEN L. SMITH

I didn't expect to live this long. My mother died when she was a hundred and my older sister died when she was ninety-three. I mean, it's the genes. Whatever I live now, it's found time.

Everybody thinks that it's your eating. I eat everything. I have a very good breakfast. I eat hot chili. But I eat in moderation. I don't overeat. I don't nibble when I watch television. And I walk.

I never took any medication. And I don't believe everything the doctors say. It's a lot of malarkey.

Nobody wants to get old, nobody likes to get old. But everybody's got to get older. I count my blessings. I have a very good family. My daughter is an angel. My two boys couldn't be any better. And my grandchildren, all my grandchildren never gave us any bad time. So that keeps me living on.

When I retired, my children sent me on a trip to Israel for two weeks, and one in Italy and one in Greece. I took up painting. I study Spanish. When I was ninety-six or ninety-seven, I moved out to Los Angeles full-time from New York. I got sciatica and I was worried about walking around in New York and not having family nearby.

I go to L.A. Laker games. I have a picture of me with Magic Johnson. James Worthy, he kissed me and gave me his autograph. When I was a hundred, I was on television and Worthy came in and they asked me who's my favorite Laker and I told them of course it was Magic Johnson, but now it's Worthy. *Now* it's Eddie Jones.

—ROSE FREEDMAN

Keep a cool head, warm feet, and open bowels. That's a big joke to tell to a doctor.

It is said that a London doctor was asked that same question. And he said, It's very simple. You select great-grandparents who live to a ripe old age. And then you select grandparents who live to a ripe old age. Then you select parents who live to a ripe old age. And then you have to be damn careful crossing streets.

—JOSEPH GOLDSTEIN

Wisdom for the Ages

You make your own advantage.

—PHILIP L. CARRET

Born November 29, 1896

Lynn, Massachusetts

Ride a motorcycle that you can ride, but be careful. When you get goin' too fast, then the motorcycle's ridin' you and you don't know what it's gonna do; and if something happens, it's your fault.

—JAMES M. DAVIS

Get an education. And free yourself. If you don't get an education now, you're out of it. You have to make decisions; you have to know what you're basing your decisions on. You have to have logic. You have to have awareness. And you're not going to get this out of the blue. You have to work at it. And you have to read, read, read.

—DELIA HARRISON-MARTIN

Get as much education as fast as you can. Then go to work.

—EDWARD J. CORCORAN

In Scarsdale, we had some neighbors who were Swiss; they went back in '36 and my wife and I visited them after the war. And Cecile told us this story:

They had three kids who were just about the same age as our children. When they returned to Switzerland, the kids, who were twelve, ten, and eight or so, were having trouble in school. So their mother complained to the teacher of one of them who was having particular problems. Do you need to work them quite so hard? she asked. And the teacher looked at her and said, Switzerland, you know, is a poor country. In order to make a living, we have to do things better than anybody else, and to do that, we have to work hard. The children had better learn that when they are young.

Damn right!

—PHILIP L. CARRET

The education is nothing. The main thing is common sense. The whole world is running by common sense.

—AARON BIRNBAUM

I have always loved art. That has brought me so much joy. If a child tells me that she's studying art, I say: You have a happy life guaranteed to you.

—LOIS CROUCH ADDY

Life essentially, basically, is purely accidental. It happens without any great architectural plan. Once you understand this, that life is full of illusions, only then can you commence to accumulate the bricks and the cement to build a home for yourself, and adapt to the environment to allow your life to more or less pleasantly pass by.

You need to make up your mind: What do you want out of life? Do you want to accumulate material goods? Or do you focus instead on the good feelings of mind and body? It all depends on what you want. But you must take the time to become what you will be.

—ALFRED LEVITT

Everybody comes in the store now, I look at 'em and I say, How long you been married? Oh, two or three years? Well, you better have children. Money's all right, but you got to have children. If I didn't have my children, what good am I? What would be the use of living? Why save money, for who? For your relatives to come enjoy themselves on your money? They don't deserve it. And suppose you live to a hundred like me?

—THERESA NIGRELLI

Make friends. There's an old saying: He who would have friends must show himself friendly.

And have good manners. Don't go flaunting around, flipping your skirts and that sort of thing. That's not good manners; that's not dignified.

—LUCY SOMERVILLE HOWORTH

Behave yourself, but flirt whenever you get the chance.

—GENEVA McDANIEL

Today, I understand that boys and girls around eleven, twelve years old are into sex. I have a saying: A few moments of pleasure does not pay the price of a long regret.

—EDDY KINCAIDE

◄ *Julia Tyler at age 107, November 1995*

Have a vision of what you want to do with your life, and develop faith in your own ability to accomplish whatever your goals might be. Be persistent. Be dependable. Follow the Golden Rule. And have faith for the comfort it will give you.

—ELLA MAY STUMPE

I taught my children the only thing my daddy left me: Keep doin' right, and right gon' follow you. And keep out of trouble: Just as sure as you do wrong, wrong gon' catch you. You may not believe it, and you can try it if you want to, but you gon' get caught. And treat people with manners and respect.

—SALLIE JORDAN

If you hear that something is going on in the world that isn't right, don't think it's happening there, it's not going to happen here and it's not going to happen to you. Pay attention. Get involved. Listen. Because history has a way of repeating itself.

—SARI MULLER

Don't ever do anything or say anything that you won't forget. God can forgive you, but you won't forget.

In your life, you've got to make decisions. And you've got to decide which road you're going to take.

—DR. LEILA DENMARK

Be reliable. Always tell the truth, so people can depend on what you say.

—KARL LONG

Keep your word. If you say you're going to do something at a certain time, do it. If for some chance you find you can't, tell people why you can't. But always be known as a person that keeps their word.

—ARTHUR W. HAMER, SR.

Don't be a smart aleck. And help everybody that you can. That way, you'll be a lot happier, and you won't go around feelin' bad about yourself.

—ADA TABOR

Don't allow yourself any time to feel sorry for yourself and think of how terrible things are. If you can do something for somebody else, it's surprising how happy it makes you feel. And keep involved, so that you don't worry.

—OSCAR C. WEBER

My father believed that right was right, and just because you were black it didn't mean that you shouldn't have every chance that any other person had—if you could qualify.

My hope is that my great-grandchildren and great-great-grandchildren get treated according to what they deserve. If they do well, treat them well. If they don't, let them jump in the pond and swim or sink.

—YORK GARRETT

It is important to learn about the past, about the roots and traditions of your family.

—ASANO KANZAKI

We had love in our home and that's the main thing. You can get along without a lot of money if you have a lot of love. If you don't have love, money don't mean anything.

And honor thy father and thy mother, that their days may be long upon the earth. That's one of the Ten Commandments.

—SARAH HUNTER JACKSON

Live a clean life.

—MARY NELL DOSSER KELLER

Live a Christian life.

—LOIS CROUCH ADDY

You have to be patient, you have to be calm, you have to try to live life the most simple way that you can, without vice. And more than that: Trust in God.

—TRINIDAD HUERTAS

Educate your soul to know God and attend to the laws of the Church. Then be charitable. Help those in need. And especially help children and keep them from bad influence.

—SR. URSULA INFANTE

God made you. You're a human being, like everybody else. Treat the other person like you want to be treated. Trust in God and have Him for your pilot all along the way. When you get to something you can't handle, just get on your knees and pray about it and say, I can't handle it, Lord, you take it. That's what I do.

—JULIA TYLER

If you're doing a problem, there is a scientific way to do it and then there's a guesstimating way of doing it. What's the right way? The scientific way.

—MILTON W. GARLAND

You can't say I want this, I want that. Or I expect this, I expect that. Don't get on that track and you won't find the going so rough.

You know what will prolong your life and what will shorten it. So do not fall victim to the thing, like tobacco, that's going to put you down.

—FRED BENSON

Take it easy. Don't worry. Take life one day at a time. Yesterday's gone; you can't do anything about it. Tomorrow you don't know what's coming up. So today you've got to see what goes on and do your best.

—HARLEY POTTER

Apply yourself and always do this: Do your work to the very best of your knowledge and ability and then say to yourself, I think I've done real good, but I'm going to do a little bit better than that. And if you reach for your zenith with that thought in mind, you'll be far better off and you'll have people that will be noticing you.

—ERNEST C. DEETJEN

Honesty is vital. But one musn't be brutal with it. Honesty with compassion is the first, absolutely important thing in your dealings with others as well as with yourself.

—BEATRICE WOOD

Don't think negatively. I had a grandfather, he was a very smart man. He used to say, A man is his own biggest enemy because he interprets everything for the worst.

—ROSE FREEDMAN

Never worry and get nervous about something before it happens. When it happens, then you'll be prepared and you'll have more strength and you'll be able to handle it.

—SAMUEL D. SCHNEIER

You have two choices in life. You can be happy, or you can crab about it. So you may as well make the best of it and be happy.

—RENATA BURT

Always remember: When something goes wrong, it could have been worse.

—AL KRAUS

Set your mind and stick to it. Don't heehaw back and forth.

—ROSIE GRIES

Keep busy.

—JOHN D. CLARK

Never look back. You always have to look forward. And whatever you do, do it well.

—GENEVA MCDANIEL

Do it yourself if you can. Ask for help if you can't—and don't be too proud to ask for help.

—VICTOR MILLS

The best thing you can do is to become proficient in some work that you can earn a living by. The sorriest thing in the world is to be unable to do anything well.

—JOHN SAILLIARD

The best thing that Eddy Kincaide ever did is put a little of what I made away for that rainy day. That rainy day is here. I'm not concerned how much money I'm going to leave behind. What I'm concerned about is how much money I can put my hands on in the morning if I wake up. Every week, every time you get a check, put some away for that rainy day. That rainy day always comes.

—EDDY KINCAIDE

Try to enjoy the many things that life has to offer. Seek out and enjoy conversations with people who think differently than you do. When one is very young, it is all too easy to be sure of everything and to defend one's opinion with revolutionary zeal—only to discover years later that one's opinion honestly has changed. It is a wonderful wisdom to be able and willing to accept that one is in error.

Never pass up the opportunity to help others, especially if you are in a kind of position to give the kind of help that is needed.

Try to attain the self-discipline never, ever to hurt someone else, for any reason. At the time of the Nazi regime, both the people in power and a vast number of ordinary citizens considered brutality and fanaticism to be admirable values and viewed the murder of helpless people a national duty.

Compare this to the essence of Mahatma Gandhi, who through his doctrine of non-violent resistance was able to defeat the mightiest empire of the time. And think about the Reverend Martin Luther King, Jr., who, by following Gandhi's teachings, was able to lead the United States out of a shameful legacy of subjugation of people because of the color of their skin.

Seek out and cherish the unexpected gifts that other people have to offer. Your life will be so much richer, as will the lives of those whom you touch.

—ERICH LEYENS

There was a rabbi named Zuma who said to his disciples, Who is rich? And the answer will not be accepted until it is unanimous, so go home and study and think.

And they came back and the first answer was: He who has money.

No.

He who has a nice family.

No.

He who has a nice family and nice children.

No.

He who has all of those things and land.

No.

He who has all of those things and money.

No.

Every answer that came up was rejected, until finally the answer came: He who is happy with the portion that the good Lord has preordained for him.

To me, that has been the most significant thing that I have come across that makes me feel that in my lifetime I haven't been as greedy or as grasping for things that I didn't deserve. Does that make sense to you?

—JOSEPH GOLDSTEIN

Take care of your own ones, but don't forget the old ones because that's what you'll become. You'll never be a baby again, and you'll never be a child again. But you will be an old person, too, someday.

—AUDREY STUBBART

As of July 1, 1998, the United States Census Bureau estimates there were 63,000 centenarians living in America in a population of just under 270 million. In 1960, when there were 180 million Americans, just three thousand of them were centenarians.

At the dawn of the new millennium, the Census Bureau projects a population of centenarians of 72,000 among almost 275 million Americans. As the so-called baby boomers begin to hit the century marker, around the year 2050, Census Bureau projections call for 834,000 centenarians—although this figure likely will range between 750,000 and 1,500,000—in a population expected to reach 394 million.

Centenographies

LOIS CROUCH ADDY has spent her life in Saluda, South Carolina, where she was born on October 24, 1892. She achieved a footnote of fame as a onetime babysitter for Senator Strom Thurmond, the longest-serving senator and the oldest person ever to serve as a member of Congress.

 FLORA ETHEL NOWELL ANDREWS was born on November 13, 1888, in Shady Side, Maryland, where she lived her entire life. "Miss Ethel," as she was affectionately known in the Shady Side community, published her autobiography, *Miss Ethel Remembers,* in 1991.

CATHERINE AVERY, née Langlands, emigrated in 1916 from Dundee, Scotland, where she was born on February 7, 1895. She has lived in New Jersey ever since she met her husband, John, while working as a domestic servant in Red Bank in the home of a governor of New Jersey.

FRED BENSON, who was born in Boston on April 14, 1895, is still known to many as "Mr. Block Island." An island institution for nine decades, a prominent black face in an overwhelmingly white community, he became the  quintessential civic activist: four-time president of the Chamber of Commerce, vice president of the Residents Association, director of the Block Island Credit Union, director of Civil Defense, captain of the rescue squad. He served as deputy registrar of motor vehicles on the island well into his nineties, making him the oldest employee in the history of Rhode Island. He wrote books, including *Research, Reflections and Recollections of Block Island,* published in 1977. An orphan who never married, he always loved children. After winning the lottery in 1975, he threw a barbecue and clambake for virtually the entire island—and established a scholarship fund for Block Island students.

AARON BIRNBAUM came to America in 1913 from the town of Skole, Austria, where he was born on July 18, 1895. He had a first career as a tailor and designer of women's clothing. In his second career, he received accolades for his prowess and vision as a self-taught artist. In the genre of "memory painting," Birnbaum's art depicts romanticized recollections of his childhood in Europe as well as scenes of Brooklyn, his home for over eighty years. His most recent exhibition, in September 1997, was at the Aldrich Museum of Contemporary Art in Ridgefield, Connecticut.

RENATA BURT, née Tetzlaff, hails from Brown County, Wisconsin. She jokes that she was born "right under the Christmas tree," on December 24, 1895. She spent a lifetime in Wisconsin raising children and animals.

PHILIP LORD CARRET was born in Lynn, Massachusetts, on November 29, 1896. In a profile of him in *The New York Times,* reporter Douglas Martin calculated that he had lived through thirty-one bull markets, thirty bear

markets, twenty recessions, and the Great Depression. In 1928, he founded the Pioneer Fund, one of only five mutual funds in existence at that time. In 1963, he launched Carret and Company in New York City, where at age one hundred he continued to manage investment accounts, commuting to his office from his home in Scarsdale. In 1991, Warren Buffett said of him: "Phil has the best long-term investment record of anyone in America." The "Lou Gehrig of investing," as Buffett also dubbed him, is the author of four books, including his 1991 autobiography, *A Money Mind at Ninety.*

Born on July 19, 1895, JOHN DODGE CLARK, the son of a minister, spent most of his boyhood in the Bronx and in the Bushwick section of Brooklyn, New York. Two months out of Amherst College, he was off to war, to a young man's adventure, participating in four major engagements involving American troops in the First World War. It was in Europe that he met and fell in love with Emma Zangler, a nurse, who was to become his first

wife. For his leadership, Second Lieutenant Clark was awarded the Silver Star. Following a career in business, he retired with his second wife, Helen, to Lakehurst, New Jersey.

ALBERT MOTT COLEMAN was born in Baltimore on December 11, 1888. In addition to having been the oldest Shriner in North America, he was, until he finally gave it up, the world's oldest driver: in his 108th year, he was still tooling along the streets of Daytona Beach, Florida.

EDWARD JOHN CORCORAN was born on July 12, 1893, in Fall River, Massachusetts. A partner in the Newport, Rhode Island, law firm of Corcoran, Peckham & Hayes, P.C., he went to his office, where he worked with his sons, every working day through his 103rd year.

 FANNIE LOU DAVIS was born Fannie Lou Hoke on March 30, 1896, in Bishop, Georgia, the tenth of fourteen children. She had eleven children of her own, and took great pride in raising them and many of *their* children as well. At last count, she had thirty-nine grandchildren, sixty-seven great-grandchildren, and sixty-one great-great-grandchildren.

JAMES MILTON DAVIS was born on March 23, 1896, in Columbus, Ohio. In his hundredth year, living in Daytona Beach, he was still traveling across the country, logging over thirty thousand miles a season, telling stories of his motorcycle-racing days to appreciative audiences. One time in Los Angeles, he said, he finished his spiel and leaned over to the president of the motorcycle association that was sponsoring the event. "I know I don't have any more time," he said, "but I do have one more story." "Jim," the president replied, "keep on goin'. You're saving the show." He still holds world records he set racing on two-mile, two-by-four board tracks—records that will last for the ages "because they don't race on boards anymore."

ERNEST CHRISTIAN DEETJEN was born in Baltimore on Friday the thirteenth of March 1896. He was named in part after his uncle, Dr. Christian Deetjen,  who discovered the X-ray with Dr. Wilhelm Conrad von Roentgen in Heidelberg, Germany, and who introduced the use of X-rays in America after emigrating and setting up a practice in Baltimore. Prior to his dual careers as a manager of A&P markets and as a salesman of insurance in western Maryland, young Ernest served as a captain in the Quartermaster Corps during

World War I. He claims to have been the only American officer present at the signing of the Treaty of Versailles.

LEILA DENMARK, M.D., holds the distinction of being one of the first women pediatricians in America and, at age one hundred, of being the oldest practicing physician in the country, according to the American Medical Association. Born Leila Alice Daughtry in Bullock County, Georgia, on February 1, 1898, she practiced for years in Atlanta before moving to, and setting up practice in, a 125-year-old farmhouse north of Alpharetta, an Atlanta suburb. Her book, *Every Child Should Have a Chance*, was published in 1971.

JUANITA DUDLEY came into the world as Juanita Friedly on a farm near Helix, in eastern Oregon, on February 18, 1898. After a friend died during the influenza pandemic, she married her friend's husband, which ended her career  as a teacher and began her life as a mother and homemaker. In her hundredth year, she was living with a daughter in Seattle.

ROSE FREEDMAN, née Rosenfeld, was born in Vienna, Austria, on March 27,  1893. A survivor of the infamous fire in 1911 that killed 146 young women at the Triangle Shirtwaist Company in lower Manhattan, she was, in her 104th year, speaking out against labor injustices affecting immigrant garment workers. After a lifetime spent in the New York area, she moved to Los Angeles to be closer to her family.

IVY FRISK, the daughter of a shipbuilder, was born in Seattle on October 21, 1896. Raised along the Duwamish River, she never lived far from the city of her birth. She worked as a bookkeeper—"and I was a good one"—before retiring "the day before yes-  terday." Friendships enriched her later years. "I talk with these people a great deal. We have coffee klatches and they are very good to me and I enjoy them and I hope they enjoy me. There's nothing in the world, you know, like good friends."

MILTON WARD GARLAND was born in Harrisburg, Pennsylvania, on August 23, 1895. In his more than seventy-eight-year career as a refrigeration engineer with the Frick Company in Waynesboro, Pennsylvania, he has been granted forty different patents on applications of refrigeration technology, all of which he assigned to Frick. Although he "retired" in 1967, he was still going to work five days a week at the age of 102, "although now I only work mornings. They keep me on as a consultant," he said, "and today I'm considered the senior consultant. My value to the company is really the fact that I've had experiences that very few other people had a chance to get." In 1998, he was honored as America's oldest-known worker. "Where would you be if you had retired at age sixty-five?" a reporter asked him at the National Press Club in Washington. "I'd be in my grave," he answered.

 YORK DAVID GARRETT was born on December 10, 1894, in Princeville, North Carolina. The son of a grocer, he learned how to deal with customers both white and black, a lesson that served him well when he opened his own business after graduating from Howard University: a pharmacy in Tarboro, North Carolina, and later in Durham.

JACOB GEWIRTZMAN was born Yankel Losice in Losice, Poland, on February 2, 1896. He arrived in the United States with his family on July 30, 1948. "I brought no earthly possessions with me from Europe," he said, "but I felt like the richest man in the world. I had my wife and my children." He worked in factories, managed a small dry-goods store in Brooklyn, struggled with the English language. "But our joy, the motivation to work hard, was always the children." He moved eventually to New Haven, Connecticut.

 ANNETTA GIBSON was born in DeKalb County, Illinois, on March 31, 1894. She taught fourth grade and later English in Rockford, Illinois, for forty years. The youngest of eight children, she never married, living with and caring for her mother, who lived to age ninety-eight.

EMIL GLAUBER was born on November 12, 1895, in Tachau, which then was part of the Austrian–Hungarian Monarchy and is now in the Czech Republic. One of the lucky ones, he escaped Europe in 1938 with his wife,  Gusti, and their children, and settled eventually in Flushing, New York.

 JOSEPH GOLDSTEIN, the son of immigrants, was born in Boston on March 1, 1895. A graduate of Harvard, he spent his working life in the family business: manufacturing slippers. He lived alone in his home in Brookline, Massachusetts, after the death of his wife of seventy-one years.

ELSIE GORDON was born Elsie Williamson in Sarnia, Canada, on August 26, 1892. After living most of her life in Indiana, she moved with her husband to Moosehaven, the retirement community for members of the Loyal Order of Moose, in Orange Park, Florida.

 ROSIE GRIES, née Moser, was born on May 2, 1896, in Eureka, South Dakota. Through her hundredth year, she was going door-to-door in the prairie communities near her home in Goodrich, North Dakota, selling Avon products, which she's done since 1938. In her nineties, she wrote *Rosie's Life Story* with the assistance of Jeff Olson, a local newspaper reporter.

ARTHUR WALTER HAMER, SR., was a carpenter and contractor—and proud union member—in and around his home town of Trenton, New Jersey, where he was born on May 10, 1896.

FRIEDA GREENE HARDIN was born in Eden Valley, Minnesota, on September 22, 1896. At age twenty-one, with the First World War on, she joined the United States Navy. Eighty years later, she had the distinction of being  the oldest female Navy veteran in the country. To those gathered for the dedication, in October 1997, of the Women in Military Service for America memorial in Arlington, Virginia, she said: "In my 101 years of living, I have observed many wonderful achievements—but none as important or as meaningful as the progress of women in taking their rightful place in society. When I served in the Navy, women were not even allowed to vote! Now, women occupy important leadership positions, not only in the military, but also in business, government, education, and in almost every form of human activity." Four times married, she has lived most of her life in and around Stockton and Modesto, California.

MARION WESLEY HARMAN hails from Canal Fulton, Ohio,
where he was born on January 2, 1897. A graduate of
Ohio State, he worked as a chemist, first for the Miller
Rubber Company in Akron, Ohio, and then with Monsanto
in Nitro, West Virginia. He was responsible for several patents of processes
involving the vulcanization of rubber. He retired to Dunbar, West Virginia.

DELIA HARRISON-MARTIN, born Adelia Harrison in Springfield, New Jersey,
on October 14, 1897, was for many years a civic and civil rights activist in
New Jersey, where she made her home and raised her family in East Orange. Among her many affiliations: From 1935 to 1990, she
was a member of the Contributory Civics Club in East Orange, for which she became secretary and then president.
She was secretary of the New Jersey NAACP for twenty
years. She was a delegate to the New Jersey State Constitutional Convention
in 1947. She was active in the New Jersey Federation of Colored Women's
Club from 1947 to 1968. And she was a board member of the regional National Committee of Christians and Jews.

A member of the Sons of the American Revolution, WILLIAM
GODFREY HINTZ, JR., is the sixth-generation grandson of
General William Graeff and his wife, Esther Leibrocke Graeff.
Born on August 2, 1896, he spent his life in and around Read-
ing, Pennsylvania. Although trained as an architect, he worked in his fa-
ther's stationery store, of which he became owner after his father's death.

LAURA HENRIETTA HOCH was born in Reading, Pennsylvania, on December 20, 1895, the daughter of a onetime newspaperman and
congressman, Daniel K. Hoch. A teacher, she ran the cafete-
rias in the Reading schools for thirty-four years before retiring in 1961 to a second "career": travel. She never married,
and lived with her father in the house in which she grew up, until he died,
well into his nineties.

CHESTER CORNELIUS ("RED") HOFF, who was born in Ossining, New
York, on May 8, 1891, was twenty when he made it to the Major Leagues
with the New York Highlanders on September 18, 1911. He
played in a total of twenty-three games in the big leagues,
going 2–4 with a 2.49 ERA for the Highlanders in 1911 and
1912, the renamed Yankees in 1913, and the St. Louis Browns

in 1915. He spent his golden years in Daytona Beach, Florida. At age 107, he was the oldest living ex-Major League baseball player.

LUCY SOMERVILLE HOWORTH was born in Greenville, Mississippi, on July 1, 1895. She was known as "Judge Lucy" after her appointment as a United States magistrate for the Southern Judicial District of Mississippi in 1927. As a national officer in the American Association of University Women in the 1940s, she was instrumental in abolishing that organization's practice of racial segregation. A trailblazer in the "spiteful" world of Washington politics, she held several positions of prominence in the nation's capital before retiring in 1954 as general counsel of the War Claims Commission.

TRINIDAD HUERTAS was born in San Lorenzo, Puerto Rico, on June 3, 1896. He followed his sons to America, arriving in Bethlehem, Pennsylvania, in 1956. He is proud to report that five generations of the Huertas family live in Bethlehem, including seven sons and daughters, fifty grandchildren, sixty-two great-grandchildren, and five great-great grandchildren—and rising.

A longtime educator, SISTER URSULA INFANTE, born Anna Lawrence Infante in Brooklyn, New York, on February 18, 1897, has advanced degrees from Fordham and Columbia Universities and an honorary degree from La Salle College. In her sixties, she organized, equipped, and opened Cabrini College in Radnor, Pennsylvania, and served as its dean and president.

SARAH HUNTER JACKSON was born on July 13, 1895, on Main Street in Johnson City, Tennessee, where she has spent her life. At age thirteen, "right out of high school," she and her sister took over her father's insurance business when he became ill. She ran the business until she got married in 1923, then worked with her husband, booking officials for intercollegiate

sporting events in the southern Appalachian region. Her one regret in life, she says, is having torn up her old love letters.

WILLIAM FRANKLIN JARNAGIN was born on December 8,
1894, on a farm in Lea Springs, now Blaine, Tennessee.
His Jarnagin Motor Company of Rutledge, Tennessee,
which he and a cousin started in 1916, is the longest-
operating Ford dealership in the world.

 SALLIE JORDAN was born Nannie Sallie Ransom on
Verona Plantation in Northampton County, North Car-
olina, on September 17, 1892. She moved to Seaboard,
North Carolina, after she got married, and was living
there with one of her daughters, Dorothy, when she reached her hundredth
year.

ASANO KANZAKI was born Asano Oshita in a suburb of Okayama, Japan,
on September 1, 1897. She accompanied her new husband to Spokane,
Washington, in 1917, where they lived before settling in Seattle. They were
separated during the Second World War, when her husband,
Kenichiro, was sent to a camp for "enemy aliens" in Missoula, Montana. Shortly thereafter, she and her children
were sent to the Minidoka Relocation Center, near Twin
Falls, Idaho. In her hundredth year, she became an American citizen.
"When I went to the Immigration and Naturalization, they gave me the
exam," she said. "Afterwards I cried. The examiner was a nice lady. She
was so kind and she passed me so easily. I was so relieved and happy. Before the test, I had been studying so hard. I was asked 'Who was the first
President?' And, 'Who is the President now?' And, 'Which President is your
favorite?' And I said, 'All of them.' "

 MARY NELL DOSSER KELLER hails from Jonesborough,
Tennessee, where she was born on January 11, 1896.
The daughter and grandaughter of merchants, she has
spent most of her life in Tennessee.

For EDDY KINCAIDE, who was born on August 25, 1895,
in New Bedford, Massachusetts, dancing was his greatest
pleasure. By the time he turned one hundred, dancing,
for the onetime seaman, had given way to connecting
with other ham-radio operators around the world from his home in
Fairhaven, Massachusetts.

ALBERT J. KRAUS was born on a farm in Dane County, Wisconsin, on December 23, 1896. He had a career in banking, much of it in Fort Atkinson, Wisconsin. "I was always quite frugal," he said. "I never got any large wages, but I never missed a chance to pick up a dollar," even clerking at country auctions on Saturday mornings. He was fifty-five years old when he finally got married.

For ALFRED LEVITT, who was born on August 15, 1894, in the town of Starodub in what is now Belarus, recognition of his achievements as an artist

was a long time coming. Twenty of his paintings, he is proud to say, are in the permanent collection of the Metropolitan Museum of Art in New York City. He received an honorary doctorate of humane letters from Mary Washington College in Fredericksburg, Virginia, when he reached one hundred. Exhibitions of his work have been held at major New York galleries. In 1997, a retrospective of his work was featured at Ellis Island, his port of entry to New York in 1911. He has lived in New York City most of his life.

ERICH LEYENS was born in Wesel, Germany, on January 13, 1898. He has written about his time in Germany during the rise of Nazism in *Years of Estrangement,* published in 1996 by Northwestern University Press.

JOSEPH LICCARDO came to the United States in 1907 from Naples, Italy, where he was born on February 12, 1897. A onetime councilman in West Paterson, New Jersey, he spent forty years as a water-generator operator for Society Useful Manufacturing, a Paterson firm specializing in silk clothing.

HENRY KARL LONG began life on his father's farm in Woodbine, Iowa, on August 3, 1894. Enchanted and excited by sports, he went from being mascot to the various teams at the Iowa State Normal School, where his father worked, to being coach of the 1927 Morton High School (Chicago) national championship basketball team. His team, basketball historians say, was influential in

changing how basketball is played, including the institution of the inbounds pass. In his later years, he lived with his second wife, Gertrude, in Holly Hill, Florida.

GENEVA MCDANIEL came into the world as Geneva O'Kelly on August 26, 1887, in Walton County, Georgia. She and her husband, a doctor, accumulated land in Gwinnett County, Georgia, where they lived in Duluth. In her 111th  year, she is the oldest centenarian to have contributed to this book.

 PAULINE HILL MASSEY was born in the Sequatchie Valley, in Etna, Tennessee, on September 3, 1896, the daughter of a doctor who tended to miners and their families. She lived most of her life in Harriman, Tennessee, where her husband first bought the local newspaper and then became the town postmaster.

VICTOR MILLS was born in Milford, Nebraska, on March 28, 1897. He spent his career with Procter and Gamble in Cincinnati, Ohio. He is responsible for twenty-five patents and is generally recognized as the most productive and innovative technologist in P&G Research and Product  Development history. He retired to Tucson, Arizona, to pursue his passion—hiking. John Pepper, the chairman of the board and chief executive officer of Procter and Gamble, acknowledged his importance to the success of the company on the occasion of his hundredth birthday. "After thirty-five years in the market, Pampers is the company's single largest brand with worldwide sales of near five billion dollars. And Pringles is now an important global brand. . . . These are just some of the great achievements that you and your colleagues accomplished during a very productive period in our history. And to add some frosting to your birthday celebration, we have just reinvented our Ivory soap business. . . . And the Victor Mills Society, which we created in 1990 in your honor, is the real legacy to your contributions. It has been an inspiration to thousands of researchers around the world who know of your accomplishments and their importance. I recall a comment you made in 1990 that is as ageless as you are. 'If it isn't innovative, it isn't much good.' You were right."

 RALPH MONTECALVO, who was born on March 3, 1895, came to the United States from Italy when he was fifteen years old. After working with his father making rubber footwear in Akron, Ohio, he "went and joined the Army instead of going to jail" because "the foreman and I argue that I sneak some samples." After his war service, during which he was gassed, he went

to work for the Converse Rubber Company in Malden, Massachusetts, and was there for thirty-five years. An inveterate horse player, he became a well-known figure around Gulfstream Park in Hallandale, Florida, where he retired after the death of his wife.

FLORENCE MORETTI started life as Filomena Pezzullo in Bellagra, Italy, on October 11, 1894. After emigrating to America with her family in 1900, she lived in Providence, Rhode Island.

 ORLANDO FESTUS MORLEY was born in the coal town of Norton, Virginia, on October 29, 1894. Growing up on a farm out of Wise, Virginia—"it used to be Gladeville then"—he worked as a paymaster for the Westmoreland Coal Company. When he retired in September 1959, "they retired my job with me. Now," he said, "they're fully computerized."

CHARLIE LUE MOSLEY was born Charlie Lue Cole in Union Springs, Alabama, on January 9, 1892. After spending most of her life in Homestead, Pennsylvania, she moved to College Park, Georgia, where, in her 106th year, she was living with her daughter, Mary Foust, and two great-granddaughters.

 SARI MULLER was born Sari Jacob in Polena, in what is now Slovakia, on September 18, 1898. A survivor of the concentration camps, she "finally got to America in January 1947, three months after my children. Here, when my children worked, I look after their children." In her hundredth year, she was living with her daughter, Idy Farber, in Union, New Jersey.

THERESA NIGRELLI, born Theresa Salimeno on March 27 or 28, 1894, in New York City, was, in her hundredth year, living in the house on Granite Street in Westerly, Rhode Island, that her husband built in 1927. "By my mother," she said, "I was born the 28th. But when my parish priest moved to New York about fifteen years ago, I asked him to see where I was baptized. When I got a letter from him, it said I was born on the 27th. So I've been celebrating two ever since."

PAUL ONESI was born in Arquata del Tronto, a village "with six or seven houses" near Catanzaro, Italy, on July 7, 1896. After coming to America to make a better life, he spent fourteen years in the coal mines of western Pennsylvania before getting a job with Union Carbide in Niagara Falls, New York. He was married at age twenty-one to Mary, who was thirteen at the time. They lived happily, blessed with six children, for over eighty years—one of the longest marriages on record in the United States.

HARLEY POTTER was born on a farm in Clinton County, Missouri, on June 26, 1892. A life of hard work was followed by an old age of hard play: at age ninety-two, twelve years after he retired, he took up golf and became a champion. He won gold medals at the 1995 National Senior Sports Championship in San Antonio, Texas. He didn't have much competition, though: he was the only golfer over the age of one hundred. In his later years, he was living with his daughter, Leta Duffin, in Winston-Salem, North Carolina.

VIRGINIA REALE was born Virginia Fiocco—"Fiocco means snowflake in Italian"—in Messina, Italy, on November 18, 1897. She emigrated to the United States to join her father after the death of her mother in 1905, and lived in New York City. In her hundredth year, she was living with one of her daughters and her son-in-law, Eleanor and John Lavarello, in Coral Springs, Florida.

JOHN HECTOR SAILLIARD hails from Allentown, Pennsylvania, where he was born on September 25, 1894. He worked much of his life for Bell Laboratories in New York City, eventually being promoted to chief draftsman. After he retired in 1959 when he turned sixty-five, he remained active, working as a volunteer Braillist and spending many hours at his lathe in his home in Madison, New Jersey, where he was living, in his 103rd year, with his second wife, Mary.

SAMUEL D. SCHNEIER, known as Dave to many in the New Brunswick–Highland Park community in New Jersey, was born on March 18, 1895, in Kreuzburg, Latvia, which then was part of Russia. A longtime philanthropist for area Jewish organizations and for Israel, he remained active in business affairs, often calling the family in for meetings to keep up with what was going on at Cream-O-Land, the dairy he founded during the Second World War.

Artist HELEN L. SMITH, born on January 21, 1894, spent her life in Frederick, Maryland. A businesswoman when most women remained in the

home, she fashioned a solid—and lifelong—career for herself. "It seems to me I've worked awful hard all my life," she said. "Not that I resent it, 'cause it's been a lot of fun, and it always came out well. Being an artist, that was me. There was nothing else possible. So it had to be art." She never married.

LENA STANLEY, née Tangen, hails from Hillsboro, North Dakota, where she was born on May 18, 1895. She spent her life slinging hash and waitressing, raising turkeys, and, finally, running a motel in Williston, North Dakota.

DIRK JAN STRUIK, a professor of mathematics at the Massachusetts Institute of Technology, was born in Rotterdam, the Netherlands, on September 30,

1894. He came to the United States with his wife in 1926 and settled in Belmont, Massachusetts. Always politically active, he kept his politics separate from his responsibilities as a teacher. He was one of the founders of *Science and Society* magazine, was a former chairman of the American–Soviet Friendship Committee and a member of the Sherlock Holmes Society. A prolific writer, he wrote, among other books, *Yankee Science in the Making,* first published in 1948.

AUDREY STUBBART was born Audrey Morford on June 9, 1895, in Newman Grove, Nebraska, to pioneer parents. Married at fifteen, a mother two years

later, she and her husband, John, homesteaded in Wyoming for twenty-eight years. After moving to Independence, Missouri, to be near her mother, she took a job as a copy reader for the Herald Publishing House. Forced to

retire when she turned sixty-five, she began a third career as a proofreader and sometime columnist for the Independence *Examiner,* for whom she was still working, five days a week, well beyond her hundredth birthday.

ELLA MAY STUMPE was born Ella May Leonard on her father's homestead near Dunseith, North Dakota, on July 12, 1895. Married three times, she has lived in Illinois, Arkansas, Washington, D.C., and Frederick, Maryland, as well as in her native state. She wrote her autobiography, *100 Years, My Story—By Ella May* for her hundredth birthday. In her 104th year, she completed her second book, *The Ladies of Record Street*.

 ADA TABOR was born Ada Ruth Cole in Ceredo, West Virginia, on May 14, 1896. She spent her whole life in the state of her birth, living in her later years with her son, Cliff, and daughter-in-law, Barbara, in St. Albans.

JESSIE TURNER was born Jessie Duffy in Henry County, Georgia, on January 29, 1894. Married to a farmer, she lived her life working the land of her native county. Although she had to move into a nursing home in McDonough, Georgia, she insisted on keeping the home she had lived in, so that any of her family "can always have a place to go."

 JULIA TYLER was born Julia Estelle Pendleton in Fredericksburg, Virginia, on June 26, 1888. Still feisty at age 108, she has resided in her later years in nursing homes in the city of her birth, where she is revered by many as "Mother Tyler."

OSCAR CHARLES WEBER was born in Tacoma, Washington, on October 8, 1897. After working as a fireman on the railroad, a baker, a salesman, and a grocer, he suffered a heart attack at age fifty-seven, which precluded any physical labor. But, he said, "I have two of the most capable hands that I believe anybody ever had. I can perform miracles with my hands."
Which he does, building dollhouses and doll furniture and giving them to charitable organizations as well as to families with little girls. At age one hundred, he was living in Seattle.

HAZEL WOLF was born Hazel Anderson in Victoria, British Columbia, on March 10, 1898. She moved to the United States—to Seattle—with her  young daughter after the First World War, as did many other Canadians, in search of a job. She had many. She gained a bit of notoriety because of her affiliation with the Communist Party, an association which caught her up in the anti-Communist mania that gripped the United States in the wake of the

Second World War. After her retirement, thanks to a small brown creeper, she found her métier—and another career—as an environmental activist, most prominently with the Audubon Society, which has created a Hazel Wolf "Kids for the Environment" endowment to help young people learn about the wonders of nature.

BEATRICE WOOD was born in San Francisco on March 3, 1893, and reared in New York City. An accomplished artist, she lived and worked in the hills of Happy Valley in Ojai, California. Her drawings and her pottery have been in numerous exhibitions and retrospectives. After a life among the glitterati of the art world, after storied affairs with Marcel Duchamp and  Henri Roché—their relationship is allegedly the basis for the book and film *Jules et Jim*—and after two less than complete marriages, her last years have been the happiest of all. Why? "For one thing, I'm not worried desperately about money. I'm not hoping anymore to hear a man call himself Mr. Wood. I have many friends, I live in beautiful surroundings, and I have something loving on my bed to sleep with. Unfortunately, it has four legs instead of two, and its name is Sheba." Her autobiography, *I Shock Myself*, was published in 1985.

About the Author

Bernard Edelman, a graduate of Brooklyn, lives with his wife and young son in Finesville, New Jersey. He is the editor of *Dear America: Letters Home from Vietnam*.

Acknowledgments

I want to thank Bill Leary, my father-in-law, for his inspiration; Ellen Leary, my wife, for her endurance; John Glusman, my editor, for his confidence and acuity; Becky Kurson, my editor's right hand, for her attention to detail; Flip Brophy, my agent, for her sticktoitiveness; Robert Santos, my friend, on general principles; John Weingart, Jeanette Eng, and the staff of the Siting Board for their accommodations; and Aidan, my son, for the joy he has given me, even if he didn't always comprehend when he was told, "Leave Daddy alone while he works on his book."

I want also to acknowledge friends, colleagues, and acquaintances near and far who clipped articles on centenarians for me and/or otherwise assisted me in my endeavors: Mark and Dee Jury; Hillary Jury; Jim Lenzo; Bill and Cheryl Ward; Mike and Anne Lund; Paul Giannone and Kate Huntley; Dick and Susan Strandberg; Hugh and Maryann Sullivan; Jerry Balcom; Jim Buckley; Pat Garvey; Dan Rosario; John Roche; John Hamill; Debby Brudno; Sally Sutphen and Rob Olick; Peter and Rayna Sachelari; Darlene and Joe Yuhas; Elliot Johnson; Bill and Kathy Couturié; Susan and Tony Shipley; Dr. Andy Weber; Debbie Good; Denny Medlin; Greta Kiernan; Prudy Gaskill; Maryann Kall; Fran Snyder; Ed Truskowski; Louise Wienckowski; Michel DeMatteis; Sharon Goldstein; Toby and Mel Steinhauser.

I am grateful to Susan Shipley and Joanne Kash and Lynn Adler, whom I met in the course of this project, who generously and graciously shared with me many of their contacts, and their trust.

I am indebted to Hillary Jury and Dee Jury, and Alyson Giantisco, who accomplished with skill and aplomb the daunting task of transcribing the interviews; to Joshua Jury, who set up and adjusted my Mac and helped me get organized; to Diane Backes, of Backes Graphic Productions, Princeton, New Jersey, for her many kindnesses; to Taylor Photo, Princeton, which processed and printed my film with intelligence and care; to Catherine DeVico, of CDL Tours & Travel, Clinton, New Jersey, who facilitated my cross-country forays.

And, for their considerations and assistance with interviews and otherwise encouraging the interviewer: Dr. Thomas Perls and Maureen Shea, the New England Centenarian Study; Meg Cliber, Williamsport Retirement Village, Williamsport, Maryland; Valerie Cole and Kay Demler, Fairhaven Retirement Community, Whitewater, Wisconsin; Cecilia Perkel, Andover Intermediate Care Center, Andover, New Jersey; Marcia Wilson, Green Thumb, Inc.; Bob Angle, American Society of Interior Designers; Tony Brula, the Shriners; H. Ross Fleet, Moosehaven; Sr. Mary Louise Sullivan, Cabrini College; the United States Naval Institute; the United States Census Bureau; the American Booksellers Association; the American Mathematical Society; Donald Davis, National Council on the Aging; Glenn Northup, AARP; Richard Howorth, Square Books, Oxford, Mississippi; Dorothy Shawhan, Delta State University; Jonett Valentine, Bolivar County (Mississippi) Library; Denise Strub, *The Bolivar Commercial*; Martha Smith, *The Providence Journal-Bulletin*; Josephine Starr Dugan, Block Island Historical Society; Kate Sexton, Newport (Rhode Island) Historical Society; Marian Beckman, Rhode Island Department of Elderly Affairs; Elizabeth Roseman, Hispanic Senior Citizens Center, Bethlehem, Pennsylvania; Susan Skinner, Northampton County (North Carolina) Agency on the Aging; Susan Riddle, River's Edge Convalescent Center, Trenton, New Jersey; Jearline F. Williams and Darlene Nowlin, District of Columbia Office on Aging; Linda Calvert, West Virginia Commission on Aging; Arnisha Norman, Atlanta Regional Commission; Pat Filer, Southwest Seattle Historical Society; Theresa Neinas; Greg Harris, National Baseball Hall of Fame; Bruce Davis, Academy of Motion Picture Arts and Sciences; Frank Betz, Carret and Company, New York City; Kerry Schuss, K.S. Art, New York City; Heinz and Sue Ann Wilms; Tiffany Wilms; Arieh Lebowitz, Jewish Labor Committee; Erika Gottfried, Robert F. Wagner Labor Archives, New York University; Marian Goldman; Beata Pozniak; the Shoah Foundation. To those whom I have inadvertently missed—and many gave me assistance and encouragement—my sincere apologies.

Finally, I am most appreciative of the centenarians, and their families, who shared with me their reminiscences, reflections, and recollections. It is my hope that this book does justice to their memories.

Credits

Excerpts from her self-published *100 Years, My Story, by Ella May*, have been incorporated into the segments of Ella May Stumpe.

Most of the segments on Beatrice Wood are taken from *I Shock Myself: The Autobiography of Beatrice Wood*, copyright © 1985 by Beatrice Wood; revised Chronicle Books edition 1988, reprinted 1992.

Early photographs were provided by the centenarians and their families. Recent photographs were taken by the author, with the following exceptions: Aaron Birnbaum, courtesy of Kerry Schuss, K. S. Art; Ivy Frisk, courtesy of Dorothy Johnson; Harley Potter, courtesy of his daughter, Leta Duffin; Oscar Weber, courtesy of Oscar Weber; Hazel Wolf, courtesy of Hazel Wolf; Ella May Stumpe at the computer, courtesy of Sue Ann Wilms.